A HISTORY OF MODERN SOUTH ASIA

A History of Modern South Asia

Politics, States, Diasporas

IAN TALBOT

Yale

UNIVERSITY PRESS

NEW HAVEN AND LONDON

Yale University Press books may be purchased in quantity for educational, business, or promotional use. For information, please e-mail sales.press@yale.edu (U.S. office) or sales@yaleup.co.uk (U.K. office).

Set in Electra type by Newgen North America.
Printed in the United States of America.

Library of Congress Control Number: 2015937886
ISBN 978-0-300-19694-8 (cloth : alk. paper)

A catalogue record for this book is available from the British Library.

This paper meets the requirements of ANSI/NISO Z39.48-1992 (Permanence of Paper).

10 9 8 7 6 5 4 3 2 1

CONTENTS

CONTENTS

ILLUSTRATIONS

ACKNOWLEDGMENTS

My personal journey of South Asian discovery, which culminated in this book, began early in September 1977. I arrived at Delhi's Palam airport armed with record cards, a portable typewriter, and a research plan. I planned to uncover the local roots of the Pakistan movement's eleventh-hour breakthrough in the key Punjab province of British India. My thesis reflected the new emphasis on region and locality in South Asian history. During the long period since then, my understanding of the compelling history of South Asia has been enriched by innumerable colleagues, friends, and students. Foremost among these are Professor Francis Robinson, Professor Judith Brown, and Professor Gurharpal Singh. Encouragement has also come from colleagues within the Punjab Research Group; at the National University of Singapore; at the University of London; and within the British Association of South Asian Studies network, which I have chaired since 2011. I would also like to record my thanks to the numerous research staffers at libraries and archives that I have used over the years, principally in India, Pakistan, Singapore, the United States, and the United Kingdom. I would also like to record thanks to my institution, the University of Southampton, for making research leave available to write this work, and to the University of Warwick, which hosted me during this period. Any errors of fact or omission are my responsibility alone.

Finally, I owe an enormous debt to Lois, for her support, encouragement, and patience over the years of my involvement with South Asian Studies.

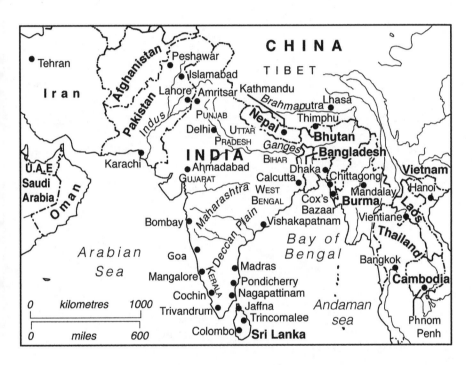

1. South Asia region after 1971

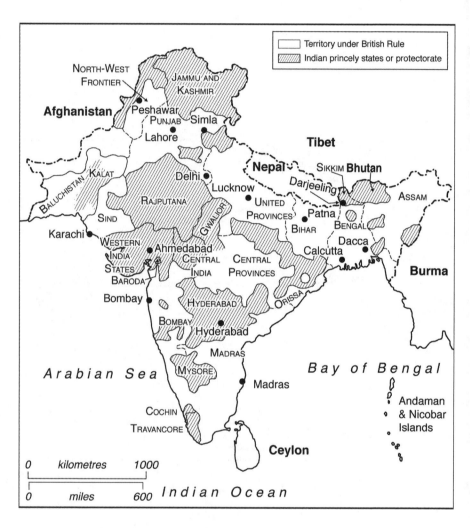

2. India before the 1947 Partition

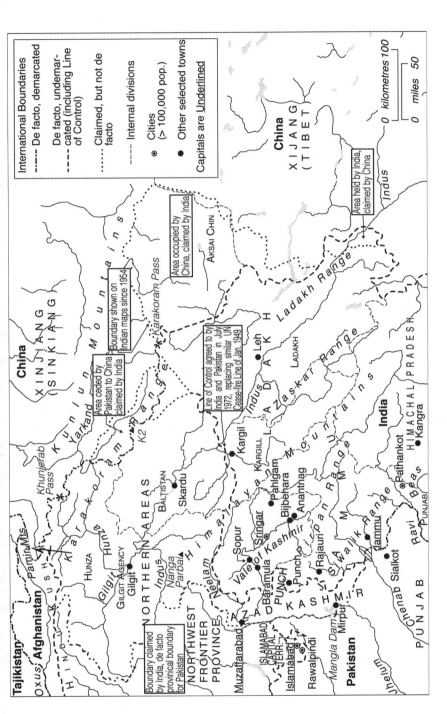

3. Contemporary Kashmir region

A HISTORY OF MODERN SOUTH ASIA

Introduction

South Asia is of immense significance to the wider world. It is home to a quarter of the global population and a third of the Islamic community. It is a major market and focus for overseas investment within which the rising economic power of India will become increasingly important in the "Asian" twenty-first century. By the end of this century's second decade, Mumbai will be the second-largest city in the world, closely followed by Delhi and Dhaka, which is currently the fastest-growing global megacity. Rapid economic growth throughout South Asia, however, exists alongside mass poverty. Six hundred million South Asians subsist on less than $1.25 per day, the greatest concentration of poverty outside Sub-Saharan Africa.[1] There are more than 300 million hungry and malnourished people in the region. Despite rapid urbanization, more than half of the population is still engaged in agriculture. Climate change is projected to reduce crop production in the region by between 10 and 40 percent by the end of the century.

The region is also an important strategic crossroads and has been the site of much bloodshed since British decolonization in 1947. Conflict between India and Pakistan alone has led to three wars and, in their wake, the development of rival nuclear weapons and delivery systems. By 2013, Pakistan's production of warheads was estimated at 100–120, India's at 90–110. It is clearly important to understand the history of this economically and strategically significant region.

The region displays immense variety in its climate, topography, and demographic characteristics. It includes some of the most densely populated and sparsely populated regions of the world. Populations are concentrated in the Indo-Gangetic plains and megadeltas of the region. Deserts and mountainous environments are largely uninhabited. Urbanization ranges from

35 percent of the population in Pakistan to just 11 percent in Bhutan. Myriad languages, religious traditions, and ethnic groups add to the region's complexity and diversity. The Indian 2011 census, for example, recorded more than fifteen hundred languages, thirty of which together were mother tongues for more than a million people. Hindi is the most widely spoken language in the region, where it is understandable in spoken form for Pakistan's Urdu-speaking population. Within the great religious traditions of Hinduism, Islam, Buddhism, Jainism, and Sikhism within the region, there are immense varieties of expression, which can prompt sectarian conflict and violence. Alongside religion, ethnicity, and language are the other great sources of identity, which in the contemporary era have become increasingly politicized.

South Asia's pluralism is the product of successive waves of migration and invasion in the region. The best-known and longest-lasting impacts have resulted from the invasions of the Aryans, Muslims, and British. The legacies of these invasions have been the source of much political as well as scholarly contest. It is important, for example, to set the British colonial tenure in the context of earlier intrusions. People from the region have also moved outward for trade and settlement, taking advantage of the monsoon winds to journey in the premodern era around the Indian Ocean rim. In the colonial and contemporary eras of globalization, large-scale migration has been mobilized, giving rise to what has become termed the South Asian diaspora.

The size and wealth of diaspora populations has multiplied in the past three decades. New Delhi, after years of condescension toward overseas Indians, has chased the "brown dollar" in its post–economic liberalization phase. Remittances from workers in the Gulf, Europe, and North America prop up Pakistan's parlous foreign-exchange reserves. Recent joint ventures in information technology between Indian and Mauritian companies can be understood only with reference to the historic Indian diaspora in Mauritius. Diasporas have, however, threatened as well as sustained their homelands. From the 1980s onward, overseas residents provided vital financial and propaganda support for Punjabi, Kashmiri, and Tamil separatist movements. Mainstream parties have also established overseas branches; London and Dubai are emerging as important hubs of Pakistani political activity. Despite the burgeoning of diaspora studies, this book represents one of the few accounts to bring together histories of overseas South Asians and their homelands.

India has experienced rapid economic growth since the abandonment of the government controls of the "license-permit Raj" in 1991. India's rising global power resulted in its being ranked fourth in the world in GDP purchasing power, with a parity of $4,784 trillion in 2012. An increasingly wealthy middle class has eagerly snapped up consumer products. The age of austerity and frugality still evident in 1970s Delhi has given way to glitzy shopping malls. Millions of Indians, though, have been left behind; ostentatious wealth exists cheek by jowl with grinding poverty. Within the region, localities that possessed advantages of education and infrastructure in the colonial era have continued to thrive alongside poorer neighbors. The countryside lags behind towns and cities, with resulting rural-urban migration across the region. Wealthier areas of the Subcontinent can be compared in development terms with Latin America, while its poorer regions are akin to sub-Saharan Africa.

The term *South Asia* possesses a complex and often confusing history. Economic commentators have often synonymously used the terms "South Asia," the "Indian Subcontinent," and even "India." The World Bank takes its cue from institutional arrangements, including in its definition the original founding members of the South Asian Association for Regional Cooperation (SAARC): Bangladesh, Bhutan, India, Maldives, Nepal, Pakistan, and Sri Lanka.[2] Afghanistan became an eighth member in 2006. The United Nations scheme for subregions includes all eight SAARC members as part of Southern Asia, but also adds Iran. The UN Population Information Network (POPIN) omits a SAARC member, Maldives, from its South Asia regional network, but includes Burma (renamed Myanmar in 1989) and Iran.[3] Burma was part of the British Indian Empire but is a member of the Association of Southeast Asian Nations trading bloc (ASEAN), which explains the confusion surrounding its inclusion in South Asia.

"South Asia" emerged as a geopolitical term during the Second World War. The *New York Times* contains scattered references in its coverage of

Japan's threat to British India. "South Asia" became more familiar following decolonization, when the term was adopted by the US Departments of State and Education as an "area studies" approach to the successor states of the British Raj. Until the late 1990s, the US State Department office for South Asia was located within the Bureau of Near Eastern Affairs. When a separate State Department office was created for South Asia, Afghanistan was included within its regional remit.

In Britain, the first official use of "South Asia" dates from the 1950 Colombo Plan.[4] This was a Commonwealth of Nations initiative designed to provide aid and technical expertise from Britain, Australia, New Zealand, and Canada for the self-governing Asian members, India, Pakistan, and Ceylon. The veteran Indian correspondent Guy Wint's explanation of the Colombo Plan to the public revealed the tentative nature of "South Asia" as a geographical label. He did not distinguish between it and "Southeast Asia" when the initiative was extended in 1952 to include such noncommonwealth countries as Burma and Laos.[5]

In this book I anchor the "nebulous entity" of South Asia in the administrative contours of the British Raj and the postcolonial Indian, Pakistani, and Bangladeshi states, which today account for about 95 percent of the region's population. By 2012, nearly one in four of the world's seven billion people lived in the Indian Subcontinent.[6] At the same time, I recognize that these entities cannot be isolated from extraterritorial spatial and imaginary connections or transnational influences, whether these are smuggling, terrorism, or flooding resulting from upstream deforestation or glacier melt. I have not examined extensively domestic politics of Ceylon (now Sri Lanka), but I do consider the long-term consequences for Indo–Sri Lankan relations of the migration of Tamils from South India to work on the island's tea plantations. The Srimavo-Shastri Pact—the 1964 agreement between the Indian and Ceylonese prime ministers—led to the repatriation of nearly half a million "Indian Tamils." Many settled in their ancestral villages, but significant communities emerged in Tamil Nadu's northwestern tea-growing areas. Repatriates played a key role in the Nilgri Hill's production boom, making up almost a third of the district's population.[7]

Large numbers of Indians were also repatriated from Burma during 1963–78.[8] While the backdrop of long-term resentment and indigenization

4

following independence was similar to conditions in Ceylon, most of these Indian returnees were urban merchants or professionals. A dangerous precedent was set for overseas Indians. Idi Amin expelled Ugandan Asians in 1972. Many Indians migrated from Fiji following the constitutional crisis of 1977 and the coups of 1987 and 2000, which were directed against their interests.[9] These population movements, Uganda aside, are below the radar of diaspora studies, which focus on the successful postcolonial Indian overseas populations. Although the repatriations have been called "involuntary mass migration," they are also neglected in literature on forced migration. The Partition-related upheaval dominates South Asian case studies.

There are numerous general narratives of British rule in India,[10] but surprisingly few volumes include the histories of all three postcolonial states: India, Pakistan, and Bangladesh.[11] Existing studies tend to be security driven, or are constructed around explanations for the different democratic trajectories of postindependence India and Pakistan.[12] Bangladesh appears rarely, except in a handful of comparisons with Pakistan.[13]

Historical perspectives are frequently reduced to stereotypes. India is portrayed as an "exceptional" democratic success story which since 1991 has also become an emerging economic power. Pakistan, despite a common colonial inheritance, conversely is a "crisis" state, mired in corruption, terrorism, and instability. Bangladesh is portrayed as a success story for overseas aid and the development role of nongovernmental organizations (NGOs). In this book I question easy assumptions regarding both the common colonial inheritance and these postindependence stereotypes. With regard to Bangladesh, for example, the country is hailed for pioneering microcredit facilities, which are seen as empowering women. Certainly, female participation in the labor market is markedly higher in Bangladesh than in India or Pakistan, but this comes at the cost of a "double burden," as women are not relieved of their domestic responsibilities. Furthermore, as I reveal, claims of empowerment through microcredit can be exaggerated. Access to loans from such world-renowned institutions as the Grameen Bank may actually increase dowry and domestic violence.

India's success in holding national polls has not prevented long-running ethnic and Maoist insurgencies in the Northeast.[14] The Punjab Crisis of the 1980s and the Kashmir insurgency at the close of the decade posed even greater threats to the state. Post-9/11 Western concerns with "Islamic terrorism" in Pakistan's tribal areas have obscured the fact that India has historically been as prone to terrorism and insurgencies as its neighbor. For example, an attack on 25 May 2013 by Naxalite insurgents on a Congress convoy rally in the thickly forested Darbha valley of the troubled state of Chhattisgarh claimed twenty-eight lives, including that of the state Congress chief Nand Kumar Patel and a former state minister Mahendra Karma. It brought home the threat of Naxalite insurgency in many other tribal areas of India.

India's contemporary growth spurt has similarly obscured the fact that throughout the first forty years of independence, its economy grew more slowly than Pakistan's. Moreover, it was Sri Lanka, not India, that pioneered South Asian economic liberalization. Despite its long-running Sinhala-Tamil ethnic conflict, Sri Lanka possesses the region's highest GDP per capita, at $6,100 in 2012, compared with India's $3,900.[15] Less than 9 percent of the island's population lives below the poverty line.

Nepal, sandwiched between the rising powers of India and China, is the poorest of the original SAARC members. One in four of its people lives below the poverty line (estimated 2012 GDP per capita: $1,300). It has experienced immense political turmoil since the 1990s Maoist insurgency. Nepal possesses the only open border with India in the South Asia region. The constant flow of populations has, however, proved a two-edged sword, increasing tensions between Indian settlers and native Nepalese in the southern Terai area and also encouraging armed criminal groups to take shelter in India.[16] Just as Sri Lanka suffers from an uneasy postethnic conflict situation, following the defeat in May 2009 of the Jaffna Tamil separatist forces (Liberation Tigers of Tamil Eelam), so Nepal has experienced an unstable aftermath to the 2006 civil war involving the Maoists.

The South Asian states are all challenged to reduce poverty by means of inclusive economic growth. Different historical patterns of development, however, present specific problems. Bangladesh and Pakistan need to diversify their exports from cotton textiles and the garment trade. Pakistan is also faced with high public debt and dependence on external finance. India has to improve its infrastructure and to encourage more labor-intensive manufacturing production. Nepal needs to generate growth through hydroelectricity production and export sale.

India's regional predominance has generated resentment and mistrust. Its neighbors' diplomatic, military, and covert attempts to challenge New Delhi's might constitute one topic of this book. Only the Maldives (with population of one hundred thousand dispersed over thirty-five thousand square miles of the Indian Ocean) and the tiny landlocked eastern Himalayan kingdom of Bhutan, which in 2008 made the transition from an absolute to a constitutional monarchy, have acted as India's "good" neighbors. The remaining SAARC countries have been periodically locked in conflict with the regional hegemon. The India-Pakistan rivalry, which found its permanent fixation in the struggle over Kashmir, has resulted in three wars, numerous military clashes, and cross-border terrorism. Mistrust and conflict have hindered regional integration and trade. It has been estimated that a normalization of relations between India and Pakistan could result in trade between them rising to $12 billion.[17] After a brief honeymoon following the 1971 liberation war, Indo-Bangladeshi tensions have also grown. Water management, illegal border crossings, and terrorism have soured relations. At various times since the mid-1970s, Bangladesh has provided hideouts and training for militant groups involved in the long-running insurgencies against the Indian state in Assam, Meghalaya, Manipur, and Tripura.[18]

Sources

Students of modern South Asian history can draw on a vast imperial archive produced by what has been termed an "ethnographic state." This was a system of governance legitimized through the enforcement of "tradition" by the codification of customary law and underpinned by the exercise of a kind of divide-and-rule strategy, through the "scientific" enumeration of difference as a result of the census and the all-India ethnographic surveys.[19] The colonial state required detailed knowledge of Indian society to recruit military auxiliaries and raise land taxes. This knowledge was, however, mediated both by values and stereotypes brought from Europe and by the input from high-caste Indian interlocutors. Eugene Irschick, in his study of nineteenth-century South India, has termed such colonial knowledge as "dialogical."[20]

Jawaharlal Nehru's increasingly frustrated efforts to transform postcolonial India into a "developmental state" are revealed in his voluminous correspondence housed in the Nehru Memorial Museum and Library in New Delhi. The Ministry of External Affairs Records recently released in the National Archives shed light on the state's cold-shouldering of the "diaspora next door." Much less material is available for the study of early postcolonial Bangladesh and Pakistan.[21] This has contributed to the Indocentric historical narrative. Primary sources are more readily available in Washington and London than in national archives in Dhaka and Islamabad.[22]

For both the colonial and postindependence eras, official documents can be supplemented by private papers, published memoirs, and newspaper accounts. Most major historical works would have been poorer without utilizing these sources. Biographies of key imperial and nationalist figures would be impossible without them. The absence of private diaries or letters for Jinnah has not prevented a cottage industry of biographical publications in Pakistan, but there are no definitive equivalents to the work on Gandhi or Nehru. South Asian historians have also deployed British and American missionary archives, not only for the purposes of church history but to provide insights into the "history from beneath" that has also been written with the aid of personal testimonies and literature.

Recent work on the history of Partition "from beneath" has, for example, derived important insights from such creative authors as Khushwant Singh, Chaman Nahal, Kartar Singh Duggal, Bhisham Sahni, and Intizar Hussain. Sadaat Hassan Manto, the celebrated Pakistani writer, has produced the greatest fictional work on Partition.[23] His portrayal of the torn identities brought by Partition in the work *Toba Tek Singh* has almost become an academic cliché.

Literature and firsthand accounts have also opened a window on diasporic experiences. Brij Lal, for example, has collected testimonies that shed light on the lives of indentured Indian laborers in Fiji.[24] Acclaimed novels by such authors as V. S. Naipaul (*A House for Mr. Biswas*), David Dabydeen (*The Counting House*), and Monica Ali (*Brick Lane*) illuminate overseas

Indians' experiences as far afield as the Caribbean and the East End of London. The largely unknown poet C. V. Velupillai has produced poignant vignettes of the lives of up-country Tamil tea plantation workers in Ceylon (*Born to Labour*).

The buoyant South Asian film industries provide another source for understanding popular culture and living conditions. The latter are featured not only in the Bollywood Mumbai noir films of the 1990s but in Satyajit Rai's earlier Bengali social realist productions such as *Pather Panchali* (1955) and *Aparajito* (1956). Films also offer insights into the construction of key historical events, whether these are the 1857 revolt (*Mangal Pandey: The Rising*), the 1947 Partition (*Earth*), or the 1971 Indo-Pakistani War (*Border*). Bollywood's influence on Western filmmakers was seen in Danny Boyle's acclaimed film *Slumdog Millionaire* (2008).

Organization and Themes

The volume, as well as focusing on key individuals, and major turning points, traces important continuities in South Asian history since the mid-eighteenth century. The British commentator Mark Tully once famously remarked that there are no "full stops" in India.[25] For Bangladesh, 1971 is the decisive moment in its history, but as William Van Schendel has expertly shown, the Bengal Delta's ecological influences continue to exert their long-run influence on the new state.[26]

My text begins with thematic chapters that address such issues as overseas migration, long-run ecological influences, and the perils of climate change. The chronological chapters focus on company and Crown rules and their legacies for the postcolonial Indian, Pakistan, and Bangladesh states. It is argued that the British Raj constructed an understanding of Indian society that laid the groundwork for future political mobilization around the ascriptive loyalties of caste and religion. The export of plantation contract workers and imperial auxiliaries to Ceylon and Burma also created the environment in the two countries for anti-Indian and Sinhala-Tamil conflict. Large-scale collective violence has been a feature of both late colonial and postindependence South Asia. It is frequently understood as being perpetrated because of primordial ethnic and religious hatreds. In this volume, however, I argue that it is primarily a tool in political contests about power, land, and resources.

Violence has been used by both the state and nonstate actors. The state has often been drawn into conflict because of local resistance to its policies of cultural, administrative, and political centralization. A legacy of the 1947 Partition has been the emergence of a "fearful" South Asian state determined to prevent further "balkanization." Democratic and authoritarian governments alike have dealt harshly with separatist demands and frequently driven those demanding greater autonomy to take arms as political negotiation has been replaced by "law and order" solutions. India, Pakistan, and Bangladesh have all at various times faced serious and lengthy insurgencies, sustained in part by the existence of cross-border sanctuaries. We shall see in the next chapter that borderland populations have been victims of the postcolonial state's resultant security arrangements and everyday violence.

PART I

ONE

Borders and Boundaries

In an uncanny echo of Saadat Hasan Manto's classic Partition short story, "Toba Tek Singh," about border identities in South Asia, 213 people, including 80 children and 65 women, were stranded for a week in 2003 on the no-man's-land between Bangladesh and India at Satgachi, in Cooch Behar, West Bengal. They sat in the open, huddled against the February cold, while the authorities argued about their future. The Indian border guards claimed that they were illegal immigrants and should be "pushed back"; their Bangladeshi counterparts refused to accept them, as there was no proof that they were Bangladeshi citizens. Newspaper investigations revealed that the nowhere people came from Poraberi in the Manikgunj subdivision of Bangladesh. They had crossed the border to entertain local Indian villagers with their snake-charming skills.[1] The "stranded people" suddenly disappeared on the foggy morning of 6 February. The Border Security Force (BSF) claimed that the Bangladesh government had taken them back under Indian pressure, but Dhaka denied any knowledge of their whereabouts.

The episode attracted headlines, because it followed the claim by the Hindu Nationalist Indian Prime Minister L. K. Advani of the "illegal immigration" of twenty million Bangladeshis. This had prompted efforts in late January 2003 by the BSF to "push in" to Bangladesh Bengali-speaking Muslims who had been reportedly collected from as far afield as Mumbai and New Delhi.[2] Local residents supported by the Bangladesh border guards had resisted these moves in an atmosphere of increasing tension.

The nomadic snake charmers' brief appearance on the historical stage is important because it puts a human face to the immigration dynamic in Indo-Bangladeshi relations. It also highlights a wider South Asian "border anxiety." This has prioritized "national security" over "human security." According to this attitude, the border is a tightly sealed boundary that separates distinct populations. Local populations living in borderland areas, in contrast, see the border as a frontier for them to cross. Everyday activities by local residents involving border crossings have become criminalized, whether this is attending local markets or providing entertainment. Such transgressions can be violently repressed, as they threaten the state's use of the border as a sign of "territorial sovereignty." Indeed, the borders of South Asian states are constituted precisely by the policing of their everyday transgressions by locals which actualize lines drawn on a map.

However, as Das and Poole argue, "Local worlds and the state do not stand as binary opposites. Even although they are locked in unequal relations, they are enmeshed in one another."[3] Border guards collude with local residents in the smuggling of goods, arms, and people. This has similarities with the "adoption" of criminals by police within their territorial jurisdictions in state heartlands. Trafficked Bangladeshis may end up in the Gulf as maids, but they are more likely to become prostitutes in Kolkata, Mumbai, and other South Asian cities. According to one estimate, half a million child prostitutes from Bangladesh are in Pakistan and India.[4]

Extrajudicial killings of "illegal" border crossers usually occur when there is some kind of grievance, for example, one arising from a lack of payment. Even extrajudicial killings do not result in widespread outrage, unless they are especially gruesome, as when the body of a fourteen-year-old Bangladeshi girl was found hanging upside down from the barbed-wire Indian fence in Phulbari, at the Kurigram, Bangladesh, border, on the morning of 6 January 2011.[5]

The Subcontinent's borders have been the site not only of human trafficking but of massive refugee movements. Eleven million people fled across the new international line that divided the Indian and Pakistan Punjab borders in 1947. India claimed that it had to support ten million refugees following the outbreak of civil war in East Pakistan in 1971. The presence of refugees in West Bengal, already disturbed by Maoist insurgents, was used to justify the military intervention that brought about the birth of Bangladesh. Three million refugees entered Pakistan during the Soviet occupation of

Afghanistan in 1979. Less well known is the forcing out of Bhutan of up to a hundred thousand Lhotshampa (Nepali Hindu) workers following the loss of their citizenship rights in the 1988 census.[6] Most recently, Rohingya boat-people refugees have attempted to cross the Teknaf River to enter Bangladesh and escape the violence in their Arakan homeland in Myanmar. The Subcontinent's borders are sites of "violence" and "resentment." They also enable the theatrical display of sovereignty.

The Punjab Border: Zero Point and the Daily Display of National Sovereignty

Wagah is the most famous of three sites in Punjab where the beating of the retreat is daily enacted as a powerful sign of sovereign statehood.[7] The Indo-Pakistani border at this point is almost equidistant from the historic cities of Lahore, now the capital of Pakistan Punjab, and Amritsar in India. These two cities were referred to as "twins" in the colonial era because of their long history of trade and communication.[8] The Wagah border post has developed from its original two sentry boxes and swing gate into an impressive complex of buildings that beginning in April 2012 has included, on the Indian side of the border, an integrated checkpoint with a passenger terminal and a cargo facility and, on the Pakistan side, a "trade gate."

The border is signified by the white line of Zero Point drawn on the tarmac. To emphasize the gulf of separation the line is intended to represent, either side of it is in a different time zone, with clocks on the Pakistan side of the border half an hour ahead. Ceremonial gateways painted in the national colors stand at either side of the border. On the Indian gate is a large sign inscribed *Mera Bharat Mahan* (My India is great); its Pakistani counterpart reads in Urdu, *Pakistan Zindabad* (Long live Pakistan). There is also a large signboard facing the Indian border that declares, "India: The largest democracy in the world welcomes you."

The nightly flag lowering ceremony displays national sovereignty. Its theatricality has been affirmed by the creation of spectator seating areas on both sides of the border. Television portrayals ensure that it is known to an international audience, so that Western tourists join the jostling throng.[9]

The flag lowering ceremony is preceded by flag brandishing and the amplification of prerecorded patriotic music. The cheerleading on the Pakistan side was orchestrated for more than half a century by Mehar Din, who became fondly known as Chacha Pakistani. He attended the ceremony every day clad in a *kurta* made out of a Pakistani flag. The ceremony itself is conducted by a dozen or so members of the BSF and Pakistan Rangers who have been carefully selected for their height, which is enhanced by the elaborate fans attached to their turbans (red for the Indians, black for their Pakistani counterparts). The goose-stepping of the lines of soldiers toward each other, followed by the clattering of boots as they wheel just short of point zero, has been termed the strut of peacocks.[10] Since July 2010 some of the more aggressive eyeballing and fist clenching has been dropped by the participants, but the whole choreography that concludes with the lowering of the national flags in unison and the clanging shut of the border gates is designed to reaffirm daily India's and Pakistan's sovereignty, each to the other.

If the retreat ceremony uses the border to theatrically underpin nationalism, the documentary regime of visas and permits represents a further sign of sovereign statehood. Because the Indian and Pakistani states mutually accepted that the virtual exchange of population in the divided province of Punjab was permanent, a permit system to enforce travel restrictions across the border in this area was introduced in October 1948. A more permissive regime prevailed in divided Bengal, where officials believed that refugees would return home. Not until 1952 were passports introduced for the eastern border. Refugees continued to cross the Bengal border nonetheless, at times of riot or Indo-Pakistani national tension. This led the Indian authorities, who received far more Bengali refugees than their Pakistani counterparts, to increasingly elaborate the documentary regime of visas and to define citizenship through migration certificates. "New migrants" who moved between January 1964 and March 1971 were eligible for relief only if they moved outside the Indian state of West Bengal.

The vast majority of Indian and Pakistan nationals who cross the Punjab border have to endure the "surveillance regime" that is the flip side to the state's theatrical display of its power. The border crossing at Wagah has been viewed by some as a "transition" for Western travelers, but a "transgression" for South Asians.[11] While "foreigners" can walk over point zero, Indian and Pakistani citizens have to endure a two-mile railway journey from the Indian station of Attari to its Wagah, Pakistan, counterpart. This can take up to seven hours because of an intrusive and intimidating customs procedure. Like the time zone difference, this expands the spatial divide between the countries. The American travel writer Stephen Alter has captured the grim conditions at Attari railway station, with its steel mesh partition of the central platform epitomizing the division of South Asia into the territorial nation states of India and Pakistan.[12]

Despite the Punjab borderland's regimes of surveillance, it has continued to be crossed by smugglers and human traffickers. In the 1980s, it was regularly "infiltrated" by Sikh separatist militants who had bases in Pakistan. Indeed, it was only when Pakistan ended its support that the Indian counterinsurgency in Punjab was able to break the militant campaign.

Sindh-Rajasthan

We continue our swing around the international border between India and Pakistan in a southerly direction. The Sindh-Rajasthan boundary stretches for more than six hundred miles, making it the longest Indo-Pakistani land boundary. The area on the Pakistan side of the boundary was part of the Bombay Presidency until the province of Sindh was created in 1935. The Indian territory formerly comprised the Princely States, which were grouped together in the Rajputana Agency. The border has been little written about in comparison with the Punjab border and the line of control in Kashmir. This reflects its relative remoteness. The area has seen little investment. Irrigation from the Indira Gandhi Canal does not reach the border villages, the land becoming browner and more barren the closer it is to Zero Point. The whole of the Sindh-Rajasthan border has become increasingly militarized since the 1965 Indo-Pakistani War. Until that time, it was still possible for refugees to cross the border at Khokhrapar without permits. Opium, which had been traditionally smuggled from western Rajasthan to Sindh, was still being smuggled across the porous border as late as 1960.

Marriage ties have continued across the international border among the Sodha Rajputs of Sindh and western Rajasthan, although they have been increasingly hemmed in by visa restrictions. Traditionally, marriage alliances were conducted between the Sodha Rajput clans of Amarkot (present-day Umerkot in Sindh Pakistan) and Rajputs outside their clan in Jodhpur and Jaipur. The Sodha Rajputs, because they were attached to their ancestral lands, did not migrate to India in 1947. The peaceful conditions meant that they were not forced to do so, as were minority populations on both sides of the Punjab border. As late as 1965, marriage parties used to cross over to India unhampered by the border security forces.[13] Since then the securitization of the border has made these long-established social ties much more difficult to sustain. Sodha girls who are married into Rajput families in the Barmer and Jaisalmer districts close to the border may never see their families and homes in Sindh again.[14]

By 2005, the entire western Rajasthan-Sindh border had been fenced; the razor wire was illuminated at night by powerful floodlights. In the wake of the 2002 Indo-Pakistani military standoff, populations were evacuated and as many as eight hundred thousand mines were laid on the Indian side of the border. Although the majority had been cleared by the following September, they caused civilian deaths and maiming and disrupted agriculture in an already poor region. Mines were laid on farming and grazing land as well as in uncultivated areas, as far as five miles from the border.[15]

In 2006, the Khokhrapar-Munabao border railway link was reopened as part of the confidence-building measures between India and Pakistan. The Thar Express ran for the first time in forty-one years on 18 February 2006.

The initial euphoria has dispelled, however, because of the bureaucratic obstacles that continue to hinder family reunions. Indians, who are the majority of the passengers, have to travel five hundred miles to the Pakistan High Commission in Delhi to secure a visa to visit their relatives. The Indian state also exerts its power by refusing to allow passengers from Pakistan to get off at Munabao, the first Indian station, although a customs check is carried out there. Passengers are not set down from the Thar Express until it reaches Bhagat ki kothi in Jodhpur, some two hours' distance from the border. Local residents of the Indian border villages have described this as

1. Thar Express at Munabao railway station at the India-Pakistan border on its first journey in forty-one years, 18 February 2006

a case of *pyase ko paani dikaya jai par pilaya na jaye*: showing water to the thirsty but not allowing him to drink.

Sindh-Gujarat: The Rann of Kutch and Sir Creek

The international boundary continues south, traveling along the Sindh and Gujarat borders. It reaches the coast at the salty marshland and black tidal mudflats of the Rann of Kutch. This is a sparsely populated area with flamingos and wild donkeys almost outnumbering the local inhabitants. It nonetheless was the site of fierce fighting at the time of the 1965 Indo-Pakistani War, following the Pakistan Army's launching of Operation Arrow Head in the early hours of 24 April.[16] In the war's aftermath, mainly the result of patient British diplomacy, India and Pakistan agreed to refer rival claims to the Rann to an international arbitration tribunal.[17] The tribunal in February 1968 upheld most of India's claim, although Pakistan had claimed half of the seven thousand–square–mile salt waste. The adjudicators did not, however, discuss Sir Creek, a sixty-mile-long estuary situated in the marshes of the Rann of Kutch. It is precisely this part of the Sindh-Gujarat border that has become a source of contention.

The Sir Creek dispute exemplifies South Asian states' border anxieties, the doleful legacies of colonial cartography, the lack of trust that undermines cooperation, and the disruptive effect of militarization on the lives of border dwellers. Fishermen are routinely arrested by both countries because they have unknowingly strayed over a hotly contested border. They have even been fired on by naval patrol boats. They can spend years in jail before being released as pawns in the chess game of Indo-Pakistani relations. Pakistan, for example, freed fifty fishermen from jails in Karachi and Lahore ahead of talks with India on the border demarcation in December 2006.[18] Charu Gupta and Mukul Sharma have recently revealed the human impact on fishermen and their families when they become "prisoners of war."[19]

India claims that the international boundary of Sir Creek should lie in the middle of the estuary, while Pakistan maintains that it should lie on the southeast bank. The situation has been further complicated by a westward shift in the course of the channel since the last colonial boundary map was drawn in 1925. If the Indian claim succeeded, Pakistan would lose a considerable amount of territory and access under maritime law to a 230-mile exclusive economic zone with potential for the commercial exploitation of oil and gas. It is hardly surprising that since 1969, there have been nine rounds of failed talks. India and Pakistan conducted a joint survey of the estuary in 2007, but the terrorist attacks in Mumbai the following year halted further dialogue until May 2011, when the maps were finally exchanged, but without any movement on the issue.

International Boundary Disputes

Boundary disputes in the Subcontinent involve not just India versus Pakistan, but Pakistan versus Afghanistan, India versus China, and the smaller Himalayan countries such as Bhutan versus China. The latter's growing power in recent years has intensified these disputes, which have their origins in colonial cartography. China refuses, for example, to acknowledge the boundaries drawn by the British in the northeast of the Subcontinent. The Chinese insist that the thirty-five thousand–square–mile Indian State of Arunachal Pradesh be included in the Tibet Autonomous Region of the People's Republic of China. Units of the People's Liberation Army overran Arunachal Pradesh, at that time known as the North East Frontier Agency, in October 1962, only to withdraw beyond the disputed 1914 McMahon line claiming victory.[20] China's claims on Arunachal Pradesh, which it calls South Tibet, have been reemphasized in recent years, although no shots have been fired on the border since 1993.

China also disputes the western end of its twenty-one hundred–mile–long border with India. This desert plateau wedged between Ladakh, Tibet, and Xinjiang, known as the Aksai Chin, was demarcated by the Johnson Line, which dates from 1865. It was used inconsistently during the colonial era as the boundary in the Karakoram region between China and Kashmir. China asserted control over the region without fully exercising that control against India's counterclaim. During the 1950s, the People's Republic of China built the strategically important road linking Xinjiang and Tibet across the Aksai Chin; New Delhi learned of the road's existence only after its completion. The construction of the road, together with India's granting asylum to the Dalai Lama in 1959 and skirmishes as India more vigorously patrolled the disputed border areas, formed the backdrop to the 1962 Sino-Indian War.[21] Hopes that India could drop its claim to Aksai Chin, with China reciprocating in the north eastern Arunachal Pradesh sector, have not materialized. On the eve of the fiftieth anniversary of the 1962 war a commentary published in the *Liberation Daily* ruled out accepting the de facto "line of actual control" as a solution to the border dispute.[22]

Successive regimes in Afghanistan have similarly refused to acknowledge the Durand Line—established in November 1893 following negotiations between Sir Mortimer Durand and Amir Abdurrahman—as constituting the boundary with what is now Pakistan. Kabul has questioned the Durand Line's legality amid claims that it was coercively imposed. There have even been inaccurate claims that the agreement was limited to a hundred years.

A twenty-six hundred–mile border divides Pakistan's North West Frontier Province (now known as Khyber Pakhtunkwha), the Federally Administered Tribal Areas, and Balochistan from Afghanistan's eastern and southern provinces. The clash between India and Pakistan over Kashmir has overshadowed the tense relations on the western border.

Only in the wake of 9/11 and Western intervention in the region was attention focused on the porous Afghan-Pakistani border. Political opinion in both countries has undermined even limited attempts at fencing the border, which is a focus not only for smuggling drugs and weapons but for trading consumer goods. Transborder attacks have been launched in both directions.[23] The Pakistan Army's interventions in such tribal agencies as Bajaur and South Waziristan to flush out Al-Qaeda militants resulted in large-scale temporary displacements of population. The borderland peoples of the Afghanistan frontier have also suffered "collateral damage" resulting from the US drone campaign against Al-Qaeda targets.

The Line of Control

We move from a disputed international border to a dotted line on the map that represents a military border not recognized in international law. The line of control separates the Indian and Pakistani administered areas of the former Princely State of Jammu and Kashmir. Our journey begins beyond its most northern point at the Siachen Glacier. The forty-five-mile-long glacier located in the eastern Karakoram Range in the Himalayan Mountains at the junction of the Pakistani, Chinese, and Turkistani borders was not included in the original cease-fire line or the later line of control in Kashmir to the south because it was considered too remote and inhospitable to become a source of conflict. Since 1984, however, India and Pakistan have been fighting each other on the world's highest battlefield, twenty-two thousand feet above sea level.

Siachen made international headlines in April 2012 when 140 Pakistani soldiers and civilian contractors were buried alive by an avalanche at Gayari some twenty miles to the west. More soldiers from both India and Pakistan have died as a result of avalanches, frostbite, or falls into crevices than in the sporadic fighting.[24] The Indian military launched Operation Meghdoot in April 1984 to preempt Pakistan from establishing a base that would have controlled the key ridges and passes in the area. The operation secured around nine hundred square miles of territory claimed by Pakistan.[25] Thereafter India has controlled around two-thirds of the glacier and the main passes and strategic Saltori ridge west of the glacier. Pakistan failed in both 1987 and 1989 to dislodge the Indian troops. Hopes that the human tragedy at Gayari might end what has been termed an "insane" military standoff have not been realized. Despite the high logistical costs, successive negotiations beginning in 1986 have failed to demarcate the area beyond the de facto line of control.

The line of control to the south of Siachen runs for six hundred miles. It replaced the cease-fire line in the Kashmir region after the signing of the Simla agreement between India and Pakistan on 3 July 1972. In later chapters, we will trace the genesis of the Kashmir dispute and its impact on Indo-Pakistani relations. Here we are concerned with the actual line of control and its impact on local populations, and on patterns of trade and communications.

Traditional Kashmiri trade routes were permanently disrupted by the armed clashes of 1947–48, which produced the current line of control. The accession of the former Princely State of Jammu and Kashmir to India was accompanied by an uprising in Poonch and a subsequent tribal invasion of the Kashmir Valley, which expanded into an Indian-Pakistani conflict. When the war ended on 1 January 1949, the cease-fire line (the current line of control) closed the well-established trade route for timber and other products from Muzaffarabad, along the Jhelum Valley via Baramulla, to the now Indian-occupied Kashmir Valley. Muzaffarabad has gained in importance as the administrative center of Pakistani Azad Kashmir, but its commercial development has been hampered. Kotli, on the alternative Mughal road route, was also cut off by the new boundary from the Kashmir Valley. Poonch, which was on the Indian side of the border, was separated from its traditional hinterland and ethnic Sudhan heartland. Such disruptions were especially damaging in a backward area that relied for its income on through trade rather than local agricultural production. State subsidies have thus been required to prop up the economy of areas that were either marginalized by the new political boundaries or, as in the case of the Neelum Valley, had long-term locational disadvantages exacerbated by proximity to a hostile border.

The two hundred–mile–long Neelum Valley, which runs north and then east along the line of control, was being constantly bombarded by mortars and indiscriminate gun fire between 1992 and the 2003 cease-fire. The crossfire caused the local residents to live in constant fear of death from stray shells. According to locals, eleven children were killed in 1993, when an Indian mortar landed in the village school at Nagdar.[26] The sense of marginalization arising from life in a war zone intensified because of the closing of road links. Because of diversions, it took eleven hours to travel from Muzaffarabad, the capital of Azad Kashmir, to Athmaquam, the district headquarters of the Neelum district.[27] Border villages were once more in the line of fire when shelling resumed in autumn 2013.

The 2003 cease-fire was followed by relaxation of some restrictions on travel across the line of control. This was one of the confidence-building measures that, as we have seen, increased transport links in the Punjab and Sindh border areas. The governments of India and Pakistan were also more open to the wishes of the local residents following the devastating 2005 earthquake in the region. The natural disaster did not respect man-made boundaries and highlighted the consequences of the poor communications links in efforts to provide assistance. Routes were opened at the border crossings at Chakothi-Uri, where the bridge across the Kalyana Khus Nallah was rebuilt; Taitri Nath-Chakan Bagh, near Poonch; and Nauseri-Teetwal, in the Neelum Valley. These border openings enabled limited barter trade at the Uri and Poonch posts and provided important opportunities for reunions among families that had been separated since 1947. Visiting Indian journalists were informed by Pakistan officials in May 2011 that twenty-three thousand trucks had been permitted from both sides since 2008, along with fifteen thousand visitors. After a verification process of some forty-five days, permits are issued only to residents of the Kashmir region for a maximum stay of a month.[28]

India's opening up of the line of control for cross-border trade and travel was accompanied by its fencing to keep out "terrorists." Until the time of the Kargil War in 1999, the Pakistani government strenuously denied that it supported militant intrusion into Indian Kashmir. This method of waging a proxy war in fact dated back to the original incursion of Pathan tribesmen in October 1947.[29] Irregular Islamic militants supported by Pakistani forces drawn from the Azad Kashmir Rifles, the Northern Light Infantry, and the Special Services Group Commandos infiltrated the line of control on 5 August 1965 in the ill-fated Operation Gibraltar.[30] Further intrusions occurred during the 1989 intifada, both by young Indian Kashmiris and, increasingly, by battle-hardened veterans from the Afghan jihad. The Kashmiri journalist Basharat Peer recounts the story of his older cousin Tariq, who had crossed the line of control in 1991 to receive arms training at a camp in Muzaffarabad run by the Pakistan military. He and his friends were led over the mountains by a guide from the border villages who knew the terrain well.[31] Tariq survived the return journey a year later, although he saw the grisly remains of those who had died in encounters with Indian patrols.[32]

By early 2004, India had fenced a seventy-five-mile stretch in the Kashmir Valley. Each mile-and-a-quarter section took a fortnight to construct. The twelve-foot-high double row of fencing was electrified and connected to a network of motion sensors. The costs were reckoned worthwhile, as it was estimated that infiltration was reduced by as much as 80 percent.[33]

The Indo-Bangladeshi River Borderland

The Indo-Bangladeshi border, which stretches for some twenty-five hundred miles, is strikingly different from the line of control in terms of its climate and topography. Nonetheless, similar issues arise from border anxiety there, including increased securitization and fencing, with its disruption of economic and social life. For about a quarter of its distance the border follows the course of rivers, which became international boundaries for the first time in 1947, separating India from East Pakistan. As a result, most boundary disputes in the region have involved rivers.[34] The problems arising from the Bengal Boundary Commission's faulty maps were compounded by the rivers' natural process of shifting their courses in the active Ganges Delta. In 1950 India and Pakistan sought arbitration through the Bagge Tribunal to resolve disputes around the boundaries marked by the Mathabhanga River on the western border between India and East Pakistan and the Kusharia River in Sylhet in the east. Just as in the Rann of Kutch, the disputed location of water borders has brought dangers to fishermen (and ferrymen who work the border rivers), and a number have died as a result of cross-border gunfire.

The Bagge Tribunal's most difficult task involved the resolution of disputes surrounding the *chars*—alluvial sandbanks—on the Ganges River and its tributary the Padma. Chars form in the middle of all the large rivers of the Ganges Delta.[35] Some of these last only a couple of monsoons, while others have provided a home for the 600,000 *char basi*—char dwellers—throughout East Pakistan and then Bangladesh for a generation or so. The biggest chars offer a precarious existence for poor farmers who risk seasonal

2. House on Char Chowmohon

and cyclonic flooding to grow betel nuts, to fish, and to graze cattle on cat-kin grass, which, when it is dried, also provides fuel and thatch.

During 1948, Indian and Pakistani police and army clashed repeatedly over the disputed jurisdiction of chars in the Murshidabad-Rajshahi border area. East Pakistani forces attempted to occupy Char Saranaspur, while their Indian counterparts seized Char Ghughumari.[36] The Bagge Tribunal did not end char disputes, as nature kept throwing up new problems. New char lands appeared in previously disputed areas. In 1953 the shifting riverscape of creeks, islets, and salt flats so confused Indian and Pakistani officials who had gone to formally demarcate a temporary national boundary established around Char Nowshera "that they could not locate the border at all [and] left thoroughly confused and disorientated."[37] The attempt to resolve char disputes through joint survey and demarcation continued after the emergence of Bangladesh. Nonetheless, local conflicts persisted, as in 2000, when the Padma shifted more than five miles to the southwest on the Nadia-Kushtia border, throwing up new chars.[38]

The Northeast and Chittagong Hill Tracts

In the northeast of the Subcontinent, Bangladesh meets Myanmar in the south and India meets Bangladesh and Myanmar in the north. This troubled area has been the site of tribal insurgencies against India, Pakistan, Bangladesh, and Burma. The focus here is not on the local roots of these insurgencies, or on their course, but on the impact of the border location.[39]

We have seen that all borderlands provide sanctuary for rebels and that India and Pakistan's post-1947 rivalry encouraged their support of insurgencies. This has kept the Kashmir dispute on the boil. The Pakhtunistan movement was similarly supported by the Afghan authorities providing refuges for Pakhtun and Baloch insurgents. India supported East Bengali insurgents in the months before the 1971 war. A decade earlier, India had trained Tibetan guerrillas. Pakistan, Bangladesh, Burma, and China have all fished in the troubled waters of India's northeast, where throughout most of the postcolonial period, tribal Nagas, Mizos, and Khasis have been battling the Indian state. The porous borders with Myanmar and Bangladesh have encouraged

3. Naga tribesmen arriving at Shillong to do war dance

what has been termed South Asia's "insurgent crossfire." This began in 1956 with Pakistani support to the Nagas.[40] New Delhi supported tribal militants from the Chittagong Hill Tracts in their struggle against the East Pakistan/ Bangladesh state. At the same time, the same area was being used to train tribal insurgents against India.

The Chittagong Hill Tracts are an area of more than five thousand square miles in southeastern Bangladesh that borders the Arakan and Chin States of Burma and the Indian states of Mizoram and Tripura. The region's hilly and jungle terrain is ideal for guerrilla training and activities. Its thirteen indigenous ethnic groups are collectively known as the Jumma people. Following the region's annexation in 1860, British rule "protected" their sociocultural practices through the upholding of customary law. The inclusion of this tribal area in East Pakistan set it on the road to repression, armed rebellion, and protracted war."[41] During the 1980s and 1990s, India supported the Shanti Bahini—the Jumma guerrilla army—in its actions against the Bangladeshi forces. During Dhaka's counterinsurgency operations, cantonments were established in the region, and settlement of population from "mainland" Bangladesh was unofficially sponsored. There are records of thirteen massacres of Jumma people between 1980 and the 1997 peace treaty, which ended the armed conflict.

India's northeastern border region has been the site of the most enduring insurgencies against the state apart from Kashmir. No fewer than 109 rebel groups were counted in the region in 2006. The Indian state has fought "little wars" against them in Nagaland, Mizoram, Assam, Tripura, and Manipur.[42] Since the launching of the armed Naga rebellion in the 1950s, this whole region has been a stage for sharpening of ethnic identity, violence against both the Indian state and smaller ethnic groups, displacement of populations, and further marginalization of minority groups. Indian counterinsurgency involved military operations (such as Operation Bajrang and Operation Rhino) and subsequent peace accords with rebels, including some that carved out new states. New groups have continually emerged to take up arms, and smaller ethnic minorities have sought their own land in emulation of the larger armed groups. Conflict has also persisted because of "insurgent crossfire." Beginning as early as 1955, the hills and jungles of East Pakistan's Sylhet, Mymensingh, and the Chittagong Hill Tracts provided safe havens and training camps for Naga insurgents. They were joined a decade later by Mizos, whose insurgency was spurred by a devastating famine caused by a burgeoning rat population (*Mautam*). While the larger tribal groups such as the Nagas and Mizos fought for secession from India, smaller ethnic communities such as the Bodos took up arms to create homelands to be carved out of the region's largest state, Assam.

Immediately after Bangladesh's independence, the Chittagong Hill Tracts were closed to Indian tribal insurgents, but military rule brought the reopening of camps. The Mizo National Front, for example, returned to the region in April 1978. Until the early 1980s China provided another training area in Yunnan for Naga and Mizo guerrillas. The Kachin Independence Army, which was fighting its own insurgency against Rangoon's military rulers on Burma's western border, provided a corridor for the long march by Naga and Mizo rebels to Yunnan in China. Manipuri rebel groups have received Chinese arms supplies through Bhutan. The tiny Himalayan Kingdom also provided a much nearer base than Bangladesh for Bodo insurgents until under Indian pressure, the Bhutan Army launched Operation All Clear against them in December 2003.

The Subcontinent's Maritime Boundaries

There are no maritime boundary disputes between India and its neighbors akin to those that bedevil Sino-Japanese relations. The Gulf of Mannar and the Palk Strait, which make up the narrow sea passage between India and Sri Lanka, have long established an interconnection between the countries. Indeed, according to the Ramayana, a land bridge existed at one time. Settlers from West Bengal reached Ceylon around the sixth century BC, and Buddhism was brought to the island by the Indian Emperor Ashoka's son three centuries later. The colonial era (the island was ceded to the British by the Dutch in 1796, but Kandy was not occupied until 1815) led to large-scale Tamil labor migration to the tea plantations that beginning in the 1870s replaced earlier coffee plantations. The presence of a significant Tamil minority in Ceylon, with a large population on the nearby India mainland, raised fears of a "long-term possibility" of Indian expansion. There were also fears in Colombo that India would occupy the Trincomalee naval base, which was finally abandoned by Britain in 1956.

Sri Lanka was strategically important to India because of its position near major Indian Ocean sea lanes. These anxieties were partially moderated by the fact that both India and Ceylon (renamed Sri Lanka in 1972) were members of the British Commonwealth. Indian security interests were threatened by the pro-West foreign policy adopted by such Sri Lankan leaders as Sir John Kotelawala (prime minister, 1953–56) and President Jayewardene (1978–89), nicknamed "Yankie Dickie."[43] From the time of Sirimavo Bandaranaike's 1970–77 premiership, China emerged as a potential counterbalance to Indian hegemony. Later chapters will reveal, however, that it was the onset of the Tamil-Sinhala civil war in 1983 that prompted eventual Indian military intervention in the neighboring island.

The Maldives lie about 450 miles from Sri Lanka's maritime coast and 250 miles southwest of India. The islands were a British protectorate from 1867 until 1965. They were first settled by Dravidian peoples from Kerela and western Sri Lanka, and Buddhism was introduced around the time of Ashoka. According to the famous Muslim traveler Ibn Battuta, who visited the Maldives in the fourteenth century, Islam had been introduced two centuries earlier by a Moroccan.[44] The Maldives' isolation reduced their strategic significance, although Britain, through its protectorate, and India, in a naval operation and airlift (Operation Cactus in November 1988), have intervened to prevent threats to these tiny remote Muslim islands.[45] The Maldives' future looked bright following the first multiparty elections in 2008, but a coup just four years later ended Mohamed Nasheed's rule and has led to turmoil and the reappearance of the former dictatorship in the controversial elections of November 2013.

The Subcontinent's borderlands differ geographically, but are similar in that they are places where guns, goods, and people illegally circulate. Borderland populations frequently face insecurity and violence as "national security" trumps "human security." Expensive fencing operations, however, fail to deliver the impermeable borders sought by nation-states. Illegal border crossings by smugglers and insurgents have continued. Periodically since 1947, India, Pakistan, Bangladesh, and China have all adopted what might be termed a policy of insurgency patronage in the border areas.

Not only are the borders porous and violent, they are of central importance for the assertion of territorial sovereignty and the development of notions of citizenship, particularly in the context of mass refugee migrations. It was also in borderland insurgencies that the modern South Asian States developed their coercive apparatus with emergency laws such as the Armed Forces Special Powers Act and the Terrorist and Disruptive Powers Act. Such laws have been physically accompanied by fencing and increased militarization. Violent border control regimes have been accompanied with discourses dominated by fears of "infiltration" and "illegal migration." Borderland populations have been continually harassed as they seek to go about their daily economic activities.

TWO

Land, Society, Environment

"The water came into our home at night and we had to swim out as quickly as possible. I carried my baby boy on my shoulders. The flood has taken everything away from me, including one of my girls. She breathed in too much water and couldn't make it."[1] The flood that turned Nizam Ali's world upside down followed record monsoon rainfall of ten inches in twenty-four hours in Peshawar at the end of June 2010.[2] The flash floods in the north of Pakistan were the prelude to an unprecedented flooding of the Indus Basin, which, by the time the waters were discharged in the Arabian Sea, had inundated nearly a fifth of Pakistan's landmass. Fourteen million people were displaced by the floods—more than the combined effects of the December 2004 Asian tsunami and the October 2005 earthquake in Kashmir. Around 875,000 homes were destroyed, along with $1 billion worth of crops.[3] Some analysts believed that up to 2 percentage points of the projected growth rate in gross domestic product would be lost.[4] The floods raised intense debate as to whether they were evidence of anthropogenic climate change or whether they fell within the natural variability of the monsoonal climate.

South Asia's high rates of poverty, dependence on Himalayan glaciers as a major source of water for its river systems, environmental degradation, and long coastlines make it vulnerable to the projected impact of climate change. This will vary across its diverse climates, locations, and populations. Nonetheless, there is mounting evidence of an increase in extreme weather events, such as droughts, intense precipitation, and rising temperatures. The last will limit water availability and encourage pests and disease, reducing crop yields and thereby affecting food security for millions of people across the region.

The Subcontinent's Natural Setting and Human Settlement

The landform of the Subcontinent, which covers a tenth of the Asian continent, emerged some fifty million years ago, when the Indian tectonic plate, having broken off from the supercontinent of Gondwana and drifted northward, collided with the Asian plate. The tremendous force created the Himalayan Mountains, the highest and youngest chain of mountains in the world. They run in a fifteen hundred–mile arc west to east. On their northwestern edge lie the Hindu Kush and Karakoram ranges. Their height has shielded the Subcontinent from the cold winds of the Tibetan Plateau, making it warmer than other temperate zones. The Himalayas have also formed a barrier for the monsoon winds, causing heavy rainfall in the foothills. The Indus, Ganges, and Brahmaputra Rivers flow out of the Himalayas and deposit huge amounts of fertile soil onto the Indo-Gangetic Plain.

Successive waves of invaders have journeyed through the dangerous passes of the northwest Himalayas before descending to the plains below. The most famous of these avenues, the Khyber Pass, became an imperial byword for the danger of the "wild" Indian frontier. The difficulties of egress meant that with the exception of Alexander the Great, the invaders settled in the land they conquered, and were to an extent imprisoned in it. In the process they added, like the river-borne sediment from the Himalayas, new layers of cultural complexity and richness. At the same time, whether it was the Aryans in the second millennium BC or the Mughals in the sixteenth century AD, they were "Indianized" during the period of settlement.

The Indo-Gangetic Plain, which has been termed the Himalayas "flattened out," is the second broad geographic area of the Subcontinent.[5] The plains suffer extreme heat before the onset of the monsoon. The British used to escape to the "hill stations" of the Himalayas to avoid it. Despite the harsh climate, the abundant water and rich soil has made this region a center of settled agriculture for millennia. The earliest archaeological evidence for the development of an Indus Valley civilization (3,300–1,300 BC), as sophisticated as that of Mesopotamia, has been found in this area, at the sites of Harappa and Moenjo Daro.[6] The Indo-Gangetic Plain's fertility has historically enabled it to support a large population, despite accounting for less than 10 percent of the Subcontinent's land mass.[7] From the time of the Mauryan Empire (300 BC) onward, rulers located their political centers in this fertile, flat, and well-watered terrain. In modern South Asia the Indo-Gangetic Plain remains the political heartland, home to more than six hundred million people.

The western areas of the plains, comprising parts of modern Pakistan and the Indian states of Punjab and Haryana, were, in the words of Bernard Cohn, both a "route" zone, through which invading armies passed, and a "nuclear" zone of settlement.[8] The resultant cultural diversity and social mobility formed a fertile soil for the emergence of Sikhism. The Muslim preponderance in the more westerly areas also took on profound political significance with the emergence of Muslim separatism in the late colonial period.

The Himalayan rivers enter the sea at the Indus basin in the west in modern-day Pakistan and the Ganges-Brahmaputra basin in the east in Bangladesh. Summer floods, although not on the scale of 2010, are a way of life in both countries, as the surge of waters from the Himalayas coincides with the monsoon deluge. The landscape of the deltas is constantly shifting with the impact on boundary demarcation that we saw in the previous chapter. Rice-based deltaic agriculture has historically supported an increasingly large population, so that today modern Bangladesh has one of the world's greatest population densities.

The Southern Peninsula is the third geographic region of the Subcontinent. The Vindhya Mountains, which run east and west across central India, separate it from the Indo-Gangetic Plain. Despite the water provided by the Godavari, Krishna, and Kaveri Rivers, it is much drier than the Indo-Gangetic Plain and is more reliant on the annual monsoon rainfall from May until September. The Western and Eastern Ghats mountain ranges form the borders of the Peninsula's Deccan Plateau heartland. Its interior is dry, but the fertile volcanic soil has encouraged human settlement from the Neolithic era. Most of the population of Peninsula India, however, has settled in the river deltas and coastal plains. The heartland of the lengthy Chola dynasty (third century BC to thirteenth century AD), for example, was in the fertile Kaveri River Valley. The fertile coastal strip known as the

Konkan lies between the Western Ghats and the Arabian Sea. This area was home to a thriving ancient civilization based in Goa and today includes districts of the Indian states of Maharashtra, Karnataka, and Kerela. The eastern side of the Peninsula is bounded by the Bay of Bengal and the Indian Ocean. The north Tamil Pallava kingdom was based around Kanchipuram in the Palar River basin on the southeast coast. Both the Cholas and the Pallavas established connections with Southeast Asia that contributed to the "indianization" of parts of what are modern Thailand, Vietnam, and Cambodia. The massive twelfth-century temple at Angkor dedicated to Vishnu by the Khmer kings remains its most lasting monument.[9]

Proximity to the sea, the barrier of the Vindhya Mountains, and the small deltas and fertile plains created by the rivers rising in the Eastern Ghats in comparison with the vast Indo-Gangetic Plain have all had an impact on Peninsula India's historical development. The rich but constricted agricultural lands account, for example, for the smaller regional kingdoms in the south, compared with the early agrarian-based large empires in North India.

Mountains, Rivers, and Sacred Geography

The importance of the Himalayas' glaciers, springs, and lakes for the great river systems that are vital to the Subcontinent's soil and agricultural prosperity helps explain the mountains' appeal to the religious imagination. Mount Kailash, at the center of the headwaters of the Indus and Brahmaputra River systems, was traditionally regarded as the center of the world and is sacred to the Hindu, Jain, and Buddhist traditions. The Himalayas generally are regarded in the Hindu tradition as the abode of gods. There is a special association with Shiva. The Amarnath cave in Kashmir, 12,756 feet above sea level, is a major pilgrimage destination because of its naturally formed stalagmite *lingam*, or image of Shiva. It is traditionally believed that in this cave Shiva explained the secret of eternity to his divine consort Paravati. A record 634,000 devotees visited the cave in the Shravani pilgrimage season, July and August, in 2011.[10] The Badrinath temple devoted to Vishnu near to the Tibet border annually attracts a similar number of pilgrims. Badrinath is on a circuit of pilgrimage sites in the Himalayas known as the Chota Char Dharm. Kedarnath, the second of the four, is another Shiva shrine and is one of twelve pilgrimage centers throughout India associated with Shiva's appearance as a pillar of light (*jyotirlinga*). Yamonitri and Gangoti are visited because they are near the glacier sources of the Yamuna and Ganges Rivers and are associated with the abodes of their two river goddesses. Haridwar and Rishikesh, made famous for Westerners by the Beatles' meditation there in February 1968, are gateways for the Himalayan pilgrimages and mark where the Ganges enters the plains. In South India, the river origins of the Godavari (Tryambakeshwar), Krishna (Kshetra Mahabaleshwar), and Bhima (Bhimashankar) are important pilgrimage places in the western Ghats.

Haridwar is also important as a ritual bathing spot during the Kumbh Mela. It is believed to be one of the four spots (with Allahabad, Ujjain, and Nashik) where drops of the nectar of immortality were split from the Kumbha (urn) during the struggle between the gods and the Asuras (demons). Bathing in the rivers Godavari (Nashik), Kshipra (Ujjain), Ganges (Haridwar), and Allahabad is believed to purify sin. The venue of the festival depends on planetary positions, although the Maha (great) Kumbh Mela is always held at Allahabad, where the confluence of the Ganges, Yamuna, and mythical Saraswati Rivers makes it especially auspicious. When the multitude of pilgrims gathered on the main bathing day at Allahabad in 2001, it was reckoned to be the biggest single gathering in history, some forty million people. The human drama surrounding the festival has made it the subject of numerous documentaries. Jonas Scheu and Philipp Eyer shot the film *Amrit Nectar of Immortality* at the 2010 Kumbh Mela at Haridwar.[11]

Varanasi is the most sacred religious spot on the Ganges and is considered the holiest Hindu place in India. The city's temples, along with ritual bathing in the Ganges, are major destinations for pilgrimage. The Kashi Vishwanath Temple is the most sacred. Varanasi has over 80 *ghats* (embankments) along the river's edge where ritual ablutions can be performed. Some of the ghats are also used in cremation. The best known and one of the oldest is the Manikarnika Ghat, which in mythology is linked with a number of stories involving Shiva and an earring dropped at this spot. It is

4. Kumbh Mela

believed that persons cremated at this ghat receive *moksha*: salvation from the cycle of birth and rebirth.[12]

We shall see in a later chapter how Hindu nationalists in the closing period of British rule deployed notions of India as a land of holy mountains, soil, and rivers to sacralize nationalist struggle. This both added an evocative symbolism to anticolonialism and provided it with a moral imperative. Nationalist action as a consequence became a form of political worship. Along with places of India-wide significance, there was a landscape of forests, earth mounds, stones, and rivers sacred to local deities. Large areas of densely wooded areas were venerated as sacred groves: gardens of the gods.

All the South Asian faith communities have sacred geography that commemorates the places associated with their leading figures, including meditation sites by holy rivers or mountains. There is, for example, the famous pipal tree at Bodh Gaya where Siddhartha Gautama achieved enlightenment and thus became the Buddha. The deer park at Sarnath, near Varanasi, is another important Buddhist pilgrimage center. It was here that the Buddha first taught the Four Noble Truths—life is suffering; suffering is caused by desire; suffering can be stopped if desire can be stopped; desire can be stopped by following the eightfold path leading to *nirvana*—and began the community life (*sangha*). The Sikh tradition does not attach importance to pilgrimage, but numerous places are linked with events associated with the lives of the gurus. The most important is at Nankana Sahib, Pakistan, which was the birthplace of the founder of the tradition, Guru Nanak.

It is now well established that Muslim sacred space in South Asia was created through its association with the lives and tombs of Sufi saints.[13] Pilgrimage was made to the localities associated with the saints, who were crucial in the spread of Islam. Places that had numerous shrines or were linked with leading saints were regarded as particularly holy. Ajmer, for example, which was linked with the leading Sufi Mu'in ad-Din Chishti, was recast in hagiographical literature surrounding his life as the "new Medina."[14] The natural setting shapes this "imagined" Islamic space only in the sense that saints often chose to set up their *khanqahs* (hospices) in strategic localities for the expanding Islamic frontier, or places that had earlier "holy" associations. The important shrine associated with the tomb of Baba Farid at Pakpattan illustrates this point. Farid established his khanqah at Pakpattan, the principal ferry crossing for the Sutlej River. The conversion of the local Hindu and Rajput tribes owed more to their gradually being drawn in to economic and kinship ties with the saint's descendants, however, than to his celebrated charisma.[15]

From time immemorial there has been an intimate relationship between local communities' engagement with their natural environment and their traditions and ritual practices. We now turn to the structure of society that interacts with, but is not confined by, natural geography.[16] Only after we have addressed this relationship can we turn to the final themes of the chapter, the historical impact of human activity on the environment and the contemporary threat of climate change to it.

The Social Setting

The Hindu tradition's long journey from an emphasis on sacrifice, to ritual devotion, and finally to a focus on text and belief has been well established.[17] The final "neo-Hindu" stage was rooted in the need to rationalize belief and practice in the context of colonial modernity.[18] Hinduism became conceived as a monotheistic faith in which the various gods in the pantheon such as Vishnu, Shiva, Krishna, Ram, and Ganesh were simply manifestations of the attributes of the one God. Reformers also sought to compensate for the lack of a central philosophical tradition or institutional focus.[19] Much Hindu devotional worship is carried out in the domestic setting. Appeals to "tradition" to legitimize change, as we shall see later, borrowed from colonial understandings of a glorious Vedic age that produced the authoritative scriptures. This pristine tradition was perceived to have been lost through so-called decadent opulence and the "destructive" impact of Muslim invaders. For millions of Hindus, however, practice rather than belief remained at the core of their tradition, and Hinduism was experienced through the caste system.

The classic fourfold *varna* division—Brahmins, who were the priests of ancient Aryan society; Kshatriyas (warriors and rulers), Vaisayas (mercantile classes), and Sudras (agriculturalists)—masks the fact that there are hundreds of castes (*jatis*).[20] A typical village could have up to twenty castes, organized around notions of common ancestry and maintaining cohesiveness through marriage restrictions. The ranking of castes depends on ritual notions of purity and impurity rooted in the traditional occupation of the caste. The most polluting occupations, including sweeping and scavenging, were held by Untouchables, who stood along with "tribal" people outside the varna system. We will examine in a later chapter the effects of British rule on the operation of the caste system.

A life in keeping with an individual's caste requirements results in the fulfillment of *dharma*, or religious duty to the fundamental laws of existence. Its neglect may result in the accumulation of bad *karma* (reflecting the moral law of cause and effect), which can result in a future rebirth at a lower stage of existence. Ritual bathing, as we have seen, can remove pollution. Devotional worship of a particular deity, fulfillment of *dharma*, and the way of knowledge or spiritual discernment can result in the goal of ending the cycle of rebirths with a return of the soul (*atman*) to God's essence.[21]

Much scholarship at one point focused on the variation between the "little tradition" of the village, where local deities are invoked to ward off disease and evil spirits, and the "great tradition" of the gods and goddesses of the pantheon.[22] There are, however, regional variations in this Great Tradition: the mother goddess as represented by Kali or Durga has a powerful influence in Bengal, while in central northern India, Vishnu and Krishna have greater popularity. In the Gujarat region, where Gandhi grew up, the Jain tradition's emphasis on *ahimsa* (absolute nonviolence) exerted a powerful influence on Hindu thought.

By the modern era, Sanskrit, the language of the Hindu scriptures, was confined to religious observances, while everyday life was carried out in a vast array of languages and local dialects. Persian remained the court language of the Muslim Mughal rulers and was the official language even of the Sikh rulers of the Punjab. The "new" language of Urdu was becoming increasingly popular in parts of North India, along with Hindi. The big linguistic divide was between the mutually incomprehensible North Indian languages, with their Indo-European roots, and the Dravidian languages such as Tamil, Telegu, Malayalam, and Kannada in the south. This underscored the geographical division between the Indo-Gangetic Plain and Peninsula India to which we have referred.

The Jain and Buddhist faiths were both sixth-century AD responses to the increasing Brahminical domination of the Hindu tradition.[23] They also possessed a common emphasis on nonviolence. Jainism's strict adherence to nonviolence involved all forms of animal life, which limited its adherents' ability to engage in agriculture. Those outside of the priesthood were traders and businessmen, occupations that are dominant to this day. Just over a millennium later, Sikhism also emerged as a response to popular Hindu forms of worship and the expression of caste. Its key tenets are release from the cycle of rebirths and spiritual union with God through meditation on the *nam* (divine name); belief in an omnipresent, universal, and timeless God; belief that all individuals are equal before God; and commitment to a balance among work, worship, and charity. The last is expressed in serving the community and is exemplified by the free kitchen open to everyone that is attached to a *gurdwara*.[24]

The tenth and last living Guru Gobind Singh (1666–1708) introduced the physical symbols of Sikhism as expressed by the "five Ks"—*Kes*, uncut hair;

kirpan, sword; *kangha*, comb; *kara*, steel bracelet; and *kaccha*, shorts—along with the initiation ceremony to become a Sikh purified by God (*khalsa*). After the guru's death, the Adi Granth—the holy Sikh scripture compiled in 1604, known by its honorific title Guru Granth Sahib—became the embodiment of the guru (preceptor). Heterodox Sikh sects since then have sprung up, each with its living guru.[25] The Sikh political trajectory in late-colonial and postcolonial India will be traced in future chapters. Suffice it to say here that Hindu claims that Sikhism was not a separate religion, along with the cultural milieu of the British rule in the Sikh Punjab heartland, contributed to reform movements that paralleled but competed with those established to forge a neo-Hindu identity.[26]

The Indian Muslim community was also involved in the competitive "modernization" and revivalism of the colonial period. Reform efforts focused on competing interpretations of Islam, as well as on the need to safeguard community boundaries from Christian and later neo-Hindu proselytization. The outcome was immense educational activity, heightened sectarianism, and communal competition. The more "Indianized" Sufi expression of Islam came under attack from Deobandi and Ahl-e-Hadith reformers, who were committed to a pristine scripturalist understanding of Islam.[27] There was, however, a reformist strand of Sufism, so it is necessary to nuance a portrayal of conflicting "great" and "little" traditions of Islam in South Asia. Similarly, the reform tradition predated the colonial impact, although colonialism accelerated the tradition, not least because of the explosion of print culture.

Muslims in the early nineteenth century were divided not only by sect, with a significant Shia presence in what would become the British Indian provinces of Punjab and the United Provinces, but ethnically and linguistically. The *ashraf* (gentle folk) were descendants of Muslim invaders. Those Muslims who were converts from Hinduism were known as *ajlaf*. The former spoke the emerging Urdu elite language, although they had originally been immersed in a Persianate cultural world. The ajlaf conversed in such regional languages as Punjabi, Bengali, and Tamil. The sense of a Muslim separate political identity in the British period emerged first among the ashraf Muslims.

Human Activity and the Natural Environment

The dramatic ecological innovations of the colonial era have obscured the fact that cutting down forests, damming and channeling rivers, and building reservoirs and lakes had been a constant feature of human activity in the Subcontinent for millennia. The Aryan clearing of the thickly forested banks of the Ganges as settled agriculture replaced pastoralism between 800 and 600 BC can be glimpsed in such texts as the Satapatha Brahmana, where the god Agni is portrayed as setting "a path of sacrificial flames from the western valley of the Ganges to the east."[28]

Population increases drove the extension of the cultivation frontier. Historians have revealed how the expansion of rice cultivation into the delta of what is now Bangladesh coincided with a shifting of the Ganges and Padma channels to the east. The Mughal state encouraged colonists to reclaim land under a system of permits. Many permit holders were Sufis, so a shifting agricultural border coincided with the expansion of the Islamic frontier in this part of the Subcontinent.[29]

Colonial rule intensified the processes of irrigation and deforestation. The expansion of canals, which irrigated more than six million acres of "crown wasteland" in the Punjab region of the Indus Basin, the heartland of contemporary Pakistan, had profound long-term political consequences. It has without exaggeration been termed "one of the world's great environmental transformations in the nineteenth and twentieth centuries."[30] Deforestation continued apace, driven by the demand for teak to build warships and later by the need for timber in railway construction. By 1905, more than twenty-eight thousand miles of track had been built, and India boasted one of the world's longest railway systems. Each mile of track required 860 crossties or sleepers, creating an annual demand of a million railway sleepers. Moreover, until coal took over in the 1880s, the locomotives were wood burning.[31] Tribal people rebelled against the intensified forestry management regime introduced in the late 1860s. Protests continued into the twentieth century, when they merged into the wider anticolonial nationalist movement.

Railways blocked natural water courses. The results were increased flooding and a rise in malaria.[32] The problems were acute in the Bengal delta, where the extensive railway network cut across the intricate river systems. The slowing of the water flow through inadequate culverts and around the pillars of bridges also provided a favorable environment for the proliferation of the Amazonian water hyacinth. This pernicious weed devastated rice paddies and jute plants in the late colonial era in large areas of modern-day Bangladesh.[33]

Postcolonial development projects have speeded up the process of environmental change. Exploitation of timber and mineral resources has been justified in the cause of development, or in the deforested Chittagong Hill Tracts in Bangladesh, of security and national integration. Within India, a stereotypical image has emerged of tribal populations attempting to defend islands of biodiversity, protected by notions of primitive "nature worship" from the depredations of global capitalism legitimized by a "Sanskritized" great tradition of formal Hindu practice. Dam projects have been especially destructive of the gardens of the gods, bringing with them not only large-scale environmental damage but land dispossession and resultant violent conflicts. The massive Narmada Valley Project in Madhya Pradesh begun in 1979 and yet to be completed, has been immensely controversial because of its environmental impact. The development was fought by regional protest groups merged into the Namarda Bachao Andolan by the redoubtable environmentalist Medha Patkar in 1987. The campaign gained further international support as a result of the intervention of the celebrated novelist Arundhati Roy, whose *The God of Small Things* was the 1997 Booker Prize winner.

Indian environmental protest had first risen to global prominence in the Chipko Andolan movement in the early 1970s. This effort to end massive deforestation, which was causing landslides, water shortages, and hardships for those engaged in firewood collection and livestock raising, in what is now the Himalayan state of Uttaranchal, drew on the Gandhian tradition of nonviolent protest. Women hugged the ash trees earmarked for felling. The powerful image inspired environmentalist movements in forest areas across

India. Chipko, like the Gandhian *satyegrahas* against the colonial state, seized the moral high ground and forced Prime Minister Indira Gandhi in 1980 to order a fifteen-year ban on tree felling in the Himalayan region.[34] Some writers have termed the struggle between states, environmentalists, and indigenous populations over forestry rights and nature as one of competing ecological nationalisms.

Bhutan leads the way in South Asia in terms of its concern for environmental preservation. Indeed, it has the largest proportion of area in the world under protected status as national parks. Conservation is one of the four pillars of its development concept model, which, since its establishment in 1972 by King Jigme Singye Wangchuck, has been based on the measurement of "Gross National Happiness." The country's international profile is increasingly rising in the promotion of environmental ethics and the establishment of accounting systems that place ecological goods alongside the market economy's activities.

The Perils of Climate Change

South Asia is vulnerable to a wide variety of manifestations of climate change, from rising sea levels, cyclones, and storm surges on its coastline to inland flooding as a result of more intense precipitation. Excessive rainfall caused more than $200 billion worth of damage in Mumbai in 2005. Temperature rises also increase the risk of the melting of glacial lakes. A survey in Bhutan, for example, identified twenty-five glaciers as threatened. Catastrophic outburst effects would be felt not only in the state's western districts but in downstream areas in West Bengal and Bangladesh.

Cyclones are also predicted to intensify in the Bay of Bengal as a result of rising temperatures.[35] They threaten the lives of the coastal populations and those who precariously inhabit the chars in the Ganges. The 1970 cyclone, which killed more than half a million people, not only brought terrible human tragedy but had, as we shall see, significant political repercussions. Bangladesh is not the only South Asian country that has suffered major cyclones. Cyclone Nargis, which hit Burma's densely populated Irrawaddy delta in November 2008, caused more than 130,000 deaths and wrought more than $10 billion worth of damage. Cyclones flood coastal areas with seawater. Increased sea levels caused by global warming also threaten the Indus and Ganges basins. Their mango forests are naturally salt resistant, but salinity could easily increase to levels that cause a decline in vegetation. The Ganges basin is particularly vulnerable because of the decline in fresh water arising from the environmental impact of the Farraka Barrage, a controversial dam on the Bhagirathi River. The fragile ecology of the Sunderbans Forest, the last refuge of the Bengal tiger, thus faces increasing risk.

Rising sea levels constitute another threat to coastal regions, including the megacity of Mumbai, built on low lying reclaimed land and home to more than seventeen million people. Rising sea level especially threatens Bangladesh, much of which is low lying. Dhaka, which is more than 125 miles from the coast, is only about twenty-five feet above sea level.[36] At the time of the 1988 floods, the capital city, with its twelve million people, was internationally cut off for eleven days when its airport was closed.[37] There is evidence that the country is already being affected by rising sea levels. A UN report in 2007 revealed that sea levels around Bangladesh had risen almost five inches since 2000. This was threatening the agricultural livelihoods of twenty million people in the southern coastal districts of Khulna, Jessore, Bagerhat, and Satkhara.[38]

The Maldives, some 250 miles off the tip of India, are the most vulnerable part of South Asia to rising sea levels. The islands and coral atolls, 80 percent of which are just three feet above sea level, could disappear beneath the waves if the Indian Ocean sea level rises as a result of global warming. President Mohamed Nasheed and eleven ministers decked out in scuba gear staged the world's first underwater cabinet meeting in October 2009 to publicize the issue of climate change. The former human rights activist and first democratically elected president had a year earlier announced that he was beginning to divert a portion of the country's annual billion dollar tourist revenue into a fund to buy a new homeland for the islands' 300,000 inhabitants.[39]

Climate change brings the risk of drought as well as flooding, as a result of increased evaporation of water supplies and unreliable seasonal rain. The human impact has already been seen. Increased problems of indebtedness

arising from crop failure in the semiarid areas of Andhra Pradesh, Karnataka, and Maharashtra led to a spate of Indian farmers' suicides in the first
decade of the twenty-first century.[40] The figures exceeded seventeen thousand in 2009, the worst year.[41] The issue of farmer suicides entered popular
culture through the story of a widowed farmer, Dayal Singh (played by the
veteran Bollywood star Jackie Shroff), in the Hindi film *Kisaan*, released in
March 2009. The deadly combination of flood and drought in a populous
poor region still heavily dependent on agriculture for its livelihood has led
some experts to maintain that the Subcontinent is the most vulnerable region of the world to the impact of climate change.[42] Water shortages arising
from climate change, urbanization, and industrialization threaten India's
economic rise.

The perils of climate change are the most dramatic example of the need
to look beyond the postcolonial boundaries in contemporary South Asian
studies. Bangladesh lies at the bottom of river systems that rise in Tibet and
India. Nine-tenths of the surface flow of water is received from outside the
country's political boundaries. Policies of neighboring states affecting forest
management and the building of dams, reservoirs, and canals thus have a
profound impact on its natural environment. Access to water more generally in the Subcontinent is affected by the management policies of countries that control headstreams. Chinese dams can affect the flow of water to
India, whose own projects have a huge impact on Pakistan and Bangladesh.
Issues pertaining to water management will in the future have a huge impact on international relations in the South Asia region, as we shall see.

Future modeling predicts that South Asia may become a region of cli-
mate-change refugees. While scenarios of millions on the move may be
exaggerated, the region already has a tradition of seasonal and large-scale
migration linked with environmental factors. This can take the form of international migration or of regional migration, as, for example, the move of
agriculturalists to Dhaka from the coastal regions of southwestern Bangladesh. In the next chapter we will examine the massive overseas migration
from the Subcontinent in the past two hundred years, and the South Asian
diasporas to which that migration has given birth.

THREE

The South Asian Diasporas

The comedy-drama film *Bhaji on the Beach* was released in 1993. Its plot follows a group of South Asian women on a trip to the British seaside resort of Blackpool, which is famous for its illuminations. The film, through the personal relationships of such characters as Simi, Ginder, and Aasha, provides insights both into the different generational outlooks of overseas South Asian communities and into the way in which immigrants and their descendants become engaged with the wider social mainstream. Less than a decade later these themes were explored in Gurinder Chadha's immensely popular film *Bend It Like Beckham*, in which Jesminder Bhamra, a young Punjabi Sikh girl living in South London, inspired by the soccer superstar David Beckham, seeks to get around her parents' disapproval and play football for her local team, the Hounslow Harriers. By the time the film was taking in $76 million at the box office, there were an estimated thirty-five million South Asians living overseas. They not only influenced their homelands economically and politically—as the Indian government, after years of indifference, discovered nonresident Indians as an important economic resource[1]—but exerted considerable impact on Western culture.[2] Before turning to the contemporary South Asian diasporas, we need first, however, to provide a historical context of migration in the age of empire.

Imperial Rule and the Movement of Indians Overseas

For centuries before the British rose to power, Indians had traded overseas, using the monsoon winds to reach the coast of Africa and to spread their culture to Southeast Asia.[3] These patterns of circular migration and trade continued throughout the relatively brief period of colonial rule. That period is nonetheless important for understanding the modern diasporas, as it increased the scale of migration, transformed its characteristics, and established regional and community patterns of overseas settlement that persist to this day.

The imperial economy's demands for labor on tea, sugar, and rubber plantations, in tin mines, and to build railways and load and unload vessels in ports created a market for Indian "coolie" labor in Ceylon, Burma, Malaysia, the Caribbean, Fiji, Mauritius, and South and East Africa.[4] This was provided by contract labor in the near neighborhood of Ceylon, Burma, and Malaysia and by indentured labor in more distant locations in the Caribbean and Indian Ocean. These indentured servants replaced the former African slaves on the sugar plantations after slavery was banned across the Empire in 1833. The pitiful existence of these workers has been dubbed a new system of slavery.[5]

Indentured laborers alone accounted for about 1.5 million workers leaving India between 1834 and 1917, when this labor system ended. More than a third of the laborers went to Mauritius.[6] Despite the circular nature of the migration to the tiny pear-shaped Indian Ocean volcanic island, its demography was totally transformed. Indians today make up more than two-thirds of the island's population, with the Bhojpuri language forming the principal mother tongue. This is a legacy of the huge migration of indentured laborers from Bihar. Many of these poorly paid workers on the European-owned sugar plantations were tribal Santals, Kols, and Dhangars. Indentured labor was ended in Mauritius in 1910. As in the plantation economies in the Caribbean, its workers were drawn from North India. In contrast, Tamils formed the bulk of the labor force for the plantations of Malaysia and Ceylon. Trusted Tamil foremen from the tea estates in Ceylon, for example, were sent back to their home villagers by the planters to secure workers.[7] Similar methods were used to recruit Telegu laborers in Burma.

The indentured laborers formed what has been termed a plantation diaspora. The large numbers of Indians in Burma and Ceylon have been called a diaspora next door. There were also trading diasporas and diasporas comprising imperial auxiliaries of clerks, soldiers, and policemen. Improved communications and an expanding imperial economy in the Indian Ocean provided opportunities for traders, merchants, and moneylenders from the Subcontinent. Chettiars from South India financed and controlled the expanding frontier of rice production in Burma's Irrawaddy delta. This previously lightly populated area had, by the eve of the Second World War, become the world's rice basket, exporting more than three million tons a year.

Parsis from Maharashtra were involved with the opium trade with China. Gujarati Patels were active in clove production in Zanzibar, and in produce trade and retailing in East Africa and Natal.[8] Memons from Gujarat settled in Port Louis, Mauritius, where they became traders in foodstuffs and textiles and later developed interests in the shipping industry. Indians not only were the shopkeepers of the Empire, they helped administer and police it. Tamil clerks beavered away in Hong Kong, Singapore, and Penang; Punjabi Sikhs manned rifles in East Africa, kept trident gangs in Hong Kong under control, and policed the wilder frontiers of the tin mines of Perak.[9]

Educational opportunities encouraged "counterflows" to colonialism, as students, including such future leading political figures as Nehru, Gandhi, Jinnah, Ambedkar, and Subhas Chandra Bose, came to Britain. In the fields of science and literature equally profound contributions were made by such "England-returned" figures as the mathematician Ramanajan and the great writers Rabindranath Tagore, Mulk Raj Anand, and the poet Iqbal. Even those who did not make their mark in such outstanding ways were shaped by their experience in England and played an important role on their return "home," not least in influencing Indian ideas about the West.[10] This dimension to the history of colonial South Asia has until recently been frequently overlooked. Students were of course "sojourners" rather than "settlers," and in this respect despite their elite status had a similarity with *lascars* (sailors) who spent time in ports between voyages and *ayahs* (nannies) who accompanied British residents of India on their furloughs.[11] Indian overseas migration was not, however, confined to the Empire in the first age of globalization. Students and farmers were drawn to California as well as British Columbia.[12] Indeed, San Francisco, as we shall see, emerged as a major hub of revolutionary action against the Raj during the First World War.

In the boom period of Indian migration to Malaya and Burma from 1921 to 1930, 4.8 million Indians entered these countries and 4 million departed in a process of circular migration.[13] Significant numbers of Indians, however (around 6 million), settled overseas for good, in such countries as Malaysia, Kenya, Uganda, South Africa, and Ceylon, laying the foundations for their postcolonial diasporas. According to an official inquiry in Ceylon in 1938, for example, there were an estimated 400,000 Tamil tea workers permanently settled on the island.[14] By that time, Malaysia, Natal, and Kenya also all had significant permanent Indian populations. Sikhs from the Punjab who had been employed in the 1890s to construct the East African railways stayed on and along with Gujarati traders accounted for more than 45,000 Indian residents in the 1921 census.[15] A decade earlier, 20,000 Indians were recorded in Natal. Growing white hostility to their presence had drawn the young Indian lawyer Mohandas Gandhi into public life. On his way back to India from South Africa in October 1901 he stopped off in Mauritius and urged its educated South Asian population to "become interested in politics" in order to help improve the community's conditions.

Well over 90 percent of all Indian overseas migrants in the imperial age went to one of three destinations: Burma, Ceylon, and Malaya. Scholars, with the exception of Sunil Amrith and Sugata Bose, have focused, however, on the North American, British, Caribbean, and African experiences. During the period from the early 1890s to the eve of the Second World War, 15.5 million contract workers, traders, and merchants left India for Ceylon and Burma.[16] Rangoon had become an Indian city in which Burmans were in a minority, despite the dominant presence of the Shwedagon Pagoda, which had been occupied for a time as a fort by the British and was the most important Buddhist pilgrimage site in the southeast Asia region. Indians monopolized Rangoon's commerce, professions, and colonial administration. They also formed the bulk of the dock labor force. In 1927, the single greatest year of migration, nearly 300,000 people journeyed from India to Burma and Malaya.[17] A further 215,000 migrated to Ceylon.[18] Three-quarters of these were tea-estate workers. By that time, however, Indian unskilled workers also dominated the dockside labor force of the important transit port of Colombo. They also accounted for three-quarters of the city's workforce regularly employed in scavenging and conservancy work, and formed a significant proportion of rickshaw pullers, domestic servants, and shop assistants.[19]

Mounting racial prejudice led to attempts to restrict Indian immigration in South Africa, Canada, Australia, New Zealand, and America in the early twentieth century. Two decades later, the Great Depression increased animosity toward overseas Indians in Burma, Zanzibar, and Ceylon. Indian financiers called in the debts of native farmers, who had seen prices collapse for their cash crops. Indians as a result increased their holdings of clove trees in Zanzibar, for example, from 152,000 in 1923 to more than 500,000 a decade later. When the Zanzibar government set up a Clove Growers' Association to wrest marketing and export from Indian hands, the Indian Congress boycotted the entry of cloves to the Indian ports; this had a crippling effect, as a third of the clove crop was exported to the Subcontinent.[20] In Burma, as the price of rice collapsed, Chettiar moneylenders foreclosed mortgages, increasing their landholding from 6 percent of all occupied land in 1930 to 25 percent in 1938.[21]

Burmese resentment against the "swindling" Chettiars and Telegu migrant Indian dockworkers in Rangoon led to the first outbreak of violence, in May 1930. This was followed by the millenarian Saya San rebellion in Lower Burma, which lasted until June 1932.[22] Rebel anger was directed not just against the British but against Indian moneylenders and shopkeepers as well. The Depression decade closed with further anti-Indian riots in July and August 1938.[23] Unrest in Ceylon did not degenerate into violence, but it prompted the inquiry that has provided the imperial archive with a rich source on the Indian presence in the island. "Repatriation and retreat" for overseas Indians persisted to the early 1950s. Nehru had visited Ceylon and encouraged trade union activity there, but both India's and Ceylon's independence disappointed Tamil activists by focusing on India's problems and development rather than providing advocacy for the "Indians abroad."

Many of the regions that experienced high overseas migration in the colonial era, however, continue to send large numbers abroad. The dominance of Bangladeshis in the ubiquitous "Indian" restaurant business in Britain can be linked, for example, to the pioneering role of Sylheti cooks

Table 1 Overview of Indian Colonial Overseas Migration

Region/Country of Migration	Region of India	Period
British Columbia	Punjab	1890–1908
Burma	Tamil Nadu, Andhra Pradesh	1870s–1940s
California	Punjab	1890s–1917
Caribbean	UP, Bihar	1830s–1917
Ceylon	Tamil Nadu	1840s–1930s
East Africa	Punjab, Gujarat	1890s–1940s
Fiji	UP, Bihar	1870s–1917
Mauritius	Bihar, UP	1840s–1917

on British ships. Table 1 sets out the broad regional patterns of migration, excluding the counterflow to Britain, Hong King, Australia, and New Zealand, where there were small mainly Punjabi Sikh overseas populations, and Natal, where there was a largely Gujarati population. (Regions in South Asia are identified by their current names.)

These broad regional migration flows can in fact be broken down into local patterns, which highlight even further the concentration of migration arising from the activities of labor contractors and more informal kin-based chain migration. To provide just one example drawn from Ceylon, three-quarters of all the Indian tea-worker migrants came from the districts around Trichinopoly.[24]

Postcolonial migration reveals a similar pattern of movement from a small number of regions, although new destinations have emerged. A significant proportion of the "new migrants" from India has consisted of well-educated professionals. The increasing wealth of the Indian overseas community, together with a major shift in domestic economic policy from the 1990s, resulted in closer ties than existed between India and its diasporas during the opening decades of independence. They were marked by a closing in of the nation's boundaries and a distancing of the state from overseas communities. This was despite the fact that the challenge to the Raj had involved overseas Indians' participation, while also drawing on the moral claim that a colonial state could not effectively protect migrants against racial discrimination and economic depredations.

Postcolonial Patterns of Migration

Four key developments since 1947 have shaped South Asian migration: decolonization, in both the Subcontinent and other parts of the British Empire settled by Indians; ethnic conflict in postcolonial Sri Lanka; the rise of the oil-rich Arab countries; and recruitment of skilled graduates by developed countries.

Indian independence generated huge migrations across the new Indo-Pakistani borders. Some of these uprooted people, especially from the Punjab and northeastern Bengal (now part of Bangladesh), were to relocate to postwar Britain, where the 1948 British Nationality Act had opened the door for entry. They came to the United Kingdom as factory workers, living as single males in shared accommodation and sending as much money back to their families as they could save. Increasing immigration restriction beginning in 1962 and growing wealth encouraged families to come to the United Kingdom while they could do so. So-called chain migration was further encouraged by the ability of relatives to sponsor male relatives and friends under a voucher system, before the migration of South Asian workers was almost completely halted. Many of the terraced streets of northern England and the Midlands in which large numbers of migrants were concentrated contained people all from the same village. Sylhetis continued to predominate among Bangladeshi migrants, many of whom settled in Tower Hamlets in London.[25] The Brick Lane area became an iconic representation of their presence.

Ethnic tensions in postcolonial Burma completed the repatriation process, which had been continuous since the early 1930s. Indians left Fiji to a backdrop of military coups and violence against them. The most dramatic departures involved the move of "twice migrants" to Britain from East Africa, as the newly independent Kenyan, Tanzanian, and Ugandan states sought to break the long-established Indian commercial and government

5. Brick Lane, London

service stranglehold. By 1968, thirty-five thousand Kenyan Asians had arrived in Britain, prompting strict immigration controls under the Commonwealth Immigrants Act. Uganda went a step farther than Kenya and not only restricted the commercial activities of Indian citizens but expelled them in 1972, triggering a dramatic exodus to Britain. Despite the traumatic forced migration, the Kenyan and Uganda Asians, many of whom were Punjabi Sikhs, brought more linguistic and entrepreneurial skills than had the earlier migrants from northwestern Punjab, northeastern Bengal, and central Punjab.

The outbreak of ethnic violence in Sri Lanka in July 1983 eventually led to a quarter of its 2 million Tamils fleeing abroad.[26] Poorer refugees returned to Tamil Nadu, but the wealthy went to Canada and the United Kingdom, where they swelled existing diaspora communities. Canada had an estimated 300,000 Tamils, most of whom were concentrated in the greater Toronto area. Britain's Tamil diaspora was estimated at around 180,000. Colombo claimed that the growing numbers of overseas Tamils were "economic migrants" who had opportunistically passed themselves off as asylum seekers. Switzerland's open-immigration policies attracted a growing Tamil population, around 50,000.

The rise of oil-rich states in the Middle East beginning in the 1970s provided a third major postcolonial influence on South Asian migration. India had well-established trading ties with the Gulf region, predating colonial rule. Under the British, there were close trading ties with southern Persia, Kuwait, Oman, and Bahrain. Indian merchants bought pearls, which were the economic mainstay of Kuwait, Oman, and Bahrain, and financed the captains of the diving boats. The Great Depression dealt a similar blow to these ties, as to the rice connection in Burma. Only when oil extraction became fully established and oil rose dramatically in price did opportunities return for South Asians in this region. Dubai and Sharjah became playgrounds for the rich. Dubai developed as the second-most-important transnational political node for Pakistanis after London. For poor South Asian workers, however, the dream of riches flowing from the black gold could become a nightmare.

The Gulf States, starting in the mid-1970s, were capital rich, but labor scarce. Migrant workers accounted for around a third of Saudi Arabia's total population. The majority came from the Subcontinent, although there were also considerable numbers from Indonesia and Sri Lanka. The Gulf States' rapid economic growth was underpinned by oil revenues, which paid for massive construction booms. Dubai's marina complexes, shopping malls, and hotels, as well as its half-mile-tall Burj tower were iconic representations of the economic rise of the United Arab Emirates.[27] By 2005, virtually the whole of the Emirate's private sector labor force were migrant workers.[28] The six states of the Gulf Cooperation Council (Bahrain, Kuwait, Qatar, Oman, Saudi Arabia, and the United Arab Emirates) had more than 10 million foreign workers. South Asians accounted for more than 60 percent of these.[29] Precise figures, let alone regional breakdowns, are difficult to obtain. There were, however, around 3.5 million Indians employed in the GCC, with the largest number (around 1.5 million) in Saudi Arabia.

Muslims accounted for fewer than a third of the Indians working in Saudi Arabia, many of whom were migrants from Kerela.[30]

Bangladesh and Pakistan each supplied around 1.5 million workers in the GCC, with Saudi Arabia being the leading destination. In 2003, the Saudi government estimated that there were between 1 million and 1.5 million Bangladeshi workers in the kingdom. This makes it the number one destination for overseas Bangladeshi workers. Within Saudi Arabia, Indians had the highest proportion of skilled jobs held by those of South Asian descent, followed at some distance by migrant workers from Pakistan and Bangladesh.

South Asians across the GCC countries were overwhelmingly employed in low-paid unskilled jobs rather than in the professions and the management and technical sectors of the oil industry. The construction industry was far and away the biggest employer.[31] Local developers circumvented existing labor laws, sometimes with deadly effect, as when, for example, they ignored the Dubai Ministry of Labour's July–August afternoon work-break regulations, thereby exposing construction workers to the dangers of heat stroke and dehydration. According to private sources, 880 construction workers died in 2004 (460 Indians, 375 Pakistanis, and 45 Bangladeshis).[32] Restrictions on migrant workers' mobility, the role of debt in their recruitment, and the spartan conditions of Dubai's construction workers' labor camps at Al Quoz and Sonapar all carry echoes of the indentured labor system.

Human rights organizations provide personal accounts of migrant experiences in which dreams of gulf riches turned into nightmares. Kattayadan Subair migrated from Kerela to Saudi Arabia as a young man, having paid $1,200 for an employment visa and received assurance of a job as a private gardener. When he arrived, he found that his job had been "substituted," and he was forced to tend sheep in a remote location that had no permanent shelter. Food and water were brought to him every other day. When he attempted to "escape," he was severely beaten by his employer.[33] Rajila, also from Kerela, went to work in Saudi Arabia to support her widowed mother and five unmarried sisters. She borrowed 35,000 rupees (about $770) to pay an agent for her employment visa. When she reached Jeddah to work as a cleaner in various hospitals, she found that her promised pay ($160 a month) had been halved. Her "free" accommodation comprised a small room lined with bunk beds, which she shared with fourteen other women. The workers were kept in "forced confinement" and were allowed out only once a week to make an escorted visit to purchase groceries at a local market.[34]

Roopa Hungund's overseas migratory experience could not be more contrasting. It is representative of the fourth major postcolonial migration development. For fourteen years she worked as a professional with multinational information technology (IT) businesses such as Oracle and Cisco in the San Francisco Bay Area, before returning to Bangalore with her husband in 2011 to set up an e-commerce business.[35] This career trajectory not only illuminates the return of a number of Silicon Valley professionals to work in India's IT sector but reflects the easing of immigration restrictions by the United States, Canada, and Australia beginning in the mid-1960s in order to attract highly qualified migrants from the Subcontinent. During the 1960s and 1970s, Canada's South Asian community grew from fewer than 7,000 to around 600,000. Five thousand new Sikh settlers from the Punjab were arriving each year.[36]

The success of Indian IT experts in California has become almost legendary. By 2007, Indians were founding more than 13 percent of all the startup IT companies in Silicon Valley although they accounted for less than 1 percent of the U.S. population.[37] The flood of engineers in the 1990s contributed to the Bay Area having the second-largest concentration of South Asians (about 235,000) outside of New York. Three-quarters of the South Asian adults have at least a bachelor's degree, and well over two-thirds are employed in management or professional occupations.[38] Many of this new generation of graduates came from regions that had not traditionally sent large numbers of migrants to North America. They now led the way because of their educational infrastructure, especially that provided by the prestigious Indian Institutes of Technology. Australia has been another overseas destination where IT professionals have carved out successful careers. Punjabis who have a longer-term presence in the country are less affluent and educated, although they may be better off than the frequently self-employed "twice migrants" from Fiji.[39]

The South Asian diasporas in North America are better educated and more prosperous than their counterparts in other areas of the world. This is reflected in the flow of remittances to the Subcontinent. There are, however, regional and national differences in the North American diasporas. The lifestyle of a Mirpuri taxi driver in New York or a Gujarati motel owner in the Midwest has little in common with that of a wealthy professional from Hyderabad living in Silicon Valley. Recent studies have begun to nuance the South Asian "success story" by exploring tensions arising from ambivalence to mainstream culture, and issues of ethnic identification and sexual orientation.[40]

Diasporas and Their Homelands

Standard histories do not always acknowledge the diasporic influence on the Subcontinent.[41] The number of overseas migrants and their growing prosperity—the median income of Indians living in the San Francisco Bay Area by 2010 was $107,000—has enabled them to send back large remittances. Second, close family ties (as a result of first-cousin marriage in the case of Punjabi Muslims), with increasing transnational marriages, have sustained connections with the Subcontinent. These have also been transformed by a third factor, the communications revolution, involving cheap mass air travel and the emergence of the internet. The internet has not only brought scattered families closer together but has afforded opportunities for online meditation, participation in *bhajans* (devotional songs in the Hindu and Sikh traditions), and watching the performance of *aarti*.[42]

In this section I will provide an overview of diasporic networks and influences, before concluding the chapter with a case study of the Bangladesh experience. Much has been written, some of it highly specialized, on migrant remittances. Worldwide migrant remittances in 2001 were double the amount of foreign aid and ten times the sum of net private capital transfers.[43] With respect to the Subcontinent, two periods of rapid economic growth in Pakistan, the 1980s and the first decade of the twenty-first century, coincided with record remittances. These increased demands for housing and transport helped pay for as much as half of all imports. Remittances from Pakistanis living in the United States, for example, stood at around

$1.7 billion by 2007–8.[44] Bangladeshis some four years earlier were remitting approximately the same amount from Saudi Arabia.[45] Accurate figures are difficult to come by, as not all money is remitted through commercial banks, some of it being transferred via informal *hundi* arrangements, which are not recorded. Ballpark figures for the early years of the twentieth century show about $3 billion remitted by Bangladeshi workers, $3.5 billion by Indians, and $4 billion by Pakistanis.[46] Sri Lankans were not far behind, with remittances of roughly $2.8 billion. In addition to these sums, diasporas have raised large amounts of charitable funds at times of national disaster, such as the 2004 tsunami and the 2005 Kashmir earthquake. The Sikh tradition's commitment to *seva* has been behind considerable charitable investment in the Punjab homeland, for example, in schools and hospitals. The Swaminarayan sect in the United Kingdom, with its impressive North London temple and its BAPS charities,[47] has been active in Gujarat, particularly in providing "uplift" for the state's tribal populations.[48]

National governments, somewhat belatedly in the Indian case, have begun to appeal to diasporas for direct investment.[49] This includes both returns on bank deposits and direct investment in manufacturing and services.[50] The Chinese diaspora's role in fueling economic growth is seen as a potential model. New Delhi's growing recognition of the diaspora populations' increasing significance was signaled by the establishment of a Ministry of Overseas Indian Affairs, the enactment of dual citizenship, and the organization of events like Pravasi Bharatiya Divas. Cultural exchanges have taken various forms; sports exchanges include diaspora support for village sports tournaments and *kabbadi* (a kind of team tag sport), which is popular in many regions of South Asia.[51] There are also exchanges in the arts and theater; musical fusion from such artists as Raghav, Panjabi MC, and Bally Sagoo, whose songs feature on the soundtrack of *Bend It Like Beckham*; and dance as represented by the Leicester-based contemporary performer Aakash Odedra. Such newspapers as *Jang, Eastern Eye*, and *India Abroad* link diasporas and their regions of origin. Websites provide information, opportunities for worship, and ways of making charitable donations. Matrimonial and bridal services also play an important role in maintaining linkages.[52] Flights to South Asia from Britain are often full in the late September to December wedding season, as diaspora couples marry in their homeland or purchase wedding items on shopping visits, which boost the price of gold by an average of 10 percent.

Some overseas South Asians have become involved in the politics of homeland. Mainstream Indian, Pakistani, and Bangladeshi parties have branches among the diaspora that raise funds and generate propaganda—as did, for example, the Indian Overseas Congress during the Emergency Period (1975–77). Secessionist groups such as the Khalistan movement have also drawn much of their strength outside of the Subcontinent. The World Sikh Organization was formed on 28 July 1984 following a meeting in Madison Square Garden in New York. Within three years its North American membership was estimated at sixteen thousand, united to popularize its aim of an independent Sikh state "by peaceful means."[53] The Kashmiri Council was created in Washington in 1990 to support Pakistan's campaign for the implementation of UN resolutions on Kashmir.

UK-based Mirpuris provided significant financial and political support for the Jammu and Kashmir Liberation Front (JKLF), which was founded in Birmingham in May 1977. Pakistani authorities by the early 1990s favored jihadist groups rather than the JKLF as a fighting force in the Kashmir Valley. The Mirpuri Jats, however, remained a long-term strategic asset for Islamabad. They greatly outnumbered Muslim migrants from the Kashmir Valley who had settled in Britain. Moreover, the latter were predominantly apolitical professionals, in contrast to the Mirpuri Jats, who had achieved social mobility through political activism.

Diaspora Tamils provided funding and ideological support for the militant secessionist group the Liberation Tigers of Tamil Eelam (LTTE). At the height of the 1983–2009 conflict, the diaspora contributed an estimated $200 million a year to LTTE. Until the late 1990s, funds were raised openly in North America and the United Kingdom to procure weapons, which were shipped via Malaysia, Singapore, Thailand, and India. Funds also came from temples, community organizations, individual "taxes," and criminal narcotics and human trafficking operations.[54] Front companies also procured weapons in Bangladesh.

Homeland struggles have sometimes been fought with deadly effects in the diaspora. The Indian deputy high commissioner in the United Kingdom was kidnapped and killed in February 1984 by Kashmiri separatists. Advocacy networks involved with human rights issues have also been active in diasporic contexts. South Asians both in Britain and in the United States have become important political lobbyists for a range of political causes, especially the vexed Kashmir issue.

A number of studies have examined the effectiveness of Mirpuri lobbying with respect to influencing Labour Party policy on Kashmir.[55] Mirpuris have exerted pressure on constituencies by enrolling as party members—most notably the Birmingham Small Heath Constituency Labour Party—and by lobbying MPs on the All-Party Parliamentary Group on Kashmir in 1990. The Blair governments did not substantively change UK policy on Kashmir, but the impact of Mirpuri lobbying did result in occasional rhetoric that leaned closer to the Pakistan position than hitherto.

Airplanes on the Walls: The Londoni Villages of Sylhet

The uniform villages of northeast Bangladesh are interspersed in such localities as Maulvi Bazaar and Nobiganj, with clusters of multistory stone dwellings, painted in bright colors. These homesteads have large airplanes painted on their walls or modeled as stone gargoyles on their roofs.[56] These spacious dwellings of British-based residents, "once completed . . . their owners' pride and joy."[57] The generic name for the migrant villages—Londoni gram—reflects the concentration of Bangladeshi/Sylheti settlers in the East London borough of Tower Hamlets, where, according to the 2001 census, they numbered a third of the total population of just under 200,000.[58] It has, however, become a term for all migrants to Britain, including the significant Bangladeshi communities in Manchester and Newcastle.

Their ancestors in many cases worked on cargo boats that plied the nearby Kusiyara River, transporting jute and rice to Calcutta. Work on local cargo boats was the first step to recruitment on British-owned oceangoing vessels and overseas settlement. Villages that had seafaring links with Britain provided the main focus of postcolonial labor recruitment in the 1950s and 1960s.

A number of detailed anthropological studies have been written on the impact of diaspora money and mores on rural Sylhet.[59] These studies reveal that pioneer migrants came from the middle strata of society. The poor lacked the resources, the local elites the incentive, for overseas travel. The new wealth remitted by the migrants, however, broadened the basis for overseas settlement in 1960s Sylhet as a result of the competitive social mobility it brought. Increasing immigration restrictions limited migration to the United Kingdom, thereby "blocking" the upward social mobility of nonmigrant families, unless they could secure short-term work contracts in the Gulf. Even the poorest subsequently risked migrating there as "illegal" workers in what has been termed a "migration mania." Migration was increasingly seen as the only vehicle for social mobility. As the wife of a sharecropper informed an anthropologist during fieldwork, "This village may be getting richer, but we shan't. People with *bideshi* (overseas) relatives may be able to improve their positions, but we can't."[60]

Land in rural Bangladesh, as elsewhere in South Asia, is a sign of status as well as an economic resource. It is therefore unsurprising that diaspora money is spent on its purchase. Following a virtual free-for-all in land acquisition among migrant households during the 1960s, a survey two decades later revealed that just 1 percent of migrant Sylheti households were landless, while more than 50 percent were prosperous enough to own more than five acres.[61] The buying power of Londoni families meant that by the early 1990s, an acre of land in Sylhet was three or four times more expensive than in nonmigration districts of Bangladesh.[62] Land, of course, is not the only mark of social status. Painted airplanes on the walls and models on the roofs of homesteads proudly proclaim the transforming effects of global migration for local Sylheti families.

PART II

FOUR

British Rule

The First Phase

Robert Clive's statue stands just outside the Foreign and Commonwealth Office, on the steps at the end of King Charles Street in London's Whitehall. His authority is expressed in holding a sword in one hand, a scroll in the other, while gazing resolutely ahead to St. James's Park. On three sides of the base are bronze reliefs depicting key moments in Clive's career and the rise of the British to power in India. The first portrays Clive's solitary reflection before the decisive victory at the Battle of Plassey on 23 June 1757; the second depicts another famous victory at the 1751 Siege of Arcot; the third portrays the moment when the administration of Bengal was granted to the East India Company by the Mughal ruler Shah Alam in 1765. Thereafter the Company collected the revenues. The resources this released created the bridgehead for the Company's further territorial expansion.

Lord Curzon, the viceroy of India from 1899 to 1905, had suggested at the 150th anniversary of Plassey that Clive should be publicly commemorated. By the time John Tweed's statue was erected in 1912, Indian nationalists objected to honoring a "looter and plunderer." The 250th anniversary rekindled anti-imperial sentiment in India and reignited the controversies that had dogged Clive's final years and precipitated his suicide. Historical understanding of the East India Company's ascent to power is far more sophisticated today than the narrative conveyed by the statue.[1] Long before Plassey, in such areas as Madras, where Mughal authority was weak, the Company had become expansive and had shed a mercantile for a militaristic character. In the popular imagination, however, Clive remains the conqueror of India.

6. Clive's statue, Whitehall

At the heart of this chapter is a concern with issues of continuity and change in the establishment of the East India Company's power in the Sub-continent. The key events in its commercial growth are well known: the establishment of a trading post or "factory" at Surat in 1612; the transfer for a large loan and a peppercorn annual rent of £10 of the "dowry" of Bombay to the Company by Charles II in 1668; the foundation of Calcutta in 1690; the establishment of Company and personal fortunes in trade in spices and textiles, followed later by opium. Along the way not only local Indian trading rivals but the Portuguese and the Dutch lost out to the Company. By the eighteenth century, only the French remained as commercial and military rivals. The French and British East India Companies supported different claimants to the succession of a number of post-Mughal states, setting the scene for Clive's triumph at Arcot commemorated in Whitehall. After entrenching its de facto rule in Bengal, and in the process terminating the remaining French and Dutch influence, the Company continued in the period up to the 1850s to conquer Mysore (1799) and defeat the Marathas (1818) and Sikhs (1849) who had risen to regional power in the late Mughal era. It also annexed key areas such as Awadh (1856) and Sindh (1843).

The collision between an expanding Company and an expansive Burmese monarchy (following the defeat of the Kingdom of Arakan in 1784–85) led to the first two Anglo-Burmese Wars, of 1824–26 and 1852. The first war was the longest and most expensive in terms of men and treasure in Anglo-Indian history. By its close, Assam, Nagaland, and Arakan were added to the Company's territories. The 1852 war resulted in the annexation of the whole of Lower Burma, with its rich teak forests. Only after the third Anglo-Burma War, of 1885, was the Konbaung dynasty ended and Upper Burma annexed. The British administered Burma as a province of India until 1937, moving its capital from Mandalay to Rangoon.[2]

During the Napoleonic Wars, Dutch territories were seized as the Company sought to protect its trade routes from French interference. The Cape of Good Hope was occupied in 1795. The Company also strengthened its hold on Ceylon, with its coastal areas becoming part of British India in 1802. British power was further projected in the Indian Ocean with expeditions to Java and Mauritius in 1810–11.

The East India Company period was also marked by growing regulation from London in response to the "excesses" of its servants. The process began as early as 1773 with the Regulation Act. There were also changing British attitudes to Indian culture as a result of the rise of Utilitarianism and Christian Evangelical thought. The period ended with the 1857 revolt, which marked a further change in British social attitudes. The "mutiny" brought down the curtain on rule by the East India Company, which had earlier been divested of its monopolistic economic powers (1813) and trade operations (1833). Despite its eventual demise, the East India Company has been seen as foreshadowing the twentieth-century rise of multinational corporations.

These important developments cannot be fully considered in a general history.[3] The aim here is to focus on key issues and to provide the reader with insights into the historical debates surrounding them. How colonial, for example, was the early East India Company state? Did it mark a radical break with the Mughal and post-Mughal states in India? How transformative was its impact? Intimately linked with this is the question of whether the Company established its power in India as a result of "negotiation" or the "force" traditionally associated with Clive. There is also growing scholarly debate whether the Company can be understood in a formal institutionalized framework. Did its seventeenth- and early-eighteenth-century trading operations work mainly through private family networks?

Eighteenth-Century India

Two interlinked questions have dominated recent writing on the Company's rise to power.[4] Did it rise to prominence because of the collapse of Mughal authority? How economically successful were the successor states to the Mughals? The eighteenth century has been traditionally viewed as a dark age marked by political chaos and economic collapse as a result of Mughal decline brought on by succession struggles (1712–20), court decadence, and the fanaticism of Aurangzeb (ruled 1658–1707). These factors undermined the alliance between the Mughals and the Hindu Rajputs that dated from the time of Aurangzeb's illustrious predecessor Akbar.[5] According to the standard account, stability and prosperity were restored only when the reluctant East India Company traders stepped into this vacuum as rulers.

This discourse served British interests. Nineteenth-century romanticism and Orientalism embellished the British accounts with their emphasis on "heroic" figures such as Clive and their portrayal of Indian "exoticism."[6] India provided a theatrical backdrop for the triumphant display of British "character." Recent research has turned this understanding upside down and shown the Subcontinent as a crucial site for generating new British identities and reimaging the British state itself.[7]

Revisionists such as C. A. Bayly have challenged the notions of eighteenth-century Indian economic and political decline. The decentralization of power attendant on Mughal weakness was, according to them, accompanied by stable, commercializing, and centralizing successor states.[8] Their dynamic economies were based on "indigenous" capitalists who oversaw the commercialization and monetization of agrarian society before the advent of East India Company rule.[9] The successor states tapped into this wealth to provide for their growing armies, establishing in the post-Mughal regional states a form of "military-fiscal" regime. The powerful trading and commercial interests, exemplified by such Hindu banking clans as the Jagat Seths, had been nurtured by Mughal rule but had hastened its decline by progressively withdrawing their support during the early eighteenth century. The parallel decline of the Ottoman and Safavid Empires may have similarities of a political order being unsettled by the rise of regional mercantile classes—in Egypt, for example, arising from the developing coffee trade.

The Transition to Colonial Rule

Revisionist understandings clearly dispel the notion of the East India Company ascending to power in the context of political decline, or that its territorial expansion represented the triumph of a dynamic capitalism over a static and feudal society. On the contrary, such writers as Bayly see preexisting commercial and landed entrepreneurs as being essential allies for the

East India Company in the transition to colonialism.[10] Burton Stein, from a South Indian perspective, reveals that following Tipu Sultan's final defeat in 1799, "the Company received substantial help from scribal, commercial and gentry groups inside Mysorean territory itself."[11] In the words of David Washbrook, another revisionist, "In a certain sense Colonialism was a logical outcome of South Asia's own history of capitalistic development."[12] This "evolutionary" understanding of state formation has important implications for the characterization of the emergent Company rule. Before turning to this topic, however, we need to be aware of the criticisms of this emphasis on "threads" of historical continuity.

One of the principal criticisms is that this narrative plays down the violence that accompanied the East India Company's rise. Military might, especially naval supremacy over the French, was a key factor in the struggle against an expanding Mysore state, which at one moment threatened the established East Indian base at Madras. Seventy years later, the British were able to bring in vital military reinforcements by sea at the time of the 1857 revolt. The rich land revenues—extracted far more uniformly and rigorously from Bengal than under the Mughals—enabled the East India Company to pay for increasingly large standing armies. These numbered more than 150,000 men at the beginning of the nineteenth century. They came from social groups that had a tradition of augmenting income and status by military service. The Madras and Bombay Presidency Armies were mainly middle caste in composition—for example, Jats and Reddis—unlike the Bengal Army, which comprised Bhumihar Brahmin and Raput *sepoys* from Awadh and Bihar. The Bengal Army's "distinctive pattern" of recruitment has been seen as explaining its leading role in the 1857 revolt.[13]

The sepoys' costs were also met by the system of so-called subsidiary alliances whereby allies paid for their protection by Company troops. Inability to keep up the payments led some states into futile resistance, which "drew the Company into further territorial expansion."[14] During Richard Wellesley's governor generalship (1798–1805), the Presidency Armies mushroomed in size. By the time of the 1840s Anglo-Sikh Wars, the Company was able to put into the field armies that dwarfed those of Clive. Indeed, the fighting at Plassey was desultory in comparison with the brutal clashes in such battles as Sabraon (10 February 1846) and Chillianwala (13 January 1849). In addition to criticism of the revisionists' "spiriting away" of the East India Company's violent expansion, opponents question their portrayal of a "weak" Company presence, adapting itself to native conditions. For many historians, it was from the outset an intrusive force that fractured society.

Company Rule: A White Indian State?

Was the Company rule merely a more efficient post-Mughal "military-fiscal" state in its operations? Or was it an interventionist, "colonial" authority? The first understanding flows from the "negotiated" view of the establishment of its rule that I have referred to above. According to this view, wealthy Indian landed and commercial elites exerted considerable agency in the Company's transition from trade to dominion. The East India Company is seen as lacking the power to unsettle the elites' interests, which were in any case responsive to its political and economic imperatives. According to the contrary perspective, Company rule almost immediately represented a qualitative break with Indian polities. The new state had been established, it is argued, because of superior technology and economic organization. The Company's "forceful" breaking into the Indian political system enabled it to restructure economy and society in keeping with its own ideas about sovereignty, rule of law, and fiscal organization with its direct "links to commercial power outside India." With respect to sovereignty, for example, the Company only paid lip service to the ritual notion of Mughal overlordship, in reality acting on the principle of absolute rather than devolved sovereignty in its dealings with Indians. Coins minted in the name of the crown and public gallows were unmistakable signs of this.

Evidence for an "interventionist" state is often drawn from the anglicizing reforms beginning in the 1820s. Innovation was seen as necessary to release Indian society from superstition and unlock individual potential. This thinking was the product of both the Evangelical revival in Britain and the Benthamite philosophy of Utilitarianism. Indeed, when Lord William Cavendish Bentinck arrived as governor general in 1828, he wrote to Jeremy Bentham, "I shall govern in name, but it will be you who govern in fact."[15]

The reforms, however, never went as far as their enthusiasts hoped. This reflected the Company's wariness of Indian resistance. Even the abolition of slavery, which Parliament enjoined in 1833, was handled in a piecemeal and nonconfrontational manner in its Indian context.[16]

The lobbying of Evangelicals was more successful when it came to the abolition of the Pilgrim Tax, which the Company collected to finance the upkeep of Hindu temples. In this instance the Board of Control overruled the Court of Directors. Both bodies were united, however, in respect to the need to intervene in the practice of *sati*, the immolation of Hindu widows in the funeral pyres of their husbands. What carried the day in the face of opposition from traditionalist Hindus, however, was support from such Indian social reformers as Raja Ram Mohan Roy. Roy was an outstanding Bengali scholar and social reformer who in August 1828 had founded the Brahmo Sabha, later renamed Brahmo Samaj (House of God). Frequently described as the "father of modern India," Roy came from the class whose position had been enhanced by the Permanent Settlement.[17] No formal statement of the Brahmo Samaj's aims and beliefs was produced before Roy's departure for England in November 1830, although it is clear that his attachment to rationalism, hostility to idolatry, and belief in a universal theism marked out the society.

Roy used the columns of his journal *Sambad Kaumudi* to attack the "social evil" of sati, which he argued had no religious sanction. Aside from testimonials at the cremation ground, women's voices went unheard during the public debate. The issue was not their suffering but the civilizing role of colonialism in the face of conflicting interpretations of religious tradition. Indeed, revisionist research has maintained that British discussions reveal a "fascinated ambivalence," and the debate strengthened the misconception of sati as being a voluntary act expressing wifely devotion.[18] Incidences continued as late as 1987. Serendipitously, the debate stimulated Indian use of print culture. As we shall see in the next chapter, this played a crucial role in the development both of later reformist organizations and the nationalist movement.

The abolition of *thugee* was another important component of the interventionist reforms of the early decades of the nineteenth century. The campaign led by Colonel W. H. Sleeman to uncover and then eradicate the elusive thugee, who preyed on travelers, strangling them with a silk handkerchief (*rumal*), signified far more than merely a desire to eradicate odious practices. It was a symbol of the Pax Britannica and of the Company's surveillance powers. The establishment of the Thugee and Dacoity Department was a forerunner of the later Central Intelligence Department. The designation of "thugs" as hereditary criminals who murdered as an act of worship to Kali displayed the essentialization of identity that was a feature of the later "ethnographic state." Indeed, the 1836 Thugee Act was in many respects a forerunner of the Criminal Tribes and Castes Act of 1872, which designated vagrant communities as criminal by birth. The thugee phenomenon, despite its essentialized colonial portrayal, was a response to socioeconomic transformations arising from the East India Company's ascendancy. These included increased revenue demands and reduced employment opportunities for officials and soldiers in the states it annexed.[19]

The settling of the countryside involved not just order and the ending of "vagrancy" but intimate knowledge of landholding systems in order to extract revenue. This understanding of rural society gave birth to the *ka-ghazi raj* (empire of paper). This was highly dependent on the role of native interlocutors drawn from the higher castes. The result was the "fixing" of supposedly immutable rigid social hierarchies onto what in the eighteenth century had been a mobile society. This understanding suited the purpose of maintaining social control through local landed classes.[20] It was articulated by an early generation of scholar-administrators. Good examples of their writings include James Tod's *Annals and Antiquities of Rajasthan.* Their work reveals the complex interplay of innovation and accommodation in the colonial impact. This was social engineering in the name of tradition, dependent on indigenous interlocutors.

Governor General Bentinck had drawn on Raja Ram Mohan Roy's support for the spread of Western education, just as he had done in the campaign to abolish sati. Roy was a first-generation member of the small elite of Western-educated Indians that had grown up around the Presidency towns but was strongest in Calcutta. It was among students from its Hindu College that Roy secured the first support for his Brahmo Samaj organization.[21]

When the East India Company's charter was renewed in 1813, it had for the first time set aside an annual sum to fund education. The hopes of Utilitarians and Evangelicals that education would result in a weakening of religious traditions and social hierarchies were never realized. The main beneficiaries of Western education were drawn from the "writer castes" of Brahmins and Kayasthas, which had long-established traditions of literacy and professional service. Education for the masses, even in the vernacular languages, remained a distant dream. Rather than having a liberating effect, English medium higher education reinforced regional, social, and gender inequalities. Most elite Indians turned to education for its material benefits, although idealists like Roy saw it as a means to regenerate Indian society. They wanted access to the administrative positions that were opening for Indians. We shall see in later chapters how Western-style education and differential responses to its opportunities helped shape politics. Ultimately, educated Indians used the ideals of liberty, equality, and "progress" they had encountered in their studies against the colonial state and its racially constructed glass ceiling.

Lack of finance as well as Indian resistance frustrated reforming and modernizing impulses. Only £10,000 was set aside for education in 1813. Bentinck's road-improvement schemes were abandoned on the grounds of cost by his successor, Lord Auckland. By the 1820s, land revenue rather than trade was the single most important income source. The Madras Presidency's shortage of funds, together with Utilitarian theories of rent, resulted in the Cornwallis Zamindari system of land revenue administration enshrined in Bengal's Permanent Settlement being disavowed in favor of what became known as the Ryotwari system. Regular settlements lasting for twenty or thirty years were to be made with *ryots* (cultivators), rather than *rentier* intermediaries. The need to identify soil types for taxation purposes, to measure plots, and to record rights thereafter involved the colonial state in constant intrusion in rural society. The Ryotwari system, however, did not in practice strengthen the power of peasant cultivators against locally powerful elites. It was nonetheless extended, with modifications, from Madras to other Company possessions.

The Ryotwari and Zamindari systems provide a useful reminder that the Madras and Bengal Presidencies in fact each had its own governing ethos and sets of accommodation with Indian society. As Barrow and Haynes remark, "Company power was rarely expressed uniformly or identically throughout its territories."[22] Washbrook, while acknowledging some "transformative" elements, draws attention to the fact that strategic alliances and involvements with local society "outlived" changes in the Madras Presidency.[23]

In sum, Company rule cannot be characterized simply either as alien and transformative or as indigenous and accommodating. Its form and impact varied over time and locality. The age of Bentinck, for example, must be regarded differently from the era, a half-century earlier, of Sir William Jones.[24] In the decades after the winding up of the Company rule came the full flowering of colonial technological transformation, and of environmental exploitation. The reconceptualization of Indian society as "Orientalist empiricism" also attained its intellectual apogee in the 1870s and 1880s. Nonetheless, these interventions were foreshadowed in the Company era. Similarly, large-scale engineering feats were presaged in the Company period. The construction of the 350-mile Ganges Canal began in 1840, its headworks featuring two enormous stone lions, evoking a symbol of imperial power. The forests of the Santhal district of the Bengal Presidency (modern-day Jharkhand) were turned into cultivable land (1839–51). India's emergence as Britain's barrack in the East was foreshadowed by the dispatch of sepoys to Java, Mauritius, and Egypt.

The 1857 Revolt

The Company had faced numerous threats to its rule from the 1780s. These included "restorative rebellions" stirred up by dispossessed rulers, disaffected *zamindars*, and former Mughal officials. These focused around Awadh in North India in the 1780s, and in the Tirunelveli District in the south from 1799 to 1805. There were also tribal movements resulting from deforestation and resistance to the settling of outsiders on tribal land. The Koli uprising occurred in 1831–32 and the Santhal uprising in 1855–56 in eastern India.

Peasant uprisings responded to high revenue demands, as in the 1783 Rang-
pur rebellion in northern Bengal. The Bengal Presidency was also the site
of religious movements inspired by Islamic reform and the call to jihad,
including the movement of Titu Mir in western Bengal (1827–31) and the
Faraizi movement led by Haji Shariatullah and his son Dudu Mian in eastern Bengal, which continued from the 1830s to the 1860s.[25] Historians have
understood these rebellions in various ways, ranging from "primary resistance" or precursors of nationalist struggle to manifestations of "the political
consciousness" of the peasant.

The civilian revolt that accompanied the sepoy mutiny which broke out
at Meerut on 10 May 1857 contained elements of these earlier rebellions. It
reflected an urge to restore the past and depended on religion for legitimization, while community ties assisted the mobilization of disgruntled peasants.
Numerous historians have rehearsed the causes and characteristics of the
uprising. For Percival Spear it was the final attempt by "traditional" India
to halt the modernizing impact of colonial rule. This interpretation draws
on the notion of grievances arising from the social and political transformations of the 1830s, as well as on the rebels' allegiance to the aged Mughal
Emperor Shah Bahadur. At the same time, the Western-educated elites of
Calcutta were studiously loyal because, writes Judith Brown, they had "material interests in the new order, and often a deep, ideological commitment
to new ideas."[26]

Agrarian change is one area of transformation that has been widely examined as a causal factor. S. B. Chaudhuri first posited the view that peasants
and gentry, who had alike lost land to moneylenders under the colonial
fiscal and legal system, united to "recover what they had lost."[27] Eric Stokes
provided a more nuanced view that revolt was caused not so much by absolute loss as by a sense of relative deprivation. Moreover, social homogeneity
rather than indebtedness promoted rebelliousness.[28]

Awadh, which was a hotbed of revolt, has drawn debate concerning the
role of its landed magnates (*taluqdars*), many of whom had lost land in the
1856 land settlement following its annexation. Stokes has provided a nuanced account, which reveals that dispossession was not the only factor in
causing the magnates to rebel. Rudrangshu Mukherjee has reinforced the

understanding that the taluqdars' participation was never universal, but depended on personal calculation.[29] Thomas Metcalf sees the local peasantry, some of whom had benefited from the new settlement, following their local taluqdars into revolt.[30] Mukherjee, however, provides evidence against this top-down explanation, providing evidence of peasants who forced taluqdars to rebel and persisted in resistance when their feudal superiors had surrendered. Partisans of this interpretation also understand the sepoys as "peasants in uniform."[31]

The role of the charismatic rebel leadership provided by the Rani Lakshmibai of Jhansi as emblematic of the top-down view of civilian mobilization has also come under question. According to the standard account, Lakshmibai, the female ruler of a Maratha Princely State in central India, was a disgruntled feudal figure who turned against the British because the East India Company in 1853 annexed her state, along with a number of others, as part of Lord Dalhousie's "Doctrine of Lapse." This policy denied inheritance rights to adopted sons. Tapti Roy's detailed district-level study, however, reveals that the sepoys took the initiative and coerced Lakshmibai to raise the standard of revolt.[32] The Rani, whatever her motivation, literally died in the saddle while fighting the British forces in the Battle of Gwalior.

The military rebellion has evoked less historical controversy. I have already referred to the sensitivity of the Bengal Army to issues of purity regarding the use of the new Enfield rifle's greased cartridges. A Brahmin sepoy, Mangal Pandey, began the unrest when he fired at Lieutenant Henry Baugh at Barrackpore on 29 March, following an alleged dispute over use of the cartridges. Pandey's hanging in April spread the disaffection. The mutineers from Meerut on 11 May proclaimed Bahadur Shah Zafar the emperor of Hindustan. Other causes of the military revolt have been variously identified as conflict over new service conditions, which forced high-caste sepoys to serve overseas and thereby become ritually polluted; resentment over reduced pay; and the decline of morale following the annexation of Awadh.

Historians have also debated the extent to which the revolt was a nationalist struggle. The rising tide of Indian nationalism in the first decade of the twentieth century was accompanied by V. D. Savarkar's attempt to portray the events of 1857 as the first Indian War of Independence.[33] He

claimed that the planned uprising had been inspired by love of country
and religion. Certainly for some Muslim rebels the struggle was seen as a
jihad. But academic historians have been divided by Sarkar's interpretation.
Evidence against a potent nationalistic influence includes Hindu-Muslim
conflict, loyalty of the Western-educated class, and the very fact of failure.
The pendulum has swung in recent years, however, in favor of Savarkar's
analysis, not just in the realm of public history, where his understanding
received full endorsement in the 250th anniversary commemorations, but
also among academic historians. C. A. Bayly, for example, has seen the uprising "as a set of patriotic revolts" picking up on the theme of Hindustan as
a valued homeland. He finds the roots for this notion in the precolonial and
early colonial past. It had been weakened by the rise of religious community
identity, but according to Bayly still persisted in 1857.[34]

The East India Company ultimately triumphed because it could call on
the support of Indian military allies, notably the Sikhs and Muslim Rajputs
in the recently annexed Punjab. These communities were to form the heart

7. Frederick Goodall, *Highland Jessie*, oil painting of an
incident during the siege of Lucknow

of the postmutiny army. The conflict was nonetheless a close-run thing, which profoundly affected the British psyche. The fall of Delhi, with its attendant European deaths, and the "transgressive" massacre of European women and children in Cawnpore (Kanpur) by Nana Sahib's bodyguards especially left an imprint. The six-month siege of the Residency at Lucknow, in which those who survived ended up eating rats and cockroaches, became the focus of Victorian accounts. Frederick Goodall's painting of the relief of the siege showing Jessie Brown, a corporal's wife, who had heard the bagpipes of the 78th Highlander's in a dream, exemplifies the sentimentality surrounding the episode, which became as firmly established in the Victorian imagination as Gordon's death at Khartoum.[35]

Indians had their own painful collective memories. They included the pillage and killings—including the execution of Bahadur Shah's sons Mirza Mughal and Mirza Khazir Sultan—which accompanied the recapture of Delhi in September 1857. British reprisals in Lucknow and Cawnpore and the "blowing away" of captured rebels from cannons—in fact, a traditional Mughal punishment—also left a powerful effect.[36] In July 1943, a volunteer female regiment of the Indian National Army in Singapore was named after the Rani of Jhansi.[37] Since independence, the events of 1857 have been commemorated in popular histories, novels, and the 2005 Bollywood film *The Rising: Ballad of Mangal Pandey*, with the celebrated actor Aamir Khan playing the lead role.[38] In Barrackpore there is a Mangal Pandey Park and cenotaph. A Mangal Pandey postage stamp and first-day cover were issued in October 1984. Feelings were running so high in September 2007, at the time of the 250th anniversary, that demonstrators prevented British descendants from visiting the site of the siege of the Lucknow Residency.[39]

Eighteen fifty-seven clearly remains a date to conjure with. The victorious British abruptly ended the Mughal "sovereignty" and the rule of the Company, although by this stage the former was a surrogate and the latter a shadow of the era of Clive and Hastings. Crown rule was accompanied by heavy financial as well as psychological burdens, including a reinforced racial divisiveness. We will see in the next chapter that the legacies of the revolt were still being felt as the Raj approached its zenith nearly half a century later.

FIVE

The "High Noon" of Empire

The clock tower and the railway station were familiar features of the Indian urban landscape in the decades following the 1857 revolt. Indeed, the new Punjabi commercial center of Lyallpur (Faisalabad) was designed by Sir Ganga Ram, with all its roads radiating out in the shape of a Union Jack from a central clock tower, commonly known as Ghanta Ghar. One hundred miles to the east, a Gothic clock tower erected to commemorate Lord Elgin's viceregal visit to Amritsar stood incongruously in the precincts of the Golden Temple. It symbolically asserted the superiority of British industrial time over the spiritual universe of a timeless and formless God.

Indian trains did not always run on time, but the platforms and stations onto which they disgorged their goods and passengers symbolized the technological prowess that "validated" imperial rule. The opposing architectural styles of Lahore and Bombay railway stations reflected the contrasting moods of postmutiny British India. The Lahore station, with its turrets and clear firing lines, revealed that the Raj was ever vigilant. Threats could come from "native" unrest or from the looming shadow of an expansive Czarist Empire.[1] The confection of neo-Gothic and Mughal styles of the Victoria terminus in Bombay—termed by one author as possibly "the central building of the entire British Empire"—on the other hand expressed the more exuberant imperial purpose and linkage with the Mughal past that followed the end of Company rule.[2] The station, which was commenced shortly after Victoria was declared empress of India, was completed in 1887. The new imperial vision of India received its final architectural flourish a generation later in the classically styled construction of the "Rome of Hindustan": New Delhi.[3]

8. Golden Temple, Amritsar

The half-century following the 1857 revolt and culminating in Lord Cur-zon's viceroyalty was marked by as many contrasts and complications as the Company Rule. The Raj sought its legitimation not only in its modernizing technological prowess but in the upholding of "tradition." The latter was based on both intimate knowledge of Indian society and Orientalist specula-tion and stereotypes. Much of the proclaimed "tradition" was a British cre-ation. Confidence bordering on racial arrogance coexisted with such deep anxieties and neuroses as those intimated in some of Kipling's ghost stories. There was both a retreat to the "safe" confines of the club and the "hill station"—a town founded in colonial Asia and Africa by Europeans at alti-tudes to escape the summer heat of the plains—and the total lack of privacy and a domestic sphere in the officials' bungalow dwellings. Women, who came to India in larger numbers after the completion of the Suez Canal (November 1869), both upheld domesticity, which underpinned social life, and actively participated in such "manly" pursuits as hunting. The business of government became ever more complex, but as that most "Imperial" of viceroys, Curzon, discovered, attempts to incorporate the Western-educated Indian elite through municipal politics led to bitterness and frustration. Before addressing some of these themes, however, we will first examine the more immediate responses to the traumatic events of 1857.

The Aftermath of the Revolt

The 1858 Government of India Act formalized the transition from Company to Crown rule. Henceforth the governor general or viceroy was answerable to Parliament through the newly established cabinet Office of Secretary of State for India. All other officials in India were subordinate to the viceroy, including the military commander in chief. This failed to prevent a clash, however, between Curzon and Commander in Chief Lord Kitchener, which resulted in the viceroy's resignation when he felt he had not received proper government backing.

Military reform headed the list of the immediate concerns after 1857. The high-caste sepoys from the Indo-Gangetic Plain were now regarded as unreliable. Recruitment shifted west to the Punjab. At the same time, the number of European troops was increased and control over artillery was put firmly in British hands. Gurkhas, who had proved their worth in 1857, also formed an important fighting component of the new army.

All these changes cost money. The army increasingly swallowed a quarter of the government of India's total budget. Education was starved of funds. In what has been termed the Conservative Reaction, the British turned increasingly to the princes and the large landowners of North India as the props for their rule. The educated classes, who had been loyal in 1857, became progressively alienated from a state that not only limited their opportunities but, apart from infrastructural development, had lost its modernizing impetus. Nevertheless, the government had created a public sphere in which Indians could protest that British rule was not living up to its liberal democratic ideals. A further complaint was that the colonialists were draining resources from India because of the high military expenditures and "home charges."

Such regions as the Punjab, Nepal, and Burma, which were to provide recruits to colonial armed forces from communities identified by the British as martial races, have experienced long-term consequences. The Pakistani Army's dominance and link with Punjab can be traced back to the new British recruitment policy from the 1880s. Nepal's history has been shaped by the employment of Gurkha troops. In Burma, the British recruited Karens and Kachins. The latter, who fought with the British against the invading Japanese in the Second World War, have been engaged in conflict with the centralizing postcolonial Burmese state in one of the longest-running ethnic conflicts in South Asia. Numerous rounds of peace talks have followed periods of conflict and short-lived cease-fires. The Kachin Independence Organization signed the most recent peace agreement with the Myanmar authorities on 30 May 2013.

By the eve of the First World War, three-fifths of the Indian Army's troops came from a handful of districts in the Punjab. The Social Darwinist ideology of "martial castes" had emerged during the period of Lord Roberts's command (1885–93) to rationalize this shift. Recruiting officers produced detailed caste handbooks, which contained genealogies and histories of the martial castes and details of their customs and physique, all set within the fashionable scientific terminology. Servicemen were rewarded with pensions and grants of land in the newly irrigated western areas of the Punjab. The Chenab Canal, for example, irrigated one million acres, with its new district headquarters of Lyallpur. Aside from military rewards, colonial stereotypes of the cultivating abilities of rural communities also influenced allotment policies, with "sturdy" Sikh Jats being favored. The migration of Sikh settlers into the Muslim-dominated western Punjab areas was to possess profound implications at the time of the 1947 Partition. The intertwining of military recruitment and canal development in the Punjab was demonstrated most clearly in the setting aside of large areas of land for "loyalist" military contractors in such districts as Shahpur. Some of this was granted on the understanding that these contractors bred mules and horses for the army's baggage trains and cavalry units.

Railway development was another immediate response to the revolt. In 1854 there were just thirty-four miles of track in India. By 1880 this had

9. Opening of the Khyber Railway, 4 November 1925

risen to eighty-five hundred miles. This rapid expansion possessed profound socioeconomic consequences. In its earlier phase, however the rail network was driven by the need to transport troops quickly in response to civil unrest. Strategic concerns overrode costs, as routes were driven through mountains with viaducts, bridges, cuttings, and tunnels. The Khyber Pass Railway, which was opened in November 1925 to allow easier movement of troops to the frontier, required thirty-four tunnels and ninety-two bridges and culverts in the ascent from Jamrood to Landi Kotal.

The railways connected India's heartland with the global economy, ending centuries of international trade dominated by the Indian Ocean littorals. Exports of cotton and wheat, for example, were shipped from the Punjab through the developing port city of Karachi. Imports from Britain grew even more rapidly. By the 1880s up to a third of the demand for cloth in eastern India was being met by imports from Lancashire. This formed the backdrop to the emergence of the native spinning wheel as a potent symbol of nationalist struggle. The opening of the Suez Canal speeded up the shipment of goods from India and, until 1937, its province of Burma. Railways in Burma had to compete with the Scottish-owned Irrawaddy Flotilla Company, which ran the largest number of riverboats in the world. The six hundred vessels annually carried around nine million passengers in the peak interwar period.

According to some critics, the railways also contributed to the famines of the second half of the nineteenth century, both by encouraging the growth of cash crops rather than food crops and by increasing the numbers of landless poor, who starved to death when food became scarce and dear.[4] The building of embankments without adequate culverts led to environmental deterioration, which affected food supply and public health in the Bengal delta.

The British, however, regarded the railways as a great achievement. Certainly the development of the Bengal and Bihar coalfields and the growth of the Bombay textile industries were dependent on the railway. Railways transported the raw cotton and the workforce to Bombay. By 1900, nineteen million people were using Bombay's stations alone. Many of these were "modern" commuters, who traveled by train from the north to the commercial and industrial areas at the south of the island city. At the beginning of the twentieth century, India, with more than twenty-eight thousand miles of track, had the fourth-largest rail network in the world.

Roads, like the railways, initially had strategic as well as commercial applications. The Fort Sandeman–Chuhar Khel road, which linked the Zhob district of Balochistan with Dera Ismail Khan in the Punjab, provides a prime example. This major engineering feat involved the blasting of a passage through the Dahana Tangi gorge. People, goods, and letters moved along the new roads and railways. According to Stanley Wolpert, the new national postal service, with its standard cheap rate, "served not only to unite the Subcontinent as nothing else had done" but became a "most important new stimulus to learning, literacy and socio-cultural change of every imaginable kind."[5]

The roads and railways were part of a wider communications revolution that not only connected regions within India but drew the Subcontinent closer to its metropolis. The telegraph linked London and Calcutta in 1870. The Suez Canal cut the journey time by steam ships from one hundred to twenty-five days. The canal made Bombay the "Gateway of India," which increasingly challenged Calcutta as India's leading port. A number of shipping lines plied between Europe and India. The Peninsular and Oriental Steam Navigation Company was always the most highly regarded. Experienced travelers chose their cabins to avoid the sun by voyaging "POSH"—Port Out, Starboard Home. Shorter journeys through the Suez Canal encouraged more visitors. Easier access also increased the number of Englishwomen in what had been a male-dominated society, heralding the Anglo-India of Mrs. Hauksbee, as portrayed in Kipling's *Plain Tales from the Hills.*[6]

The Raj, "Tradition," and Its Collaborative Allies

While technology "validated" the Indian Empire, the system rested also on the upholding of "tradition." Eric Hobsbawm's classic study illuminated the most spectacular manifestation of the "invention" of tradition in the adaptation of Mughal pageantry in the Delhi Darbars of 1877, 1903, and 1911.[7] The darbar ceremonials, which in Mughal times, with their gift exchange of clothes, were acts of reciprocity, under the Raj became acts of subordination. The reviews of troops and parades, including those of veterans from 1857, underlined the military basis of British rule. The 1877 darbar, at which the Viceroy Lord Lytton proclaimed Victoria as empress of India, was attended by more than four hundred princes and their retinues. Fifteen thousand troops were drawn up to witness Lytton's declaration on New Year's Day. The banners, heraldry, and costumes evoked Victorian medievalism with its tropes of order, harmony, and benign hierarchy.

Curzon held a darbar in 1903 to celebrate Edward VII's coronation. The darbar surpassed Lytton's pageantry, thanks to the viceroy's meticulous arrangements. These included the extension of the site to a five-mile arena linked by a light railway. Temporary buildings were decorated in an Indo-Saracenic architectural style. Curzon paraded through Old Delhi on an elephant before entering the amphitheater in a carriage. He was greeted by a 101-gun salute before making his speech. The nationalist newspapers, to his chagrin, termed the darbar "an extravagant waste" and found the speech "full of platitudes."[8] The pageantry was mockingly dubbed by some

86

10. Delhi Darbar, 1903

"Curzonation Darbar." The 1911 darbar was the only one attended by the reigning monarch. George V and Queen Mary were guests at a glittering ceremony at which it was officially announced that India's capital would be transferred from Calcutta to Delhi.

A more subtle example of the invention of tradition is provided by Sir Robert Sandeman's introduction of the jirga (council of elders) as a key institution of tribal governance in Balochistan. The jirga was an institution with no history in the region. It was imported from the very different circumstances of the North West Frontier Province. Even there, the jirga was part of the Deputy Commissioners' armory of powers under the Frontier Crimes Regulation. The census (begun in 1865), which was the apogee of the "ethnographic state's" Orientalist empiricism, further invented "tradition." It provided the bedrock for the late-nineteenth-century British portrayal of a static rural India hidebound by caste distinctions and deeply divided along religious lines. British rule in these circumstances acted as a neutral adjudicator.

The essentialization of religious community by the census operations is brought out most clearly by the statement of Denzil Ibbertson, who supervised the 1881 enumeration in the Punjab. "Every native who was unable to define his creed," he declared, "or described it by any name *other than that of a recognized religion*, was held to be classed as a Hindu.[9] Two decades later, the Indian census commissioner E. A. Gait expressed a similar attitude when he rapped the knuckles the Bombay census superintendent for using the hybrid term "Hindu-Muhammadans" for groups who did not fit easily into any category. Gait was of the view that each Indian should be assigned to "the one religion or the other as best he could."[10] It was the British census operations that spurred Sikh revivalists to reconstitute the Sikh tradition around the "Khalsa sub-tradition," as until the 1901 census only Khalsa Sikhs were defined as Sikhs. Finally, the census established an overarching identity of the "depressed classes," which for the first time lumped together Untouchables from different regions and communities into a single social category. The process was completed in 1936, when a list of scheduled castes was promulgated.

The census was accompanied by other intellectual products of colonial ethnography, such as the codification of customary laws. According to a government census report, "The codification and elevation of Brahminical practices" over local custom and practice made Indian society more "knowable" and hence more controllable from a British perspective. For the Brahmins themselves, codification provided an opportunity to consolidate their position in the social and ritual hierarchy.[11] In the Punjab, however, a different scenario arose. There a codified tribal customary law was privileged over Islamic personal law with respect to inheritance. This played a key role in binding rural intermediaries to the Raj in a strategically crucial region.

From the outset, the Punjab colonial state balanced commercial agriculture with the stability of the traditional order. On the one hand, it recorded individual property rights and guaranteed them by law; on the other, the state safeguarded traditional hierarchies through the application of a codified system of customary law. Sir Charles Louis Tupper's codification was a monumental exercise, as customary law varied from district to district. Women were routinely excluded from the inheritance of agricultural land despite their rights under Islamic personal law. Land nonetheless moved out of the traditional classes as its rising value was used to secure loans for "unproductive" use, such as wedding expenditures. Fearing instability, the British overrode laissez-faire scruples to halt the process. Legislation introduced in 1900 divided the population into "agriculturalist" and "nonagriculturalist" tribes. Land could not pass permanently from the former to the latter. The protected landowners formed a loyal set of intermediaries down to the end of the Raj.

The Punjabi military contractors, as epitomized by such loyalist families as the Noons and the Tiwanas, were not the only post-1857 British allies. The princes also formed an important pillar of the Raj. They were bound to the British Paramount Power in what has been termed Victorian "feudalism." Their subordination, as we have seen, was symbolically enacted in the darbars. In return, for control over foreign affairs, the British exerted only indirect power in the domestic matters of the 560 odd states that had survived Dalhousie's doctrine of lapse. The Princely State of Hyderabad was larger than France; the smallest states were only a few acres in extent. A handful of rulers, most notably the Wodeyar Maharajas of Mysore, who had been returned after the defeat of Tipu Sultan, implemented educational and industrial development policies that were in advance of those in neighboring British districts. Most states, however, were economically backward. They also lacked the developing public spheres of the British territories. The Raj kept watch on them through the appointment of residents from the Political Service to the native courts. They intervened only in situations of gross misgovernment or moral turpitude.

The British and Indian Society

Britons interacted with Indians in more complex ways than that presented in some standard histories. There is post-1857 evidence of a retreat to the bungalow and the sanctuary of the hill station, but the ruling classes were also always on display, leading very public private lives. Similarly, the memsahib was as much a "partner" in empire as a cocooned dependent. Finally, despite their imperial mythology of being places apart, hill stations, like other urban settlements, depended on Indian capital and enterprise for their maintenance and development during the Raj.

The first hill stations had been created in the 1820s. They proliferated in the decades after 1857 to well over a hundred, clinging to the spurs of the Himalayas and the Ghats. Railway development enabled easier access. The narrow-gauge "toy train" railways that are today's tourist attractions, at such places as Darjeeling and Simla, played a vital role in the development of the larger hill stations. The sixty miles of track from Kalka to Simla ran across precipitous viaducts and through a series of 107 tunnels. Like the railways, the hill stations had a military as well as a civilian purpose, as they were seen to offer a healthy climate for the convalescence of British troops. "The temperature is such," the British army officer William Gowan wrote, "that Europeans may be out of doors all day with comfort and advantage—partaking of occupations and diversions the same as at home, and delighting in the association excited by scenery and climate . . . resembling so exactly those which distinguish and exult in his mind his distant and Dear Native Land."[12]

Simla, which became known as "The Abode of the Little Tin Gods," was the most famous hill station, as each summer, from 1864 onward, the government of India shifted there to escape the heat of the plains.[13] The atmosphere of gaiety and scandal during the summer season was immortalized in Kipling's short stories of the 1880s. Simla's increasing "bustle" after the completion of the railway line from Kalka (1903) was not, however, to Curzon's liking, and he moved his summer headquarters to an "elaborate camp" some distance from the town. Simla, with its faux Swiss chalets, mock Tudor official buildings, and imposing Anglican church on its main ridge, should not be taken as an uncomplicated symbol of post-1857 British "retreat" from India. Its existence demonstrated the imperium's command of military, financial, and technological resources. Without these, thirty-five thousand people could not have perched on a Himalayan ridge each summer to escape the heat and dust of the plains below.

The bungalow, the adaptation of a traditional Bengali dwelling into a building form exported throughout the world, was also a more complex symbol of British postmutiny culture than has sometimes been portrayed. The fact that bungalows were surrounded by large plots of land that sepa-

11. Viceregal lodge, Simla

rated servants and living quarters, and were also set back from the road with entrances guarded by the ubiquitous *chowkidar* (night watchman), could be read as representing a desire for separation from a chaotic and disease-ridden India.[14] However, as such scholars as Procida and Collingham have revealed, far from being a place of refuge, the bungalow was neither a private nor a domestic space. In the words of Procida, "Private life was on permanent display, the home was an arena for political discussion and administrative action."[15] Collingham adds, "No bungalow was ever free of various Indian servants. . . . The structure of the bungalow and the habits of the Indian servants meant that the bungalow was flawed as a private space. . . . A sphere which the British claimed to cherish as a closed area of life was laid open to Indian view and judgement."[16]

Procida has also revised attitudes regarding the role of the memsahib.[17] A traditional view, derived in part from literary representations, is that British women in India lived in a "cultural cocoon," were lazy, pampered, and "ultra-domestic." Procida portrays them, however, as "partners" in empire. They "integrated" themselves with the public world of the empire "by adopting more masculinized personae and embracing masculine activities."[18] These even included the dangerous sport of "pig-sticking," the spearing of wild boar. Isabel Savory at the turn of the twentieth century thus captured the excitement of the chase and kill: "It is a case of riding as never before one has ridden: and the excitement of the break-neck gallop only gives place at the finish to a battle royal, fraught with danger."[19] A woman's involvement in such activities, in which she dressed in male attire, allowed her to be a comrade, not just a companion, to her husband. Closer ties with her spouse came, however, at the cost of separation from children, who usually from the age of eight were dispatched to boarding school in the United Kingdom.

British social life in India has been explored through the lens of the civil servants and the army. The Anglo-Indian population, however, also included teachers, governesses, shopkeepers, skilled factory workers, engineers, journalists, accountants, businessmen, and large numbers of missionaries. Calcutta, which by the end of the nineteenth century had grown to be the second city of the Empire, was always the most "British" of Indian cities. It was here that the famous managing agencies, such as Andrew Yule, Bird and Co., Gillanders, Arbuthnot, Jardine Skinner, and Mackinnon, Mackenzie and Co., had their headquarters. They had originated as commission agents but went on to control mines, plantations, railways, and shipping lines. British managing agencies controlled all fifty jute mill companies scattered along the Hooghly River, which increasingly undercut the Dundee firms' markets in Europe and North America. The private-partner management agencies acted as bankers, entrepreneurs, and managers for their joint-stock companies. The most successful houses, such as Andrew Yule, could manage up to sixty companies with capital investments of £20 million.[20] The British commercial grip began to decline in the interwar period, although the beneficiaries were Marwari capitalists from western India rather than native Bengalis. Calcutta's prominent position under the Raj as both administrative capital and financial center encouraged an early growth of the "politics of association," which increasingly took a nationalist and militant turn.

The Raj in Excelsis: Curzon's Viceroyalty

George Nathaniel Curzon's viceroyalty (1899–1905) is seen as the "high noon" of the Raj. Curzon not only organized the ten-day Coronation Darbar, with its million onlookers, he laid the foundations for the Victoria Memorial, which, set in its sixty acres of gardens, remains one of modern Kolkata's most famous landmarks.[21] He is held to have taken to their extremes both the post-1857 paternalism that we have seen at work in the Punjab and the sense of imperial destiny that was materialized in the Indo-Saracenic architectural style. There is no doubt that Curzon cared about India's cultural heritage, as seen in his creation of a directorate general of archaeology and the funding for the restoration of the Taj Mahal. Nonetheless, his insensitivity to educated Indian opinion over a range of issues culminating in the 1905 partition of Bengal undermined the British ruling authority that he so trumpeted.

Recent research has rightly pointed out that Curzon was not a universally controversial figure and that there is a tendency to read back the rancor of his final days as viceroy to earlier times.[22] Nonetheless, there is a common thread of antipathy to the political activities of the educated classes. The racial barriers to the administrative advancement of some of their ablest representatives (for example, Surendranath Banerji) led to demands both for reform in the Indian Civil Service examination system and for greater political representation. The latter was partially addressed by the liberal Viceroy Lord Ripon (1880–84), who increased the representation of elected Indians in municipal and rural local bodies. We will examine in a later chapter the circumstances that led regional associations—which had strong roots not only in Calcutta but in the old Presidency towns of Madras and Bombay—to the formation of a Subcontinent-wide Congress in 1885. Curzon shared the view of the Punjab School of Administration that the "real" India was that of the sturdy peasants, and that the Congress was "unrepresentative" of that world.

He acted upon this outlook soon after his arrival in Calcutta. While Curzon's role in the decision to halve the elected element in the city's corporation was obscured from the general public, it bore all the hallmarks of later decisions that evoked Indian outrage. The Calcutta Corporation was a body with two-thirds of its members elected by Indian ratepayers (13,890 in 1898), operating cheek by jowl with the bureaucratic government of India. Civil servants and British residents alike increasingly balked at its becoming a base

12. Lord and Lady Curzon, tiger hunt, 1902

for political opposition led by such figures as Surendranath Banerji. There were claims that the corporation's "Hindu clique" was halting municipal projects by playing politics with them. Curzon inherited this rancorous situation. His predecessor, Lord Elgin, had stymied the Bengali government's reform proposals. Curzon's temperamental hostility to the "Baboo" party was reinforced by his desire to root out inefficiency. He therefore pushed ahead to reduce the elective element without consulting Bengali opinion. His Chicago-born wife Mary Leitner was far more able to reach out to Indians. Curzon's aloofness led him to seriously underestimate political opposition. In the event Banerji and twenty-seven commissioners resigned from the Calcutta Corporation in what Curzon airily dismissed as an "act of petulance."[23] He justified the act of disenfranchisement in a letter to the accommodating secretary of state, George Hamilton, in terms of the unrepresentative character of the elected commissioners—"the helm had been seized and worked in their own interest by a clique of Bengali Hindus"—and the resulting "swamping" of the interests of "the European mercantile interests who have made Calcutta what it is."[24]

Curzon's role in the Indian Universities Act of 1904 was more immediately controversial. The legislation reduced the autonomy of the universities, including the oldest established of them, Calcutta University, by instituting greater government control over their senates and their territorial jurisdiction. The act was regarded with suspicion, as a means to control nationalist sentiments in those institutions, especially because there had been no Indian representation on the committee of inquiry that preceded the act. The following year Curzon encountered even more opposition when he decided to partition Bengal. The viceroy denied that this was an attempt to "divide and rule" by separating a Muslim-majority East Bengal and Assam from Hindu-majority West Bengal. The decision seems to have been taken on purely administrative grounds. Only after nationalist protests mounted did British officials attempt to rally Muslim support for the measure in East Bengal. The protests, which involved boycotting British goods, are known as the *swadeshi* movement.

The swadeshi protests were focused in Bengal but spread farther as Congress "extremists" like the Maharashtrian Tilak sought to convert them into a national campaign. The partition proposals were roundly condemned in such newspapers as the *Bengalee* and *Sanjibani*. The latter's editor, Krishna-kumar Mitra, was popularly credited with originating the idea of a boycott of British goods. Calcutta observed a *hartal* (strike) on 16 October 1905, the day on which the partition took effect. Surendranath Banerji addressed an audience of more than seventy-five thousand, the largest political gathering ever seen at that time in the imperial capital.

The great Bengali writer Rabrindranath Tagore (1861–1941), in a famous speech, debated how the *bhadralok* (educated upper classes) could put across their political message to the uneducated masses. He suggested the popular-ization of swadeshi goods at traditional *melas* (fairs) and the use of *jatras* (folk dramas), *kathakata* (recitals), and *suhrid* (magic lantern shows) to spread patriotic feelings, along with oral readings from newspapers.[25] Jatras became so effective at spreading "seditious doctrines" that the Bengali government arrested Mukunda Das, the author of *Matri Puja*, one of the most famous plays, in which Matangi, the goddess of war, prepared herself to rid a foreign-ruled India. "Patriotic ideas" were woven into traditional recitals from the Hindu epics. For example, Girin Mukherji, a priest of the Calcutta Kalighat Temple in 1907, wrote a *Swadeshi Ramayana*. Many people were in fact drawn into the swadeshi movement through *Kali Pujas* (religious devotions). The bloodthirsty Kali, who was believed to stalk the cremation ground, was invoked to incite violence by the revolutionary weekly publication *Jugantar* in March 1908: "Without bloodshed the worship of the goddess will not be accomplished. . . . With firm resolve you can bring English rule to an end in a single day. . . . Begin yielding up a life after taking a life."[26]

Fifty thousand people took the swadeshi pledge at the Kalighat Temple on 28 September 1905. These were predominantly male gatherings, but women embraced such symbolic actions as the refusal to light household fires when public protests were held over the partition. Female mobilization in nationalist struggle became more sustained in the Gandhian era, but Sarla Debi Choudhurani, Rabindranath Tagore's niece, organized swadeshi meetings in Calcutta and started the Lakshmi Bhandar store for popular-izing indigenous goods.[27]

The singing of *Bande Mataram* (Hail, Mother) became the movement's rallying cry. This patriotic song was a source of great inspiration for educated Bengali youths brought up on the historical novels of Bankim Chandra Chatterjee, including the 1882 publication *Ananda Math* (The abbey of bliss), from which the song came. The song's aggressive Hindu imagery alienated Muslims, however, as did the social boycott of community members who still used and sold British goods. Girischandra Ghosh's "patriotic plays" *Sirajuddoulah* and *Mir Kasim* had Muslim heroes but were swimming against the tide of opinion, as was the revolutionary paper *Jugantar's* hailing the 1857 revolt as the first Hindu-Muslim war of independence. Despite the presence of leading Muslim swadeshi orators such as Liakat Husain, who was described by the *Sandhya* as a "lion among men," Muslims remained aloof from the campaign.

By the time that the partition of Bengal was annulled, in 1911, Indian nationalism had dug deep cultural roots in the region. Once mobilization moved beyond the narrow circle of Western-educated elites, however, it took on a Hinduized form that alienated Muslims. Much of Gandhi's later public life was to be spent grappling with this tension and its consequences.

A sense of "Indianness" in the post-Mughal states predated the rise of the East India Company. This "old patriotism" was challenged by British rule, which through such innovations as the census essentialized religious communities. The postmutiny Raj created the conditions for both "communalism" and modern nationalism. The latter was rooted in European ideas of the "nation," "liberty," and "democracy," which were communicated to the English-educated elite. The desire for self-government increased as a result of racial exclusion and the insensitivities to educated Indian opinion exemplified by Curzon's viceroyalty. It was communicated to a wider audience in terms of "traditional" religious iconography.

In succeeding chapters we shall examine in more detail the self-conscious efforts made by educated Indians to strengthen and institutionalize "imagined" collectivities of community and nation. They constructively engaged with the new definitions of community and arenas for political participation provided by the colonial state. This process was far more nuanced than "diffusionist" understandings of nationalism would allow.

SIX

Indians and the Raj

The British Raj depended on Indian taxes, labor, and capital. Its self-proclaimed greatest achievement, the railways, relied on Indian contractors, unskilled laborers, quarry gangs, and timber merchants. The postal service, which also knit the country together, depended initially on *dak* runners, then later on Indian postmen and postmasters, who for many subjects were the most visible representation of the Raj. The elites were the main beneficiaries of the Raj's informal and formal networks of collaboration, but military service provided opportunities for the martial castes of the Punjab peasantry. It would be facile to divide colonial Indian society into winners and losers arising from the imperial connection. Relative rather than absolute gains were in any case frequently more important in community perceptions. In this chapter we shall look, rather, at the ways in which Indian commercial and cultural interaction with the Raj had long-term and often unforeseen consequences. The first part will focus on the emergence of leading Indian capitalist communities, which continue to exert a powerful influence. Their commitment to a strong state to oversee economic growth was important in influencing the political economy of independence and partition. In the second section we examine the emergence of cultural and community associations, which were important in the transition to a politics of national and communal identity.

Tata, Jamshedpur, and Indian Business in Colonial India

The township of Jamshedpur grew up in the early years of the twentieth century on a 25-square-mile plot of land on the Chota Nagpur plateau in the Singbhum district of Bihar, some 155 miles west of Calcutta. By 1911 its population stood at six thousand, who inhabited two distinct parts known as north town and south town. At the township's heart was a square ringed by a number of bungalows and offices; in its middle was a *maidan* (park). About a mile to the east of the town was the "overgrown and very dirty" village of Sakchi.[1] Clues to the town's identity were provided by the name of its station (Tatanagar) and the large works whose principal entrance lay at its center. This was the pioneering steel township established by the Tata Steel Company. The first steel ingot was rolled in 1912. By the early 1970s Jamshedpur had expanded from this original site and grown to a population of half a million people, almost all employed in the steelworks and the truck-making Tata Engineering and Locomotive Company. Today, Jamshedpur is the major industrial city of eastern India and is home to numerous Tata companies, including the multinational giant Tata Motors, as well as hundreds of medium- and small-scale industries. With a population of more than 2.3 million, the Jamshedpur urban agglomeration is the third-largest city in eastern India, after Kolkata and Patna.

"Steel City" is both a major success story for its company and a symbol of twenty-first-century Indian industrial and economic power. Its early development relied not just on the entrepreneurial genius of its founder Jamsetji Nusserwanji Tata (1839–1904), "the father of Indian industry," but on the business conditions of the later colonial era.

J. N. Tata did not live to see the development of the Jamshedpur project that he had initiated. He had appointed a well-known American consultancy engineering firm to design the plant, and the search for a site had begun before his death, although the final location was not chosen until 1907. The area was underdeveloped but accessible and had an assured perennial water supply from the Khorkai and Subarnarekha Rivers. Most important, there was abundant land that the company could acquire for extensions to the original plant. The local tribal population provided a ready-made and cheap labor supply, although workers were to be drawn from all of India. Iron ore was transported from the Tata-managed Gorumashisani deposits just under 40 miles away. Coal was brought from the Jharia field 115 miles distant. These locational advantages, when allied to a cheap labor force, meant that Jamshedpur was one of the lowest-cost steel producers in the world. An American expert, when he visited the works in 1912, reckoned that the production cost of a ton of pig iron was only seventy-five cents, compared with eight dollars in Pittsburgh.[2]

Jamsetji Tata was the most famous Indian industrialist and Parsi of his generation. Following his death on a business trip to Germany in 1904, Curzon declared that "no Indian of the present generation had done more for the commerce and industry of India."[3] In addition to his laying the pioneering foundations for the Indian iron and steel industry and for the development of company steel towns, Jamsetji had been active in cotton manufacturing in Nagpur and Bombay in the 1870s. In Bombay he had built and opened in December 1903 the luxury Taj Hotel on the Colaba waterfront, which was to become as famous for travelers in the imperial age as Raffles Hotel in Singapore. He also had plans for a science institute and for hydroelectric power generation. A draft plan for the latter was submitted to Curzon in 1898, just five years after Tata had broached the idea during a chance meeting with Swami Vivekananda, the founder of the Ramakrishna Mission, during a sea voyage. The Tata Company was to fulfill these goals with the later establishment of the leading Indian Institute of Science at Bangalore in 1909 and the creation of the Tata Hydroelectric Power Supply Company (now Tata Power Company Ltd.).[4] The first batch of students was admitted to the Indian Institute of Science in July 1911. Bangalore's leading technological role in contemporary India has its historical roots in J. N. Tata's vision.

In some respects, Jamsetji was typical of Parsi businessmen who invested fortunes made in trade in Indian industrial development. Parsis dominated Bombay's early textile industry, founding nine of the thirteen cotton mills that were established between 1854 and 1870.[5] The Petits were among the foremost Parsi textile mill owners. The future founder of Pakistan, Muhammad Ali Jinnah, married Rattanbai, the only daughter of Sir Dinshaw Petit, in April 1918. The wealth of the fifty thousand or so Parsis living in Bombay and their pioneering roles in industry, the development of the stock exchange, or even Indian cricket had almost become a cliché.[6] A 1900 tourist guide to Bombay, for example, described the city as the "Paris of the East" and Parsis as a "Persian sect of fireworshippers: a very rich, commercial and influential part of Indian cosmopolitan population."[7]

Most Parsi businessmen were apolitical and have been understood as "comprador capitalists."[8] A few Parsis engaged in "moderate" nationalist politics, most notably Dadabhai Naoroji (three times Congress president and a British MP) and Pherozeshah Mehta (Congress president, 1890).[9] J. N. Tata's career clearly contained a nationalistic motivation. There is the apocryphal story that when he was a young man and was asked to leave the exclusive Watson's Club in Bombay, he swore to build a hotel to outdo it, an ambition he achieved when he opened the Taj. This aside, there is a strong nation-building element in the plans for the steel mills at Jamshedpur and the technical and research institute at Bangalore. While the latter enterprise was able to thrive in the environment of the progressive Princely state of Mysore, the development of the Tata Iron and Steel Company (TISCO), in the generation after its founder, owed much to the supportive environment of the colonial state. Its early development was boosted by British demands, during the First World War especially, for military operations in the Middle East.[10] The postwar slump threatened the company's existence, but long-term railway contracts and the government of India's tariff protection from 1924 onward saved the day. Cheap production costs enabled expansion even in the depressed 1930s, before the Second World War generated further growth.[11]

The Bombay Dockyards and the Wadia Builders

The Wadia industrial group in contemporary India is dwarfed by the Tata conglomerate. It is, however, one of the oldest Indian industrial houses. It is primarily known today for its budget airline GOAir, Bombay Dyeing, and its popular Britannia and Tiger biscuits. The current chairman of the group, Nusli Wadia, is the son of Dina Wadia, the only daughter of Muhammad Ali Jinnah. The Wadias, like many Parsis, originated from Surat, but they moved to Bombay as it eventually eclipsed the East India Company's original foothold on India's western coast. Sir Lovji Nusserwanjee Wadia established the family's fortune when he secured contracts from the Company in 1736 to build naval vessels for its Bombay Marine, which protected trade routes from European rivals and the Angria pirates. Fourteen years later he selected the site and supervised, along with his younger brother

Sorabji, the laying down of the dry dock in Bombay, which was the first of its kind in Asia. Until 1885, the Wadias ran the dockyard, which was vital to British strategic as well as commercial interests. The dockyard enabled Royal Navy vessels to be repaired and to patrol the Indian Ocean.

The Wadias not only built ships, but until 1808 acted as contractors for the supply of teak for their construction. Shipbuilding did not demand timber as voraciously as the railways, but the teak forests of the Malabar Coast were depleted before the dockyard turned to Burmese timber. The Wadias' first commissions were for the East India Company, but by the beginning of the nineteenth century they were also entrusted to build Royal Navy frigates. The Treaty of Nanking, which ceded Hong Kong, was signed on one of these ships, HMS *Cornwallis*. According to folklore, most of Nelson's ships at the Battle of Trafalgar were Parsi-built.[12] The Wadias' reputation as master carpenters in England was in fact fully established only by their successful commission in 1810 to build HMS *Minden* for the Royal Navy.[13] Its completion coincided with the expeditions to Reunion and Mauritius and the siege of Java, which projected British power into the Indian Ocean.

By the middle of the nineteenth century some family members had moved into ship owning. They traded with China, or acted as agents for the French vessels that visited Bombay.[14] They also owned large areas of Bombay, providing the historical roots of the contemporary Bombay Realty Company. Pestonjee Bomanjee Wadia was one of the promoters of the Bank of Bombay. At this time the Parsis were well established as one of the leading business communities of Bombay. Their preeminence was to be challenged, however, by the Marwaris, who were beginning to arrive in search of commercial opportunities.

The Rise of Marwari Enterprise

The Marwaris were bankers and traders from the Hindu commercial castes—Agarwal, Maheshwari, Oswal, and Khandewal—of western Rajasthan, which in the colonial era encompassed the Rajput Princely States of Jodhpur, Jaipur, and Bikaner. There were also Marwari Jains, who later became active in the Ahmedabad textile industry. Before the rise of the

East India Company, Marwaris had been mobile throughout North India, in part because of their geographical proximity to the Ganges-Jumna trade route, but also because Princely rulers sought out their commercial expertise. Unlike other kinship-based commercial castes from Sindh, Gujarat, and the Tamil region, however, they did not develop as a trading diaspora. India remained their field of commercial activity. They so successfully challenged the Parsis' long-established hold in textile manufacture that shortly after independence, they controlled more than half of the productive capacity of the Bombay cotton mills. The Marwaris' grip was even tighter in the Ahmedabad textile industry. Calcutta had become another major focus of their activities. By the 1980s, twenty-eight of India's "top industrial giants" were Marwari owned, with the Birlas accounting for no fewer than twelve of these.[15]

Colonial rule reduced court patronage but provided the Marwaris with new economic opportunities in Bombay and Calcutta for trade in grain, jute, and British piece-goods. By the early twentieth century there were around thirty thousand Marwaris living in the two cities. New arrivals were housed in community-run hostels (*bassas*). The Marwaris' "clannishness" was crucial to their economic dealings, which used indigenous financial instruments such as the *hundi* where trust (*sakh*) was paramount in the absence of colonial legal regulation.[16] The Marwaris increasingly bought up property in the Bara Bazaar (Great bazaar) in Calcutta and took over its diverse business activities. The Marwaris were never a totally monolithic community, of course, as revealed by the splits between Arya Samajists and the majority Sanatan Dharmis in the Marwari Association (established around 1898).

Marwaris frequently worked as intermediaries between domestic producers and consumers and foreign exporters and importers.[17] They acted as selling or purchasing commission agents for European firms at the port linking them with Indian businessmen in the hinterland. Marwaris increasingly replaced Bengali Banias and also eased out competition from Punjabi Khatris because of their superior networks and access to commercial intelligence. Like the Parsis, many leading Marwari businessmen made their initial fortunes in the opium trade, but as price speculators, not dealers.

The huge volume in trade ensured profits, but it was extremely risky, as it depended on news from the China market as well as on supply factors. Calcutta eclipsed Bombay as the main auction center beginning in the 1830s, and speculation there was a "matter of wild excitement." The successful playing of the futures market on the Calcutta Stock Exchange was a notable feature of Marwari commercial activity. Speculation on prices of grain and cotton, as well as "rain bargains"—wagers on when the first day of the rains would arrive—was, however, more common among Marwari migrants from Bikaner, where there was an indigenous speculative tradition, than among those from Jodhpur.[18]

First World War speculative windfall gains, especially in jute, as the Indian industry supplied 1378 million sandbags, but also in silver, provided the capital for Marwari traders to move into industry. They made inroads into the former British-dominated jute industry. This was a natural progression, as they had experience in the brokerage of jute. By the 1930s as a result of "distress" sales, Marwaris also began acquiring British-owned mines and tea plantations in eastern India. This has led some scholars to see economic decolonization preceding the later transfer of political power by the British.[19]

G. D. Birla: Industrialist and Congress Financier

The move into industrial ownership was led by the Birlas, Dalmias, Poddars, and Singhanias. Ghanshyamdas "G. D." Birla established the Birla Jute Mills in south Calcutta in 1920. In the same year, he bought a cotton mill in Delhi. At the invitation of the Maharaja of Gwalior, he also set up the Jiyajee Rao Cotton Mills in the Princely State. Before entering manufacturing, the Birlas, like other Marwari merchants, had traded cloth with Japanese firms. The Singhanias established a cotton mill in Cawnpore (Kanpur) before moving into jute and sugar mills and engineering. Ramakrishna Dalmia also entered the sugar industry in addition to investing heavily in cement manufacturing. Anandilal Poddar joined hands with Japanese partners to establish cotton textile mills in Bombay.[20] By the early 1950s, Marwaris and Gujaratis together owned half of the productive capacity of the Bombay mills.

The Birlas rose from humble roots in rural Rajasthan to become the most prominent Marwari family. G. D. Birla's grandfather Shivnarain Birla profited from speculation in opium in Bombay. The August 1896 bubonic plague epidemic prompted him and his only son, Baldeodas, to relocate their business activities to Calcutta. Like many other Maheshwaris, they were latecomers in a city that already had a considerable Agarwal and Os-wal Marwari presence. This may explain their continued involvement in speculative commercial activities alongside growing trade in silver, grain, and cloth. Baldeodas retired in 1911 and handed over the family business to Ghanshyamadas. In his retirement he devoted himself to philanthropy and religion, including the Birla tradition of temple building across India. The famous Lakshmi Narayan Temple in New Delhi (now a leading tourist attraction) was constructed by him between 1933 and 1939. Ghanshymadas Birla became the most famous Marwari businessman of his generation be-cause of his involvement in public life and his transformation of the Birla house from a trading to a major industrial player.

G. D. Birla was involved in public social and charitable activities from as early as 1913 through a social service organization known as the Marwari Sahayak Samiti. It extended activities far beyond its Bara Bazaar base to in-clude the provision of medical camps at the Kumbh Mela. Ghanshymadas Birla's religious devotion and personal experiences of racial insults at the hands of British businessmen led him briefly into involvement with extrem-ist and revolutionary politics in Calcutta, and he had to "abscond" after be-ing implicated in the Rodda Conspiracy Case of August 1914.[21] He fell under Gandhi's "spell" in 1916, having been brought to the Mahatma's notice by a fellow Marwari businessman, Jamnalal Bajaj. Thereafter Birla maintained a close personal association with Gandhi, which was "of a quasi-filial and religious character."[22] Standard accounts of Gandhi's transformation of the Congress into a mass movement from 1918 onward often overlook the fact that its organizational costs were funded by rich industrialists and traders headed by G. D. Birla, who stood to gain from the boycott of British goods. Birla as a mill owner wanted indigenous factory–produced cloth rather than homespun khadi to replace British imports.[23]

Birla funded not only Congress but the *Hindustan Times* newspaper, which began in the mid-1920s to promote the nationalist cause. Association with Gandhi brought Birla valuable political connections with such lead-ing congressmen as C. Rajagopalachari, Rajendra Prasad, and Vallabhbhai

Patel. Birla became a key fund-raiser for the Congress among the commercial castes and was a frequent visitor to Patel in this capacity. Between 1921 and 1923 the Congress collected more than thirteen million rupees. The money helped the Congress pay full-time organizers as it developed a base that reached down to the villages. By the eve of the Second World War, the Congress boasted a membership of more than 4.5 million. No other anticolonial nationalist movement was ever to attain this level of support. When Gandhi expressed qualms about the vigorous fund-raising, Patel characteristically informed Birla, "This is not his concern. Gandhi is a Mahatma. I am not. I have to do the job."[24] Birla's greatest political influence was in the immediate postindependence period, when Patel was deputy prime minister.

Birla opened his homes in New Delhi, Calcutta, Bombay, Ranchi, and Simla to Congress politicians. Birla House in Delhi was the scene of numerous Congress parleys, leading an important British official to remark, "The real capital of India is not just New Delhi but Birla House, where Mahatma Gandhi and other Congress leaders stay and where the Congress Working Committee meets and major political decisions are taken."[25] Gandhi was to spend the last four months of his life as a guest there, opening the exclusive residence at 5 Albuquerque Road to streams of well-wishers and those seeking his assistance in the aftermath of the Partition. On Friday, 30 January, just after 5 P.M. as Gandhi walked down the garden path at Birla House to his evening prayer, he was assassinated by the Hindu right-wing activist Nathuram Godse. Birla himself was not at home but in his native Pilani to visit the educational institutions he was establishing there. The Martyr's Column today marks the spot where Gandhi fell, and the house has been a museum dedicated to Gandhi since 1973.[26]

It is increasingly recognized that Birla and J. D. Tata exercised an important influence on the "political economy" of India's Partition. Their commitment to a state-led "dash for growth," which was institutionalized in the Bombay Plan (January 1944), required a strong central government that would manage a phased industrialization. We shall see later that Congress was ultimately to accept Partition in preference to an "enfeebled" center distracted by disputes with the Muslim League. Birla's legacy was also important in two other areas that have not always been acknowledged. First, along

13. Gandhi's body being brought out of Birla House, New Delhi

with other representatives of big business, he strengthened the conservative elements in Congress, as represented by such figures as Vallabhbhai Patel, Rajendra Prasad, and Rajagopalachari. This made Nehru water down the radical leftist stance that had been evident in the mid-1930s, leaving him isolated in the party and dependent on Gandhi's patronage. This helps explain Nehru's postindependence difficulties in "modernizing" Indian society and polity. Second, big business's support for state-led capitalist development, together with the unanticipated trauma of Partition, completed the process of narrowing down Indian nationalism from its earlier transnational "imagining" to a territorialized conception that was strongly influenced by a legal-juridical approach to citizenship.

Associations, Anjumans, and Print Culture

The Marwari Association in Calcutta, like other community associations in India at the high noon of empire, blended elements of "tradition" and "modernity." It was community-based in its membership, but at the same time possessed elements of a modern voluntary organization. It had, for example, an executive committee, dominated by rich traders, and it held regular meetings, whose agendas and reports were products of print culture. These features were present even in such organizations as the Sanatanist Dharma, which was dedicated to an avowedly Hindu traditional religious agenda.

Jatis, religious reformist and revivalist organizations, developed a rich associational life. They all responded to the challenges brought by colonial rule, but in complex and often highly creative ways. The phrase "strategic syncretism" has been coined for the Arya Samaj movement's adoption of Christian missionary critiques of traditional Hindu outlooks in its reform program. The Arya Samaj, founded in 1875, within a generation became a significant force among the upwardly mobile commercial castes of the Punjab. In part, this was because it enabled religious commitment to go hand in hand with a Western "rationalist" mindset, necessary for professional life. The criticisms of Christian missionaries regarding treatment of widows and Brahminical caste distinctions were addressed in the name of tradition by restoring a purified practice based on the Vedas. Arya Samaj founder Swami Dayananda maintained in his work *Satyarth Prakash*, published in 1875, that Western scientific knowledge was predated by Hinduism's oldest scriptures. By the time Dayananda left the Punjab in 1878, there were eleven Arya Samaj branches in the Punjab. Thereafter the numbers mushroomed. A Dayananda Anglo-Vedic school (later a college affiliated with Punjab University) was established in Lahore in June 1886 in memory of the movement's founder. It taught "modern" subjects, thus equipping its graduates for sought-after employment in the government services, but at the same time remained independent of British control and influence.

The Punjab Arya Samaj split in 1893 between the so-called College and Vegetarian factions. The divisions were ideological as well as factional. The differences had to do, first, with the significance attached to Sanskrit in the DAV College established in Dayananda's memory; second, with the emphasis to be placed on the reconversion (*shuddhi*) of "low-caste" Muslims and Sikhs to Hinduism; and, third, with the strictness with which vegetarianism should be observed. On the last point the "militant" Vegetarian faction, led by Guru Dutt and Munshi Ram (later known as Swami Shraddhananda), believed that any compromise was a betrayal of Dayananda's inheritance. The "moderate" College faction (so-called because it controlled the Management Committee of DAV College), led by Lal Chand and Hans Raj, maintained that a nonmeat diet repeated the errors of Jains, who had deprived non-Muslim India of its manhood by their attachment to *ahimsa*. Numerous Indians equated eating meat with physical strength. The attitude was summed up in the ditty "Behold the mighty Englishman! He rules the Indian small; because being a meat eater, he is five cubits tall."[27] B. S. Moonje, the leader of the Hindu Sabha in the Central Provinces in 1923, placed himself in stark opposition to Gandhi's teaching by attributing Muslims' "virility" and "readiness to kill and be killed" to their meat diet. He attempted to popularize Vedic animal sacrifice so that Hindus would be accustomed to the sight "of spilling blood and killing."

The search for physical prowess through gymnastic exercises was a prominent feature of educated Hindu middle-class youth. This was especially the case in Bengal, where the colonial state had constructed a racial stereotype of Hindu effeminacy. Subhas Chandra Bose was to challenge this in the later colonial period, in opposition to Gandhi's attachment to the "strength" of nonviolence. G. D. Birla's earliest public activities in Calcutta involved the creation of the Marwari Sporting Club to "encourage a culture of fitness." In 1916, he began a long interest in wrestling, following the formation of the Bara Bazaar Yuwak Sangh. He not only funded the organization and its wrestlers in Calcutta, but along with his brother supported similar institutions elsewhere in India.

The Arya Samaj's contribution to the rise of communalism in the Punjab, which had gained the epithet the Ulster of India because of its religious tensions and riots, has been extensively researched.[28] Scholars have pointed out the acrimonious debates generated by its tracts and pamphlets, including the English weekly *The Regenerator of the Aryavatra*, and how the adaptation of the technique of ritual purification, *shuddhi*, into a weapon of conversion caused conflict not only with Muslims and Sikhs but with the Sanatanist guardians of Hindu orthodoxy. Despite the supremacist stance of the Arya Samaj, however, the local context of factional rivalries prompted possibilities of cooperation with Muslim organizations. The creation of a "new" Arya woman was a key project of "strategic syncretism" for both College and Vegetarian factions. Female education was promoted on grounds not of equality of opportunity but of community identity and pride, just as the Arya women's illiterate degraded sisters represented for the organization the "degeneracy" of contemporary Hinduism. The Vegetarian faction led the way with the establishment of the K. M. V. Girls' High School with the first female hostel at Jullundur in 1891.[29] The College faction, under Pandit Mehr Chand's leadership, attempted to establish a rival institution but found its efforts stymied by its own militant faction, which was especially influential in the Jullundur district. Land for a boys' and girls' school and financial support were eventually provided by the local Muslim Khoja elite. Well-off Muslims continued to send their sons to the D. A. V. College in Jullundur, even after the opening of a local Islamia College. This situation reveals the complexities surrounding "communal" relations, which are not always appreciated in conventional understandings.[30]

In Bengal, the Rama Krishna Mission began in 1897 to propagate the colonial high noon Indian messages of "self-strengthening and social service."[31] Its founder, Swami Vivekananda, was attracted to the informal group of disciples who had gathered around the charismatic teacher and mystic Ramakrishna, who lived at the Kali Temple at Dakshineshwar.[32] Ramakrishna blended traditional *bhakti* devotionalism to Kali with the importance of the realization of "God-consciousness" in each individual in keeping with the Monist philosophy of Advaita Vedanta. When Vivekananda succeeded Ramakrishna, he systematized these elements into a structured doctrine and institutionalized them in the Ramakrishna Mission.[33] Vivekananda moved beyond the confines of Bengal to popularize his message with Western audiences. He cut a dashing and exotic appearance, with his flowing orange robe and saffron turban, at the September 1893 World Parliament of Religions held in Chicago. Vivekananda did much to popularize the binary opposites of a "spiritual India" and the "materialist West," a dichotomy that still exerted a powerful influence on Western hippies in the mid-twentieth century. Vivekananda used funds raised in the West to establish two monasteries, the second at Mayavati in the Himalayas. He overturned Ramakrishna's quietist spiritual practice by plunging the Ramakrishna Mission into relief work during Calcutta's 1899 plague epidemic.

Pakistani nationalist historiography has emphasized the role of the Aligarh movement in the forging of a modern Muslim collective consciousness. Its support for Western education radiated outward from the college established by Sir Syed Ahmad Khan in 1875. After the trauma of the 1857 revolt, he worked to both improve Anglo-Muslim understanding and to enable Muslims to meet the new intellectual and social changes of colonial rule. Successive generations of Aligarh students assumed leadership roles in the Indian Muslim community. Sir Sayed is even more honored in Pakistan for giving birth to the two-nation theory that underpinned the Pakistan demand than for his educational activities. Beginning in the late 1880s he spelled out the incompatibility of the interests of the North Indian Muslim elite and the Bengali "babus who dominated the new nationalist organization.

Alongside the Aligarh movement, numerous Muslim *anjumans* (associations) had their own agendas and independent institutional lives. Within the Punjab, the Anjuman-i-Matalib-i-Mufidah-i-Punjab (Society for the propagation of useful knowledge), later known as the Anjuman-i-Punjab, was founded in 1865. It sought to promote "modern" knowledge and successfully agitated for the establishment of a Punjab University College. The Anjuman-i-Himayat-i-Islam, founded in September 1884, played an even greater role in educational development. Its efforts culminated in the foundation of the "Aligarh of the Punjab," Islamia College, in Lahore. Like many reformist bodies of this period it published its own magazine, tracts, and textbooks.

The Ahmadiyah movement was the most divisive of the Punjabi Muslim organizations. Its members (Ahmadis) are no longer regarded as Muslims in Pakistan. The movement initially led Muslim resistance to the activities of the Arya Samaj. It became increasingly criticized by Muslims, however, as its founder Ghulam Mirza Ahmad claimed revelations concerning the birth of his son and the death of Dayananda that challenged the central Islamic doctrine regarding Muhammad as the "seal" (last) of the Prophets.

The Emergence of the Indian National Congress

The Congress's roots lay in the associations in the presidencies of Madras, Bombay, and Bengal, which predated 1857. These associations represented the interests of the Western-educated elites, landed and business communities. Many of their members were also active in the Brahmo Samaj and Arya Samaj. Not until 1876, when the Indian Association was founded in Calcutta, were there attempts to move beyond the regional to an all-India organization. The catalyst for the emergence of the Indian Association was Lord Lytton's reduction of the age limit for civil service entrance examinations from twenty-one to nineteen, making it difficult for Indians to enter unless they had spent all their education in England.

The final push for all-India organization came with the resistance from English residents in eastern India to the attempt by the liberal Ripon viceroyalty (1880–84) to enable Indian judges to preside over cases involving Europeans. The so-called Ilbert Bill controversy (named after the member of the government of India, Sir Courtney Ilbert, who moved the legislation) revealed to educated Indians both the underlying racial prejudice of the British and the impact of organized protests. Ripon watered down the measure in the face of European opposition. At the same time, the government of India saw the need for the representation of Indian national views as both a "safety valve" and a counterweight to European interests. The incoming Viceroy Lord Dufferin favored the efforts of a retired official, Allan Octavian Hume, to found a "responsible" Indian organization. Hume acted as the president of the Congress's inaugural session, which was held in Bombay in December 1885.

The seventy-two founding members represented the Western-educated classes, primarily of Bombay, Madras, and Calcutta. Many were lawyers, although there were also teachers and journalists. Muslims were underrepresented in these professions and regions, and as a result only two were in attendance. This set a pattern of Muslim underrepresentation, which contributed to the creation of a separate Muslim political organization. The inaugural Congress session lasted for three days and concluded with Hume leading "Three cheers for her majesty the Queen Empress." The first generation of congressmen were "moderate" in their aims and outlook. They did not want to break India's connection with Britain, but rather sought a larger role for Indians in governance. This outlook was eventually questioned by such "extremists" as Aurobindo Ghosh, from Bengal, Lalal Lajpat Rai, a leading Arya Samajist from Punjab, and the Maharashtrian G. B. Tilak.

The Formation of the All-India Muslim League

The rise of Muslim separatism was rooted both in the North Indian Muslims' responses to the loss of political power and in Hindu resurgence. We have already seen that the standard-bearer was the Aligarh movement of Sir Syed Ahmad Khan. The old-boy Aligarh network facilitated greater transregional Muslim cooperation than had been provided by the earlier *anjumans*, most of which were localized in membership and influence. Indeed, it was at the 1906 Dacca meeting of Syed Ahmad Khan's Muhammadan Educational Conference that the All-India Muslim League was founded.

There were two principal precipitating factors: first, the prospect of further British constitutional reform and its likely impact on Muslim interests, and second, the effects of the rise of the "extremist" wing of the Congress and especially the impact of the *swadeshi* movement on Muslim opinion. The prospect of further constitutional reform in the post-Curzon era was unwelcome for Muslim elites in the United Provinces (UP), where they numbered around 15 percent of the total population. The region had already been the site of political mobilization of Hindus in the Hindi-Urdu language controversy and the 1893 anti–cow killing riots. The system of elective government which was introduced with the Indian Councils Act (1861) had brought the devolved powers used by Hindu leaders to control butchers' shops and slaughterhouses and to alter procession routes at festival times in such towns as Agra, Moradabad, and Chandpur. Muslim leaders were concerned not just about the local exercise of power by Hindu representatives but about its future reproduction at provincial levels. Muslims had been consistently underrepresented in municipal committees because they failed to meet property and educational voting qualifications.

Exploitation of Hindu religious and historical symbols, such as Tilak's politically motivated popularization of the Ganesh and Shivaji festivals, had accompanied the rise of the "extremists" in Congress. As we have seen during the swadeshi movement, activists evoked Kali and adopted "Bande Mataram" as their rallying cry. It was against this background that the famous Simla deputation led by the Agha Khan met the Viceroy Lord Minto on 1 October 1906. The delegation pressed for the recognition of a distinct

Muslim political interest. The deputation comprised mainly Muslims from Hindu-majority provinces, where fears about future Hindu domination were most apparent. This established a pattern for the future development of the All-India Muslim League. Its initial membership was limited to four hundred, seventy of whom came from the UP quota. There were few members from the main centers of Muslim population.

Pakistani authors portray an inevitable progression from the Muslim League's formation to the birth of their state in 1947. We shall see in the next two chapters, however, that political separatism based on religion was an ideology that resonated only in particular contexts. Moreover, the territorial nationalism of the Congress and the separatism of the Muslim League were not the only expressions of political struggle against the Raj in the closing decades of colonial rule.

PART III

SEVEN

The Nation and Beyond

Transnational Anticolonial Struggle

During the early years of the twentieth century, the Raj's opponents extended the freedom struggle far beyond its borders, with "India Houses" serving as meeting places for revolutionary students in London, Paris, and New York. By 1914 such activities had spread to the Pacific Coast of North America and as far afield as Tokyo.[1] The First World War and the Russian Revolution further stimulated transnational revolutionary networks. Constantinople, Berlin, Kabul, neutral Stockholm, and revolutionary Moscow emerged as new centers. The German wartime conspiracies to ship arms to India gave prominence to Batavia, Bangkok, Shanghai, and briefly Hilo in Hawai'i. The First World War was also marked by the famous Silk Letter conspiracy, involving pan-Islamic revolutionaries and the establishment of a provisional government in Kabul in 1915 by Raja Mahendra Pratap Singh, following the Indo-German-Turkish mission to Afghanistan.[2]

The Pacific Coast of North America was another wartime revolutionary hub as a result of the Ghadr movement, in which mainly Punjabi Sikhs returned to India from North America in the hope of raising a revolution in their homeland. The failed attempt led the Bengali revolutionary Rash Bihari Bose to flee to Japan, where in the 1920s he orchestrated the creation of Indian Independence Leagues among the diaspora populations of Southeast Asia. His leadership role continued until the Second World War, when Subhas Chandra Bose arrived in Malaya following an epic submarine journey from Kiel in May 1943. Subhas Chandra Bose revived the Indian National Army, which, together with the Indian Independence Leagues, formed the basis for the establishment of a provisional government of Azad Hind (Free India) in Singapore on 21 October 1943. It sought Japanese military support to free the homeland.

The independence of India and Pakistan came about, however, not by revolution or armed invasion but as a result of a transfer of power from postwar Britain. The triumph of territorial nationalism overshadowed the long history of transnational revolt. Nationalist historiography focused on events in Lahore, Delhi, and Bombay rather than Kabul, San Francisco, or Tokyo. But there was, in fact, a strong transnational element to Indian nationalism, in terms both of the participation of overseas Indians and of the Congress's "conviction" late in the colonial era that "the problems faced by the Indian nation were not restricted to the territory of mainland India."[3] Leading nationalists such as Gandhi and Gokhale concerned themselves with the conditions of indentured laborers in distant Mauritius. Gandhi visited the island on his way to India from South Africa in October 1901. Six years later he persuaded a fellow Gujarati lawyer, Manilal Manganlal Doctor, to take up residence in Port Louis and campaign for Indian rights. Manilal later moved on to Fiji to organize Indian opinion there through the Indian Imperial Association.[4] Only on the eve of independence was the nationalist movement's perspective "narrowed down" to concern with construction of a strong sovereign territorialized nation-state. This preoccupation contributed to Congress's difficulties in acknowledging the intensely transnational struggle for freedom of Subhas Chandra Bose. It also set the scene for a decoupling of the Indian state from the diaspora. Not until early in the twenty-first century did the relationship begin to be reestablished. In 2002, 9 January—the date of Gandhi's permanent return from South Africa in 1915—was chosen for annually celebrating the contribution of overseas Indians, *Pravasi Bharatiya Divas*, to the nation.

The narrowing down of Indian nationalism was mirrored with respect to the mobilization of Indian Muslims. The universalistic pan-Islamic approach of the early twentieth century received its last manifestation in the Khilafat movement (1920–22). Thereafter, mainstream Muslim separatism focused on concerns for minority rights within India. Ultimately, it was believed that these could be safeguarded only within a territorially defined state. But the failure to clarify Pakistan's physical or ideological boundaries in the colonial era had damaging long-term consequences.

India House

Unless one looks closely at its blue plaque, 65 Cromwell Avenue, Highgate, would pass as any other North London Victorian villa. From 1905 to 1910, however, it was India House, the base of revolutionary activity. Activists at the house published its own "seditious" newspaper, *The Indian Sociologist*, and in the later stages it was home to not only incendiary lectures on colonial exploitation but experiments in bomb making and rifle practice. India House had been established as a hostel for nationalist students whose scholarships were paid for by its patron, Shyami Krishna Varma, the Balliol-educated lawyer, disciple of Swami Dayananda Saraswati, and admirer of Herbert Spencer. The writings of Spencer provided the masthead motto of *The Indian Sociologist*: "Resistance to aggression is not simply justifiable but imperative."

In addition to the twenty-four permanent residents, numerous members of London's growing Indian student population passed through its doors, with Gandhi, Lala Lajpat Rai, Har Dayal, and Virendranath Chattopadhyaya all finding their way to Highgate. The last was the younger brother of Sarojini Naidu, "the nightingale of India." Chattopadhyaya went on to have a long revolutionary career in Europe and was a leading figure in the German mission to Afghanistan in 1915. A Punjabi student who had resided at India House, Madan Lal Dhingra assassinated Sir Curzon Wyllie, political aide-de-camp to the secretary of state for India, after a meeting of the National Indian Association on the evening of 1 July 1909. Dhingra confronted Wylie on the landing outside the main Jehangir Hall of the Institute of Imperial Studies and shot him four times at point-blank range. After a single day's trial at the Old Bailey, in which Dhingra offered no defense, he went to the gallows at Pentonville Prison on 17 August. Gandhi, who was in London at the time, joined the chorus of Indian disapproval at Dhingra's action. India House was closed. The revolutionary baton passed to Paris, New York, and Tokyo, where India Houses were established.

The Ghadr Movement

Five Wood Street is a refurbished three-story building in the Laurel Heights neighborhood of San Francisco, not far from the University of San Francisco Lone Mountain campus. Its historical significance becomes apparent only when one climbs a flight of steps to the entrance, above which is written in Hindi and English, "Ghadr Memorial." The Ghadr Party, which was dedicated to the violent overthrow of British rule in India, in fact started its operations from 436 Hill Street in 1913 before moving to the Wood Street address. The building was handed over to the Indian consulate in San Francisco in 1952 and completely renovated into its current utilitarian style in the mid-1970s. It has in recent years become, along with sites in Sacramento and Stockton, the focus of Indo-US organizations as the new generation of South Asians connect with their forebears' heritage.

The Ghadr movement's centenary has revived interest in its history of international revolutionary struggle.[5] It is still seen largely as a movement of Sikh Jats from the rural Punjab who had migrated to North America, where their experience of racism impelled them into an abortive attempt during the First World War to overthrow the Raj. In the first decade of the twentieth century as many as fifteen thousand Indians had migrated to the Pacific Coast, where they worked as fruit farmers, in the lumber industry, and as laborers. Sikhs from the Punjab predominated. Increasing legal restrictions and the 1907–8 anti-Asian riots in British Columbia and Oregon radicalized the migrants. Eventually the Ghadr movement crystallized in San Francisco under the inspirational leadership of the mercurial Har Dayal.[6] The youngest of four brothers, Har Dayal had grown up in Delhi, where his father was employed at the district court. After graduating from St. Stephen's College, he migrated to Lahore in 1903 to attend the Punjab University. While in Lahore he displayed the freethinking and intellectual brilliance that became his hallmark. It was no surprise that he won the state scholarship in 1905, which enabled him to travel to England to study at Balliol College. It was during his weekend trips from Oxford to London that he began attending the meetings of the revolutionary nationalists based at India House in Highgate. He refused to accept the "tainted money" of the state scholarship following the news of the 1907 disturbances in the Punjab, and he returned to Lahore the following year. He stayed in the city's Sutar Mandi locality, where for a time he lived austerely, dressing like a sadhu. His charismatic appearance and intellectual brilliance attracted students to visit him as he preached the need for a "national education" based on Hindu values.

Har Dayal left Lahore under the threat of arrest to once more embark on a transnational journey that was to lead him via radical revolutionary circles in Paris, where in 1909 he edited the *Bande Mataram*, to Algiers, Martinique, and Honolulu, where he lived as a Hindu renunciate. The efforts by Bhai Parmanand to bring him back into political activity form part of Indian nationalist folklore. Parmanand's overseas activities were initially linked with lecture tours for the Arya Samaj. In 1905 he visited South Africa, where he stayed for a time with Gandhi. Five years later he visited Guyana, which was the center of the Arya Samaj's outreach to the Indian population in the Caribbean. He famously persuaded Har Dayal to abandon his Waikiki Beach retreat in Honolulu and take up activism in San Francisco. Parmanand joined him and became a founding member of the Ghadr Party. He returned to India in 1915 as part of the Ghadr uprising with the intention of raising revolt in Peshawar. Parmanand was initially sentenced to death after his conviction in the first Lahore Conspiracy Case. His execution was commuted, and he served a sentence in the notorious Circular Jail at Port Blair in the Andaman Islands until his pardon in 1920.[7]

In California, Har Dayal's success lay in linking Indian students' revolutionary enthusiasm with the racial grievances of the immigrant Sikh farmworkers and laborers of the Pacific Coast. He also built on the tradition of the overseas Sikh communities' establishment of direct links with Punjab through the circulation of newspapers and magazines, converting the conservative media ties established by the Singh Sabha and the Chief Khalsa Diwan to revolutionary purposes. The outcome was the celebrated publication in 1913 of the *Ghadr* newspaper. It transmitted back to Punjab from its San Francisco press an urgent battle cry:

> Time for prayer is gone,
> take the sword in the hand,

time is now to plunge in a battle,
mere talk serves no purpose,
those who long for martyrdom.
will live for ever as shining guideposts.[8]

Action matched rhetoric. More than three thousand Indians answered Har
Dayal's call in meetings at Fresno and Sacramento early in August 1914 to
return to the Punjab and raise the standard of revolt. While the province's
militarization increased the state's surveillance, it also held out the hope
that a sepoy revolt could pave the way for freedom. Propaganda was constantly directed at the sepoys. This took the form of such revolutionary publications as *Bande Mataram* and *Madan's Talwar*, which were published in
Paris from 1909 and smuggled into India through Pondicherry. The *Ghadr*
newspaper joined in with the following advertisement:

> Wanted: Enthusiastic and heroic soldiers for organizing Ghadr
> in Hindustan
> Remuneration: Death
> Reward: Martyrdom
> Pension: Freedom
> Field of Work: Hindustan

Turkey's entry into the First World War on the side of the Central Powers
intensified efforts to sway Muslim soldiers against their colonial masters.
The Ghadrites attempted unsuccessfully in 1915 to suborn Punjabi troops,
in Burma, Malaya, Bombay, and Meerut. Four Rajput companies of the
Indian 5th Light Infantry in Singapore did mutiny on 15 February. The British were caught unawares and needed to call on French and Russian naval
assistance before reinforcements could arrive from Rangoon. Only after a
fierce battle were the mutineers defeated. Forty-seven sepoys went to the gallows after a subsequent court-martial. This event both provided a warning to
the British and sustained hope among their revolutionary opponents.

The general rising of the population and army mutiny anticipated by the
Ghadrites, however, failed to materialize. Eighteen of the returnees from
the Pacific States were hanged and another fifty-eight were transported for

life. Kartar Singh Sarabha was the youngest and most famous martyr. He had first migrated to the United States in January 1912 at the age of sixteen. He eventually enrolled at the University of California, Berkeley, to study chemistry. He was one of a number of West Coast students and lecturers who became leaders of the Ghadr movement. In addition to Har Dayal, these included Tarak Nath Das and Vishnu Ganesh Pingle, who was also hanged in Lahore. Sarabha's execution on 16 November 1915 inspired the even more famous Punjabi revolutionary martyr Bhagat Singh.[9]

The Ghadr headquarters in California was raided and its occupants were arrested and tried for conspiracy in San Francisco. Har Dayal escaped arrest and went to Germany, where he worked for a time with revolutionaries on what became known as the Berlin Committee. He left for neutral Sweden when he became disillusioned with factional fighting in the committee and its cynical manipulation by the German authorities. After many years of poverty-stricken exile in Sweden, he was granted permission to return to London in 1927 under the surveillance of the India Office. Har Dayal now devoted himself to the world of study, receiving a doctorate from the School of Oriental and African Studies and accumulating a five thousand–book library in his Edgware study.[10] Despite his hopes of a return to India, Har Dayal lived his final years of exile in the United States, where he died in Philadelphia early in March 1939. By this time, the Ghadr Party had ceased to provide an overseas revolutionary threat, although it still possessed significant support in the diaspora.

Pan-Islam

The First World War also intensified pan-Islamic revolutionary activity. Western encroachment on the declining power of the Ottomans began to increase with the outbreak of the Russo-Turkish War of 1877–88. The Ottoman emperor was regarded as the spiritual head (*khalifa*) of the Islamic world, and Muslims regarded it as vital that he should continue to act as custodian over the Muslim holy places in Mecca and Medina. Fears about threats to his temporal power created an ideological environment that encouraged Indian Muslims to resist European imperialism in the name of

Islamic universalism.[11] Pan-Islamic sentiment intensified in India during the first decade of the twentieth century as a result of the journalistic activities of Mohamed Ali, Maulana Zafar Khan, and Maulana Abul Kalam Azad, "the foremost Indian Muslim intellectual to blend the politics of Islamic universalism with a comprehensive anti-colonial vision."[12]

The fiery editorials of the *Zamindar* newspaper, published in Lahore, had sounded the alarm.[13] Another local paper, *Paisa Akhbar*, echoed the theme. This paper, which had a larger circulation than *Zamindar*, had first rolled off the press in 1887 and was to have a whole Lahore residential locality named after it.[14] Both papers published accounts of the Balkan Wars and raised funds for the Red Crescent Society, which had been established to provide medical aid for the Turkish forces. *Paisa Akhbar*'s proprietor, Maulvi Mahbub Alam, in 1913–14 visited both Cairo and Constantinople, where, according to intelligence reports, he expressed anti-British sentiments.[15] The outbreak of the world war encouraged further disaffection among Indian Muslims, as Turkey was pitted against the British forces, with their considerable numbers of Punjabi Muslim soldiers.[16] The head of the Deoband School of Ulema, Mahmudul Hasan, requested Maulana Obaidallah Sindhi to go to Afghanistan in 1915 to secure support from Emir Habibullah Khan. Obaidallah had been active in pan-Islamic causes since the Balkan Wars.[17] Although Afghanistan was neutral, it had become a center of German and Turkish intrigues. Mahmudul Hasan went to the Hejaz on the pretext of pilgrimage to secure support for jihad against the British. He secured a proclamation of jihad from Ghalib Pasha, the Turkish commander in chief (the so-called Ghalibnama). Obaidullah sent secret details to Mahmudul Hasan for the formation of an Army of God (Hezbollah) in letters woven into yellow silk handkerchiefs. When these were intercepted in August 1916, the Silk Letters conspiracy, as the colonial state termed it, was thwarted. Mahmudul Hasan was arrested in Mecca and imprisoned in Malta for three years. Obaidullah had encouraged a number of Lahore students to "abscond" to the tribal areas, where they spent a time in the long-established colonies of so-called Hindustani fanatics. In Kabul, a number took minor roles in Mahendra's provisional government. After a long intellectual and physical odyssey, some eventually found their way to the

University of the Toilers of the East, set up in Tashkent by Russia's new Bolshevik rulers.

The Khilafat movement continued pan-Islamic sentiment in the wake of Ottoman Turkey's defeat. Gandhi's declaration that he supported the "just cause" of the Khilafat movement was followed by well-publicized displays of Hindu-Muslim unity.[18] The Khilafat campaign ran alongside Gandhi's noncooperation movement, although apart from anti-British sentiment, many of its participants adhered to a totally different worldview from the Gandhians'. There are some parallels here with the contemporaneous Akali Dal–sponsored Gurdwara reform movement, which also had links with the mainstream nationalist struggle, but a distinctive communitarian base.[19] Liberals such as Jinnah, who had been the architect of the Lucknow Pact, in which Congress recognized separate electorates in return for Muslim League support, were alienated by the prominence the ulama acquired during the Khilafat campaign. There were also growing tensions between Khilafatists and Gandhians over nonviolence as a strategy. The Hindu-Muslim alliance was further tested by the outbreak of violence in Malabar, where poor Muslim peasants in the fevered Khilafat environment violently attacked both symbols of British rule and "hated" Hindu moneylenders.[20] There were communal riots elsewhere in India in 1922. The Khilafat campaign received its coup de grâce in March 1924, when the Turkish National Assembly abolished the office of caliph.

The post-Khilafat estrangement between the Congress and Muslim League was never as complete as some Pakistani historians aver. However, Muslim influence in the Congress organization waned, reducing its appeal, despite the continued rhetoric of a "composite culture." Not all Muslims were as alienated as the strapping former Khilafatist Shaukat Ali when he declared in 1929 that "Congress ha[d] become an adjunct of the Hindu Mahasabha," but the Congress's reversion from struggle to electoral politics had encouraged a greater presence within its ranks of those who sympathized with the Mahasabha's pro-Hindu platform.[21] Simultaneously, the Muslim political elites' abandonment of a concern with Islamic Universalism for a minority rights discourse in India premised on a weak center with devolved power to provincial governments stood in the way of the Hindu capitalists' growing interest in a strong central government to lead economic development.

Gandhi and the Transformation of the Congress

Gandhi has been termed an "expatriate patriot" in recognition of the formative influence of his twenty-one years spent in South Africa as a "coolie barrister."[22] In the South African Transvaal, Gandhi first used the technique of *satyagraha* (nonviolent civil disobedience) in 1907.[23] For Gandhi, satyagraha was not merely a useful tactic in a struggle against a powerful colonial state, it was integral to the individual's self-realization. Moreover, because no individuals or groups knew truth completely, no one should use force to press his view of the truth. The goal of independence could not be achieved by the morally wrong means of violence.

It was also in South Africa that Gandhi first experimented with community living, first at the Phoenix Settlement (near Durban 1904) and then at Tolstoy Farm (Transvaal 1910), as a microcosm for his vision of future social development. These ideas were disseminated in numerous publications, beginning with the weekly *Indian Opinion*, thereby establishing what was to become a hallmark of Gandhi's career. The South Africa experience enabled Gandhi to transcend the regional and factional affiliations that had accompanied the Congress's development. While he emphasized the Gujarati Hindu tradition of *ahimsa*, he was always seen as a national, rather than a Gujarati, figure. Gandhi also sidestepped the "moderate" or "extremist" camps, although he used the latter's weapons of British boycott and encouragement of swadeshi goods and enterprises.

Gandhi's most important work on the national struggle and independence was also written outside of his Indian homeland. The seminal study *Hind Swaraj*, first published in English in 1910, had been written the previous November during the course of a sea voyage from London to South Africa. In the book, whose Gujarati version was banned, Gandhi not only expounded the notion of satyagraha but argued against a modernizing pattern of economic development for an independent India. The "mundane sphere" of spinning and wearing of homespun cloth (khadi) was later to become an important element in the nationalist struggle.[24] Women were to play leading roles in spinning clubs, and in the 1928 Bardoli campaign they were involved in much larger public demonstrations and lawbreaking.[25] Women volunteers also took part in large numbers two years later in Gandhi's celebrated 240-mile Salt March, undertaken at the age of sixty-one. The international press and film coverage of the dramatic march severely undermined the government of India's moral authority. In this respect the march was matched only by the Amritsar Massacre.

Even as Gandhi was shaped by his transnational experiences, he influenced the Congress's attitude toward overseas Indians during the postwar period. In order to reinforce what were seen as inadequate attempts by the British-controlled government of India to safeguard Indian diasporas against institutionalized racial and economic discrimination within the Empire, the Congress sent overseas missions to such places as South Africa, Ceylon, Fiji, Malaya, and Zanzibar. Nehru visited Colombo in both 1939 and 1946. Sarojini Naidu journeyed to Kenya in 1923. The Congress not only regularly debated the conditions of Indians in such dominions as Canada and South Africa but linked the situations they faced with the fact that the colonial state was unrepresentative of the people of India. Its inability to safeguard overseas Indians was unfavorably contrasted with the role of Nationalist China on behalf of its diaspora. The logic was that subjugation overseas could be ended only by freedom at home.[26] The colonial state responded to such attacks on its moral authority by establishing a Department of Overseas Indians in 1936. The office was impotent, however, as the Union of South Africa continued to whittle away the rights of Indians that Gandhi had fought so hard to protect. As a result, "Colonial subjugation . . . came to be regarded as the main reason not only for government inaction but also the manner in which the members of the diaspora were looked upon in their new places of settlement."[27]

Subhas Chandra Bose and Azad Hind

Subhas Chandra Bose remains a controversial and complex figure in Indian nationalism. Although he is revered by his followers as Netaji (the leader), and as the architect of freedom, opponents viewed him as a traitor who flirted with fascism and sought freedom not through nonviolent struggle but through foreign invasion. Following a dramatic escape from house arrest in Calcutta in January 1941 and a journey to Berlin via Afghanistan and the Soviet Union, Bose founded the Indian Legion from soldiers who had surrendered in North Africa. He made impassioned calls for revolt in daily broadcasts from Germany on Azad Hind Radio. It soon became clear, however, that Japan rather than Nazi Germany provided the best opportunity for freeing India. After an epic submarine journey, Bose arrived in Japanese-dominated Southeast Asia. He assumed leadership of the Indian Independence League and the Indian National Army. His reinvigoration of the latter organization from among not only Japanese prisoners of war but Indians settled in Malaya called into question the notion of a narrow territorially bound nationalism.[28] Bose's provisional government of Azad Hind (Free India) declared war on Britain. An invasion of India was launched from Rangoon early in 1944. The Japanese and INA forces were driven back with heavy losses by the British in the Battle of Imphal (March–July 1944) in the northeastern state of Manipur. This was the nearest Bose was to get in his drive for Delhi.

Subhas Chandra Bose's career has been most expertly and extensively covered in the writings of his grandnephew Sugata Bose.[29] Sugata Bose reveals that by June 1944, nearly a quarter of a million Indians in Malaya had written oaths of allegiance to the provisional government of Azad Hind, which succeeded in bridging the divides of language and religion that had so profoundly affected nationalism in the Subcontinent.[30] The mixture of Urdu and Hindi (Hindustani) became the national language accessible to all those of North Indian descent because it was written in the Roman script. Bose's speeches were simultaneously translated into Tamil for South Indians. Rabindranath Tagore's *Jana Gana Mana* was translated into Hindustani and served as a national anthem that transcended religious identities. *Jai Hind* (Victory to India) became a common salutation. The national flag looked beyond the Congress spinning wheel with its emblem of a leaping tiger, recalling Tipu Sultan's resistance to the East India Company. The transnationalism, which crossed community barriers, was finally summed up in the Urdu words *itmad* (faith), *ittefaq* (unity), and *kurbani* (sacrifice).[31]

Bose's "failure" because of the INA's dependence on the Japanese military, the distractions surrounding his plane crash in Taiwan, and the extent to which he espoused or rejected fascist ideology and Nazi racism have all dominated writing on his career.[32] Sugata Bose has pointed, however, to the significance of his grand-uncle's challenge to a linear territorial nationalist account of India's freedom. Bose exemplifies the diverse histories of an immensely complex late-colonial India that cannot be reduced simply to the triumph of Congress and the Muslim League. Sugata Bose also raises the "what if" of Subhas's career. If he had survived the war, could Gandhi's "most rebellious son" have worked with him to avert "the catastrophe that engulfed the subcontinent in 1947?"[33] It is to the climacteric of independence and its accompaniment with the partition of the Subcontinent that we will turn in our next chapter.

EIGHT

Independence with Partition

The penultimate viceroy of India, Archibald Wavell, noted in his diary at the close of 1946 that Britain was "still legally and morally responsible for what happens in India . . . [but lacking] nearly all power to control events; we are simply running on the momentum of our previous prestige."[1] Six years of global conflict had exhausted British military and economic power. The fall of Singapore to the Japanese on 15 February 1942 had dealt a severe blow to British prestige throughout Asia. Churchill termed it "the worst disaster" and "largest capitulation in British history." In India, the 1942 Quit India movement had severely stretched resources. The Raj's sea of troubles had not ended with victory over Germany and Japan; the trials of Indian National Army personnel created a furor, and the Royal Indian Navy mutiny of February 1946 revealed the danger of Britain clinging onto power too long. By the time that Wavell was writing, it was simply a case of when and how, not whether, Britain would depart.

In the event, the British left honorably and on good terms with the Indian political elite, thereby safeguarding commercial and strategic interests, which still remained considerable in the postindependence decade. The triumph of Indian nationalism had been soured, however, as Partition had accompanied independence while bringing in its wake terrible human suffering. The division of the Subcontinent into the dominions of India and Pakistan internationalized the Congress-Muslim League conflict. This increasingly centered on the dispute over the former Princely State of Jammu and Kashmir. The creation of a truncated Pakistan, according to some revisionist historians, may not even have been Jinnah's intention. Ayesha Jalal has argued, for example, that his espousal of the Pakistan demand from 1940 onward was a bargaining chip to secure greater influence for Muslims in a postcolonial Indian state.

In the first part of this chapter, we will seek to explain the circumstances in which the British decided to quit India. We will then turn to the division that accompanied decolonization. This was by no means a foregone conclusion even after the Muslim League had sought to mobilize mass support around the demand for a separate state. The chapter concludes with a brief assessment of the consequences of the British departure for the Princely States.

The Path to Independence

The Congress in the late colonial period adopted a "struggle-truce-struggle" strategy. This was marked by periods of both direct action and entry into the legislatures established by the constitutional reforms of 1919 and 1935. Council entry, especially in the wake of provincial autonomy, enabled Congress to establish parallel administrations to the Raj. The process was also assisted by the activities of full-time workers, who, we have seen, were funded by Indian industrialists. Recourse to direct action along the lines of Gandhian noncooperation meant that the propertied classes could throw their weight behind nationalist struggle without fear of social revolution, even as nonviolence corroded the moral authority of colonial rule. The British had always prided themselves on this moral high ground. Such episodes as the firing on unarmed crowds at the time of the 1919 Amritsar Massacre, or the beating of peaceful protestors at the time of Gandhi's 1930 Salt Satyagraha, severely diminished British authority. The 1942 Quit India movement was the last and the least Gandhian of noncooperation campaigns, employing violence as it did. Well over one thousand post offices and police stations had been destroyed by the end of 1943. In all, more than ninety-two thousand people were arrested.

The Quit India movement included students, peasants, and workers. Thirty thousand workers went on strike at TISCO in Jamshedpur. Bihar and eastern United Provinces were the sites of the most intense mobilization, although British rule also almost collapsed in the coastal Midnapore districts of Bengal. The patchy mobilization elsewhere reflected the prevailing aloofness of Muslims, Dalits, and supporters of the Hindu Mahasabha and the right wing Hindu nationalist Rashtriya Swayam Sevak Sangh (RSS). The recently legalized Communist Party was also a bystander, in keeping with its "Peoples' War" strategy. Nonetheless, more than fifty battalions of troops were required to suppress the movement. These were additional wartime troops in a Subcontinent threatened by Japanese invasion. It was clear that mass struggle could not be indefinitely faced down in this way. The Congress leadership was also bruised by the wave of arrests and by the experience of a movement running out of their control. It has been argued that Quit India strengthened the resolve of the conservative elements in Congress to seek a "friendly" and swift transfer of power, even at the cost of Partition. Moreover, we have seen earlier that plans for state-sponsored economic development were inconsistent with the degree of devolved power required to maintain India's unity.

Nationalist struggle, although crucially important, did not by itself cause the British departure. Protective tariffs and the British taxpayer's new burden of paying for the imperial costs of the Indian Army diminished India's value. Britain ended the Second World War in debt to India for the first time. The new economic landscape, itself a response to nationalist demands, was accompanied by a gradual process of "Indianization" of the civil service and army elites. The Raj's fabled "steel frame" was further weakened by the wartime halt to British recruitment. Quit India and later mounting communal conflict called into question the willingness of Indian civil servants to do the bidding of an outgoing colonial state. While the British had, since the August 1917 Montagu Declaration, held out the eventual goal of self-government, the Second World War's strains had brought this outcome much closer. Sir Stafford Cripps, in his 1942 mission prompted partly by US pressure and by the need to secure greater Indian support, following the catastrophic loss of Singapore, had promised Dominion status at the war's conclusion. Without a massive postwar reinforcement of British forces, collaboration began to unravel and communal conflict intensified as the end of the Raj loomed in sight. The final decision to both divide and quit became interlinked with the fear of being caught in the middle of a civil war.

London also had changed priorities following the election of a postwar Labour government. Perhaps too much should not be made of this, however, as the Attlee administration did not see India's freedom as leading to a general end of empire. Moreover, within South Asia, Whitehall had key commercial and strategic long-term interests. Any thoughts of a reinforcement of the British presence in India itself were halted, however, by the widespread disturbances of November 1945 to February 1946. These were sparked by attempts to prosecute the officers and men who had been captured in Singapore and subsequently joined Bose's INA.

The cycle began with the protests arising from the announcement of the guilty verdict on charges that had been brought against Captain Abdul Rashid of the 14th Punjab regiment. Calcutta, with its long revolutionary tradition and links with Subhas Chandra Bose, was at the heart of violent protests on Abdul Rashid Day (12 February). Clashes between British troops and protestors resulted in eight deaths and more than ninety injuries. Protestors attacked US Army trucks, injuring three soldiers. US troops were confined after these episodes to the barracks in which they had been based during the war against Japan. A couple of weeks later, thousands of students went on strike in Lahore in protest at the seven years' sentence imposed on another INA officer, Captain Burhanuddin. The governor's car was stoned on the Mall; its windshield was smashed and the Union Jack torn from the hood. Such "hooliganism" paled into insignificance, however, with the serious threat posed by the Royal Indian Navy mutiny.

The February 1946 mutiny began with a strike on the vessel *Talwar*, which was more about local grievances than about nationalist demands. The strike spread to twenty other ships in the harbor and to twelve shore establishments. Ships in the harbor began flying the Indian flag rather than the Union Jack. Gunfire was exchanged for seven hours between the Indian naval enlisted men and British military personnel, but by far the greatest violence accompanied the strike in Bombay in support of the enlisted men. There were widespread looting, strikes by textile workers, and the burning of trams, buses, and post offices. The Congress and Muslim League sent out peace brigades to try to restore order. The enlisted men decided to surrender their arms after the mediation of the Congress deputy president, the pugnacious Sardar Vallabhbhai Patel. He had no wish to see industrial production halted, or to inherit armed services that were in disarray.

While the *People's Age* condemned the Congress policy of "compromise," Gandhi publicly stated that Hindu-Muslim unity for purposes of violence was "unholy."[2] Patel, in a private letter at the beginning of March 1946, emphasized that the discipline in the armed forces could not be "tampered with." "We will want an army," he declared, "even in a free India."[3]

Gandhi would not have concurred, but it was a shared feeling among the Indian elite that too much would be put at risk if there were a revolutionary seizure of power. This was best summed up in another private letter at the time written by Nehru's fellow Kashmiri, the Indian Liberal party leader T. B. Sapru, who had acted as a defense counsel in the Delhi INA trials. "What awful times we have been passing through!" he wrote. "The strike of the Naval ratings led to a terrible chaos and disorder in Bombay. . . . These are bad omens of the time. Speaking for myself I have no doubt whatsoever that these disturbances are being deliberately fomented by the Communists, who, having been driven out of the Congress, are very disgruntled with it. The Communists to my mind are playing the game of Russia."[4]

The INA disturbances dispelled any lingering thoughts of reinforcing the Raj. Instead, attention turned to what would now be termed an "exit strategy." The Attlee administration's "new imperialism" put good relations with independent India's future rulers at the heart of this. The wartime policy of raising Jinnah's status, however, now stood in the way of an ordered decolonization. There was constitutional gridlock over the Pakistan issue. In an endeavor to resolve this, the secretary of state, Pethick-Lawrence, Sir Stafford Cripps, and A. V. Alexander, the first lord of the Admiralty, hauled up in New Delhi on 25 March 1946. The "three magi" attempted to secure compromise around the idea of a "three-tier wedding cake": of a federal union whose powers would be limited to defense and foreign affairs, provinces in which all other powers would reside, and three groupings of provinces with their own legislatures. When Nehru publicly doubted the feasibility of the groupings, the Muslim League reversed its earlier acceptance of the scheme. The viceroy invited Congress to join an interim government without the Muslim League's participation, whereby a furious All-India

Muslim League Council meeting in Bombay on 28 July bade goodbye to "constitutions and constitutional methods." Large-scale violence on "Direct Action Day" occurred only in Bengal, where the Muslim League ran the government.

Wavell's inability to resolve this deteriorating situation and provide any prospect other than an "ignominious scuttle" cost him the viceroyalty. It was left to Victoria's great-grandson, Lord Mountbatten, to bring down the curtain on the Raj. Mountbatten would agree to take on the role of viceroy only if a deadline was announced for the British transfer of power in India. The impending British departure improved relations with Congress, but it also raised the stakes in the struggle over Pakistan. A cycle of violence began with the four thousand deaths of the August 1946 Great Calcutta Killings and culminated in the Partition killings a year later, which may have claimed as many as a million victims. The Partition-related violence differed from earlier Hindu-Muslim riots in its intensity, its clear political purpose of driving out minority populations, and its attacks on vulnerable women and children. Police failures led to British troops having to be deployed in Calcutta and later, in March 1947, in the Rawalpindi district of the Punjab, which was also the scene of gruesome violence.

Unfortunately, the Indian leaders' acceptance of the 3 June Partition Plan did not halt the endemic violence in the Punjab region. This was to spiral out of control when the British departed. The Sikh involvement has been explained by historians in terms of desire for revenge following the March 1947 Rawalpindi Massacres and the attempt to secure a Sikh majority area by ethnically cleansing Muslims. Sikh hopes for a separate state had crashed on the rocks of British and Congress concerns about "Balkanization." These had also resulted in a reduction of Pakistan, with the division of the Muslim-majority Bengal and Punjab provinces. Many Pakistani scholars blame the British for Pakistan's emergence as a "moth-eaten" country. The final British viceroy, Lord Mountbatten, is portrayed as pro-Indian in his dealings because of his closeness to Nehru, in contrast with his frosty and formal approach to Jinnah.[5]

Western scholars have also debated Mountbatten's viceroyalty.[6] Aside from the "blame game" as to whether his moving forward the date of

14. Mountbatten heart to heart with Jinnah, 5 April 1947

independence to August 1947 from June 1948 added to the violence and the chaos, there are the fundamental questions: Were the British reluctant partitioners? Did they have real influence over the course of events, or was their ability to transfer power an illusion?

The Path to Partition

Pakistani accounts often portray Muhammad Ali Jinnah as singlehandedly creating Pakistan in fulfillment of the primordial divisions between Muslims and Hindus. Jinnah was a great leader in terms of his tactics in constitutional negotiations. He relied, however, on favorable political circumstances during the Second World War to increase his bargaining power.

It was convenient for the British to delay further constitutional reform as a show of respect for Muslim opinion. Moreover, while the Congress was decimated by the mass arrests of the Quit India movement, the Muslim League could continue to build its strength. The anglicized Jinnah was, of course, in many respects an unlikely figure to lead a demand for a state in the name of religion. Some revisionist scholars maintain that he never abandoned his earlier stance in favor of Hindu-Muslim unity, raising the Pakistan demand as a bargaining counter for a greater Muslim voice in postcolonial India. Jinnah spent the first half of the 1930s in London. His Muslim League Party not only struggled to fend off local Muslim parties in Bengal and Punjab but was eclipsed by the Punjab Unionists in All-India deliberations.[7] But the 1935 Government of India Act, followed by the outbreak of the Second World War, created new opportunities for the League and its president.

The 1935 Government of India Act culminated the process of introducing local representative politics while the British firmly maintained the levers of power at the national level. The act introduced provincial autonomy in which, apart from the constitutional backstop of a governor, full legislative power lay in the hands of popularly elected Indian ministers. The Congress swept the polls in the first elections under this new arrangement, in 1937. It won 716 out of 1,585 seats in the provincial assemblies, enabling it to form governments in seven of the eleven Indian provinces. Power presented its own problems. Congress ministries not only disappointed the heightened expectations of workers and peasants but were drawn into conflict in Bombay (epitomized by the 1938 Trade Disputes Act) and in Bihar, where a militant peasant movement was led by the Kisan Sabha. Gaps appeared between the governing Ministerialist wings and the Organisational wings of provincial Congress parties. Differences were usually factional rather than ideological, but in their wake Congress membership declined. It was therefore with some relief that the Congress ministries resigned in October 1939, under the orders of the national leadership, in order to protest the British declaration of war. This had been made on India's behalf by the Viceroy Linlithgow without any consultation.

Congress rule in Muslim minority provinces intensified fears about a future national government. Representatives of the Muslim landholding elite in the United Provinces were unsettled by the hurly-burly of the new legislatures, with their noisy public galleries and Gandhian-clad congress-men.[8] Even watered-down commitments to tenancy reform were threatening. Most historians agree that the failure to establish a Muslim League coalition government in the UP also heightened separatist anxieties. UP was the only region in which the Muslim League had performed reasonably well in the 1937 polls. It had captured twenty-nine of the sixty-four Muslim seats. In the Muslim heartland of the Punjab, in contrast, it had won just two seats. The UP Congress leadership, however, wanted the League to cooperate on terms that would have ended its autonomous existence. There were good parliamentary and ideological reasons for such a stance, but it was a grave political blunder. A number of other Congress ministries displayed insensitivity to Muslim anxieties in encouraging Gandhian-inspired educational reform, which Muslims saw as an attempt at "Hinduization." The Muslim League made political capital out of investigations into Congress misrule (in the Pirpur Report of 1938 and the Sharif Report of 1939). When the Congress ministries resigned, Jinnah celebrated a "Day of Deliverance." Separate electorates had manifestly failed to safeguard Muslim political interests. Congress rule in the provinces had inadvertently boosted Chaudhary Rahmat Ali's call for a separate Muslim homeland.

The outbreak of the Second World War further framed Indian political developments. The Congress abandoned its strategy of parliamentary politics for popular resistance. This began with strictly controlled individual protests against the war. It culminated in the 1942 Quit India movement. While the Congress was pitted against the Raj, the Muslim League was accorded increased status. This process had begun in 1940, when the Viceroy Lord Linlithgow had in his August offer clarified that the British would not transfer power to any system of government whose authority was "denied by large and powerful elements of India's national life."[9] Jinnah's constitutional veto was further extended at the time of the March 1942 Cripps mission. Indeed, R. J. Moore has gone so far as to describe it "as a watershed in the history of partition."[10] Cripps's proposals had included a proviso that no part of India would be forced to join the postwar Indian Dominion. A furious Gandhi informed him that this amounted to "an invitation to the Moslems to create Pakistan."[11] It gave Jinnah immense bargaining power, which he skillfully exploited. When the war ended, the British focused on securing support of the Congress to ensure an orderly transfer of power. But by this time, Jinnah had so extended his influence that he could not be easily brushed aside.

Gandhi, who was an increasingly isolated figure, never contemplated Partition as anything other than a defeat for his vision of India. It was only through the press that he got to hear about the Congress Working Committee's Resolution adopted in Match 1947—that Punjab should be partitioned if Pakistan was created. He publicly stated that he could not "tolerate" any plan which involved the "vivisection" of India. The Mahatma maintained that Britain did not possess the moral right to impose division on an "India temporarily gone mad."[12] Other Congress leaders, in a mixture of pragmatism and cynicism, came to accept Partition as the means to secure freedom and end the violence that had spread from Calcutta to Noakhali, then Bihar, and eventually to the Punjab. Women were increasingly targeted for humiliation, as they were believed to represent community "honour."[13] Parts of India were already ablaze by the time that Lord Mountbatten was received at Palam Airport on 22nd March.

15. Reception of Mountbatten, left, by Nehru, Liaquat Ali Khan, and Auchinleck, Palam Airport, 22 March 1947

The final viceroy quickly realized that a return to the federal arrangements of the Cabinet Mission Plan was impossible and the British would have to divide and quit. While Partition came about along the lines sketched out above, it is important to realize that the outcome was not preordained. The Muslim League had to defeat its powerful Unionist rivals in the Punjab. It was able to achieve a breakthrough in the 1946 elections, but only first, through compromising with local Muslim elites, which were to cause long-term problems for Pakistan's political development, and second, by deploying electioneering methods that prevented it from forming the alliances required to run the government in the province.[14] The March–June 1946 Cabinet Mission was tantalizingly close to achieving a constitutional settlement that safeguarded Muslim interests in a loose federal arrangement.

A combination of local and national factors ensured that India's Partition was accompanied by the division of the Muslim majority provinces of Punjab and Bengal. The Muslim League's and local congressmen's attempts to prevent this in Bengal were frustrated by the local *bhadralok* resolve for division, arising from the highly charged class conflict in the East Bengal countryside, and the Congress High Command's veto of the United Bengal scheme. Jinnah had adopted a flexible position, although it contradicted the two-nation theory, in a bid to improve the Muslim League position and avoid provincial partition. The Radcliffe Boundary Commission was created to demarcate the boundaries along religious demographic lines in Punjab and Bengal. Its proceedings, like the division of assets by the Partition Council, encouraged rancor rather than compromise following the national leaders' acceptance of what became known as the 3 June Partition Plan.

The Punjab boundary award remains controversial. Pakistani writers claim that far from the award's being an independent judicial decision, Mountbatten influenced Radcliffe to grant the Muslim-majority *tehsils* of Ferozepore and Zira to India. They also maintain that the Gurdaspur district, which had a bare (0.8 percent) Muslim majority, was awarded to India because of the access it provided to Jammu and Kashmir, with the Hindu-majority Chittagong Hill Tracts in the east going to Pakistan to "balance" the award. It is also claimed that the award's delayed publication generated confusion and contributed to post-Partition violence.

16. The seven leaders accept the Partition plan, 3 June 1947, in the viceroy's study. Clockwise from left: Nishtar, Baldev Singh, Kripalani, Patel, Nehru, Mountbatten, Jinnah, and Liaquat

Recent research has demonstrated that the Pakistani claims over Gurdaspur were unfounded, although Mountbatten may have influenced the award of Ferozepore to India. Even if this occurred, Lucy Chester maintains, rather than being regarded as "improper," it was symptomatic of a process shot through with politics, despite the façade of judicial objectivity.[15] She maintains that the Punjab award, "rushed and inexpert" as it was, may have minimalized the violence. The Boundary Report was not published until 17 August. The new Dominions of India and Pakistan thus came into existence without knowing the full extent of their territory.

If a criticism is to be made of Mountbatten's machinery for Partition, however, it lies more with the inadequacy of the Punjab Boundary Force to maintain order than with the Boundary Committee.[16] Joya Chatterji's study of the Bengal Boundary Committee has revealed that demands placed before it ignored potential economic dislocation and population movements. Carefully laid plans for a "right sized" bhadralok-dominated state were

17. Coming out of the Constituent Assembly, Karachi, with
Jinnah now governor general of Pakistan

undone by the loss of the jute supplies from East Bengal and by the influx
of refugees into what became, with a total area of just twenty-eight thousand
square miles, one of the smallest Indian states. The bhadralok expectations
of Partition delivering a "small, manageable Hindu-dominated state," a "lost
golden age of . . . power and influence," were to be cruelly unrealized.[17] We
shall see later that East Punjab was similarly marginalized by Partition, unlike its West Punjab "twin," which became the core of the Pakistan state.

Chatterji's work also reveals that the "minimalist" dissident Congress
groups' attempts to influence the framing of a future West Bengal state so
as to increase their postindependence prospects clearly dispels the orthodox
view that Radcliffe imposed his "fiat from above."[18] Contrary to the portrayal
in Auden's famous poem "Partition," Radcliffe did not singly settle the fate
of millions by the stroke of his pen. In fact, he provided a useful "screen" for
the Indian politicians to hide behind when the new boundary lines evoked
their inevitable hostility.

Independence and the Princely States

The British departure had profound implications for the Princely States, which covered almost a third of the Subcontinent. As rulers of nominally independent territories, the princes had direct treaty relations with the British Crown. Their apprehensions had increased as a result of the Congress support for political reform within their boundaries and the collapse of their hopes for a role as a conservative bulwark in an All-India Federation. Following the acceptance of the 3 June Plan, the British attempted to ensure that each of the Princely States accede to the dominion of either India or Pakistan. Some princes, however, harbored hopes for independence. Accession was made more difficult in cases like Hyderabad, Junagadh, isolated on the tip of the Kathiawar peninsula, and Jammu and Kashmir, where the ruler came from a different religious community from the majority of his subjects. These states' eventual incorporation in India resulted in bitter recriminations. There was armed conflict between India and Pakistan in the case of Jammu and Kashmir.

Mountbatten charmed, while Patel and V. P. Menon bullied rulers to accede. The Princely States' absorption added more than ninety million people to the Indian Union. The bitter pill of the ending of the old order was sugared by granting tax-free pensions linked to the former state's revenue levels and by making some of the rulers of the larger states *rajpramukhs* (governors). The dispute between India and Pakistan over Jammu and Kashmir was not so easily resolved, with profound long-term consequences.

Pakistan also needed to address the problem of the amalgamation of Princely States, some of which, such as Bahawalpur and Kalat, had pretensions of independence. The issue was further complicated by the fact that small tribal states such as Swat and Dir occupied strategically sensitive locations in the borderland regions with Afghanistan. Bahawalpur, the largest of the Pakistan-region Princely States, lay on the sensitive Punjab border with India. Its ruler reluctantly signed an instrument of accession to Pakistan on 5 October 1947, but not until the beginning of 1951 were the last vestiges of his power removed. Kalat provided a greater problem and unconditionally acceded only in March 1948. The ruler's younger brother was involved in military clashes with Pakistani forces until his eventual arrest on 16 June. This was the first of the troubles in the area, as Baloch nationalists supported the state's stance. In October 1958, the khan, in response to the centralizing impact of the One Unit Plan, announced his secession from Pakistan, claiming that a government of nonbelievers led by Jinnah had forced him to accede. The tribal revolt had repercussions far beyond the remote region, for Pakistani President Iskander Mirza used the episode to justify the coup that ended Pakistan's first experiment with democracy.[19]

The Second World War accelerated the British departure from India. It also created the conditions for an agreed transfer of power, rather than a nationalist revolution. The British, however, were never as much in control of the process as that terminology implies. Mountbatten raced to free India to ensure that there was a perception of British initiative. Responsibility without power was to be avoided at all costs. Leading congressmen supported the British rush for the exit door, as they feared both Communist revolution and an unraveling of national unity if the process became protracted. Jinnah got what he could in the less propitious postwar circumstances.

Partition was not the inevitable outcome of entrenched Hindu-Muslim differences. Even at the height of communal polarization in 1946–47, there were well-documented cases of people, parties, and leaders refusing to accept the official registers that defined the political categories of Hindus and Muslims.[20] Nor was Partition the inevitable fulfillment of British so-called divide-and-rule policies. It was contingent on a range of political choices made by both the British and the Indian elites within the context of the impact of the Second World War. None of the protagonists anticipated the scale of the social dislocation which Partition would bring, or factored in the economic consequences. For Gandhi especially, Partition was a bitter blow to his life's work, and he refused to celebrate it. His presence in previously riot-torn Calcutta served as a "one man boundary force," but created bitterness in the eyes of some right-wing Hindus. This culminated in the tragedy of his assassination on 31 January 1948.

The division of territory forced millions of people to abandon their homes in a frantic two-way flight over the new international boundaries in North

India. These unforeseen consequences possessed immense repercussions for both state construction and community formation in the postcolonial era. They also soured the relations of the fledgling Indian and Pakistani states. The legacies of Partition continue to have an impact on the contemporary Subcontinent, as we will discover in the remainder of this volume.

PART IV

NINE

Nehru and the "New" India

In 1995 the Swiss government issued a new series of ten-franc notes de-signed by Jörg Zintzmeyer. They featured such individuals as the Dadaist artist Sophie Tauber-Arp and the sculptor Alberto Giacometti. The note commemorating the architect and urbanist Le Corbusier's contribution to Swiss cultural history had on its reverse side representations of the iconic buildings of the Chandigarh Capitol, which he had designed. The banknote evoked both irony and controversy. Le Corbusier had stressed his French rather than Swiss citizenship from 1930 onward.[1] Such Indian writers as Vikramaditya Prakash were "outraged" by the Swiss government's claiming the Chandigarh Capitol as its own.[2]

The controversy represented a posthumous victory of sorts for Jawaharlal Nehru, who had taken a close interest in the building of the new city, which had grown up in the 1950s on the Punjab plains at the foot of the Sivalik Mountains, some 150 miles northwest of New Delhi. "The site chosen," Nehru noted, "is free from the existing encumbrances of old towns and old traditions. Let it be the first large expression of our creative genius flowering on our newly earned freedom."[3]

Chandigarh was intended by the Indian prime minister not just to sym-bolize the Punjab's recovery from the trauma of Partition and the loss of La-hore, but to make an international statement about the "new" India.[4] When he laid the foundation stone for the legislative assembly building in April 1958, Nehru proudly declared, "The world's architects come to see what is going on in Chandigarh."[5] Nehru originally commissioned Albert Mayer, who had pioneered American new town development, but Le Corbusier took over the planning of Chandigarh from him when Mayer's architectural partner Matthew Nowicki died in a plane crash. Le Corbusier significantly modified the original plan, with its use of Indian building types and adaptation to the landscape. The city was instead laid out in a rectangular grid "based in the metaphor of the human body." Its plan can still be seen on the handcrafted cast-iron manhole covers, which remain one of Chandigarh's trademarks. In the words of a leading architectural historian, "To Nehru and Le Corbusier, the machine age held the promise of liberating individuals and improving society. . . . Modernism offered a shimmering vision of escape from everything conservative, traditional and limited."[6] As Sunil Khilnani has aptly judged, Nehru sought a "productive" and "universal modernism," not the "inauthentic modernism" represented by the colonial city.[7]

Chandigarh's deliberate renunciation of a "national style" was part of what Nehru saw as a necessary shock of the new. "It hits you on the head, and makes you think," he declared. "You may squirm at the impact but it has made you think and imbibe new ideas, and the one thing which India requires is being hit on the head so that it may think. . . . Therefore Chandigarh is of enormous importance."[8] Nehru emphatically endorsed modern architecture, which he saw as both a symbol and a vehicle for the technological and social programs of the new Indian state's modernization.

By the time the Le Corbusier banknote was in circulation, Nehru's foundational vision was under attack. Indeed, some critics saw Chandigarh's "celebration of an alien form style and material" as symbolic of a sterile and implanted national identity. Nehru had not been alone in Asia and Africa in seeing modernist architectural styles as symbolic of a break with the colonial past. Indeed, the development of Islamabad had followed a similar pattern of relying on Western expertise and seeking to build a modern city on a site unencumbered with past urban development. Nor was Chandigarh the only embodiment of this new vision for India. Bhubaneswar, the capital of Odisha (formerly Orissa), was also designed as a modern city, planned by the German architect Otto Königsberger, although unlike Chandigarh it emerged alongside a temple town dominated by the towering sandstone structure of the Lingaraja dedicated to the city's presiding deity Shiva. Königsberger, who had been recruited by the Tatas to replan an increasingly congested Jamshedpur, had worked as the chief architect for the Princely State of Mysore from 1939 until Nehru appointed him as federal director of housing in 1948. As Ravi Kalia has revealed in an excellent study, Königsberger's commitment to a "secular" modernist architectural style had to compromise with Indian influences.[9] While Nehru may have seen the city as a modern nationalist statement, Oriyans who had fought hard for a separate province in British India (finally granted on 3 March 1936) wanted the new capital to reflect a romanticized and religiously saturated representation of their past. The architectural compromises that ensued reveal in microcosm the limitations to the transformation of India in Nehru's image.

The clash between the "optimistic promises" of a liberating modernism and the realities of entrenched interests, continuing poverty, and disparities of power that haunted the Nehruvian era were also displayed in the building of Gandhinagar as a new capital for Gujarat. The desire to rival Le Corbusier's Chandigarh led wealthy Ahmedabad mill owners and architects influenced by modernism (for example, Balkrishna Doshi) to attempt to commission the American Louis Kahn, who had designed the modernist Indian Institute of Management in the city. Disputes over payment in local currency and Kahn's autonomy prevented his employment.[10] H. K. Mewada, who had worked with Le Corbusier in Chandigarh as a draughtsman, eventually sought to recapture Gujarati history and Gandhian ideals in Gandhinagar's capitol complex. It has been termed, however, an "outright failure,"[11] "a cruel concrete homage to Gandhi."[12]

Nehruvian India's "love affair" with concrete received its greatest expression not in public buildings but in dam construction. The environmental consequences of the dams' development have been discussed. To Nehru, however, dams, even more than new cities, represented the modernizing postcolonial state. Pride of place was given to the Bhakra Dam in the Bilaspur district of what is now Himachel Pradesh.[13] Construction of the 750-foot-high concrete wall stretching three-tenths of a mile across the Sutlej River began in 1954. By the time of its completion at the end of 1963, 4.5 million cubic yards of concrete had been produced. If Chandigarh was the aesthetic response to Lahore's loss at Partition, Bhakra was the engineering response to the breakup of the colonial Punjab's integrated irrigation system. Nehru's enthusiasm for the project as a symbol of the New India was as great as for Chandigarh. He visited the construction site no fewer than ten times. When he dedicated it to the nation on 22 October 1963, he declared Bhakra the "symbol of India's progress" and "the new temple of resurgent India."[14]

Key Ideas and Institutions of the Nehruvian Era

Dams and cities physically embodied a new India awakening "to life and freedom." For real progress to occur, however, Nehru realized that "restrictive social customs" had to be broken down and there had to be "emotional awareness" not only of political but of "economic and social equality."[15] He turned to his long-standing beliefs in democracy, socialism, and secularism to inspire this transformation. While it is right to draw attention to the "improvised" nature of Nehru's responses to the "constrained circumstances" postindependence, this should not obscure the vision he held for India and its unifying consequences.[16] Above all, Nehru's commitment to modernization led him to use the power of the Indian state to secure secularism and to remove social and economic inequalities. An increasingly pervasive state reduced to the margins of national life the Gandhian vision of a decentralized polity and economy based on the village, although the Mahatma was mythologized as the founder of the nation.

Nehru's vision for India's future rested in part on his reading of its past. This was laid out most clearly in the book he wrote in prison on the eve of independence, *The Discovery of India*. In this "living history," he celebrated what became known as a "composite culture" in which "layer upon layer" of thought had been laid down on India's ancient "palimpsest." This vision of a plural and eclectic Indian past may appear unremarkable, but it was highly significant at the time, when the agonies of Partition encouraged the voices of Hindu majoritarianism. Indeed, Nehru's insistence that Indian Muslims were not a "fifth column" but equal citizens embittered his relations with the saffron-tinged Sardar Patel so much that Gandhi had to admonish the deputy prime minister in the fevered post-Partition atmosphere.[17]

Nehru's personal impress on the nation-building process was greatly strengthened following Gandhi's assassination (30 January 1948), which enabled him to ban the communal RSS organization, and by the death of his

Is this generous to Nehru?

potential rival Patel (15 December 1950). Successive election victories (1952, 1957, 1962) in which the Congress won three-quarters of the seats in the lower house (Lok Sabha, literally house of the people) cemented Nehru's national authority. The 1952 polls, when more than eighty million votes were cast, in more than 130,000 polling stations, established the now clichéd claim that India was the world's largest democracy. Nehru used the opportunity to convey his ideas about the new India. In ten weeks of electioneering, beginning in mid-November 1951, he covered around twenty-five thousand miles and in his own estimation addressed about thirty million people.[18] Nehru also used broadcasts on radio and state television (Doordarshan) to exhort his compatriots. The first television broadcast was made in 1959.

Cinema, though always driven by commercial rather than state forces, also played a role in the nation-building process. Early postindependence Bollywood films (*Mughal-e-Azam, Taj Mahal*) stressed the themes of Hindu-Muslim unity and in their iconography and patriotic songs (as, for example, in Satyen Bose's 1954 production *Jagriti*) encouraged nationalist sentiment. Mehboob Khan's 1957 production *Mother India* was not only the greatest box-office success of its day, running for fifty weeks in Bombay, but has been widely recognized as a nation-building picture. While it borrowed its title from the freedom movement's identification of India with the mother, it projects through the character of Radha, played by the leading Muslim actress Nargis, the stereotype of the suffering woman who keeps her family together despite the depredations of the village moneylender, Sukhilala. This stereotype of suffering motherhood, as we have seen, was deployed by Gandhi to good effect. Radha, despite losing two of her sons and her husband in a flood, refuses Sukhilala's offers of support in return for becoming his mistress. She eventually rebuilds her life and is acknowledged as the "mother of the whole village." As she sings to the peasants in the name of the mother, a map of pre-Partition India appears on the screen. The film is, however, more than a celebration of Hindu-tinged nationalism. It also alludes to the Nehruvian goals of nation building through modernization with its shots of tractors, machinery, and dams.

The key ideas Nehru articulated were largely unchallenged until the emergence in the 1980s of Hindu nationalism and globalization. Nehru anchored secularism not in Western notions of a separation of religion and politics but in the belief in the equality of religions that was the natural outcome of a composite culture developed through the ages. Equality of opportunity, regardless of religion, was at the heart of Nehru's secularism. Secular principles were embodied in the fundamental rights in part III of the new constitution, which was introduced in January 1950. These included cultural and educational rights, along with freedom of religion. Separate electorates and reserved seats for Muslims were abolished as barriers to national integration. (They were, however, retained for Untouchables.) Partly to reassure the Muslim minority, and to the chagrin of Hindu nationalist critics, the *shariat* was retained in Muslim personal law. This resulted in Muslim women being deprived of the equal status provided by the constitution in matters of divorce, maintenance, and inheritance. State Congress governments in UP and Bihar continued to enforce bans on cow slaughter. More damaging in the long term, however, was Muslim marginalization in the bureaucracy, the police, and the ranks of the Congress, even in the heyday of Nehruvian secularism. This limitation reflected not only that many national politicians did not share the prime minister's vision, but that the federal arrangements established by the 1950 Constitution delivered considerable powers to conservative state-level politicians. They were to thwart Nehru's ambitions regarding agrarian reform, just as they did with respect to Muslim recruitment to the services and the privileging of Hindi over Urdu.

The Congress's co-opting local elites and accommodating a range of conflicting interests and ideas delivered remarkable electoral success in the 1950s and early 1960s. Paradoxically, though, this stood in the way of top-down initiated reform. Nehru's unwavering commitment to democracy meant that he could not force through major agrarian reforms as in neighboring China. At the same time, democracy was little more than a paper promise for those at the base of society, where inequalities arising from gender, class, and caste persisted, despite the promises of the Constitution and the periodic round of elections. Nehru's liberal democracy meant that despite his socialist rhetoric, property relations remained basically unchanged. Privileged social groups who had supported the Congress during the freedom movement thus continued to feel comfortable with it, despite its redistributionary pretensions. In the longer run, however, the growing gap between rhetoric and reality injected cynicism into a once highly idealistic political culture.

Congress dominated the political scene down to Nehru's death, winning national and state elections. The Congress system of one-party dominance, as political scientists have termed it, spared the Indian political system the crises of legitimacy that bedeviled its Pakistani neighbor and most South Asian states. The linguistic reorganization of state boundaries following the States Reorganization Act of 1956 is held up as an example of Nehruvian accommodationist politics that stands in stark contrast to the handling of linguistic demands in Pakistan. In reality, Nehru acceded to this process with extreme reluctance. Nevertheless, the creation of the new southern linguistic states of Andhra Pradesh and Tamil Nadu helped "domesticate" regional linguistic loyalties. In Robert Hardgrave's words, the Dravida Munnetra Kazhagam (DMK) "was transformed from a secessionist movement, nurtured on vague dreams of a glorious past and an impossible hope for the future, to a party of increasing political maturity and parliamentary discipline. As it was drawn into the political system, interests became more specific and were formulated as pragmatic political demands."[19]

Self-reliance, the encouragement of heavy industry, and the belief in state control of key sectors of the economy continued the freedom movement's quest for a "new" and modern India. It continued to hold in tension the prospect of greater social equality and the interests of a nationalist-minded industrial elite. The Planning Commission that sought to institutionalize these goals was the heir to the National Planning Committee, which had first met in December 1939. With its headquarters at Yojana Bhavan in New Delhi, the commission, with Nehru as its ex officio chairman, acted as a kind of "supercabinet" that was unaccountable to Parliament.[20] The three five-year plans (1951–66) of the Nehru era were increasingly more ambitious in scope. They shared the characteristic of emphasizing industry rather than agriculture as the key to development, although the latter continued to provide a livelihood for more than 70 percent of the population. Low agriculture productivity depressed economic growth rates and made India reliant on US food aid. The five-year plans did not have the force of law, but Nehru championed them, and government intervention extended into the fields of consumption, production, investment, and trade, finally giving birth to what became known as the "licence-permit raj."

The planning exercise achieved the goal of self-reliance, but it was at the cost of highly subsidized and inefficient state enterprises. The public sector's poor productivity, along with that of agriculture, limited the GDP rate of growth to around 3 percent, dubbed by some economists "the Hindu rate of growth." The neglect of agriculture in favor of industrial development could have resulted in famine without the supply of huge amounts of discounted wheat and rice initiated by the Eisenhower administration under Public Law 480, the Food for Peace Program. Despite its failings, the planning process had some successes. The sinews of the nation were knit more closely together by the allocation of twenty-one billion rupees for transport and communications by the third five-year plan (1961–66). This plan had benefited from liberal Western and US economic funding. In the sphere of human development there were rising literacy rates, increases in life expectancy, and reductions in infant mortality, although literacy gains were mitigated by a rapid rise in population (from 361.1 million in 1951 to 439.2 million a decade later).[21]

Most important, the plans, whatever their economic weaknesses, served important "legitimation functions" for the Indian state. Intervention in the economy for the purpose of development distinguished independent India from the Raj, which until the Second World War had been committed to laissez-faire economics.

For Nehru, the "new" India rested not just on planning and democratic routines but on the resolute defense of India's borders. We have seen in earlier chapters that India inherited a number of boundary disputes. China's claims against the colonial legacy of the McMahon Line resulted in Nehru's greatest defeat. In Jammu and Kashmir and the northeastern states, a distinctive pattern began to emerge under which political accommodation gave way to coercion, electoral manipulation, and direct administration from New Delhi. As early as August 1947, Nehru's response to self-determination movements in the northeast was blunt: "We can give you complete autonomy but never independence. No state, big or small, in India will be allowed to remain independent. We will use all our influence and power to suppress such tendencies."[22] A variety of administrative and constitutional provisions were adopted to placate tribal sentiment—the creation of tribal zones, of autonomous districts, union territories, and even new states. According to one commentator, state building in the face of separatist pressure has followed three strategies: "to fight the insurgency with military force for some time; then when the rebels seem to be tiring, offer negotiations; and finally, when the rebels are convinced that no matter what the casualties are on either side, they are not going to be able to secede, win them over with constitutional sops, invariably resulting in power being given to them in the resulting elections."[23] Quite frequently these "sops" have been followed by renewed struggles, violence, and endemic terrorism. Since the 1950s, the history of Assam, Mizoram, Nagaland, Tripura, and Manipur is littered with accords signed by New Delhi with separatists.

Nonalignment was the one foreign policy area in which Nehru carved out a fresh approach. It led to endemic tensions with Washington but enabled India to punch above its weight in international relations. In addition to securing a claim to moral authority, it also enabled New Delhi to secure aid from both the Western and the Soviet-led blocs. Unlike in the domestic sphere, where Nehru found the ideas of secularism and socialism being constantly contested, he was more or less given free rein in the pursuit of nonalignment. This reflected at least in part the fact that well before independence he had become widely acknowledged as a foreign affairs expert in Congress circles. His decision to act as minister of external affairs as well as prime minister thus went unchallenged. By the late 1950s, however, these two responsibilities were leading to overwork, which placed a strain on India's aging leader.

Nehru had headed the Congress's Foreign Department since 1928. By the end of the Second World War, it had the established outlook that India's freedom could influence the wider international system and that a free India could exert leadership in Asia. An Asian-relations conference in New Delhi in March 1947, which was attended by more than two hundred delegates from twenty-eight countries, was a dress rehearsal for this role. Within a year of independence, Nehru was articulating to such international bodies as the United Nations that India was committed to both anticolonial struggle and nonalignment. The latter was not simply neutrality or a diplomatic strategy but, according to Nehru, a moral imperative rooted in Indian traditional values of tolerance and nonviolence. By the time that the Non-Aligned Movement formally came into being at the 1955 Bandung Conference in Indonesia, India had secured a standing in international relations far in excess of its material resources. As with secularism and democracy, it provided India with a sense of moral superiority vis-à-vis its Pakistani neighbor.

By the end of Nehru's life, however, the luster was wearing off nonalignment. Following the outbreak of a disastrous war with China in October 1962, India had pressed for Western military aid.[24] Moral posturing on the international stage calling for peaceful resolutions of conflicts had also been belied by the 17 December 1961 invasion of the Portuguese enclave of Goa. Duncan Sandys, the British secretary of state for commonwealth relations, termed it "a very real shock," adding, "It may not be such a bad thing that Nehru should have fallen off his undeserved pedestal."[25] A resolution of the Kashmir dispute remained as distant as ever. Pakistan may have introduced the Cold War into South Asia by its security pacts with the United States, but there were already signs following the dramatic increase of Soviet economic aid after Nehru's June 1955 visit that India might reply by moving into a closer relationship with the Soviet Union.

The Limits of Power

Nehru's vision of "secularism" was not shared by Patel, his deputy prime minister, or by Rajendra Prasad, who had become the first president of India in 1950. Prasad opposed the Hindu Code Bill, which threatened male domination in such family matters as property rights. While Patel acknowledged the need for industrial development, unlike Gandhi, he was uneasy about the emphasis Nehru placed on the role of the state. Nehru had to contend not only with national opposition to his reforming vision but with the ultimately more damaging ability of state-level leaders to block reforms.

The 1950 Constitution gave the center the power to create new states and to take over their government by the mechanism of President's Rule, which was a throwback to the imperial regime. The center also had control, through what was known as the Union List, over matters of national importance, including defense, foreign affairs, and income tax. The center and the states in the Concurrent List shared authority for such issues as social and economic planning. The states' list devolved authority over such items as agriculture, land revenue, welfare, public order, and the police. This meant that key areas of national development could be unwittingly or willfully blocked by state politicians. Governance required cooperation between the center and the states. This was not always forthcoming, even when Congress ruled both. The rise of regional opposition after Nehru's death was to make it more difficult. His successor, Indira Gandhi, sought to bypass this through populism and by use of President's Rule to unseat opponents. This was not without precedent, as Nehru himself in July 1959 had removed the democratically elected Communist government of Kerela, headed by E. M. S. Namboodiripad.[26] On the whole, however, Nehru displayed tolerance of regional impediments to his rule provided that they were untainted by "communal" or "secessionist" undertones. This created a paradoxical state of affairs in which "Delhi was dependent on theoretically subordinate states for the successful pursuit of programmes deemed essential for the new nation."[27]

Even when policies were established in support of social equality, they were not always vigorously implemented. The issue of Untouchability is a good example. The 1955 Untouchability Offences Act made it illegal to discriminate against Untouchables with respect to temple entry and access to shops, restaurants, and wells. Throughout the Nehruvian era, only around three hundred cases were annually brought to court under the act. Penalties on conviction could be as little as fines of three or four rupees. Legislation in favor of female rights in 1956 similarly failed to transform everyday experiences in the face of entrenched conservatism regarding such issues as marriage, maintenance, and property rights. Few women possessed the wealth and education to use the law to protect their rights. Finally, in such backward states as Bihar, laws to abolish large Zamindari landholdings were patchy in their implementation. The rural poor scarcely benefited, although middling farmers did make some gains. Thereafter they acted as a further barrier to the transformation of the poor, who remained trapped in poverty and exploitation.

By early 1962, Nehru was facing a "restless" country and a political class that had begun a whispering campaign about the prime minister's "loss of grip and the shadow of the succession."[28] The disastrous and unexpected war following the Chinese invasion of northeastern India on 20 October 1962 not only undermined Nehru's international vision but dealt a severe blow to his domestic authority. The ignominious military setbacks led to the departure of Nehru's longtime close ally, the irascible Krishna Menon, as defense minister. Nehru's judgment on China—characterized by the slogan "Hindi-Chini-bhai-bhai," Indians and Chinese are brothers—was called into question. The needs for a vastly expanded defense budget threatened the third five-year plan. India had to compromise its nonaligned stance by looking to the United States and the United Kingdom for arms. Following its military humiliation, New Delhi was also faced with Washington's efforts to mediate in the Kashmir dispute. These came to naught but were disturbing, as India did not want to give ground. For the first time, Nehru had to face a no-confidence motion in the Lok Sabha (August 1963). The motion was defeated, but as a US intelligence report noted, "Indian politicians, both within his party and outside it, seemed to be increasingly willing to contemplate a period when Nehru would not be around."[29]

Nehru's increasing political vulnerability was mirrored by his declining health, after years of overwork. In a letter to Mountbatten he had admitted as early as March 1951 that "to be Prime Minister of India is to be a beast of burden."[30] The death of Mountbatten's wife, Edwina, in February 1960 added to Nehru's increasing gloomy isolation. "She came as a star brightening our lives," he condoled her husband in a handwritten letter.[31]

Nehru visited the Broadlands home of Lord Mountbatten shortly thereafter on the eve of the London Commonwealth Prime Ministers' Conference. In his last letter, written just three days before his death, in May 1964,

18. Edwina Mountbatten takes tea with Jawaharlal Nehru and his daughter Indira and her son during I.L.O. Conference.

Nehru expressed the hope that he could again visit Broadlands later in the summer.[32] He was reluctant, however, to take the former viceroy's advice and groom a successor.[33] The subject of the political succession privately perturbed British and American policymakers, while the Western media increasingly speculated on the issue. *Time* magazine named the home minister Lalal Bahadur Shastri as the favorite, while the NBC journalist Welles Hangen plumped for the finance minister Moraji Desai.[34] Other commentators touted Nehru's daughter Indira Gandhi, despite her political inexperience. Mountbatten, on a visit to India early in 1964, had urged Nehru to give up his day-to-day administrative burdens, although he prophetically noted that Nehru "would like to go on working at full pressure and die in full harness."[35] Hypertension led to a stroke and later to the ruptured aorta that claimed Nehru's life on 27 May 1964. In the words of one biographer, "He thus in a sense killed himself rather than lay aside what he had felt was a vocation."[36]

Nehru was a man of ideas who succeeded in steering the Indian ship of state damaged by the buffetings of Partition through its most "dangerous decade." He made pragmatic compromises, as in the Muslim civil code and reservations of government jobs and educational places for the Untouchables, even when those compromises stood against the "modern" concept of common citizenship based on individual rights. Similarly, despite initial misgivings, he accepted the linguistic reorganization of India's internal boundaries. Despite discomfort at the slow pace of socioeconomic change, because of the entrenched power of local elites, he remained committed to democracy as the means to build a new India. Under his watch, India became acclaimed as the world's largest democracy, although this was constructed against the grain of poverty, inequality, and, according to some theorists, an equally unpropitious ethnic and linguistic diversity.

Nehru was not only a convinced democrat but an internationalist. He ensured that a newly independent India did not turn in on itself, or have a weak voice in international politics as it emerged from the Raj's shadow. India played a leading role in the United Nations and in the British Commonwealth, despite its status as a republic. Nehru's vision of peaceful coexistence in a bipolar world order found its highest expression in the concept of nonalignment. If reorganizing India's internal borders was one of his greatest successes, then his greatest failure was the failure to defend India's boundary with China. This dealt a blow to his authority that was never restored.

Nehru's role in the formative phase of postindependence India highlighted the importance of political leadership. Not only did Nehru cling on to power too long, but he made no plans for a successor. His daughter Indira was a confidante, a "nursemaid," and an appointments secretary during his painful decline. Chester Bowles, America's ambassador to India, compared her role to that of Woodrow Wilson's wife, Edith Bolling Wilson, following the twenty-eighth US president's stroke, and asserted that Indira would "probably drift out of politics in a year or two."[37] This reasoning ignored her formidable determination and ambition. American diplomats and Indian politicians alike were to underestimate her at their peril. We will see that Indira Gandhi both played down connections with London and Washington in favor of Moscow and domestically threatened her father's democratic legacy.

TEN

Pakistan's Failure in Democratic Consolidation

A n oasis of calm lies in the heart of the chaotic city of Karachi. This is
a building of white marble topped by a dome resting on an elevated
platform that is approached by terraced avenues and fountains. The main
platform is reached by a flight of stairs from which the building can be entered through four arched entrances. At night, the structure is illuminated by
dazzling spotlights. The building, which is an iconic symbol of the Arabian
Sea port, is the last resting place of Mohammad Ali Jinnah, the founder of
Pakistan. A large four-tiered crystal chandelier gifted by China sits above
the tomb. People crowd around the railings that surround the sarcopha-
gus, which is guarded by uniformed naval servicemen.[1] Fatima Jinnah, the
founder's sister and confidante, and Liaquat Ali Khan, the first prime minister of Pakistan, are buried beside the Quaid-i-Azam—the Great Leader.

It is widely believed in Pakistan that Jinnah's premature death, on 11 September 1948, followed by Liaquat's assassination in Rawalpindi just over
three years later, dealt a crippling blow to the state's fledgling democracy.
We will see in this chapter, however, that Pakistan's failure to consolidate
democracy, in such marked contrast with India's experience, had far more
complex causes. We will begin with an examination of the strategic, institutional, economic, and political inheritances from British rule and the
decolonization process. This will be followed by a consideration of the
search for a national identity and vision. We shall see that the collapse of
democracy was not inevitable, but that institutional weaknesses and a denial
of Pakistan's pluralism resulted in power slipping into the hands of the bureaucracy over a number of years. The country's first military coup, of 1958,
culminated this process. We will turn first, however, to the main geographical and economic inheritances of the new Dominion of Pakistan.

19. Pakistan Day at the Residency in Ramzak

Geographical and Economic Inheritance

Even the "moth-eaten" Pakistan following the division of Punjab and Bengal was by no means a small country. It had a combined area almost four times that of the United Kingdom, or equal to that of Texas and Arizona in the United States. In a different regional context, it would have appeared a significant power, with a population according to the 1951 census of seventy-three million. India, however, dwarfed Pakistan—inheriting 77 percent of the landmass and 82 percent of the population of the undivided Subcontinent—creating a sense of insecurity that has dogged the smaller nation's history.

Disputes over Kashmir and the division of assets and water in the aftermath of Partition increased Pakistan's anxieties regarding its much larger neighbor. Kashmir's significance for Pakistan far exceeded its strategic value; its "illegal" accession to India challenged the state's ideological foundations and pointed to a lack of sovereign fulfillment. The "K" in Pakistan's name stood for Kashmir. Of less symbolic significance was the division of post-Partition assets. Not until December 1947 was an agreement reached on Pakistan's share of the sterling assets held by the undivided Government of India at the time of independence. The bulk of these (550 million rupees) was held back by New Delhi because of the Kashmir conflict and paid only following Gandhi's intervention and fasting. India delivered Pakistan's military equipment even more tardily, and less than a sixth of the 160,000 tons of ordnance allotted to Pakistan by the Joint Defence Council was actually delivered.[2] The Pakistan state was cash strapped, as it sought to improvise its federal capital in Karachi, short of basic office equipment and even accommodation space. India, conversely, had inherited the colonial state's central apparatus in New Delhi. Pakistan's sense of inferiority was exacerbated by the fact that unlike India, which had inherited membership of such international organizations as the United Nations, it had to apply for admission.

The emergence of the Pakistani military-bureaucratic combine has been frequently linked with perception of an Indian threat. This has given rise, it is argued, to a "garrison state," in which the military role is inevitably "overdeveloped" and scarce resources are diverted from a "political economy of development" to a "political economy of defence."[3]

Aside from its relatively small share of the Indian Subcontinent, the most significant features of Pakistan's political geography were the distance between its eastern and western wings and their different economic inheritances. One thousand miles of Indian territory separated East Bengal and West Pakistan. This created a sense of isolation in the eastern wing, as the centers of power lay in West Pakistan. It also reinforced regional perspectives, with East Bengal increasingly looking toward Southeast Asia and West Pakistan toward the Middle East. Partition disrupted trade in the Bengal region and cut off the textile mills of the Calcutta area from their supplies of raw jute in East Bengal. There was also disruption in West Pakistan, as the cotton-producing areas of Punjab had supplied raw materials to mills in Bombay and Ahmedabad. This was more easily overcome, as the Pakistani Punjab already possessed textile mills. There was not a single factory, however, in East Bengal. The western wing of the country forged ahead industrially in the 1950s and 1960s, with increasingly dangerous consequences for national consolidation. Even West Pakistan, however, inherited a lower economic base than India. There was no equivalent of the Tata works at Jamshedpur or the concentrated development around Calcutta and Bombay. Indeed, on the eve of Partition just one of the fifty-seven leading industrial companies was owned by a Muslim.[4] The future Pakistan areas of the northwest have been termed an "agrarian appendix" to the Subcontinent. Within them were the rich canal colony regions of the Punjab, but elsewhere capitalist farming was thinly spread among subsistence agriculture and nomadism.

Pakistan's northwest was not only home to potentially troublesome tribal populations in the Tribal Area "buffer zone" with Afghanistan but, as we have seen, the site of a disputed border with Afghanistan. Kabul supported the secessionist Pakhtunistan demand and voted against Pakistan's admission to the United Nations. Pakistan inherited a system of rule in the region that was based on the *jirgas*, the power of the political agent and frontier crimes regulation. In Balochistan, electoral politics were restricted to the Quetta municipality until independence. Political participation was also delayed in the North West Frontier Province (NWFP). As late as 1927, the Simon Commission argued that the Frontier's strategic location made it unsuitable for self-government. It was only after the widespread unrest of 1930–32 that the system of dyarchy was introduced. Pakistan thus inherited a "democratic deficit" in much of its future territory because of the needs of the local "security state."[5] This "slow growth" in elective politics in important areas of Pakistan "must be taken into account," Muhammad Waseem has argued, "in any study of electoral democracy . . . especially when [Pakistan] is compared with India."[6] A tradition of bureaucratic authoritarianism was deeply rooted in the future Pakistan areas. Its hallmarks were paternalism, wide discretionary powers, and the personalization of authority. In the Punjab heartland, as we have seen, the army had established its main recruiting activities. A special relationship between the peasantry and the army had been established, which Clive Dewey has argued holds the key to military dominance in independent Pakistan.[7]

Inherited authoritarian attitudes prevailed among leading Pakistani bureaucrats in the 1950s. Indeed, Allen McGrath primarily understands

Pakistan's early democratic failure in terms of the willingness of such seasoned bureaucrats as Iskander Mirza (president 1956–58) and Ghulam Muhammad (governor general 1951–55) to dismiss elected governments.[8] "Creeping authoritarianism" at the national level was presaged by the bureaucratic control exerted over the formerly Princely States, which occupied a considerable proportion of West Pakistan's landmass. Security considerations were used to justify a bureaucratic grip, which contrasted starkly with the Indian experience.[9] The thwarting of democratic activity created not only antagonism toward the center but space for the flowering of ethnic and linguistic nationalism in parts of Bahawalpur and Kalat.

Colonial governance was not, however, the only historical inheritance that affected Pakistan's political development, along with its geography and economy. In the next section, we shall turn to institutional and political influences arising from the freedom movement and the immediate aftermath of Partition.

The Legacy of the Pakistan Movement

The creation of Pakistan by a transformed Muslim League came at the cost of weak political institutionalization and a culture of intolerance, which were inimical to future democratic consolidation. The Muslim League was a latecomer in many of the future Pakistan regions. With the exception of Bengal, it did not establish a mass organizational base akin to that of Congress. Consequently, it was not well placed to act as a focus for postcolonial political development. This situation was exacerbated by the unrealistic, almost millenarian expectations aroused during the final stages of the Pakistan struggle.

The Muslim League raised the expectations of a population wearied by its contributions to the war effort and resentful of the Hindu and Sikh domination of economic life. Traditional resentments were given a new twist by the growing wartime prosperity of non-Muslim traders and contractors in such provinces as the Punjab. Moreover, Hindu civil supplies officers were further charged with discriminating against Muslims in their distribution of rationed goods.[10] When Muslim League propagandists sought to break the Unionist Party's grip on the countryside, they presented Pakistan as a panacea for wartime and longer-standing grievances. Propagandists were directed, when they visited a village, to "find out its social problems and difficulties to tell [the villagers] that the main cause of their problems was the Unionists [and] give them the solution—Pakistan."[11]

Grassroots propaganda was accompanied by the Punjab Muslim League's utilization of the influence of local Sufi *pirs*, landowners, and *biraderi* heads to mobilize voters in the 1946 polls. Its parent organization portrayed the elections as a referendum on Pakistan.[12] This process was equally present in Sindh and the NWFP.[13] By accepting elite converts to its ranks, the Muslim League was able to overcome its weak institutional base: its membership in Punjab stood at just 150,000; in Sindh it had only 48,500 members. Elite opportunistic converts, however, brought poor discipline and factionalism. In Sindh, the shallow roots of the Pakistan movement paved the way for a separatism based on hostility to potential Punjabi domination. The massive post-Partition migration of "outsiders" into the province was to further strengthen Sindhi separatist sentiments. The Provincial Muslim Leagues in the future West Pakistan areas were in reality ramshackle organizations beset by factional infighting and parochial insights that were hard to reconcile with Jinnah's all-India understanding of the Pakistan demand.

Bengal was the exception. In this province, like the Congress, the League possessed paid, full-time members. Primary branches were established even in remote villages. During 1944 alone, the Bengal Muslim League enrolled more than 500,000 members. Unlike in Sindh, the progressive organizational wing of the Muslim League triumphed over the Ministerialists to such an extent that Khawajah Nazimuddin, the former prime minister (March 1943–March 1945), did not stand for election in 1946. Yet this platform was dismantled rather than built on after independence. In fact, it was even threatened during the Pakistan movement as conservative Muslim Leaguers claimed that the dynamic Secretary Abul Hashim and his close followers were Communists. The Muslim League's postcolonial demise in Bengal owed much to its recapture by the conservative old guard, who opposed agrarian transformation and emphasized a national Urdu-based Pakistani identity rather than a regional Bengali one.

The language issue dominated East-West Pakistan relations shortly after independence. Its emergence contributed to the antidemocratic centralizing tendencies in the latter wing. Rather than seeing pluralism as a source of strength, Pakistan's national elite plowed on with a policy that looked to Islam and Urdu as the sole nation building blocks. Regional identities and loyalties were delegitimized. This attitude was expressed as early as January 1948 by the Federal Communications Minister Abdur Rab Nishtar during a visit to East Bengal. "Regional patriotism [is] simply repugnant to Islam," he intoned. "Pakistan was established on the basis that Muslims were one nation, and the tendency to think in terms of Bengali, Punjabi and Bihari would undermine the very foundations of Pakistan. . . . These disruptive ideas [are] being spread by enemies of Pakistan who [are] working as fifth columnists amongst the Muslims."[14]

Conflicting understandings of the Pakistan demand meant that unity could be achieved only around Jinnah's towering personality and by falling back on a "negative" basis for nationalism. Hostility was primarily directed toward the "Hindu" Congress, but regional opponents were also demonized. Mock funerals were conducted for the Unionist leader Khizr Tiwana.[15] Pirs threatened that Tiwana would become "a fiend in Hell" if he separated himself from the Islamic movement for Pakistan.[16] League propagandists declared that anyone who voted against it were *kafirs* (unbelievers) and would not be buried in a Muslim graveyard. It was thus hardly surprising that after independence, the Muslim League equated opposition to its rule as being "against the interest" of Pakistan.[17]

The All-India Muslim League's long-term domination by the interests of the minority Muslim population areas was reflected in its internal organization. Bengal, with its thirty-three million Muslims, possessed just ten more seats on the All-India Muslim League Council than UP, with its seven million. This meant that many in the League's hierarchy lacked a power base in postindependence Pakistan. Liaquat Ali Khan, who came from the UP, had to be nominated to a place in the Pakistan Constituent Assembly from East Bengal. As Yunas Samad has pointed out, "The establishment of a strong centre was a lifeline" for "many *mohajir* [refugee] politicians who lacked electoral support in the country."[18] Lacking a local base, migrant

politicians had little incentive to hold elections in the immediate postindependence period. It was not until 1970 that Pakistan conducted its first
national election. This contrasted starkly with the situation in India. The
parliamentary system was unable to put down roots. Prime ministers moved
through the revolving doors of office with increasing rapidity. One of these,
the former Bombay businessman I. I. Chundrigar, survived scarcely two
months in office in late 1957.

In sum, three important inheritances from the freedom struggle exerted a profound influence on postcolonial political developments. First,
the Muslim League was poorly institutionalized. The pyramid of branches
stretching from the villages to the national level, which was the Congress's
hallmark, was absent in the League, which was thus far less able to form a
democratic pillar in the postcolonial state. Second, there was an incipient
clash between regional and "Pakistani" identities. Within Bengal especially,
there were different priorities from Jinnah's all-India perspective in terms of
cultural and economic policy. The third legacy was the low level of political culture in the Muslim-majority areas. Even at the height of the Pakistan
struggle, many landlords were primarily concerned with local interests and
self-aggrandizement. Factionalism and opportunism encouraged antidemocratic sentiments that were also born of the desperate struggle to quickly
secure popular support for the Pakistan demand.

The Legacy of Partition

Authoritarianism was further encouraged by the chaotic conditions that followed Partition. The unanticipated refugee influx and military conflict with
India over Kashmir threatened the fledgling Pakistan state. Resources and
energies were diverted from building up political institutions to strengthening the bureaucracy and the army. Tensions increased between the center and the provinces over the settlement of the huge number of refugees,
nearly five million of whom crossed from the Punjab Indian border alone
between August and November 1947.

The West Punjab and urban Sindh were the main refugee destinations.
East Punjab farmers settled on the rich canal colony lands vacated by

Sikh agriculturalists. The capital Karachi attracted educated UP migrants. Within six years of independence the city's population had tripled to 1.3 million. The creation of an Urdu-speaking enclave in the sands of Sindh had profound long-term implications for Pakistan's politics. The Sindhi Prime Minister Ayub Khuhro had dragged his heels in accepting refugees and was eventually removed over the issue. This not only strengthened Sindhi sentiment against the center but also created the precedent of executive action against elected representatives, which boded ill for the future. Sindh continued to receive waves of refugees in the years after Partition. By the end of 1950, the authorities had withdrawn all refugee assistance at the Khokrapar border in an attempt to stem the tide. There were even allegations that Sindh's inspector general of police had requested permission for his officers to fire on the refugees should the need arise.[19]

The Kashmir Conflict

The decision of Hari Singh to accede to India in October 1947 led to war between India and Pakistan, the United Nations' intervention, and a de facto division of the former Princely State of Jammu and Kashmir along the cease-fire line. Three long-running themes in Pakistan's domestic history resulted from the conflict, all of which have undermined democratic consolidation. First, the priority to build up the army was established. This was spelled out by Liaquat Ali Khan in a national broadcast early in October 1948: "The defence of the State is our foremost consideration . . . and has dominated all other governmental activities. We will not begrudge any amount on the defence of our country."[20] In fact, during 1947–50 up to 70 percent of the national income was allocated to defense.[21] The weakness of the postindependence Pakistani Army had been brought home by the fact that almost five hundred British officers had to be employed to make up the shortfall in qualified Pakistanis. Some in Pakistan believed that the British Commander in Chief Sir Douglas Gracey's initial reluctance to commit troops to assist the invading "Pakhtun tribesmen" represented a "missed opportunity" for a lasting military solution to the Kashmir issue.

Second, the invasion of October 1947 marked the beginning of the use of Islamic proxies to achieve Pakistan's strategic goals. Pakhtun tribesmen loyal to the pir of Manki Sharif were assisted by irregular Pakistani forces. Much contemporary analysis links Pakistan's patronizing of such forces to military regimes and in particular the Zia era (1977–88). It is, however, much more historically deep-rooted than this.

Finally, following the 1947–48 conflict, Pakistan looked for external assistance to counterbalance India. This culminated in Pakistan joining the Western Cold War alliances SEATO and CENTO in the mid-1950s. Pakistan's entrance into these alliances was followed by US financial and military aid, which strengthened the army's position vis-à-vis other state institutions. A template was laid down, arising from security concerns, in which democratic governance would always play second fiddle to the military and bureaucracy. Indeed, one understanding of the 1958 military intervention is that it was a preemptive coup to prevent a challenge to the West Pakistan elites' strategic approach. Bengalis had a "democratic majority," accounting for more than 55 percent of the population, and national elections could have brought to power Bengali-led democratic interests who embraced a different vision for Pakistan.[22]

The Failure of Democracy

There are a number of signposts on the way to Pakistan's first coup: the dismissal of elected provincial governments in the NWFP (August 1947) and Sindh (April 1948); the encouragement of a discourse of political corruption by creating categories of political crimes that would result in disqualification from public office (the Public and Representative Office Disqualification Act, PRODA, 1949); intervention of the army following the East Pakistan language riots (February 1952) and anti-Ahmadi riots in Lahore (March 1953); the defeat of the Muslim League in the East Bengal elections (April 1954); the Supreme Court's legitimization of Governor General Ghulam Muhammad's dismissal of the first Constituent Assembly (October 1954); the desertion of West Punjab landlords from the Muslim League to the

Republican Party (May 1956); the resignation of the bureaucrat–turned–prime minister Chaudhuri Muhammad Ali (September 1946).

Lying behind these events were not just colonial administrative, political, and strategic inheritances, but competing visions of the state. Was it to be a homeland for Indian Muslims, or an Islamic state? Was centralization or pluralism to lie at the heart of state construction? Conflicting visions were expressed in the Constituent Assembly debates around such issues as the adoption of separate or joint electorates and the role of Urdu and Bengali as national languages. The ensuing wrangling delayed the ratification of a Constitution. While the state could be practically governed under the terms of the 1935 Government of India Act, the delays reduced parliamentary legitimacy and opened the way for "creeping authoritarianism." The Muslim League's decline further aided it.

The language issue reemerged in East Bengal in 1952 following the publication of the Interim Report on the Constitution, which declared Urdu as the national language, although the majority of Pakistanis spoke Bengali. The death of four university student protestors at the Dhaka University campus on 21 February 1952 gave the language movement its first martyrs. From this time onward the Muslim League was seen as an "outsider." The party that had created Pakistan was humiliated two years later in provincial elections in East Pakistan, when it was reduced to holding just 10 of 309 Assembly seats.

It was in West, not East, Pakistan, however, that martial law was first introduced. This followed the March 1953 anti-Ahmadi disturbances in Lahore. They were led by Ahrar and Barelvi ulema who sought the dismissal of the Ahmadi Pakistan Foreign Minister Zafarullah Khan and the declaration that Ahmadis were non-Muslims. The movement gained momentum from the establishment following Partition of a new Ahmadi center at Rabwah in the Jhang district. It was also a useful vehicle for Ahrar leaders to reestablish the influence they had lost because of their opposition to the Pakistan struggle. The two months of martial rule in Lahore set a precedent. At the same time, the direct action revealed both the street power of the ulema and their divisions, which were to hinder attempts to Islamicize Pakistan.

In October 1954 Governor-General Ghulam Mohammad dismissed the Constituent Assembly. His action was prompted by proposed constitutional amendments that would have stripped his office of the power to dismiss the cabinet and nullified the use of PRODA proceedings against politicians. The Supreme Court in an important ruling gave legal cover to Ghulam Mohammad's action under the doctrine of necessity. The façade of a parliamentary system lingered on until 1958, but its heart had been cut out. The new "cabinet of talents" that followed the dissolution of the Constituent Assembly included the later executors of the coup, Iskander Mirza and Ayub Khan, in the important interior ministry and defense posts.

Symptomatic of the passing of power from the politicians to the bureaucracy and their military allies was the creation of the One Unit scheme. This established, in October 1955, a unified West Pakistan province by dissolving the historic provinces to enforce interwing parity and thus deny the majority Bengali population from implementing its interests in national politics. West Pakistan politics now became even more unstable and fractious than in the past. Leaders who could not be bought off from the now defunct smaller provinces rallied against Punjabi domination. Provincial politics fed into a national scene marked by shifting coalitions. Prime ministers came and went with increasing regularity. "Yesterdays 'traitors,'" the Pakistan Army commander in chief Ayub Khan noted, "[are] today's Chief Ministers, indistinguishable as Tweedledum and Tweedledee!"[23] These sentiments became public only in 1967 and could be dismissed as a post hoc justification for martial law. Nonetheless, they reveal that by the mid-1950s there was a growing sense in the military that the country was sliding into chaos because of the actions of self-seeking politicians. Officers increasingly felt that the army was the only properly functioning institution and that its responsibility was to protect the state from both external and internal dangers. These attitudes have remained more or less constant throughout Pakistan's history.

The army had secured a Trojan horse in the shape of the Republican Party, which emerged in the Punjab in May 1956. It was a prototype of future pro-establishment parties, such as the Convention Muslim League and more recently the Pakistan Muslim League–Q (PML-Q). Henceforth, as the Punjab increasingly became the core of the state, a section of its leadership willingly acceded to the centrist designs of the military and the bureaucracy in return for a share of power. This process accompanied the marginalization of Mohajir influence that gathered pace following Ayub's coup. Not surprisingly, the most sustained resistance to this emerging polity came from politicians outside the Punjab's charmed circle.

The elevation of the civil servant Chaudhri Muhammad Ali to the post of prime minister in October 1955 was seen by the British high commissioner as a "deplorable" departure from the established parliamentary norms.[24] It fell to Chaudhri Muhammad Ali to see the Constitution Bill through the Assembly. Six years after India and nearly a decade after independence, Pakistan had its own constitution. Iskander Mirza took the post of president of the Islamic Republic of Pakistan. Promised elections were never held, partly because of delays over the issue of joint or separate electorates. The Constituent Assembly thus carried on for a further two years as an interim National Assembly.

Ibrahim Ismail Chundrigar's brief period (17 October–16 December 1957) as prime minister illustrated the political decline of the Constituent Assembly in terms of accountability and disunity. Chundrigar, who had one of Karachi's main thoroughfares named after him, had no political base in Pakistan. A native of Ahmedabad, he had worked closely with Jinnah in the pre-Partition decade as president of the Bombay Muslim League. Mirza nominated him as prime minister after removing the combative veteran Bengali Prime Minister Suhrawardy. The new government, an unlikely combination of the Muslim League and the Republican Party, was weak from the outset. Brief though it was, Chundrigar stayed in office long enough to further widen the gulf between the eastern and western wings by reversing Suhrawardy's decision to distribute the lion's share of an American $10 million aid package to East Pakistani industrialists.

The veteran West Punjab politician Firoz Khan Noon headed the final ministry before the October 1958 coup. The rivalries between him and former Muslim League colleagues prevented cooperation, despite common landlord interests. The Byzantine goings-on in Karachi were positively gentlemanly, however, compared with the bear pit of the East Pakistan Assembly in Dacca. In a debate on 21 September, verbal assaults turned into blows, resulting in the death of the deputy speaker. This disgraceful episode provided a pretext for military intervention. More than four months earlier, Mirza and Ayub had separately conveyed to the US ambassador that "only a dictatorship would work in Pakistan."[25] The country's first experiment with democracy was terminated in the early hours of 8 October.

President Mirza survived a mere nineteen days, as the army, under Ayub Khan's command, was not prepared to take a junior role in the new authoritarian setup. The first strains in the Mirza-Ayub duumvirate emerged with the publication of contradictory statements regarding the timing of the lifting of martial law. The catalysts for Mirza's dismissal were his alleged meddling in army affairs and attempt to instigate a countercoup.[26] At around 10 PM on 27 October the startled president was summoned in his dressing gown to receive a delegation of generals, who informed him to leave Pakistan "in the interests of the country." The bridge-loving Mirza had played his final rubber. The ex-president and his Iranian wife Khanum Naheed were shunted into a London exile in indecent haste, even having to purchase their own airline tickets and secure their own passports.

Pakistan now entered a new era with Ayub Khan at the helm. This ushered in what some political scientists have termed a path of dependency that has been responsible for the country's thwarted democratization, military interventions, and post–military withdrawal crises.[27] Military rule also exacerbated the tensions between the eastern and western wings of the country, which culminated in the emergence of Bangladesh.

PART V

ELEVEN

Challenges to Nehruvian India

The period from 1964 until 1991 brought significant changes in eco-nomic policy and political practice from the foundational Nehruvian era. These changes pointed the way to further and even more profound transformations in India's political, social, and economic landscape in the twentieth century's closing decade. The break with Nehru's vision has not, however, been merely a straightforward repudiation by a resurgent Hindu right that had always opposed it. Congress oversaw many of the transforma-tions, from economic reform to the shift away from nonalignment or secu-larism. Indira Gandhi posed the greatest challenge to the parliamentary democracy espoused by her father. Before turning to this, we will examine the brief Shastri premiership, which followed Nehru's death.[1] Although it was tragically short-lived (9 June 1964–11 January 1966), it marked the first tentative steps away from the path laid out since independence.

Lal Bahadur Shastri was part of the Congress old guard who had made considerable personal sacrifices during the nationalist movement. He had spent nine years in jail. Short in stature and unassuming, he was nicknamed the Sparrow. He had loyally served as railways minister (1951–56) and home minister (1961–63). His hard work earned him Nehru's favor, but had come at the expense of a heart attack in October 1959.[2] When Nehru died, this modest son of UP, who had never traveled outside of South Asia, became the unanimous choice for prime minister of the "Syndicate"—regional Con-gress bosses headed by K. Kamaraj, chief minister of Madras. Just as later with Indira Gandhi, the Syndicate saw the elevation of an unassuming fig-ure as prime minister as the best means to establish a collective leadership.

Shastri confronted a worsening economic situation. Its immediate manifes-tations were a foreign-exchange problem and mounting military expenditure.

Longer-term problems arose from low agricultural productivity coupled with the lack of economic diversification. Most important, India lacked the export-led growth that at this juncture was propelling the Asian "tiger" economies. The growing Indian population was reliant on American-subsidized wheat shipments under the Food for Peace Program. By the time Shastri became prime minister, there was increasing aid "weariness" in Washington and skepticism about India's economic planning policy.[3] Shastri responded by modifying Nehru's economic strategy in a number of important respects. First, he gave a renewed influence to agriculture in the planning process following its earlier neglect. Second, he sought a technological, rather than institutional, solution to low productivity. Where Nehru had encouraged cooperative farming, Shastri turned to the Green Revolution to raise yields.[4] Within the period 1965–70, wheat production doubled, greatly increasing national food security. Punjab, because of its existing irrigational infrastructure, was seen as the best region to pilot the new "package" of improved seeds, fertilizers, and tractors. The Green Revolution brought rapid gains in wheat production, enabling the region to forge ahead. Later, rice was also developed as a Green Revolution crop. Not all regions and classes in Punjab shared in the agricultural bonanza.[5] The consequences of a "wheat whisky" culture were to be felt in the rise of a "fundamentalist" Sikh outlook, which spilled over into militancy a decade or so later.[6] Other regions of North India that shared in the Green Revolution, such as Haryana, saw the rise of "bullock capitalists," whose political assertiveness was rewarded by subsidized agricultural inputs, electrical power, easy credit, and low taxes.

Shastri further deviated from Nehru's policies when he accepted that the private sector and foreign investment should play larger economic roles. He also sought to reduce the influence of the Planning Commission in policy making. This was partly achieved by establishing a parallel National Planning Council in February 1965. Finally Shastri attempted to shift some decision making to the states. These moves presaged a number of the post-1991 economic reforms. Indira Gandhi and long-standing Nehruvians disapproved. Within three months of taking office, Shastri faced a no-confidence motion in the Lok Sabha. This did not deter him from attempting to chart a new course. Further evidence that he meant business was seen when he moved to increase the size of the Prime Minister's Office, to be headed by the high-ranking civil servant L. K. Jha.[7] Shortly afterward, in the wake of the first Chinese tests, Shastri initiated a modest nuclear-weapons program.[8]

These moves were largely unnoticed by the Indian voters. Shastri began to emerge from Nehru's shadow only with his leadership during the 1965 Pakistan War. On 6 September, Shastri decisively directed the Indian Army to advance toward Lahore (Operation Riddle) when the tide of battle was going in Pakistan's favor in Chhamb, Kashmir. Thereafter, Pakistan found itself on the back foot; with its stocks of ammunition running out, and faced with a US embargo, it had to reluctantly agree to a UN cease-fire on 22 September. The United States was happy to see the Soviet Union host peace talks. Dean Rusk, the secretary of state, reportedly offered "in a semi-joking way" all the paperwork the United States had built up in twenty years of trying to resolve the Kashmir issue.[9] Shastri traveled to Tashkent to attend the peace conference hosted by the Soviet Premier Alexi Kosygin. Triumph turned to tragedy when Shastri died of a heart attack in the early morning of 11 January, shortly after signing the Tashkent Agreement with Ayub Khan.[10] India faced a second succession crisis. The Syndicate now turned to the reserved Indira Gandhi, in the expectation that they could control her.

"Indira Is India"

Indira Gandhi has divided opinion in India as much as her populist contemporary Zulfiqar Ali Bhutto has done in Pakistan. Both leaders have received uncritical admiration and unremitting criticism.[11] In Bhutto's case opponents have focused on the loss of East Pakistan and the rigging of the 1977 elections. Critics of Mrs. Gandhi have highlighted her interrupting the democratic process through the proclamation of emergency in June 1975. The successes and failures of the two leaders need to be understood not simply in terms of personality traits, populism tinged with authoritarianism. We must also take account of the context of rapid socioeconomic change across the Subcontinent, and the profound shocks to the global economy as a result of the fourfold increase in oil prices by OPEC.

India's long 1970s, which began in 1969 and ended in 1984, were the period of Indira Gandhi's towering successes and greatest defeats, culminating in her violent death at the hands of her own Sikh bodyguards. In this period she shattered the old-style Congress, experimented with authoritarian rule, moved away from a nonaligned stance to develop close ties with the Soviet Union, and abandoned Shastri's halting steps toward economic liberalization in favor of state control. It was also during this period when Gandhi achieved her greatest success, via her astute response to the unrest in East Pakistan, which spilled over into civil war in 1971. That war occurred, as we shall see, against the backdrop of a mounting Maoist insurgency. The breakup of Pakistan not only decisively tipped the strategic balance in India's favor but cut short Islamabad's sponsorship of the Naga and Mizo insurgencies in the troubled northeastern periphery. The threat of a "foreign hand" there also prompted Gandhi's acquisition of Sikkim (1975), in a break with her father's policy.

Prithvi Nath Dhar, who headed the Prime Minister's Secretariat, provides an engaging if partisan account of Gandhi's role in the merger with India of the sparsely populated but strategically significant Himalayan Kingdom of Sikkim. Security briefings allowed her to follow closely the situation arising from the movement against its ruler, the Chogyal Palden Thondup Namgyal. Dhar also maintains that Gandhi believed that her father had blundered when he overruled Patel's desire to secure Sikkim's accession in 1947–48.[12] Despite the mounting pressures of the "J. P. Movement," she reversed the traditional policy in New Delhi of backing the chogyal in any conflict with the Sikkim State Congress, which represented the majority Nepali population. The chogyal was seen as an "undependable ally" when he sought greater autonomy in the wake of India's diminished prestige following the 1962 conflict with China. Activism against his rule increased with New Delhi's tacit support, culminating in the ending of the 333-year-old Namgyal dynasty when Sikkim became the twenty-second state of the Indian Union on 16 May 1975. Although this was not as dramatic a change to South Asia's political map as the emergence of Bangladesh, in Dhar's words it "closed a dangerous gap" in India's northern defenses.

Aside from the Pakistani threat, India faced an internal Maoist insurgency. In one sense its development was a legacy of the low economic growth rates that Nehru bequeathed. The disturbed conditions of the mid-1960s gave birth to what became known as the Naxalite movement. This Maoist peasant revolutionary movement began with the occupation of landlords' fields at Naxalbari in the Darjeeling hills of West Bengal. The initial support base among tribal Santhals was extended to the radical student population of Calcutta.[13] The original Naxalite movement had been repressed and driven underground by the mid-1970s, but it has recently emerged in a number of states, including Jharkhand, Odosha, Maharashtra, and Chattisgarh, each with hill tracts that provide ideal guerrilla terrain. Gandhi used the refugee influx into a West Bengal menaced by the Naxalites to justify military intervention in East Pakistan in 1971.

Before turning to the tumultuous events of the (1975–77) emergency period, it is necessary to frame them with the first years of Indira Gandhi's premiership, as the start of her tenure provides clues to her later willingness to break with democracy. Humiliation at the hands of the Syndicate and a bullish US President Johnson, who sought to use the renewal of the Food for Peace agreement as a means of economic leverage, undoubtedly influenced her metamorphosis. The two issues intersected following President Kamaraj's criticism of her devaluation of the rupee, which discouraged the anticipated flow of foreign aid. The 1967 general elections were consequently conducted in an atmosphere of economic frustration with inflation, uncertainty, and near-famine conditions in Bihar. While Congress retained power, with around 55 percent of the seats (compared with 73 percent in 1962), the one-party dominance was ended in the states. The DMK won a majority in Tamil Nadu; in Kerela the Communist-led United Front triumphed; and in Punjab the Akali Dal led a shaky coalition, which included dissident congressmen and the Hindu Jana Sangh. These electoral reversals would in any case have resulted in soul searching. Gandhi, however, used the defeat of the Congress old guard, including Kamaraj, to strengthen her grip on the party. She took it in a leftward and populist direction, announcing the nationalization of major commercial banks and a program of land reform. Ultimately this resulted in 1969 in a split, with the Syndicate leading the Congress (Organization). Gandhi's Congress now had to cling to national power with the support of the Communist Party of India and the Tamil nationalist DMK. Contemporary India's trend toward coalition politics and regional bases of power began at this time, although it was to be masked by the "Indira Wave" at the time of the 1971 parliamentary and state elections.

The 1971 polls marked the beginning of Gandhi's personalization of power, as she sought to bypass the traditional vote banks and the elites who delivered them. The simple populist slogan "Garibi Hatao"—Abolish poverty—was at the heart of her campaign. The delinking of parliamentary and state elections further assisted the turn away from old-style patronage politics. The four-party opposition alliance played into her hands by personalizing the campaign with the slogan "Indira Hatao," Abolish Indira.[14] Gandhi's striking success accelerated the process of offering herself as an "object of adulation, identification, and trust." In Dhar's words, "a personality cult evolved and a court came into existence."[15] Gandhi's diffidence was now transformed into a reputation for being secretive and haughty. This was undoubtedly accentuated by the "fact that she was a woman at the top of a male dominated society." Never one to engage in complicated arguments, she surrounded herself with yes men.[16] Her common sense compensated for this failing, and according to the head of her secretariat, she was "too mistrustful a person to have swallowed the flatterer's opinion entirely." Indeed, according to him, Indira Gandhi "knew more about the situation in the country during the Emergency than she was prepared to admit."[17]

The 1971 Lok Sabha polls reduced the Syndicate's Congress (Organization) to just 16 seats, while Gandhi, with 352, commanded a two-thirds majority. The Communist Party of India, confined to its West Bengal power base, was the second-largest party in Parliament, with just 25 seats. Indira Gandhi further consolidated her power in the March 1972 "khaki" state elections, which followed close on the heels of the crushing defeat of Pakistan and the emergence of Bangladesh. The Indira Wave swept across the states, engulfing its opponents. Gandhi's Congress captured 70 percent of the seats, even eclipsing its performance in the 1952 polls, when it still possessed the "glow of freedom." She was publicly hailed as the incarnation of the Goddess Durga.[18] Within three years, however, as popular movements swept Gujarat and Bihar and legal challenges mounted to her rule, Gandhi, without consulting any of her cabinet ministers, decided to proclaim an emergency.[19] Her father's legacy of parliamentary democracy faced its gravest challenge.

The Emergency

There are numerous accounts of the background to the imposition of emergency rule.[20] The sequence of events is laid out clearly in the first report of the Shah Commission following the Janata Party's assumption of power in 1977. These include the agitation led by veteran Gandhian Jayaprakash Narayan against the "corrupt" Congress governments in Gujarat and Bihar.[21] Narayan drew on a wide spectrum of support from the Communists to the RSS. His call for "total revolution" drew considerable support from students, especially in Gujarat, where they formed a "Nav Nirman Samiti" (reconstruction association) to spearhead the struggle.[22] In the face of the protests, the Gujarat Congress Government stepped down, and the state was placed under presidential rule.

To the old Gandhian weapon of *satyagraha*, Narayan added statewide strikes (*bandh*) and the *gherao*, or surrounding by crowds of administrative buildings or factories. The gherao had become a feature of strikes since the late 1960s.[23] The protest movements in Gujarat and Bihar occurred against a backdrop of food shortages and inflation that had both global (world energy crisis) and domestic roots. Narayan's campaign, which claimed the moral high ground, followed hard on the heels of a three-week-long nationwide strike in May 1974 against India's largest public sector undertaking, the railways. They employed nearly 1.5 million workers at the time. The army had to be called in to man key installations. The photograph of a defiant George Fernandes, head of the All India Railwaymen's Federation, with a raised shackled fist later became one of the iconic photographs of the emergency period.

Those who at least initially approved the proclamation of the emergency claimed that India was becoming "ungovernable" and that it was time for "discipline." Explanations that focus on Gandhi's authoritarian traits emphasize the personal slights arising from legal action against her and the humiliating Congress defeat in the 1975 Gujarat State elections.

The Gujarat polls had been supportive of a threatened "fast unto death" by the opposition leader Moraji Desai. The Congress defeat at the hands of a combined opposition was in many respects a dress rehearsal for the 1977 national polls. Gandhi had campaigned actively but to no avail.[24] An even greater personal blow was the Allahabad High Court judgment that she had been guilty of electioneering violations during her contest at Rai Bareilly in 1971 against the Socialist Party candidate Raj Narain. Gandhi appealed to the Supreme Court against her disqualification, which would not only force her to step down as prime minister but bar her from elective office for six years.

Dhar provides a gripping account of the tense period after the Court judgment and reveals the influence of her younger son Sanjay to resist resignation over "minor" legal technical irregularities.[25] Gandhi's agonizing was ended by the Supreme Court ruling, which granted her only a conditional rather than an absolute stay of the Allahabad judgment. This meant that she could continue as prime minister but could not vote or participate in parliamentary proceedings. The formal declaration of the emergency by President Fakhruddin Ali Ahmed was preceded by the arrest of leading opposition figures under the terms of the Maintenance of Internal Security Act. They included Jayaprakash Narain, Moraji Desai, and Raj Narain. Opinion remains divided as to whether Gandhi sought primarily to save herself or to bring the country back from the brink of chaos. Whatever her motives, this was the biggest challenge yet to her father's faith in parliamentary democracy and the rule of law.

Gandhi publicly justified the emergency in terms of the need for order and discipline to build a new India. During its early months inflation abated and trains ran on time. The press was curbed. Political dissent was contained by the arrest of leading figures and the banning of such organizations as the RSS and Jamaat-i-Islami. Nonetheless, Gandhi allowed back-channel approaches to opposition figures, most notably Jayaprakash Naryan. Sanjay Gandhi and other "radical" congressmen, however, disapproved of such overtures. They favored a prolonged period of emergency rule as the prelude to the establishment of a new constitution, which would jettison Westminster-style democracy.

Gandhi introduced the Twenty-Point Program within five days of the emergency, in order to provide the declaration "with some legitimate political and social purpose." The Program promised land reform and new minimum agricultural wages for the rural population. It also offered tax relief and price reductions for the urban population. Some progress was also made in the implementation of land reform, but these emergency "gains" were outweighed by the "losses" arising from its excesses.

The emergency's excesses are linked with the pet projects of Sanjay Gandhi, who became an increasingly powerful figure. His mother loyally supported her younger son and earmarked him as her successor. Sanjay built up his own power base in the Youth Congress. He also secured influential ministerial allies, including Bansi Lal, who had been moved to Delhi as defense minister from his post as chief minister of Haryana, and Om Mehta, minister of state in the Home Ministry. Sanjay took a particular interest in family planning and slum clearance. Indeed, he personally supervised demolition work in Delhi, including the razing of squatter settlements around the Jama Masjid. Family planning had pride of place in his Five-Point Program. Whether he was "beautifying" Delhi or limiting families to two children, his "lumpen bourgeois" sentiment was that the poor, not poverty, were the problem. The government's vasectomy program was increasingly driven by attempts to meet quotas by rounding up minorities and poorer classes for forcible sterilization. The program was pursued most vigorously in Delhi, which had become Sanjay's personal fiefdom through his influence over its new lieutenant governor, Kishen Chand. It was also active in north Indian states like Haryana, Bihar, and UP, "where chief ministers were anxious to do his bidding."[26] Police firing on an antivasectomy riot by the Muslim population of Turkoman Gate, Delhi, came to symbolize the emergency's excesses. Gandhi initially maintained that claims of compulsion were "baseless" but later became privately uneasy about the human and political costs involved. Dhar raises the intriguing possibility that she called for early elections in 1977 not because of a miscalculation but because she was disquieted by the "arbitrary power" wielded by some of Sanjay's supporters.[27]

A number of novels provide insights into the prevailing atmosphere of fear and repression. The Parsi novelist Rohinton Mistry reveals the horrors of forced sterilization through the characters of the tailors Ishvar Darji and Omprakash Darji in his melodrama, A *Fine Balance*.[28] Ishvar becomes infected after his sterilization and has to have his legs amputated. Omprakash is castrated by the medical staff at the behest of a local landlord who has been put in charge of the Congress sterilization program and has an old score to settle. The protagonist Saleem Sinai in Salman Rushdie's *Midnight's Children* also suffers the fate of sterilization, and like the tailors has his home destroyed as part of a "beautification" program.[29] Nayantara Saghal's work *Rich Like Us* similarly includes the emergency period in its historical sweep and emphasizes the now-conventional historical understanding that the poorest classes and castes were the victims of the sterilization program.[30] Shortly after the end of the emergency, Rahi Masoom Raza produced a searing indictment in his Urdu novel *Katraa Bi Arzoo*.[31] This work, which has since been translated into Hindi but not yet into English, is set in a locality of Allahabad and examines the impact of the emergency both on the poor and on the protagonist Desh, who initially resists its repression but is ultimately crushed by it.

The 1977 Parliamentary Elections

Indira Gandhi's decision to call elections, which had been twice postponed, inspired almost as much surprise as the emergency proclamation. The opposition parties (Congress [Organization], Socialist, Jana Sangh, Bharatiya Lok Dal) united as what became known as the Janata Front.[32] This in itself would have made it difficult for Congress, which had always profited from a divided opposition vote. Gandhi's challenge further increased when Jagjivan Ram, the most prominent Untouchable in Indian politics, resigned from the Congress government and founded the short-lived Congress for Democracy. He was joined by two other "defectors," H. N. Bahuguna, the former chief minister of UP, and Nandini Satpathy, whom Sanjay had ousted as chief minister of Orissa. The Congress for Democracy agreed to campaign with the Janata Front. It garnered further regional allies in the DMK in Tamil Nadu and the Akali Dal in Punjab and finally entered an alliance with the Communist Party (Marxist). Congress allied with a rival Tamil Party (All-India Anna DMK) and with the mainstream Moscow-oriented Communist Party of India, which had defended the imposition of the emergency.[33] The disparate character of the Janata-led opposition was to undermine its prospects in government. However, its electoral platform to "revive democracy" was a rallying call to voters. Moreover, Congress found that it could no longer rely on its traditional Muslim and Untouchable voters because of their victimization during the sterilization campaign.

Sanjay and Indira suffered personal defeats, the latter humiliatingly at the hands of Raj Narain. Stunned and "forlorn," Gandhi remained silent when an angry Rajiv told his mother that his younger brother Sanjay had brought her "to this pass."[34] She remained protective as cases were brought against him. Just a month before Sanjay's death following a failed air stunt, near Safdarjung Airport, he had been made secretary general of the Congress Party. The accident in June 1980 led the reluctant Rajiv to assume the mantle of the Nehru political dynasty. His Italian-born wife, Sonia, who had been working as a waitress in Cambridge when they first met some fifteen years earlier, had supported Rajiv's desire to stay away from politics.

The 1977 polls reduced the Congress to just 154 seats in the 542-member Parliament. Janata and its allies captured 330 constituencies. For the first time since independence, Congress had lost a national election. Its percentage of the popular vote, 34.5 percent, was well below the previous weakest performance in 1967, when it had captured 40.7 percent of the votes. The fractious Janata government was to allow Gandhi to stage what in March 1977 appeared to be an unlikely comeback. Nonetheless, the elections marked a further stage in both the rise of the backward caste farmers in North India (exemplified by Charan Singh's prominence) and the regionalization of Indian politics.[35] This was reflected in the Congress's own performance. It had captured just a handful of seats in the Hindi heartland. It survived as a powerful player in South India in part because the Janata Front was seen as a northern pro-Hindi movement, and also because it had popular local allies, or powerful chief ministers as in Karnataka and Andhra Pradesh.[36]

The Janata Interlude

The Janata Government was riven from the outset by factional dissent. Jagjivam Ram, the candidate of the left, was passed over as prime minister in favor of the octogenarian Moraji Desai, who was more acceptable to the right-wing Jana Sangh. Desai, who was austere and puritanical, gained a certain amount of Western notoriety because he attributed his longevity to drinking his own urine. Raj Narain, however, was the real joker in the pack. Despite his buffoonery, his victory over Gandhi ensured a ministerial appointment. The government sought to reverse the Congress's authoritarianism (press freedom was restored) and its economic and foreign-policy approaches. In an attempt to go back to the future, nonalignment was favored over the closer ties Gandhi had established with the Soviet Union. Rural development and industry more labor intensive than capital intensive were encouraged, although this did not amount to the trumpeted "Gandhian alternative." Despite the election of individual candidates ideologically committed to free enterprise, the coalition remained dependent on the classes in both town and countryside that had benefited from the land reforms of the mid-1950s, a culture of subsidy, and the operations of the "licence permit Raj." Symptomatic of the new power of the North Indian peasantry was the establishment in January 1979 of a commission headed by the Bihari Bindeshwari Prasad Mandal to consider the extension of reservations for government employment for the "intermediate castes" or "other backward classes" (OBCs). But the Janata government had fallen before the report could be implemented.

It was not the government's failure to break with the past, however, so much as increasing inflation and communalism that sapped its popularity. There were also mounting corruption scandals, which swirled around Moraji Desai's son Kanti. The public soon lost interest in the cases and in inquiries into Gandhi's conduct, which expended much time and energy. Ultimately, rather than discrediting Gandhi, they helped rehabilitate her, making her seem to be a persecuted victim. A brief period in prison further increased her air of martyrdom. Nonetheless, her comeback was by no means straightforward. There was a split between those congressmen (led by former ministers Y. B. Chavan and Swaran Singh) who repudiated the emergency and those who remained loyal to her in the party that was now known as Congress (I). The Congress rebellion could have proved fatal. In the event the Janata government's disunity and incompetence provided Gandhi with the chance of a second coming.

Moraji Desai stepped down from office amid growing disaffection. Nonetheless, he did all in his power to prevent Jagjivan Ram from succeeding him. Charan Singh, who was concerned by the growing Hindu nationalist Jana Sangh influence, quit the Janata Party to form a rival Janata (Secular) Party. In July 1979 he cobbled together a weak coalition government opposed by many of his former colleagues. It was, paradoxically, propped up by the outside support of the Congress (I), led by Gandhi, who had jailed him during the emergency. Charan Singh survived for just twenty-four days, as Gandhi withdrew her support when he refused to drop the legal cases against her.

Indira Gandhi's Second Coming

The 1980 polls restored Indira Gandhi to power. The Congress's resurgence in North India did not, however, presage a decline in the growing political influence of the rural lower-caste groups. Rather, it demonstrated that Congress in propitious circumstances could splinter its vote.[37] Gandhi seemed to have learned little from the emergency era. She continued to see centralization as the means to stability. This further deinstitutionalized the Congress and weakened Indian federalism. Constant recourse to Article 356 of the Constitution to dismiss state governments was accompanied by neglect of regional Congress Party organizations. In such circumstances, new, powerful regional rivals emerged alongside the long-standing Akali and DMK, AIDMK parties in the form of the Telegu Desam Party in Andhra Pradesh. Like the AIDMK, this was led by a charismatic film actor (N. T. Rama Rao).[38]

In the aftermath of Gandhi's emergency, the political climate encouraged the rise not only of regional and caste-based politics but of communalism. The Jana Sangh and RSS had strengthened their presence as a result of their opposition to her authoritarianism. Jana Sangh was an important element in the Janata Front. Communal conflict had never entirely disappeared, even in the Nehruvian era. It was to intensify in the 1980s as a result of a number of factors, including the Congress's organizational decline; exploitation by the Jana Sangh's successor, the Bharatiya Janata Party, of upper-caste anxieties arising from not only Muslim assertion, but that of the lower castes; the "utility" of conflict for consolidation of vote banks; and the impact of Islamization in neighboring Pakistan.[39] Gandhi encouraged the mounting tide of communal mobilization through her involvement in the Punjab crisis. This was to cost her life and to leave long-lasting scars in the Green Revolution heartland state. Gandhi's role remains controversial. It is best understood in terms of her wider intolerance of non-Congress state governments and her political opportunism; resistance to a Sikh "threat" in Punjab was seen as a useful means to undercut the rising power of the Hindu Right in North India.

Gandhi ousted the Punjab's Akali-Janata coalition, led by Parkash Singh Badal, just as she did other non-Congress state governments. In a further effort to undermine the Akali Dal, she encouraged the charismatic "neo-fundamentalist" preacher Jarnail Singh Bhindranwale, who had risen to prominence following clashes with the heterodox Nirankari sect in 1978.[40] Bhindranwale also drew on the All-India Sikh Students' Federation for support. Simultaneously Gandhi cultivated Hindu voters by exaggerating the threats posed by the Akalis' moderate demands for greater Punjabi autonomy, which had been raised in the 1973 Anandpur Sahib Resolution.

The Akalis turned to civil disobedience when their negotiations with Gandhi stalled. These were undermined by police harassment of Sikhs entering Delhi at the time of the November 1982 Asian Games. Civil disobedience ran parallel to an increasingly violent campaign by Bhindranwale, who took sanctuary in the Golden Temple Amritsar. At his daily congregations, he dispensed justice, issued statements on religious and political matters, and granted interviews to foreign journalists. He rapidly converted the Akal Takht—a shrine representing the temporal power of God—into an armory. Although he was publicly ambivalent toward the demand for a separate Sikh state of Khalistan, which had been supported by a splinter group of the Akali Dal since 1981, it was clear that Bhindranwale espoused the need to achieve sovereign authority for the khalsa.

Operation Bluestar, the seriously bungled army action against the Golden Temple in June 1984, resulted in Bhindranwale's death. Sikhs around the world were outraged by the physical destruction and the civilian casualties that resulted from the fierce fighting.[41] On 31 October 1984, Indira Gandhi was assassinated by two of her Sikh bodyguards. The Punjab crisis continued for another ten years of militant struggle. The Sikh community was also faced with the further tragedy of a four-day pogrom in Delhi in the wake of Gandhi's assassination; two thousand people died in the anti-Sikh riots.[42]

Gandhi's death lowered the curtain on a tumultuous era. This was a period in which India, rather than pursuing a different political and economic trajectory from those of its Pakistani and Bangladeshi neighbors, relied on a similar mix of populism, nationalization, and charismatic power, which turned authoritarian. India's democratic "exceptionalism" appeared to have vanished. Indira Gandhi, like the two other South Asian populist leaders, Zulfiqar Ali Bhutto and Sheikh Mujibur Rahman, met an untimely death. Her untried son Rajiv was unable to arrest the long-term Congress decline as Indian politics developed further along caste and regional lines. His halting economic reforms proved incapable of heading off the 1991 fiscal crisis. This, as we shall see, resulted in a decisive break with the economic policies inherited from Jawaharlal Nehru.

TWELVE

Pakistan's National Crisis and the Birth of Bangladesh

The Indian and Pakistani states have experienced violent ethnic and ethnonationalist movements, which have claimed the lives of hundreds of thousands of militants, members of the security services, and civilians caught in the cross-fire. The emergence of Bangladesh in 1971, however, has been the only successful secessionist movement on the postcolonial Subcontinent. Some writers have seen the "geographical absurdity" of the separation of the western and eastern wings of Pakistan and the existence of a strongly defined Bengali collective consciousness as making the creation of Bangladesh inevitable. The reality was far less clear-cut. In this chapter I argue that the breakup of Pakistan was not a foregone conclusion. It resulted from the failure to accommodate Bengali demands for greater autonomy, which the West Pakistan establishment treated as illegitimate. Nation building was premised on a coercive centralization rather than the recognition of pluralism. A united Pakistan could have survived, but it would have been a very different state from that conceived by the West Pakistan power holders.

In this chapter we shall examine the key events and turning points that led to the disastrous military intervention of Operation Searchlight on 25 March 1971. The operation ended nine months later with the humiliating surrender of Pakistani forces in Dhaka after a fourteen-day war with India. The immediate circumstances that led to the political breakup still remain fiercely contested.[1] Controversies surrounding the Pakistani government's long-standing denial of charges of genocide have been exacerbated by the publication of Sarmila Bose's provocatively revisionist work.[2]

Legacies of the Freedom Struggle for the Future of East Pakistan

The leading Bangladeshi historian Harun-or-Rashid has pointed to a number of features of the Pakistani struggle that "foreshadowed" postindependence problems in national consolidation. He points, for example, to the marginalization of Bengali influence within the Muslim League Council and Working Committee. He also links activists' hopes of a future sovereign eastern Pakistan within a Pakistan confederation to the 1940 Lahore Resolution's ambiguous reference to Muslim states.[3] I have mentioned briefly the political and cultural tensions between the Bengali- and Urdu-speaking Muslim elites; here we will look in more detail at this important legacy from the freedom movement.

The Urdu-speaking business classes of Calcutta, along with the landholding Khawajas of Dacca, were wedded to Jinnah's conception of an East Pakistan zone in a single Pakistani state. They also subscribed to the belief expressed as early as July 1933 by the All-Bengal Urdu association that "Bengali is a Hinduized and Sanskritized language" and that "in the interests of the Muslims themselves it is necessary to have one language which cannot but be Urdu."[4] Herein lay the roots of the damaging postindependence language dispute. The East Pakistan Renaissance Society was founded in 1942 to counter this pro-Urdu stance. Its public pronouncements increasingly contradicted the Muslim League's official ideology. At its May 1944 meeting, President Abul Mansur Ahmed, a journalist-cum–politician, declared that Bengali Muslims were different not only from Hindus but from other Indian Muslims. "Religion and culture are not the same thing," he maintained. "Religion transgresses the geographical boundary, but *tamaddum* [culture] cannot go beyond the geographical boundary. . . . Here . . . lies the differences between *Purba* [East] Pakistan and Pakistan. For this reason the people of Purba Pakistan are a different nation from the people of the other provinces of India and from the "religious brothers" of Pakistan.[5]

Political and cultural tensions between the Bengali- and Urdu-speaking elites did not hinder the Muslim League's advance because it rested on the almost millenarian hopes of the poor that the creation of Pakistan would transform their conditions. Although nearly 90 percent of Bengali Muslims were ineligible to vote in the 1946 provincial elections, crowds turned out in large numbers to greet the League's candidates. The party won 104 of 111 seats in the rural areas. Independence and Partition, however, cut away the ground from the West Bengal leadership of the "progressive" Hashim-Suhrawardy group. Khawaja Nazimuddin, who had Jinnah's ear and was committed to a one-nation, one-culture policy, returned to the limelight as prime minister.

The Language Movement and the Collapse of the Muslim League in East Pakistan

Urdu became the state-sponsored language of Pakistan, despite the fact that Bengali was the mother tongue of more than half the state's population, and within East Pakistan itself, only around 1 percent of the population regarded Urdu as their first language. From March until September 1948, students in Dhaka led a widespread popular movement in favor of Bengali. Among those arrested was Sheikh Mujibur Rahman, the future leader of Bangladesh. The language movement reemerged early in 1952 following the publication of the interim report on the constitution which declared Urdu as the state language. The death of four student protestors at Dhaka University led to the erection of a memorial, Shahid Minar, and the annual commemoration of their death on 21 February.

The center's "Pakistanization" program was continuously counterproductive. In July 1948 popular protests forced the director of broadcasting to end the highly unpopular practice of introducing Arabic and Persian words and phrases into the Bengali news bulletins of Radio Pakistan Dhaka.[6] The protracted constitution-making process kept disputes over language and the economy on the boil. Bengali counterproposals to the center were increasingly articulated by the Awami League, led by the veteran Suhrawardy after its foundation in 1950. The opposition parties, including the octogenarian Fazlul Haq's Krishak Sramik Party, coalesced with the Awami League. Huq's still formidable oratorical skills propelled him to the forefront of the opposition United Front formed to contest the 1954 provincial elections; its institutional backbone was provided by Suhrawardy's Awami League.[7]

The United Front campaigned on a twenty-one-point manifesto, which called for the regional devolution of all powers except defense, foreign affairs, and currency control. It also promised "fair" agricultural prices and the elimination of income disparities among white-collar workers. Such demands addressed the rising inflation that had followed the collapse of the Korean War boom. Finally, by calling for the nationalization of the jute industry the manifesto attacked the leading symbol of East Bengal's "colonial" status. The manifesto was presented to the people as a "charter of freedom." All later opposition programs were merely shorter versions of this seminal document.[8]

The Muslim League's close identification with the center resulted in a humiliating defeat. In comparison to its meager haul of 10 seats, the United Front captured 223, winning more than 65 percent of the total vote.[9] Haq, however, was dismissed within a month of taking office, charged with pro-Communist and pro-India leadings. He split within a year from the Awami League and ended his career as governor of East Pakistan. Nonetheless, the Muslim League failed to make up lost ground in an increasingly acrimonious and chaotic political environment.

Pakistan's First Military Dictatorship and the Consequences for National Integration

Ayub Khan reintroduced colonial ideas of political tutelage through indirect elections and official nomination of representatives. His distrust of the political class resembled Curzon's. He famously asserted that democracy was not suited to the "genius of the people." As in the colonial era, the elite civil service formed the backbone of a system of governance that privileged administration over popular participation. At the union council and committee level of the Basic Democracies scheme that Ayub promulgated in 1959, the government could nominate up to one-third of the members.[10] A report on the workings of the Basic Democracies revealed that government officials initiated 85 percent of the agenda items at union council meetings.[11] The eighty thousand Basic Democrats collectively formed the Electoral College, which affirmed Ayub as president in January 1960. Following the introduction of the 1962 Constitution, the Basic Democrats were also the electorate for the national and provincial assemblies. The indirect elections in 1962 were held on a "partyless" basis. This further entrenched the power of local elites. It was only after July 1962 that Ayub reluctantly legalized party organization. Even then the political system bore his imprint, in that the Convention Muslim League emerged as a pro-regime party, with Ayub as its president beginning in December 1963.

Ayub further clipped the politicians' wings by the introduction in 1959 of the Public Offices Disqualification Order (PODO) and the Elective Bodies Disqualification Order (EBDO). These established the concept of "accountability"—in theory to root out corruption, in practice to hamstring political opponents. Politicians who were indicted could either be tried by a tribunal or voluntarily "withdraw" from public life. Well over four hundred politicians were disqualified by EBDO.[12] Muhammad Waseem has maintained that EBDO was one of Ayub's strongest weapons of depoliticization. Its stifling of meaningful opposition explains his longevity in power.[13] Maulana Bhashani, Hamidul Huq Chowdhury, and Sheikh Mujibur Rahman were all influential Bengali leaders who were disqualified. Students renewed protests in Dhaka in late January 1962 when Suhrawady was arrested. The Punjab regiment had to be dispatched to bring peace to the campus. Ayub, who was in Dhaka to chair a governor's conference, was virtually imprisoned in the President's House for the last three days of his visit.[14]

The Pakistani president used the media to malign the politicians and later, without much success, to trumpet the achievements of his regime. He promulgated the Press and Publications Ordinance in 1963 to "make the press conform to recognized principles of journalism and patriotism."[15] News management was further enhanced the following year with the establishment of the supposedly independent National Press Trust. It acquired ownership of such former radical papers as the *Pakistan Times* and turned them into government mouthpieces. The press and the wider nation-building process suffered in the long run. The National Press Trust was dismantled only in 1996.

The stifling of democracy had an especially pernicious impact in East Pakistan. Bengalis were grossly underrepresented in the powerful army and bureaucracy. This reflected both the region's continuing educational and economic underdevelopment and the dominant "martial races" approach to army recruitment. Official figures confirm that Bengalis provided just 5 percent of the Army Officer Corps and around 30 percent of the elite civil service cadre. Bengalis were also marginalized in the numerous commissions of inquiry into such varied fields as land reform, franchise, constitutional recommendations, and the press, accounting for just 75 of the 280 members. None of the president's key aides was from Bengal. He thus "had no one around to advise him adequately or intelligently." The lack of expert advice was compounded by the fact that, as a high-ranking army officer informed the American consul general in January 1963, "East Pakistanis in the Cabinet are men of no particular stature and competence and are only trying to please Ayub and say what they think he might like to hear."[16]

In a classic case of too little too late, the civil service recruitment system was changed, so that ten of the sixteen probationers for entry to the central secretariat in 1968 were drawn from East Pakistan. By this stage, however, there was mounting unrest throughout Pakistan. Ayub's star had begun to wane following the ill-advised launching of Operation Gibraltar (1965) in an attempt to wrest Kashmir from India.[17] He had been encouraged by his brash young foreign minister Zulfiqar Ali Bhutto.[18] Bhutto was to form the Pakistan People's Party (PPP) in November 1967 to coordinate the growing campaign against Ayub.[19] The Pakistani public had been fed a diet of victory reports during the conflict, so were stunned when the Soviet Union acted as an honest broker in sponsoring a cease-fire that restored the status quo ante bellum. Students and Kashmiri migrants rioted in Lahore when the Tashkent Declaration of 10 January 1966 revealed the extent of Ayub's "surrender." A photograph of a somber Ayub lifting the coffin of the Indian Prime Minister Lal Bahadur Shastri onto an airplane following his sudden death at Tashkent the next day created further outrage.[20] The British high commissioner noted the general sentiment that "Ayub had betrayed the nation and inexcusably lost face to Indians."[21]

The 1965 war not only led to the rise of the populist PPP but left a legacy of anti-Americanism and the army's engagement with jihadist groups.[22] It also exacerbated the tensions between the two wings of Pakistan. East

Pakistan's sense of defenselessness led to demands for the first time for the creation of a separate militia or paramilitary force.

Ayub continued the policies of cultural integration pursued by his civilian predecessors. We shall turn first to their impact in Sindh before considering in more depth their consequences for East Bengal. The 1959 Report on National Education emphasized the importance of Urdu for national integration in both provinces, with predictable counterproductive consequences. In Sindh, there were widespread protests at the decision to introduce Urdu as a medium of instruction from Class Six upward. Ayub eventually backed down, but the closure of a number of Sindhi medium schools was seized on by linguistic nationalists. They claimed that Sindhi radio broadcasts were being reduced and that government advertising revenue was being denied to Sindhi publications. Further disputes followed in 1965, when the Municipal Corporation in Hyderabad, where there was a large Mohajir (North Indian refugee) population, made Urdu its working language. The following year, there was a dispute at the local university over the language of instruction and examination. The arrest of Sindhi-language activists by the Urdu-speaking commissioner for Hyderabad Division, Masroor Hasan Khan, further alienated Sindhis from Ayub's regime.[23]

In Bengal, the official aim was to deemphasize the distinctiveness of Bengali by bringing it closer to Urdu "by increasing the common element in their vocabularies and by putting such common elements to extensive use."[24] In this atmosphere, the center played down the centenary celebrations of the great Bengali poet Rabindranath Tagore in 1961. It later banned the broadcasting of his poetry. Activists retaliated by changing street names and nameplates from Urdu to Bengali throughout Dhaka.

Modernization was the third element of Ayub's vision for Pakistan, alongside depoliticization and centralization. This was physically expressed in the construction of a new federal capital of Islamabad, deep in the Punjab beside the Margalla Hills (conveniently close to army headquarters in Rawalpindi). The social expression was the Muslim Family Laws Ordinance, which was promulgated on 15 July 1961. Its establishment of an Arbitration Council to resolve issues such as divorce and polygamous marriages was regarded as "un-Islamic" by the ulema. While Ayub refused to budge on this issue, the ulema was more successful in getting him to reinstate the title of "Islamic," which had been dropped from the title of the Republic of Pakistan in the 1962 Constitution. Modernization was economically expressed with the introduction of land reforms in 1959. They had a limited impact because of their high ceilings and numerous irregularities and loopholes. Ultimately, Ayub's land reforms were used to penalize opponents rather than to abolish "feudalism."

Rapid economic growth was to be the cornerstone of a "modern" Pakistan. In an echo of Nehru's approach, Ayub assumed the chairmanship of the Planning Commission in 1961. The emphasis on private sector–led development, however, starkly contrasted with India's approach. It delivered higher rates of growth than those achieved by its neighbor, an average of 5.5 percent during the Ayub era, but it strained national cohesion. Wealth became highly concentrated, and economic growth exacerbated the existing east-west disparities. The Planning Commission, which played a key role in coordinating the state's import substitution and export promotion policies, was assisted by the Development Advisory Service of Harvard University. In a real sense, therefore, Pakistan was a laboratory for modernization theory's prescription for a "takeoff" into sustained economic growth through massive infusions of capital to industry and the establishment of a cultural, political, and economic environment conducive to the release of entrepreneurial energies.

Ayub's vaunted "development decade" saw a staggering concentration of capital in the hands of Gujarati-speaking Khojas and Memons, leavened with a sprinkling of Punjabi Chiniotis. Absolute poverty increased, despite high growth rates. The regime was to reap the whirlwind of growing social tensions and regional conflicts. Disenchantment intensified as the 1965 war dampened growth. Throughout the Ayub era, economic growth proceeded more slowly in East than in West Pakistan. Most of the rapidly expanding private businesses were based in the west. Their owners were reluctant, on climatic, cultural, and infrastructural grounds, to set up in the East. They benefited from tax breaks and easy credit supplied by the Industrial Development Bank of Pakistan and the Pakistan Industrial and Credit and Investment Corporation (PICIC). In the five years beginning in 1961–62, only around a fifth of PICIC loans went to East Pakistani entrepreneurs.[25] Ayub, it is true, stepped up public sector investment in East Pakistan, but this could not keep pace with the private sector advances in urban Sindh and Punjab. Moreover, the profits from the army-run Fauji Foundation's rice, flour, and jute mills in East Pakistan were reinvested in welfare projects for servicemen in the main Punjab recruitment areas.[26] This naturally fueled claims of the "Punjabization" of Pakistan.

The Awami League's demands for regional autonomy reflected the existence of two distinct economies with different needs and requirements. A six-point program in May 1966 called for East Pakistan to raise its own taxes, mint its own currency, and operate its own foreign exchange account. The center was left only with responsibility for defense and foreign affairs. Ayub attempted to haul in the Awami League by involving its leader Sheikh Mujibur Rahman in what became known as the Agartala conspiracy case. The charges brought in an open court that he and fifty or so other codefendants had sought Indian aid to secede provided the perfect platform to expound Bengali regionalist views. Mujib had indeed met Indian officials in the capital of Tripura, but the prosecution's bungling put Ayub on the back foot. Mounting evidence of torture cast Mujib and his codefendants as martyrs. Popular hostility peaked when one of the defendants, Sergeant Zahurul Haq, was murdered while in custody. The case was eventually dropped, to Ayub's acute embarrassment. Mujib was included in talks to the backdrop of mounting disturbances. They contributed to Ayub's resignation on 25 March 1969. But his successor, the army commander in chief Yahya Khan, failed to profit from the lesson that it was better to co-opt Bengali aspirations than to confront them.

The 1970 Elections and Their Aftermath

Yahya Khan allowed Pakistan's first national elections to take place in December 1970. Nearly a quarter of a century had elapsed since independence, and a whole generation had grown up without an opportunity to choose the national government. The polls showed the abandonment of the principle of parity between the two wings in the National Assembly, giving East

Pakistan its long-denied demographic majority (162 of 300 members). This move represented a considerable gamble on Yahya Khan's behalf, as the 1958 coup had been prompted precisely by the desire to preempt a Bengali democratic challenge to the establishment's economic and foreign policy interests.

Yahya was no khaki democrat. This decision was one of a number of costly miscalculations and blunders. These have been linked by critics to his alcohol-induced befuddlement. More important, he lacked political acumen and a vision for the country. After his first broadcast to the nation, Yahya reportedly "sat down holding his head in dismay . . . woefully remark[ing], 'What should we do now?' "[27] He did make some provision to safeguard the constitutional outcome of the election through the promulgation of the Legal Framework Order (LFO) on 30 March 1970. It set a deadline of 120 days for the framing of a constitution by the National Assembly and reserved to the president the right to authenticate it. This could not prevent a deadlock, however, when the Awami League secured a landslide victory, an outcome that Yahya had resolutely discounted from the time in November 1969 when he had promised to hold direct elections.

Yahya was not entirely to blame, as he was badly misled by the intelligence agencies, which, a week before the Awami League landslide, were projecting that it would win no more than eighty seats. This misreading of the outcome resulted in part from an overestimation of the Islamic parties' impact. In West Pakistan they were eclipsed by Bhutto's populism, epitomized by the ringing slogan "Roti, Kapra, aur Makan": food, clothes, and shelter. In the East, Sheikh Mujibur Rahman campaigned on the regionalist six-point program. The Pakistan establishment also had high hopes for the fortunes of the Muslim League, which had been formed by the former chief minister of the NWFP, Abdul Qayyum Khan. It allegedly received an election war chest of four million rupees from the spy masters. It failed miserably, despite having been projected to win as many as seventy seats.[28]

The elections were delayed by the terrible cyclone disaster of November 1970, which claimed up to a million victims. The government's response to this massive human tragedy became a political football between the Awami League and the establishment. The slow official response summed up for many a long-term callous indifference to Bengali interests. The Awami League portrayed the candidates of parties from the western wing as descendants of Mir Jaffar, whose traitorous action had secured Clive's pivotal victory at Plassey. A more recent historical connection was made through the use of the slogan "Shonar Bangla," Golden Bengal, taken from a song by Rabindranath Tagore, evoking love for the Bengal Motherland. Rallies of rival parties were broken up by crowds chanting "Joy Bangla," Victory to Bengal.[29]

Iftikhar Ahmad and J. K. Bashir have provided detailed studies of the 1970 elections.[30] Their headline features were the Awami League landslide in the East, where it won 160 of 162 seats, and Bhutto's breakthrough in West Pakistan, where he captured 81 of 140 seats at the expense of the Muslim League and religious parties. The long-established political cleavages between East and West Pakistan were laid bare. No party had seats in both wings of Pakistan. The Bengalis had responded to years of exclusion by projecting to power a party that stood diametrically opposed to the interests of the West Pakistani civil-military establishment. The latter had expected to play a mediating role among a large number of equally balanced parties. Pakistan's future now rested on the complex negotiations that were to be held between Bhutto, Mujib, and Yahya.

Conflict, War, and the Independence of Bangladesh

Failed negotiations and a sense of impending crisis marked the period from the elections to the launching of a military crackdown on 25 March 1971. The meeting of the National Assembly was increasingly delayed. Mistrust hindered compromise. The first meeting between Mujib and Yahya, for example, had to take place in the bathroom off the main bedroom in the president's house, as the Awami League leader would not hold discussions in the drawing room in case it was bugged. The conflicting visions of the main protagonists also hindered accommodation. Bhutto's decision to stay away from the National Assembly strengthened the hand of those who wished to postpone it. Popular pressures for independence became almost uncontrollable when Yahya, against advice, announced on 1 March the postponement of the National Assembly. Days of clashes between troops and protestors led him to backtrack, but at a mass rally at the Ramna Race Course on 7 March, Mujib raised the bar for the Awami League's participation, while falling short of declaring independence.

Both Yahya and Bhutto made a final visit to Dhaka, but this bid to maintain Pakistan's integrity has been likened to "giving oxygen to a dying patient when the doctors have declared him a lost cause."[31] By teatime on 23 March the army command had recommended that military action was essential. Even as the 1940 Lahore Resolution was commemorated, student militias paraded with the Bangladesh flag. This may explain the ferocity of the army assault on the Dhaka campus two days later, following the launch of Operation Searchlight. The army also turned its weapons on the headquarters of the police and the East Pakistan Rifles. These massacres led to the "mutiny" of the East Bengali regiment under Major Ziaur Rahman, who just four years later was to head Bangladesh's military government.

The unfolding massacres and humanitarian crisis internationalized the "civil war" as millions of Bengalis fled to India. In a forerunner of the later Live Aid concerts, a fund-raising Concert for Bangladesh was held in New York by George Harrison and Ravi Shankar, supported by Bob Dylan. In the White House, Richard Nixon sympathized with the Pakistani government, which had been helpful in forwarding US diplomatic overtures to China. Congressional opinion, however, was hostile to Nixon's "tilt" to Pakistan, and there were differences of opinion between the White House and the State Department concerning criticism of Yahya's repression.

The emerging crisis provided Indira Gandhi with the opportunity to cut Pakistan down to size and to close the transborder camps for Naga and Mizo rebels. After some initial hesitation, New Delhi provided military and diplomatic support to the Bengali rebels. Thousands of Mukhti Bahini freedom fighters were trained in camps in West Bengal, Tripura, Meghalaya, and Assam. India also provided sanctuary for a Bangladeshi government in exile. This did not, however, include Mujib, who had been arrested and flown to West Pakistan. By October 1971 it was clear that Pakistan could not regain control of the whole of East Bengal. The freedom fighters were able to wage successful guerrilla campaigns but could not defeat the better-equipped government forces in a pitched battle. The US stance prevented India from declaring war, although international opinion was carefully prepared for military intervention by stressing the humanitarian problems arising from the refugee influx. Indira Gandhi's remaining doubts about an all-out offensive to capture Dhaka were ended by Pakistani Air Force's raids on northwestern Indian airfields on 3 December.

The third Indo-Pakistani War lasted just two weeks. During its course, Pakistan lost half its navy, a third of its army, and a quarter of its air force. Yahya, under intense diplomatic pressure from Washington, agreed to accept the Indian terms for an unconditional surrender. General Niazi surrendered on 16 December, along with ninety-three thousand troops who had been surrounded in Dhaka. While Mujib returned in triumph to lead an independent Bangladesh, West Pakistani generals faced the humiliation of seeing their men languishing as prisoners of war. With Indian forbearance, Mukti Bahini militants took revenge on civilian, mainly Bihari, collaborators.

The causes of the drift to civil war, the extent to which the Pakistani Army activities after 25 March 1971 can be called genocide, and the circumstances of the Indian military intervention on 3 December 1971 are the subject of massive historical controversy. Some Pakistani writers blame the drift to civil war on Bhutto's intransigence and Yahya's incompetence. Bhutto is claimed to have possessed an "elemental" drive for power and an anxiety that the PPP would "unravel" if it was denied the fruits of power in the National Assembly.[32] Bhutto maintained in his defense that the postponement of the National Assembly, which was the catalyst for the crisis, was not his responsibility. Yahya's critics claim that it was "impolitic" to accept Bhutto's hospitality at his Larkana estate on 17–18 January, as it convinced some Awami Leaguers that the PPP leader was the cat's-paw of the military. Yahya is also censured for his counterproductive efforts to tough out the situation and make Mujib "see sense."[33] After a meeting with Mujib in Dhaka in mid-January, Yahya reportedly expressed the opinion that Mujib was a "clever bastard" who wanted an early National Assembly meeting in order to bulldoze through the constitution.[34]

Conspiracy theories have long seen Indian engineering behind the breakup of Pakistan. While India sought international support for its action by highlighting the refugee crisis in West Bengal and Tripura arising from the Pakistani Army's "terror," the action was not taken "under duress." Despite her many policy failings, Indira Gandhi's response to the East Pakistani crisis was sagacious. It contrasts dramatically with Pakistani blundering into armed conflict. Nonetheless, Pakistan did not fall apart because of Indian machinations. The crisis was homemade. Pakistani chauvinism compounded folly in the dangerous denial of Bengali democratic urges.

Early Bangladesh accounts focused on the role of Mujib as the "Father of the Nation" (*jatir janak*), and on the sacrifices and sufferings of the "martyrs" of the struggle, not only military combatants but also victims of Pakistani Army atrocities, including rape victims known as "brave heroines," *birangona*. A more complex history of the struggle has emerged more recently, in terms of its regional dimensions, of the local fighters who remained outside of the Mukhti Bahini (such as the Siraj Sikdar group in Barisal), and of the contrasting experiences between those "on the ground" in East Bengal and the Bangladeshi government in exile in India. Common to all Bangladeshi historiography is the significance that colonial rule continued until 1971. This date, rather than 1947, is the key moment in modern history. Bangladeshi nationalist history thus serves a dual purpose. It both legitimizes the Bangladesh state and "challenges the hegemony of Indo-Pakistani understandings of modern South Asian history."[35]

THIRTEEN

Bangladesh Since Independence

During the three decades following its birth, Bangladesh slipped from the international media's view. It lacked Pakistan's geopolitical Cold War significance. India possessed more colorful dynastic politics and greater economic potential even in the days of the "Hindu" rate of growth. In the fields of cultural and sporting endeavor, Pakistan and India overshadowed Bangladesh. A domestic cinema (Dhallywood) producing more than sixty films a year was dwarfed by Bollywood; coveted cricket test-match playing status was not achieved until 2000. Attention turned toward Bangladesh when natural disasters struck, or at the time of military coups, but was quickly averted thereafter. Bangladesh was largely left to the writings of experts in development. Excellent work has been produced on a vast array of topics, from aid, dependency, and resource ownership to environmental degradation and the "mass poisoning" arising from arsenic contamination of groundwater used for drinking.[1]

In the wake of the terrorist attacks of 9/11, the international spotlight began to shine on Bangladesh, which possessed the third-largest Muslim population in the world and elected an Islamist government in October 2001, especially when an upsurge of violence against women, minorities, and "secular" NGOs ensued. Previous inattention seesawed into exaggeration of linkages between indigenous militant groups such as the Ja'amatul Mujaheedin Bangladesh (JMB) and Al-Qaeda. Political complexities were overlooked in the portrayal of a straightforward clash between a "secular" Awami League and an "Islamist" Bangladesh National Party and its allies. When India emphasized the "Talibanization" threat and claimed that Pakistan's ISI was attempting to use Bangladesh as a terrorist base, its possible motives went unexamined.[2]

Just as in Pakistan, Bangladeshi militancy had not sprung up overnight. It was the culmination of long-term influences, some of which dated from the early years of independence. These created an environment in which the Islamist Jamaat-i-Islami (JI) and a host of smaller Islamist parties (fifteen contested the 2001 elections) entered the mainstream and militant groups emerged on the fringes of society.[3] The struggle over the history of the liberation war and its legacy for nation building has been so acute that it has undermined the legitimacy of civilian governments. Violent confrontations have reduced the state's capacity to govern. Since 2010 these have focused on attempts to try war criminals. NGOs have filled some of the space the state has vacated. Militant Islamic groups have also moved in. Their violence, despite its new forms, can be fully understood only in the historical context of conflict in Bangladesh.[4] The military has also benefited from this situation. The men in uniform, like their Pakistani counterparts, have used Islam for political legitimization.

State- and society-sponsored Islamization has adversely affected minorities and women who have been caught up in "cultural wars." These have been played out in terms of dress, gender relations, and cultural expression. They attracted international attention with the fatwas calling for the death of the feminist writer Taslima Nasrin following the publication of her controversial novel *Shame* (about anti-Hindu violence in Bangladesh), leading her to flee to Sweden in 1994. She later also had to leave West Bengal because of hostility to her work.[5] Minorities have also been victimized. Buddhist temples and properties were destroyed in Cox's Bazaar and Chittagong in September and October 2012. There are parallels between the attacks on Ahmadis in Bangladesh and in Pakistan.

Bangladesh's crisis deepened during 2013 with mounting political polarization and violence. This culminated early the following year in elections, which were boycotted by the opposition Bangladesh Nationalist Party and from which the main religiopolitical party Jamaat-i-Islami was barred following a high court ruling. Bangladeshi history cannot be reduced, however, to a narrative of political violence and creeping Islamization. The state from its war-torn beginnings has made considerable socioeconomic advances. Raising living standards for a population of some 160 million people packed into an area slightly smaller than the size of Iowa is a remarkable achievement. Despite political instability, economic growth rates have been running at more than 5 percent during the past two decades. A burgeoning export trade, together with considerable amounts of overseas aid, have raised living standards. Bangladesh has led the developing world in the pioneering concept of microfinance. Its two leading NGOs, Grameen Bank and the Bangladesh Rural Advancement Committee (BRAC), have become agents of its provision in other parts of South Asia.

Before turning to these overarching themes in Bangladeshi history, we will first examine the immediate background to the 2013–14 crisis, which commenced with the Shahbagh movement; its use of social media recalled the earlier Arab Spring. The movement attested to the continuing bitter struggles over the history of the liberation war in the defining of Bengali/Bangladeshi national identity.

The Shahbagh Movement

Bangladesh's forty-first Victory Day was celebrated in Dhaka on Sunday, 16 December 2012. The annual commemoration of independence was the occasion for the parading of placards and large model caricatures of 1971 war criminals. Young men dressed in black robes held aloft fake bloody swords. Conflict intensified over the sentences faced by those being tried for crimes against humanity by the International Crimes Tribunal. This body had been established by Sheikh Hasina Wazed's Awami League government, and was sitting in the Old High Court Building in Dhaka.[6] The defendants included senior figures in the Islamist Jamaat-i-Islami party (JI). Its activists and the student wing Islami Chhatra Shibir (ICS) claimed that the trials were a witch hunt and called for the release of their leader, Abdul Quader Molla. Strikes and pitched battles with the police broke out in the Motijheel commercial district of Dhaka. The key Shahbagh intersection of central Dhaka became the scene of a mass sit-in when Abdul Quader Molla, the so-called Butcher of Mirpur, was sentenced to life imprisonment on 5 February, after being convicted of killing 344 people.[7] In the following weeks mass gatherings took place that were reminiscent of those in Cairo's Tahrir Square during the

Arab Spring. Young activists used social media (Blogger and Online Activists Network) to organize their protests and to call for capital punishment for the war criminals. A candlelight vigil on 14 February included a huge image of the writer Jahanara Imam, who had campaigned in the 1990s through the Nirmal Committee (Committee for the Uprooting of Traitors and Collaborators of 1971) to bring alleged war criminals to court.[8]

Overseas Bangladeshis joined in the Shahbagh protests as far afield as Sydney, Stuttgart, and Diversity Plaza in Jackson Heights, New York. A small park in the Bangladeshi area of Whitechapel in London (Altab Ali Park) was the site of a weekly vigil and eventual clashes between the protestors and supporters of JI.[9] The East London Mosque had links with JI leaders in Bangladesh.

Protests in Dhaka intensified following the murder of Ahmed Rajib Haider, a prominent internet activist and blogger. There were calls for the

20. Altab Ali Park, London

banning of ICS. Further signs of polarization emerged after a number of leaders of former Premier Khaleda Zia's Bangladesh National Party were arrested; JI had been its leading partner in the coalition that ruled Bangladesh from 2001 to 2007. The unfolding situation acutely revealed the continuing struggle for the soul of the nation. Violence increased in October 2013, when Prime Minister Sheikh Hasina rejected the calls for a "neutral" caretaker government to oversee the polls. When Abdul Quader Molla was hanged in mid-December, thousands of JI supporters took to the streets. The polarization of Bangladesh's politics has resulted in instability and failure to consolidate democracy, despite the euphoria of the immediate postindependence period.

Democracy, Dictatorship, and the Struggle over Bangladeshi Identity

Bangladesh emerged with high democratic hopes. A jubilant Sheikh Mujibur Rahman made a triumphal return to Dhaka. Within three years, however, the nation's founding father declared a state of emergency. The intervening period had been marked by economic chaos and an almost complete breakdown of law and order in parts of the country. Nationalization, as in Bhutto's Pakistan, undermined business confidence, with industrialists sending money overseas. An overexpansionary fiscal policy contributed to runaway inflation, which peaked at 59 percent in 1974. The politicization of the bureaucracy and the doling out of patronage to party loyalists bore further similarities with Bhutto's populism. The comment made of Mujib's regime that "political connections and proximity to the seat of power determined access to resources" could stand as readily for Bhutto's Pakistan.[10]

Mujib's political capital was also expended by the claims of widespread rigging of the March 1973 elections.[11] Not for the first time in the region's history, natural disaster, in the shape of the 1974 floods, exacerbated a mounting political crisis. Mujib, like Indira Gandhi shortly afterward, responded to mounting political disorder by declaring a state of emergency. He used this crisis to curb the judiciary and limit press freedom. He went farther than Gandhi, however, in that in January 1975 he amended the Constitution, replacing the prime ministerial system with a presidential one, in which he was to hold office for a further five years. Rival political parties were banned.

These moves provided a pretext for military intervention. The Bangladeshi Army felt aggrieved when Mujib sought to establish a rival military organization (the National Security Force). He had also favored "freedom fighters" over "repatriates" (those army officers who were interned in West Pakistan until 1973) when making promotions. These divisions meant that the Bangladeshi Army did not possess its Pakistani counterpart's discipline. It helps explain the much bloodier nature of the coups and countercoups involving the Bangladeshi Army. While Bangladesh's first military ruler, Ziaur Rahman, had freedom-fighter credentials, the second prolonged period of military rule was to be led by Hussain Muhammad Ershad, who was a repatriate.

Mujib's fall was swift and bloody. He died along with eighteen other members of his family when junior officers seized power on 15 August 1975.[12] His daughter Sheikh Hasina Wazed survived because she was in India. There were two more coups before Ziaur Rahman (Zia) established his regime in November. It lasted four years until he was assassinated in Chittagong.[13] Zia provided an Islamic gloss to the state, favoring Bangladeshi over Bengali nationalism. He also reopened the Chittagong Hill Tracts as a training area for tribal insurgents fighting India. Simultaneously, he stepped up military action against the CHT's indigenous tribal insurgents, which continued under successive governments for over two decades.

Zia took the office of president in April 1977. Within months he faced a serious mutiny in Dhaka led mainly by air force officers. The dangers of the politicized military were to be fully revealed at the time of Zia's assassination. In an attempt to civilianize his rule, Zia stepped down as chief of army staff (to be replaced by Major General Hussain Muhammad Ershad) and formed his own political party, the Bangladesh National Party (BNP). It won the elections that were held in February 1979 before martial law was lifted.[14] Like the anti-PPP forces in Pakistan a decade later, the BNP was held together by opportunism and the "politics of grievance" against a deceased populist leader whose legacy was now being carried by his daughter.

The Awami League captured just thirty-nine of the three hundred parliamentary seats.[15] Despite this victory, Zia's position remained precarious. However, he visited Chittagong in May 1981 with only a light guard, despite the fact that it was the headquarters of his scarcely concealed rival Major General Muhammad Manzur. Zia was gunned down in the Chittagong Circuit House early on the morning of 30 May. His widow, Begum Khaleda Zia, was to take over the leadership of the BNP from her husband's civilian right-hand man Abdus Sattar. The former lawyer and election commissioner Sattar won elections held in mid-November 1981. His attempts to move from a military backed regime to a fully fledged democracy were halted by Ershad's coup the following March.

Ershad's regime (1982–90) sought legitimization in the new industrial policy announced in June 1982. Its centerpiece was the privatization of the industrial assets that Mujib had taken into state ownership just a decade earlier. Nonetheless, Ershad faced continuous opposition from both the Awami League and the BNP. Khaleda Zia believed that Ershad had a hand in her husband's death. Ershad's response was to form his own political party, the Jatiyo (National) Party, in 1986. It duly won rigged parliamentary elections that May. The BNP boycotted those elections; the Awami League did not, but it sat out the presidential polls that followed in October, in which Ershad predictably triumphed. The court of public opinion, however, continued to hold him to account. Even his successful handling of the devastating floods in 1988 did not improve his popularity.

Bangladesh's military rulers resembled their Pakistani counterparts in turning to Islam to legitimatize their rule. It was during Zia's regime (1975–81) that JI leaders were allowed to return from exile in Pakistan. Ershad amended the Constitution in 1988 so that Islam was declared the state religion. He also talked about implementing sharia law. Islamization went nowhere near as far as in Pakistan, but it was nonetheless divisive because of the significant Hindu population and the Awami League's historic commitment to secularism. This had been summed up in the 1972 Constitution, with its four principles of "Mujibism"—nationalism, socialism, secularism, and democracy.[16] Forty years on, rival Islamist and secularist visions of Bangladesh remain unresolved.

Ershad was overthrown in a popular uprising in late November 1990. Students were at the forefront. Demonstrations spread from university campuses and paralyzed the economy. When the army refused to back him, Ershad had to step down. He made a comeback, however, after imprisonment for corruption. The 1991 parliamentary elections were dominated by the struggle for power between Sheikh Hasina's Awami League and the BNP of Khaleda Zia.[17] Like Benazir Bhutto, Indira Gandhi, and Sirimavo Bandaranaike in Sri Lanka, they had inherited charisma from male members of their political families. This was routinized as they secured control of their respective party organizations. Sheikh Hasina did not compromise the party's foundational principles as much as Benazir Bhutto. Khaleda provided a rallying point for conservative forces, thereby perpetuating the struggle against the populism of the Mujib period.

The BNP narrowly polled the most votes in 1991, but because of the first-past-the-post system ended up with a comfortable majority of 52 seats over the Awami League, which had won 140. Khaleda Zia ruled for the next five years, but the restoration of parliamentary democracy, as in Pakistan in 1988, ushered in a period of "disloyal opposition" and "bad governance." The opposition Awami League early in 1992 began street protests against prominent JI "war criminals" (principally the newly elected leader Golam Azad), beginning a long campaign that culminated in the Shahbagh movement. Bangladesh became increasingly ungovernable. Street protests were accompanied by frequent walkouts and boycotts of Parliament. In late December 1994, Awami League members finally resigned en masse. They also refused to contest the by-elections that became mandatory for those MPs who were absent for more than ninety days. When the BNP government resigned and proceeded with parliamentary elections in February 1996, the opposition boycotted these, resulting in the formation of what it termed the "illegal parliament" of February 1996. Its only legislation was a constitutional amendment that permitted the formation of an interim neutral caretaker government and the holding of a fresh round of elections within ninety days.

The Awami League, having just failed to secure a majority in the June 1996 polls, formed a coalition government with Ershad's Jatiyo Party.[18] The twenty-five-year insurgency in the Chittagong Hill Tracts was ended by an accord with the armed wing of the United People's Party (the Shanti Bahini). Sheikh Hasina's government also implemented long-awaited local government reforms. The BNP used the same tactics it had formerly faced. The power struggle revolved around such issues as the lifting of criminal cases against opposition MPs and the government's removal of the floating footbridge that led to Zia's tomb. The Awami League increasingly returned to the theme of its role in the Liberation War, especially as the JI became a powerful opposition presence. Tareque Masud's documentary films *Mukthir Gaan* (Song of freedom) and *Muktir Katha* (Words of freedom) reflected the public visibility of this foundational event in the nation's history. The first was released in the twilight period of the BNP government and escaped halfhearted attempts at banning.

The BNP and its JI partner promised the voters a restoration of law and order at the time of the October 2001 polls. The anti–Awami League alliance emerged with a massive parliamentary majority. The BNP captured 193 of 300 Assembly seats. JI won just 17 but increased its influence in government. Ershad's Jatiyo Party also joined the government after switching sides. Once again an opportunity for democratic consolidation was missed. The army was brought back into the mainstream through the crackdown on rural crime known as Operation Clean Heart (October 2002). Political violence grew, and attacks on minorities were common. Critics attributed the latter to the influence of JI. The government also acquired an unenviable reputation for corruption and factional rivalries. Intensification of the rivalries coincided with the increasing prominence of Khaleda Zia's son Tareque Rahman. Bangladesh was no more immune to dynastic politics than neighboring India and Pakistan. Rahman sought to position himself as future prime minister. Like Sanjay Gandhi earlier in India, he also created an independent power base by pitting a younger generation of party activists against longtime stalwarts.

The opposition Awami League reverted to its traditional tactics of street protests and parliamentary boycotts. It returned to Parliament in mid-June 2004 only because in its absence the government had passed the 14th amendment to the Constitution. The amendment's raising of the retirement age of Supreme Court judges was seen as an attempt to ensure that a pro-BNP judge would serve as chief adviser in the caretaker government required to oversee the next national elections.[19]

The economy continued to grow (around 6 percent per year, beginning in 2001), despite the prevailing political instability. This achievement rested on the export sector, in which the garment industry played a leading role, especially through its sales to the US market. Total exports of all goods in 2002–3 to the United States stood at more than $2.3 billion, making America Bangladesh's largest export market.[20] Frogs and shrimps were also important exports, eclipsing the once-dominant jute. Farmers, however, had to increase the use of pesticides to control insects as frogs disappeared from the rice paddies. In addition to ecological and environmental problems, Bangladesh faced similar structural economic problems to those of Pakistan, such as a low tax-to-GDP ratio and major problems in electricity production arising from corruption and lack of investment. The resulting power cuts undermined the BNP government's popularity, as they were to do later under the Zardari regime (2008–13) in Pakistan.

Time-honored South Asian tactics of transferring officials as a prelude to poll rigging became increasingly apparent in 2006. There were also attempts to tamper with the voters' lists. Tareque Rahman coordinated administrative actions to maximize the BNP's prospects. The Awami League took to the streets. Public protests intensified when Ershad, who had thrown in his lot with the opposition once again, was prevented from standing because of a criminal case being brought against him. Moreover, the BNP appointed the loyalist president, Iajuddin Ahmed, as head of the caretaker government that would oversee the polls.

Sixteen years of political infighting, including more than six hundred days of strikes, was ended by military intervention on 11 January 2007. The army backed an administration headed by a former World Bank executive, Fakhruddin Ahmed. He proclaimed the independence of the judiciary and sought to root out corruption and reform the politicized Electoral Commission. The "two begums," Sheikh Hasina and Khaleda Zia, were detained, along with Tareque Rahman. The fifth intervention by the army in Bangladesh's history raised fears that it would be as reluctant as its Pakistani counterpart to return to the barracks.[21]

Sheikh Hasina was the first of the leading figures to be released from detention, in time-honored tradition being sent abroad for medical treatment in June 2008. Three months later Khaleda Zia and Tareque Rahman were released on bail as part of Fakhruddin Ahmed's preparation for national elections. Tareque Rahman was to spend more than five years in exile. The ballots were cast on 29 December 2008. The Awami League returned to the theme of the liberation war as a rallying cry for secular forces. This formed the backdrop to the later attempts to prosecute JI "war criminals." The Awami League dominated a fourteen-party "grand alliance," which once again included Ershad's Jatiyo Party. In an election that had the highest turnout in Bangladesh's history, 80 percent, the Awami League and its allies swept aside the BNP, which was reduced to 30 seats; JI fared even worse, capturing just 2 constituencies. Sheikh Hasina's captured 49 percent of the total vote and won 231 of 300 assembly seats.[22]

NGOs, Development, and Female Empowerment

During the early weeks of the military-backed Fakhruddin Ahmed administration, it was announced that Bangladesh's first Nobel Peace Prize winner (2006), the celebrated developmental economist Muhammad Yunus, was going to launch a new political party. Citizen's Power was to pursue an anticorruption agenda. The Grameen Bank founder abandoned this plan in May 2007. It was too late to prevent conflict with the incoming Awami League government. The government claimed that Yunus had misappropriated funds and also seized on revisionist debates within development economics about the Grameen Bank's "microfinance." By this time, the bank was lending money to around four million borrowers (96 percent of whom were women) in forty-six thousand villages. Critics challenged the Grameen Bank's claims of female empowerment, the extent to which loans were in fact "noncollateral," and the neoliberal agenda that microfinance advanced.[23] Sheikh Hasina could even draw on Foucaldian discourse analysis, which purported to see the same "disciplinary gaze" and construction of "bound productive subjects" in the villages of rural Bangladesh as in the factories of nineteenth-century western Europe.[24]

Grameen Bank had started out in the mid-1970s as a local development enterprise. It was one among thousands of aid-supported enterprises in a social landscape dominated by NGOs.[25] Local development programs and agencies predate Bangladesh's independence and can be traced back to the famous Comilla Model for rural development in the 1960s.[26] The contemporary proliferation of NGOs reflects their ability to project an image as "honest brokers" in comparison with government agencies that have become mired in corruption as a result of their capture by vested bureaucratic and political interests. NGOs have also filled the vacuum resulting from the state's diminishing reach.

Grameen Bank's main NGO adversary, the Bangladesh Rural Advancement Committee (BRAC), has moved from furnishing microcredit to providing a number of health care and educational services that were previously in the state's purview. By 2004, for example, it provided primary health care to thirty-one million people. It had also founded and was running more than thirty-four thousand village schools, whose pupils made up around 11 percent of all primary schoolchildren in Bangladesh.[27] This figure is in line with the total NGO reach of service provision for the Bangladeshi population.[28] Indeed, BRAC, with its bank, university, and internet services alongside development, educational, and health programs, has journeyed so far from its liberation-war relief and rehabilitation origins that it almost resembles a state within a state.

Increasing international interest in microfinance as a tool for development and social empowerment assisted the rise of BRAC and the Grameen Bank. A Microcredit Summit was held in Washington, DC, in 1997, and the UN General Assembly proclaimed 2005 as the International Year of Microcredit." Grameen Bank's and BRAC's microcredit activities have been copied elsewhere.[29] BRAC, for example, has worked in Afghanistan, Sri Lanka, and Pakistan. Muhammad Yunus was to be rewarded with a Nobel Peace Prize. His counterpart at BRAC, Fazle Hasan Abed, who had begun his career as an accountant, received British knighthood in February 2010.

The impact of the Grameen Bank and BRAC on female empowerment has been increasingly debated. Both organizations' microcredit activities target women who would be unable to secure loans from formal banks. According to the Grameen Bank, household incomes of its members are 50 percent above those nonmembers in the same social category. Twenty percent of Grameen Bank members live below the poverty line, compared with a figure of 56 percent for nonmembers nationally.[30] Women make up two-thirds of all BRAC's recipients of microcredit. BRAC also runs income-generating programs for women, such as poultry keeping and vegetable farming. Women's rights and other women's issues are addressed in BRAC's legal aid workshops and clinics and through the performances of visiting theater groups.[31] BRAC-run schools actively enroll "hard-to-reach children," those from economically disadvantaged communities, and have almost two-thirds female pupils. Such initiatives enable Bangladesh to perform relatively better in human development indicators than its more prosperous South Asian neighbors. Female literacy was estimated at 52.2 percent and 40.3 percent in Bangladesh and Pakistan, respectively (2010 and 2009 figures), although GDP per capita was much lower for Bangladesh ($1,900) than for Pakistan ($2,800, est. 2011). There is also a much greater female participation in the labor force in Bangladesh than in Pakistan. This female participation, which had reached 50 percent by 2000, has contributed to the growth of national income, especially through employment in the ready- made garments and shrimp-export industries, although women's overall employment status has remained low. Microcredit was designed to address this by encouraging a switch from rural day labor to self-employment. Proponents also argue that providing women with economic resources would increase their power in domestic decision making.

Nonetheless, critics maintain that little has been achieved in the way of empowerment. Local studies point out that while women secure loans and are responsible for their repayment, men use the money that the household acquires.[32] New economic opportunities for women have to be set alongside the continuing traditional burdens of child care and other domestic responsibilities. We have already referred to the "disciplinary gaze" of the organizations that, according to some writers, make women dependent on them and thus disempower them. "Bicycle bankers" may exert as much pressure as traditional loan sharks in enforcing regular weekly repayments. Some critics even claim that domestic violence, which remains a marked feature of rural Bangladeshi life, has increased because of these financial pressures.[33] While microcredit interest rates are considerably lower than those of traditional moneylenders, their demands are unrelenting. One respondent to a village survey maintained, for example, that "the Grameen Bank is a kind of British Raj" that takes advantage of "poverty." "For poor people there is no difference between money-lenders and the Grameen Bank."[34] Local studies have also revealed that, contrary to the expressed policy of the microcredit lenders, loans have been taken out for dowry purposes.

Women, Minorities, and the Threat of Islamic Militancy

An unexpected consequence of increased affluence arising from microcredit activities has been the increased use by rural women of the face-and-body-concealing *burkha*.[35] This is a sign not just of upward social mobility but, as Elora Shehabuddin has revealed, of a complex process in which women socially mobilized through the activities of secular NGOs seek to reclaim and reshape, rather than reject, their faith.[36]

There is a trend across all sections of Bangladeshi Muslim society in favor of greater conservatism. Dress code is a visible symbol of this. Attempts to reform a "corrupted" religious practice, as we have seen, have occurred in the Bengal delta since the early nineteenth century. They have been bolstered in recent decades by labor migration to the Gulf and the increasing influence of such reformist organizations as the Tabligh movement, with its massive annual gatherings at Tongi, north of Dhaka. When coercion has replaced persuasion in the enforcement of a narrowly conceived Islamic propriety, women have been victimized. While the fatwas against Taslima Nasrin attracted international attention, there have been locally reported episodes of Islamic judgments against rural women. In some instances, women have been flogged or even stoned to death for sexual transgressions. A young woman named Noorjahan in northeastern Bangladesh was stoned in 1993 following the implementation of a fatwa.[37]

Dramatic attacks on symbols of "secularism" have taken place in the early twenty-first century, such as the bombing of an open-air concert in Dhaka in 2001 celebrating Bengali New Year (14 April). Four hundred simultaneous bomb attacks across Bangladesh in August 2005 revealed the ability of militant groups such as JMB to coordinate their activities. The BNP government eventually cracked down on JMB, but not before alarm bells had sounded in Washington and other Western capitals regarding the "Talibanization" of Bangladesh.

Leaders in their quest for power have used Islam. Military regimes have been especially prone. Zia, like his Pakistani namesake, made Islamic studies a mandatory part of the curriculum for Muslim students. He also developed close ties with religious figures, most notably Maulana Abdul Mannan, leader of the Association of Madrassah Teachers. The Awami League was as ready to use Islamic slogans as its BNP rival in the 1991 elections.[38] Alongside such political expediency, there has been, as in Pakistan, a proliferation of madrassahs, especially from the Deobandi school of Islam, which have also created an environment conducive to radicalism.

The retreat from pluralism has affected women, minorities, and the heterodox Ahmadi community. Hindus have responded to persecution by a continuous outward migration. Claims of rape and violence intensified with the election of the BNP-led coalition in 2001, with evidence of state inactivity at best, and at worst complicity in these assaults. Anti-Ahmadi activities dated from the early 1990s and had never abated during the Awami League rule (1996–2001), but they intensified with the BNP coalition coming to power. An Islamist umbrella organization called Khatme Nabawat had links with the BNP's coalition partners JI and Islami Okye Jote (IOJ). Throughout 2004–5, Khatme Nabawat, dedicated to the preservation of "the finality of the Prophethood," attacked Ahmadi mosques in a campaign designed to get Ahmadis declared non-Muslims. One clash at Joytidrianagar, a remote village in the southwestern Satkhira district, was prompted by KN activists placing a signboard on an Ahmadi mosque that read, "This is a place of worship for Kadianis [Ahmadis]; no Muslim should mistake it for a mosque."[39] While the Ahmadi community numbered only around 100,000, civil society activists saw their persecution as part of a wider assault on pluralism in Bangladesh.

The question whether being Bangladeshi is vested in identification with the Bengali region or with territorially bounded Islam has thus fueled domestic political violence. The conflict reached a crescendo in late 2013 over the issues of war trials and the impending elections. Sheikh Hasina's government had passed the 15th Constitutional Amendment, which abolished the caretaker system that had been in place for fifteen years to ensure free and fair elections. When the Awami-led government refused to back down, the main opposition party boycotted the polls. Bangladesh thus entered 2014 with its long-standing problems of democratic consolidation and national identity unresolved. Political polarization threatened its hard-won economic advances.

FOURTEEN

Pakistan Since 1971

Despite a seemingly chaotic rush of events and enduring crises, much has remained unchanged in Pakistan since 1971. Personalities and patronage continue to dominate politics, rather than programs and policies. Problems that preoccupy contemporary analysts, such as the distribution of power between the executive and the legislature, the issue of weak political institutionalization, and the state's involvement with Islamic militants as "strategic assets," were present at the beginning of this period. In the Bangladesh civil war, for example, which ushered in the "new" Pakistan, the West Pakistan elite used Islamic paramilitary proxies such as Al-Shams and Al-Badr alongside regular forces. In this chapter I offer a consideration of important themes in this period rather than a detailed narrative.[1] We will turn first, however, to the legacies arising from the 1971 war with India and the resultant emergence of Bangladesh.

The Downsized Pakistan State

Pakistan lost one-sixth of its territory with the East Bengal breakaway. It was subsequently around twice the size of California in area. The state's asymmetrical power relationship with India was further exaggerated, but the West Pakistan establishment, which blamed India for the course of events, refused to bow to Indian hegemony. Three longer-term policies were thus intensified: first, the search for external allies to counterbalance India; second, the channeling of resources for defense expenditure; third, the use of Islamic proxies to destabilize India's position in Kashmir. These reactions to the new geopolitical "threat" have remained constant throughout the post-

1971 period, revealing that even during periods of civilian rule, the army maintains control of security and strategic policy.

The new demographic contours of the Pakistani state also exaggerated two other preexisting historical trends: first, the important role of Punjab in national affairs; second, the drive to Islamicize Pakistan. As we have seen, a dominant political theme had been the attempts by the Punjabi-dominated political establishment of West Pakistan to nullify the Bengali numerical majority. This problem no longer existed in the downsized Pakistan. Punjab now accounted for over 56 percent of the total population. The region's economic predominance was also firmly established. Punjab accounted for 65 percent of food grain production and 50 percent of manufacturing output.[2] Long-established patterns of army service and overseas migration further added to the region's relative wealth.

Punjab's "big brother" status in the post-1971 state created increasing re-sentment among Sindhi, Baloch, Pakhtun, and Mohajir ethnonationalists. They complained of the "Punjabization" of Pakistan. In reality, Punjab is not monolithic. Agriculturally poorer areas in the south and the north of the province each have distinctive linguistic cultures (Hindko and Seraiki, re-spectively). Further ethnic heterogeneity comes from the presence of Kash-miris, Mohajirs, and Pakhtuns. Army recruitment, although traditionally linked with the whole of the province, is concentrated both geographically (Jhelum and Shahpur districts) and ethnically (Rajput, Awan).

With the emergence of Bangladesh, the tensions were intensified be-tween an Islamic discourse identified with the nation-state and one that rested on a transnational vision. The "denationalizing" tendencies of the Islamic discourse were further strengthened by the Afghan jihad. Zia rode the Islamic tiger to both legitimize his regime and further his regional secu-rity agenda. However, a radicalized and politicized religious establishment proved an uneasy ally. Moreover, the long-term seeds were sown for grass-roots radical resistance to the state and its vision of a top-down Islamization process, within the parameters of Pakistani nationalism.[3]

The post-1971 Islamic discourse has also been marked by intensified sectarianism. The trend toward "Sunnification" in the Zia era (1977–88) increased sectarian tension and violence. "Traditional" sectarian riots as at the time of Muharram have been replaced by the targeted killings and bombings. Heavily armed militias such as Sipah-i-Sahaba-i-Pakistan (SSP, the Pakistani force of the companions of the Prophet Muhammad) have secured political protection and influence. Violence has been further intensified by what some have termed a "proxy war" between Saudi Arabia and Iran being fought on Pakistani soil.[4]

Zulfiqar Ali Bhutto's Pakistan: A Missed Opportunity for Democratization

Zulfiqar Ali Bhutto's rule (1971–77) remains both controversial and definitional for contemporary Pakistan. The military debacle and breakup of the country provided an opportunity to establish civilian supremacy when he formally replaced Yahya Khan as president on 20 December 1971.[5] Following the lifting of martial law and the National Assembly's approval of a new Constitution, Bhutto became prime minister in August 1973. Bhutto, however, paradoxically required a strong army, as he retained a hawkish attitude toward India. He toyed for a while with the possibility of a "people's army" but eventually devoted a disproportionate portion of the state's resources to the army's reequipment. Pakistan's defense expenditure rose by more than 200 percent during the Bhutto period. Eight dollars per citizen was being spent on the armed forces.[6] Pakistan was spending on defense almost twice as great a percentage of its gross national product as India. This failed, however, to endear Bhutto to the generals. Like other conservative elites, they opposed his populist land reforms, nationalization of industries, and rhetoric of political empowerment. Moreover, he threatened their institutional interests with the establishment of a private army, the Federal Security Force, designed to assist the police in the maintenance of law and order.

Every dollar Pakistan spent on arms reduced funding for education, health care, and housing. Attempts to rein in growing budget deficits led to the curbing of food subsidies from April 1974 onward; this from a party that had promised to provide "roti, kapra, aur makan": food, clothes, and shelter. The failure to meet raised expectations increased Bhutto's vulnerability, especially after he rehabilitated the army by using it to cow legitimate Baloch political demands.

Bhutto was presented with an opportunity not only to reframe civil-military relations but to reconstruct the country around the acceptance of pluralism. As a Sindhi he might have been expected to take up the latter task. Increasingly, however, although he advanced the cause of Sindhi speakers in his native province, he returned to the centralizing impulses of his predecessors at the national level. The resulting disturbances between Mohajirs and Sindhis in 1972 led to a pattern, which was to be repeated in the 1990s, of civilian politicians approaching the army to intervene against their detested opponents.

Bhutto was not the first Pakistan ruler, nor was he to be the last, to use force to suppress Baloch nationalism. A confrontation in 1973–77 that claimed at least nine thousand lives not only damaged hopes of decentralization but opened the door to the army. Like the Bengalis earlier, the Baloch were underrepresented in state institutions. They felt economically exploited as the region's natural resources such as gas were turned to national rather than local economic development. The immediate catalyst for the tribal insurgency was Bhutto's unwillingness to allow political rivals to rule the region. The pretext for the dismissal of Ataullah Khan Mengel's National Awami Party government was the discovery of weapons in the Iraqi embassy in Islamabad, which Bhutto's supporters claimed were part of a gun-running operation for separatists in Balochistan. Eventually, fifty-five thousand Baloch were pitted against seventy thousand Pakistan troops in a conflict whose memory continues to influence Baloch nationalist struggle. In his testament from his "stinking death cell," Bhutto claimed that the army overrode his plans for a withdrawal because the generals wanted to "spread their tentacles throughout Balochistan."[7]

The dismissal of the NAP government in Balochistan was symptomatic of growing authoritarianism. Bhutto brooked no rivals outside or within his own party. The radicals of the early PPP period who had developed the ideas of "Islamic socialism" and structural reform were shunted to one side. Like the earlier Muslim League movement, Bhutto increasingly turned to the traditional power holders, who injected factionalism and opportunism into his party.[8] Rather than representing a break with the time-honored patron-client politics, the PPP looked increasingly like any other weakly institutionalized Pakistani party. Violence or its threat marked political life, exposing Bhutto to charges concerning the death of Nawab Muhammad Ahmad Khan, the father of one of his fiercest critics. Zia later alleged that Bhutto had had a hand in this killing and hanged the former prime minister. He removed a rival but thereby burnished a legend that overshadowed Bhutto's failings in office. Bhutto is revered as a martyr, especially in Sindh, where the execution by Punjabi generals of the country's first prime minister from this region evokes strong nationalist sentiment.

The bloodless military coup of 5 July 1977 has been well documented.[9] The disturbances and campaign led by the Pakistan National Alliance (PNA) that formed its backdrop were catalyzed by persistent claims that Bhutto had rigged the March elections. The PNA campaign was also driven by the underlying resentment of small-scale industrialists whose businesses had been nationalized and hit by increased labor costs. Bhutto had raised wages, but because of inflation, his working-class supporters were little better off. He had made the tall claim, impossible to fulfill, that nationalization would "eliminate, once and for all, poverty and discrimination in Pakistan."[10] He had similarly claimed grandiosely that the 1972 land reforms would remove the "remaining vestiges of feudalism." According to one estimate, the reforms released just 1 percent of cultivable land to tenants.[11] Bhutto's populism had threatened established interests and tantalized the masses with a glimpse of a more egalitarian society but had been largely cosmetic. This also increased his vulnerability.

Furthermore, Bhutto's concessions to Islamist parties by such actions as the stripping of the Ahmadis' status as Muslims (1974) only emboldened fundamentalists. The PNA campaign against him coalesced around the call for the introduction of "the rule of the Prophet" (Nizam-i-Mustapha). Following clashes between protestors and the security services, martial law was declared in Lahore and urban Sindh. As talks became deadlocked between the government and opposition early in June 1977, the army chief Zia-ul-Haq intervened in the coup, code-named Operation Fair Play. Bhutto was briefly released from protective custody in August. The large crowds that greeted him led a fearful Zia to cancel the promised early elections and rearrest the former prime minister on a charge of conspiracy to murder.

Zia-ul-Haq: A Doleful Legacy

The Zia era is consistently linked with contemporary Pakistan's ills of intolerance, sectarianism, and Islamic militancy. We have seen that longer-term influences contributed to these features. It is undeniable, however, that Zia bequeathed both the "Kalashnikov culture" and closer ties between the army, the ISI, and militant Islamic groups. Zia's grip on power was strengthened following the Soviet occupation of Afghanistan. Pakistan now became a front-line state in the United States' renewed Cold War struggle with Moscow. Zia's diplomatic isolation was ended. The Reagan administration provided aid and turned a blind eye to Pakistan's human rights violations and nuclear proliferation.[12]

Domestic developments also shaped Zia's Pakistan. We have seen the reemergence of the question of Islamic identity in the wake of the 1971 national catastrophe. The period was also shaped by rapid processes of migration, urbanization, and population growth. By 1980 Pakistan's population was among the highest in the world and was increasing at an annual rate of 3 percent. Zia reflected the conservative values of an emerging urban middle class. According to that view, Islam provided an anchor of stability among the currents of rapid social change and contrasted in its simplicity with the ostentation and decadence of the upper classes. The diplomat Iqbal Akhund wrote a series of anecdotes in which he recalled Zia's frequent claim to being a "simple man." On one occasion, he broke off from an envoy's meeting to join junior office staff for midday prayers, while the ambassadors, federal secretaries, and senior officials "kept walking back and forth and chatting on the terrace alongside the prayer tent."[13]

The extent to which Zia's Islamization policy was motivated by his Deobandi-influenced religious piety or by instrumentalist political concerns has been frequently debated. In August 1983, the Advisory Council of Islamic Ideology conveniently pronounced that a presidential form of government was the "nearest to Islam." It was to later rule that political parties were non-Islamic.

A less remarked-upon feature of the 1977–88 period was the continued underfunding of social welfare, despite remittance- and investment-fueled economic growth. By the early 1980s, overseas workers were annually remitting $2.2 billion to Pakistan. Informal transfers through the *hundi* system meant that the real figures were considerably higher. Pakistan still outperformed India at this time in terms of economic growth (with rates of more than 6 percent) and per capita income. But its uneven development and lack of human capital investment meant that it was more poorly equipped than India to take advantage of the rapidly approaching late-twentieth-century era of globalization.

State-sponsored Islamization was the cornerstone of the Zia regime. By 1983, a range of measures had been introduced. Judicial reform introduced shariat courts at both federal and lower levels to try cases and to assess laws for their consistency with Islam. An Islamic penal code, the Hudood Ordinances, was also implemented. Attempts to Islamicize economic activity included the introduction of interest-free banking and Islamic taxes, including *zakat* (alms) and *ushr* (agricultural tax). In educational policy there was an emphasis on Urdu as the language of instruction, the establishment of an Islamic University in Islamabad, and state support for mosque schools. Traditional ulema, along with the Islamist Jamaat-i-Islami, regarded the reforms as insufficient and tardy. Co-opted early in the regime, they increasingly parted from it. Nonetheless, the measures radically altered the social and religious landscape with respect to sectarianism, gender, and minority relations.

The mushrooming of mosques—nearly twelve thousand were opened in 1983–84 alone—encouraged sectarianism. Some mosques were militarized during the Afghan jihad and bequeathed a militant jihadist legacy. Zia patronized the Deobandi mosque at Binora in Karachi, which was at the forefront of mobilizing support for the Afghan jihad. Many of its former students became leading figures in jihadist organizations from the 1990s onward.[14] Successive post-Zia governments have been unable to rein in the radical mosques and their militants. While Zia was forced by protests to exempt Shia from paying an obligatory alms tax (which came into effect on 20 June 1980) to support Sunni charitable institutions, the resulting bitter sectarian divisions have never healed. Shia self-assertion was institutionalized as a result of the dispute around the Zakat Ordinance in the Tehreek-i-Nifaz-i-Fiqh Jafria (TNJF, Movement for the implementation of Shia law).

Islamization also deepened the divisions between the Barelvi representatives of traditionalist Sufi-influenced Islam and the Deobandis. Sindh's Sufi tradition fed into the opposition's struggle in 1983. Massive repression was required to crush agitation by the Movement for the Restoration of Democracy in the Sukkur, Larkana, Jacobad, and Khairpur districts.

Women were disadvantaged by the Islamic law of evidence, Qanoon-o-Shahadat, which regarded the value of a woman's testimony in court to be half that of a man, and by a definition of sexual crimes that failed to distinguish between rape and adultery. Women's groups also opposed the Diyat Ordinance, which set the blood money compensation for a female at half that for a male. Protests were coordinated by Liaquat's widow, Begum Raana Liaquat Ali Khan, the founder of the All-Pakistan Women's Association (APWA). The police tear-gassed and used *lathi* batons against a public protest by APWA and Women's Action Forum in Lahore on 12 February 1983. The episode polarized opinion, with ulema describing the protest as an act of apostasy that challenged Quranic injunctions, while the Lahore Court Bar Association condemned police brutality.

The marginalization of minorities was displayed in the introduction of separate electorates and their increasing vulnerability to charges of blasphemy. An amendment to the Pakistani penal code introduced by presidential ordinance made it a criminal offence for Ahmadis to "pose" as Muslims and to use Islamic terminology or Muslim practices of worship.

Zia's authoritarianism perpetuated the weakness of political parties and civil society organizations. He took the brutal repression of dissent to new depths when four journalists were flogged in public in May 1978 by bare-chested wrestlers because they had gone on strike to protest the closure of the leading PPP newspaper, *Musawat*. Martial law regulation no. 48 of October 1979 invoked a maximum penalty of twenty-five lashes for participating in banned political activities. Torture was so widespread at the time of the 1981 and 1983 military crackdowns that it attracted international condemnation.

When elections were finally held, ninety months after the coup, not ninety days, as Zia had initially promised, they were organized on a non-party basis. Even more than in Ayub's earlier partyless polls, they encouraged biraderi loyalties and patron-client ties that had traditionally stood in the way of modern-style politics. The partyless elections, alongside developments in Sindh, contributed to an ethnicization of political identity.

The February 1985 National Assembly elections paved the way for the lifting of martial law ten months later. Zia, however, armed himself, through the Eighth Amendment to the Constitution, with the discretionary power to dismiss the prime minister and National Assembly. He handpicked his prime minister, Muhammad Khan Junejo, and was careful to ensure that the Assembly indemnified all his acts after the 1977 coup. Thus fortified, Zia allowed Benazir Bhutto, who had spent the years after her father's death in prison and exile, to return to Pakistan in April 1986. She received a tumultuous welcome. Yet all was not plain sailing, as fissures emerged between the PPP old guard and Benazir's younger supporters. Zia demonstrated where power still lay in Pakistan when he unexpectedly dismissed Junejo and dissolved the assemblies on 29 May 1988. He also began strengthening groups opposed to the PPP in advance of a fresh round of partyless elections. The ISI was to play a role in organizing anti-Bhutto figures into a coherent grouping in advance of the polls that followed Zia's death in a mysterious plane crash. As we shall see, when Benazir became Pakistan's youngest and first female prime minister, it was, as she acknowledged, with one hand tied behind her back.

Pakistan in the 1990s: Failure in Democratic Consolidation

A transition to democracy followed Zia's unexpected death and the victory of the PPP, led by Benazir Bhutto, in the 1988 election. It raised hopes of a new era, with the beginnings of a modern party system, the addressing of persistent social and gender inequalities, and the removal of the smaller provinces' long-standing alienation from the center. It was also hoped that relations between Pakistan and India would be improved with the advent of two leaders in Benazir Bhutto and Rajiv Gandhi who had been born after the trauma of Partition.

None of these expectations was realized. The period from 1988 was marked by political infighting, a continuation of personality-based politics, and the use of selective accountability to intimidate opponents. During Benazir Bhutto's first administration (1988–90), Nawaz Sharif and other opponents faced as many as 160 charges of tax evasion and loan default. When she had lost power, Benazir Bhutto and her controversial spouse, Asif Ali Zardari, faced charges relating to bank loans, kickbacks, and the misuse of secret service funds. Such politically motivated cases were designed to hamstring opponents. The persistence of patron-client politics made all leaders vulnerable to charges of corruption. Parliament was at worst a bear pit, at best the fountainhead of patronage politics, with legislation being restricted to presidential ordinance.

Democracy did not reverse Zia's doleful inheritance. The gender discrimination in the Hudood Ordinances remained unchallenged. Persecution of Ahmadi and Christian minorities besmirched Pakistan's international reputation.[15] Ethnic conflict in Sindh between Pakhtuns, Sindhis, and Mohajirs evolved into a mini-insurgency in Karachi directed by the Muttahida Qaumi Movement (MQM) against the state. Violence in the country's main commercial center limited the economic gains derived from the privatization process that was a response to globalization.

Civilian leaders also presided over the intensifying military involvement with armed militias in Afghanistan, which spawned the Taliban (during the second Bhutto government, 1993–96), and over the mounting missile race with India. Many of contemporary Pakistan's leading militant organizations emerged in the democratic 1990s, including Lashkar-e-Taiba (LeT) in 1997 and Lashkar-e-Jhangvi (LeJ) in 1990. LeT was to achieve international prominence following the audacious Mumbai attacks on 26 November 2008; LeJ was involved in numerous sectarian atrocities and in the attack on the Sri Lankan cricket team in Lahore in 2009. Pakistan and India stood on the brink of war over Kashmir at the outset of the 1990s and fought each other at Kargil at its close. This was the first conflict after the two countries had tested nuclear weapons in May 1998.

Partly because US aid ceased because of the inability to certify under the Pressler Amendment that Pakistan did not possess a nuclear weapons program, the economy entered a tailspin and required IMF bailouts. The structural problems, hidden during the years of US aid to Pakistan as a front-line state, brought growing problems. Taxation continued to fall on the middle classes, while large landowners like the Bhuttos themselves paid virtually nothing in agricultural taxes. A series of financial crises with loan defaults and misappropriation of public funds further reduced foreign investment and brought ignominy on the political elites. The collapse of cooperative societies in Punjab (during Nawaz Sharif's first government, 1990–93) led to depositors losing twenty billion rupees. In August 1993, the caretaker government of Mooen Qureshi published a list of more than five thousand defaulters and beneficiaries of sixty-two billion rupees' worth of written-off loans.[16]

Such evidence superficially supports the claim of Pervez Musharraf at the time of his October 1999 coup that politicians had plundered the country in a period of "sham democracy." The army was in reality part of the problem rather than its solution. It sought to exert influence behind the scenes through "understandings" that the defense budget was sacrosanct, and vital security and foreign policy issues remained in its hands. Election outcomes were influenced by the military and security establishment.[17] The military also exerted leverage through the office of the president, who formed along with the chief of army staff and the prime minister a ruling troika. It is widely claimed that the security services fished in the troubled waters of Karachi's increasingly violent ethnic politics with its support for the MQM Haqiqi ("Genuine") Group in July 1992. "Constitutional coups" enacted by Presidents Ghulam Ishaq Khan and Farooq Leghari, unseating both Benazir Bhutto (1990, 1996) and Nawaz Sharif (1993), were ostensibly justified not only by corruption but by failure to maintain law and order in the troubled province of Sindh.

The constitutional coups were not, as the army averred, motivated by the desire to uphold the national interest but by sometimes clumsy and ill-advised efforts by Bhutto and Sharif to exert control over what was seen as the military's internal promotional preserves. Since the pioneering work of Ayesha Siddiqa, the encroachment of the military into all spheres of Pakistan's life has been laid bare and the military's need to protect these interests has become apparent.[18] Stephen Cohen has argued that Nawaz Sharif's rapid privatization program in the early 1990s may have upset the military because it increased competition with its businesses.[19]

This does not absolve the politicians for the failure to consolidate democracy. Personal vendettas took precedence. These, along with failures of governance and a worsening economy, meant that both Bhutto and Sharif were seen as partisan figures rather than symbols of democratic struggle. They were not averse to stifling the media and packing the judiciary to consolidate power. Moreover, elected leaders were as prone as the military to creating strategic alliances with Islamic militants. Democratic governments did not always crack down on sectarian militants if they were politically useful. Moreover, when violence got out of hand and there was the pressing need to do so, governments continued support for their transnational Islamist allies. Naseerullah Babar's crackdown on sectarian violence in 1994–96, as part of his Operation Save Punjab, coincided with the organization of the Taliban in order to secure "strategic depth" against India by securing a friendly regime in power in Kabul.

Nawaz Sharif's abrogation of the Eight Amendment, following his crushing victory in the 1997 polls, meant that the army had to dismiss him by direct intervention rather than via a constitutional coup.[20] In his second ministry (1997–99) this former military protégé had revealed an increasing tendency to accumulate power at the expense of rival institutions such as the presidency and the judiciary. While his easing out of the chief justice and the resignation of President Farooq Leghari in December 1997 were victories in Nawaz Sharif's personal quest for power, they did littler to further Pakistan's democratic development. Opponents claimed that Nawaz Sharif was bent on an "elective dictatorship." His relations with the chief of army staff, Pervez Musharraf, who was the architect behind the Kargil conflict, worsened in the wake of this episode. The democratic interlude ended when Musharraf came to power on 13 October 1999. Nawaz Sharif's attempt to sack him in a national television broadcast and "hijack" his plane en route from Colombo to Karachi enabled the former commando to pose as a reluctant coup maker.

Contemporary Pakistan: Governance, Security, and Economy

Pervez Musharraf promised to improve Pakistan's governance and economy. In the early stages of his regime, local government reform and a return to healthy rates of economic growth seemed to justify his claims to be the state's savior.[21] Musharraf also talked in terms of Pakistan being a moderate Islamic country and cultivated a liberal image that starkly contrasted with Zia's.[22] Just as the Soviet occupation of Afghanistan shaped Zia's regime, so Musharraf's was affected by the events of 9/11. In both instances, authoritarian rule was prolonged by developments in the regional neighborhood. I will address some of the security aspects in the concluding chapter. Here, it is important to note three legacies of 9/11 for Pakistan: first, the problems this raised for the state's long-term engagement with Islamic militants; second, the unpopularity that accrued from what critics saw as the pro-Western policy pursued by Musharraf; third, the short-term economic boom based on foreign inflows, which masked the long-term structural economic problems. By the end of Musharraf's regime, the economic bubble had burst. There were also mounting security problems as the state maintained an ambiguous approach to dealing with the numerous militant groups that had established themselves not only in border areas but even in the Punjab heartland.

Musharraf failed to acquire political legitimacy. This laid him open to attacks not only from liberal opponents but from Islamic traditionalists and Islamists. Paradoxically, his liberalism in allowing the flowering of an electronic media and freer press than at any time since the late 1940s opened him up to a barrage of criticism. Musharraf's approach to the press compared well with Nawaz Sharif's harassment of the Jang Press Group in 1998–99 and of Najam Sethi and the *Friday Times*.

Just as Bhutto had promised much and delivered little, so Musharraf failed to address Pakistan's long-term problems. Political institutions had been further weakened in the experiment with guided democracy. There had been at best halfhearted measures to roll back Zia's Islamization legacy. Initial hopes of dialogue with India had stalled. Similarly, the political empowerment of the masses through political reform had proved a chimera. In sum, Pakistan still had to resolve the issues that had blocked off its economic and political development since independence. The opportunity for structural reform had been missed. After Benazir Bhutto's widower, Asif Ali Zardari, assumed the office of president in 2008, his administration's failures of governance led some to see Musharraf's era as one of stability.[23] But if Pakistan was not a failed state under Musharraf's stewardship, it remained immobilized.

Benazir Bhutto's assassination on 27 December 2007 brought the party leaderships closer together than ever before. It also preempted any election rigging; the 2008 polls were the fairest since those of 1971. The unexpected result was the rise of Bhutto's controversial widower, Asif Ali Zardari, to a position of political leadership in Pakistan. As had happened after Bhutto's victory in 1988, the expectations that elections would usher in a new era failed to materialize. The postelection coalition of PPP and Pakistan Muslim League–N (PML-N) proved short-lived, although it had functioned long enough to force President Musharraf to step down under the threat of impeachment. Once again a lengthy period of military-backed rule gave way only to a fragile democracy. Claims of corruption were reminiscent of the 1990s, although this time it seemed that judicial activism, rather than executive action, could signal the end of a democratically elected government. The post-2008 period also shared with the 1990s the specter of economic crisis and a continuing decline in governance.

It would be wrong, however, to see the Zardari era as merely a repetition of the failed democratization of the late twentieth century. Some political lessons had been learned in that the PPP and PML-N avoided the zero-sum game in which they had engaged in the 1990s. Despite periods of tension and outright confrontation, the official opposition was critical of the military, rather than seeking to connive with it to remove the government. President Zardari's public commitment to a politics of reconciliation was not merely rhetoric. He attempted to roll back presidential power, and to address long-standing grievances arising from relations between the center and the provinces. Alongside these achievements, his government served its full term in office; the May 2013 elections thus historically marked Pakistan's first democratic transition of power. The polls did not, however, sweep the former cricketer turned anticorruption and antidrone campaigner Imran Khan to power, as some commentators had expected. Rather, they brought back Nawaz Sharif for a third term in office. His mandate raised hopes that Pakistan might be able to embark on further democratic consolidation.

From 2007 onward, however, militant groups linked with Al Qaeda had increasingly turned their firepower on Pakistan's "apostate" rulers. The state was to pay the price for its long-term strategy of utilizing Islamist proxies. The military found that it could not even secure its own facilities against attack, whether on the army headquarters in Rawalpindi in October 2009 or on the Mehran naval base near Shahrah-e-Faisal in Karachi on 22 May 2011.

The attacks on the state's installations and security services and on "soft" civilian targets were orchestrated by the Pakistani Taliban (TTP). It had been formed in December 2007 and brought together several groups under the leadership of Baitullah Mehsud, who based his power in South Waziristan. The state claimed that Mehsud was the instigator of numerous suicide attacks, including the assassination of Benazir Bhutto. The TTP was not a monolithic organization but rather coordinated the activities of existing radical Sunni jihadist and sectarian groups. After the postelection lull, a new upsurge in activity began in late 2008. It was focused in the Swat region, which for a while slipped out of government control. The mounting violence in Pakistan formed the backdrop to protracted negotiations in 2014 between Nawaz Sharif's government and representatives of the Pakistani Taliban.

Pakistan's postcolonial history is much more nuanced than its journalistic portrayal in terms of the binary opposites of authoritarianism and democracy, secularism and Islamism, tradition and modernity. For these reasons, simplistic hopes of Western policy analysts—that the conduct of a single fair and free election or the ability of an elected government to serve out its term would somehow transform the country's politics and society—have been misplaced. Pakistan is not only much more complex than monochrome portrayals admit, but it is in rapid transition as a result of population growth and urbanization. Because census data are inadequate, these transformations are not fully appreciated. Environmental changes will also make it unlikely that Pakistan will be able to "muddle through" future crises both natural and man-made, as it has done in the past.

A second major theme of the country's history which we have studied in this and other chapters is that of interconnectedness. Events in Afghanistan, changing policies in Washington, the cold war with India, and the remittances and political stances of overseas Pakistanis have all shaped domestic development. Despite the siren call of nationalist historiography, Pakistan is best understood in terms of the interplay among local, regional, national, and global networks of political, economic, and religious influence.

Finally, it is important to understand Pakistan on its terms and not to regard it as the "other" of Indian secularism or democratic achievement. This exaggerates the differences in the political trajectories of the two successors to the Raj.[24] It also reinforces a stereotypical understanding of Pakistan that flounders when confronted with the paradoxes that abound in the country's history—whether, as we have seen, it involves a more liberal response to the media from a general than that of his elected predecessor, or the espousal of Islamic socialism by one of the leading landowners of Sindh, or the cultivation of the Taliban and sectarian extremists by Benazir Bhutto, the face of liberal Pakistan.

FIFTEEN

India Shining

The marketing slogan India Shining was popularized by the ruling Bharatiya Janata Party (BJP) as part of its 2004 election strategy. The International Technology Park (IRP) in Bangalore exemplified the optimism and the rebranding of India trumpeted by the artistic director Prathap Suthan's campaign. The seventy-acre site housed offices for the multinational software giants Microsoft and Google. Buildings with such names as Discoverer, Innovator, and Explorer provided space for spin-off companies. The Ascendas Park Mall, situated at the entrance of the complex, had numerous food outlets, a bowling alley, and a movie multiplex. The ITP infrastructure included its own power plant, sewage treatment plant, and several parking lots.[1] The first world had come to India, and not in a Bollywood dream factory production.

India's Silent Revolution

One clue to the BJP's 2004 election defeat, which astounded analysts, lay in the parkland surrounding a developing rival internet technologies hub, with its multiplexes and shopping malls at Gomti Nagar in Lucknow. The city lay in the heart of India's most populous state, the UP, and was a vital swing state for the BJP. In the event the proponents of India Shining placed in third place in the polls. The Ambedkar Park in Lucknow surrounding the IT hub had been renamed the Ambedkar Memorial in June 2002. Work began on creating the double-domed sandstone stupa that currently dominates the site, whose main entrance is guarded by the statues of sixty elephants. The elephant is the election symbol of the Bahajan Samaj Party (BSP), whose charismatic female leader Mayawati had ordered the memorial's construction in honor of the Dalit leader.[2] The BSP kept the BJP out of power by providing external support to the Congress-led coalition of Manmohan Singh, which formed the new government.

The rise of the Dalit-based BSP symbolized the new India as much as did the IT boom. It formed part of a resurgent caste-based politics that mushroomed in a competitive environment of government patronage and affirmative action.[3] The Dalits, under the astute leadership of Kanshi Ram and Mayawati, triumphed by turning to upper-caste support in order to fend off the more numerous lower castes, who had increasingly organized themselves in UP and elsewhere in India outside of the Congress. The Dalit–upper caste combine enabled Mayawati during her period as chief minister (2002–3; 2007–12) to build her statues and thousands of her Dalit supporters to secure government jobs.

In other parts of India, lower-caste groups actively sought similar benefits. Politics increasingly revolved around collective caste identity and quota politics, the so-called Mandalization of politics.[4] Christophe Jaffrelot has provided an authoritative account of the rise of the 3,743 castes listed as Other Backward Castes (OBCs). The short-lived National Front government of Vishwanath Pratap Singh (2 December 1989–10 November 1990), following Rajiv Gandhi's 1989 electoral setback in the wake of the Bofors Scandal, accelerated this process.[5] V. P. Singh implemented the Mandal Commission Report, with its recommendation that 27 percent of all government posts be reserved for OBCs, and 15 percent for Dalits. This generated immense upper-caste resentment, as government administration had always been seen as its monopoly.

Under Mandalization, huge numbers of jobs became available under the new reservation policy, but more important, a politics of identity was encouraged that replaced the old clientalistic Congress politics. Formerly the Congress had established patron-client links with the Dalits and Muslims at the bottom of society, while also relying on the dominant castes at the top. These varied from state to state. In Andhra Pradesh, for example, they were the Reddys; in Karnataka, Vokkaligas and Lingayats; Kshatriyas in Gujarat; and Brahmins in Uttar Pradesh. Mandalization dealt a major blow to this type of politics.

Parties could no longer ignore the OBCs because of their new assertiveness and numerical strength. In northern India, the number of OBC
parliamentary representatives more than doubled to 25 percent between
1984 and 1996. OBCs not only aligned with variations of the Janata Party,
which formed their original political vehicle, but clambered on board Congress and the BJP. These two parties consequently had to adjust their politics. Caste identities did not, of course, sit well with the BJP's emphasis on
Hindu identity. The consolidation of caste also strengthened Dalit-based
politics, although Dalits did not have the numbers to become as influential
as the OBCs, and in the Punjab, where they were more numerous, they
lacked the organization, outside of the Doaba region, to strengthen their
political presence.[6]

OBC political interests in UP resided in the Samawaji Party. The party's
leader, a former wrestler, Mulayam Singh Yadav, was originally a protégé of
Raj Narain. He first became chief minister of UP in 1989. The OBCs also
became a powerful force in Bihar. Here successive governments were led
by the Janata Dal and the Rashtriya Janata Dal Party. The colorful politician Laloo Prasad Yadav was their dominant figure. He became known for
his rustic language and appearance, addressing journalists while wearing
a sleeveless *ganji* (vest) and a dhoti while chewing paan. Laloo had first
entered the Lok Sabha in 1977, when the Janata Party had swept up all the
seats from Bihar. He had, as president of the Patna University Students'
Union, been actively involved in the 1974 movement led by Jayaprakash
Narayan against the Congress state government. He served as chief minister
of Bihar from 1990 to 1997, consolidating political support during this time
not only from the OBCs but from the Muslims who had traditionally supported Congress. After he became embroiled in what was known as the Fodder Scam, Laloo handed over power to his semiliterate wife, Rabri Devi.[7]
In July 1977 she became Bihar's first female chief minister.[8] Laloo moved
to national politics in 1998 and six years later became an extremely successful railways minister in Manmohan Singh's United Progressive Alliance.[9]
Opponents, however, pointed to the criminalization of Bihar's politics under the Rashtriya Janata Dal regime, terming it a "jungle raj." Laloo was
eventually convicted for his role in the Fodder Scam in autumn of 2013 but

was freed on bail by the Supreme Court within two months. Close family members fought the 2014 Indian general election on his behalf, but the BJP triumphed in Bihar over the Rashtriya Janata Dal, as it did elsewhere in India, where it rode the Modi wave.

The BJP in UP, partly in response to the BSP's co-option of its own upper-caste base of support, was eventually driven with mixed results to play the OBC card through the figure of Kalyan Singh.[10] His government pioneered the BJP rewriting of history textbooks for use in state schools to include a stereotyped view of Muslim destruction of Hindu temples in the "Medieval" period. Most controversially, Kalyan Singh's government was complicit in the December 1992 destruction by temple volunteers (*kar sevaks*) from the Rashtriya Swayam Sevak Sangh (RSS) of the Babri Masjid constructed on the ruins of Ram's temple in the pilgrimage town of Ayodhya. The BJP had reinvigorated the Babri Masjid issue in an attempt to counter caste-based politics with Hindu communal assertion. "Mandir," the movement to restore Hindu sacred temple sites occupied by Muslims, came to be opposed to "Mandal" as the locus of political mobilization.

Mandir and the Rise of the BJP

The recovery of Ram's Ayodhya birthplace from its Muslim "occupation" by Babur's Mosque and the building of a temple there became symbolic of the BJP's campaign to restore national Hindu pride.[11] Inchoate upper-caste anxieties, arising from the Punjab and Kashmir insurgencies[12] and the reports of large-scale conversions of Hindus to Islam in Tamil Nadu,[13] were displaced onto a demonized Muslim "other." Muslims not only were blamed for Babur's past iconoclastic behavior but were dubbed as a "pampered" minority. This claim, in fact, inverted the reality of Muslim marginalization so explicitly revealed by the 2005 Sachar Committee.[14] Hindu nationalists in the BJP and its associated "family," which included RSS and the Visha Hindu Parishad (VHP), argued that India would be strong only if it acknowledged the genius of its Hindu culture.[15] The BJP's will to power in domestic politics was to be matched on the international stage with the nuclear weapons testing of the Atal Bihari Vajpayee–BJP government in

May 1998. The BJP's cult of manliness and virility, rooted in nineteenth-century rejections of colonialist charges of Hindu effeminacy, was reflected in popular headlines that hailed the tests as "Vajpayee's Viagra."

The BJP's initial breakthrough occurred in the 1989 general elections, when it secured eighty-nine seats in the Lok Sabha, although it polled less than 12 percent of the votes. From the outset its growing popularity was linked not just with the long-term RSS organizational base but with the emotive issue of the Babri Masjid. The Congress government in UP made the campaign to "liberate" Ram's alleged birthplace at Ayodhya possible in 1986 by encouraging the unlocking of the mosque. The screening on national television (Doordarshan) of the religious epic the Ramayana—broadcast to a spellbound nation on Sunday mornings from 25 January 1987 to 31 July 1988—intensified interest in the religious site. The popular reception of the broadcasts appears to bear out that Doordarshan "inadvertently" assisted the BJP's "project of fundamentalism."[16] The ceremonial chariot processions (*rath yatras*) that accompanied the BJP's intensification of the campaign significantly copied aspects of the costuming and iconography of the Doordarshan series. Lal Krishna Advani, the BJP party president, began his rath yatra in late September 1990 from the Somnath Temple in Gujarat, whose destruction in January 1025 by Mahmud Ghaznavi had become a shorthand for Muslim aggression. The procession route was accompanied by Hindu-Muslim riots. Advani, who had entered public life as an RSS volunteer in pre-Partition Karachi, was finally arrested at Samastipur in Bihar on 23 October 23 at the behest of the chief minister, Laloo Prasad Yadav. Troops stationed at Ayodhya prevented the large number of kar sevaks who massed there a week later from destroying the temple.

These events reprieved the Babri Masjid but toppled the National Front government following the BJP's withdrawal of support. The short-lived Samajwadi Janata Party government of Chandra Shekhar fell when Rajiv Gandhi withdrew his support. During the ensuing election campaign, on 21 May 1991, Rajiv was assassinated at Sriperumbudar by Thenmozhi Raja-ratnam, a member of the Liberation Tigers of Tamil Eelam. This Sri Lankan Tamil extremist group had opposed the Congress leader's sending an Indian peacekeeping force to the island.[17] Rajiv Gandhi was cremated following a state funeral at Vir Bhumi on the banks of the Yamuna River, close to his mother's *Samadhi*, or funeral cremation ground. His death influenced the poll outcome, allowing the veteran Telegu congressman Narasimha Rao to become India's ninth prime minister on 21 June 1991.[18] Rao, whose role in India's economic liberalization will be examined later, also had to deal with the rising crescendo of the BJP's campaign. The polls had seen almost a doubling of the support for the BJP to 21 percent of the vote, although it won only an additional 30 seats, giving it a total of 119 in the Lok Sabha. This performance seemed to justify the party's Ayodhya strategy and encouraged its intensification.

On 2 December 1992, thousands of kar sevaks broke through the police cordon and swarmed over the Babri Masjid. In pictures relayed around the world, they tore it down, using pickaxes, shovels, and their bare hands. Nehru's vision of a secular India tumbled along with the domed structures. Several months of Hindu-Muslim violence followed in such cities as Surat, Ahmedabad, and Delhi. The worst violence was in Bombay. Riots there were organized against the Muslims by Shiv Sena activists. Shiv Sena, under the leadership of Bal Thackeray, a former political cartoonist, had originally risen to power in the late 1960s by articulating local Maharashtrian hostility to South Indian migrant workers.[19] With the growth of the BJP, however, it switched to a demonization of the Muslim population. Shiv Sena activists, just as Congress Party members had done in the anti-Sikh pogrom of 1984, used electoral registers to identify businesses and residences to be attacked.[20] The party was also assisted by its links with the city's criminal gangs and developers eager to clear Muslim shanty dwellers from plots whose value was rocketing during the city's real estate boom.[21]

Ayodhya did not, however, mark a decisive political triumph for the BJP. Its state governments in Uttar Pradesh, Himachel Pradesh, and Madhya Pradesh were all defeated in 1993. The BJP national government lasted just thirteen days in office after the 1996 polls, as it could not find regional and caste-based allies. This lesson was learned. The establishment of a BJP-led government two years later resulted in the main from making alliances more effectively than had Congress. It linked not only with established regional parties like the AIADMK in Tamil Nadu and the TDP in Andhra

Pradesh but with OBC-dominated parties such as the Samata Party and the Lok Shakti. The BJP had finally come to power, as head of a National Democratic Alliance coalition but paradoxically through a process that has been termed Indirect Mandalization.

The Vajpayee government (1998–2004), as we have seen, did develop the "Hindu bomb." But to the dismay of RSS purists, the National Democratic Alliance coalition backtracked on earlier promises regarding the repeal of Kashmir's special constitutional status and on establishing a uniform civil code, which would have abolished Muslim personal law. The Vajpayee government was also committed to economic reform, with its attendant consumerism, and a "calibrated globalization," despite the RSS-dominated Swadeshi Jagaran Manch, which emphasized austerity and indigenous culture. One scholar wittily labeled such differences in outlook as "Kar Sevaks Versus Car Sevaks."[22]

The BJP national leaders fell silent when its state administrations permitted attacks against minorities. Some of these were directed against Christian tribal populations, but the most notorious episode involved the 2002 pogrom against the Gujarati Muslims. There were claims that Gujarat's BJP Chief Minister Narendra Modi was complicit in the attacks which over a three-month period claimed as many as two thousand lives.[23] He was shunned by both the United States and Britain as a result, but the "Modi brand" of development in Gujarat was eventually to secure his triumphant national election in May 2014. The attacks were claimed to have been a "reaction" to the torching by Muslims on 27 February at Godhra of a train that was carrying a group of *kar sevaks* from Ayodhya. In the words of an experienced analyst of postindependence Indian communal violence, this was no mere reaction but exploitation of "an opportunity to provoke Hindi communal sentiments to draw political advantage."[24] "It was a pogrom," Asghar Ali Engineer continues, "and a pogrom more sustained than at the time of the Delhi Riots. Indeed one would need to look at the involvement of the civil authorities and the Police in the Partition-related violence to find parallels of the state machinery along with criminal elements wreaking havoc with impunity."[25]

kar sevaks?

Modi called state assembly elections in December 2002, and the BJP secured a two-thirds majority. The party captured most of the seats precisely in areas affected worst by the riots, revealing once again the utility of communal violence in electioneering. Modi's two further state victories ensured that, despite his controversial reputation both nationally and internationally, he became the BJP national prime ministerial candidate for the 2014 polls. His slick public relations campaigns, adroit use of social media, and ability to attract overseas investment all contributed to a Modi brand.[26] Opponents argued that close examination of the much vaunted economic record of "NAMO" in Gujarat revealed rates of growth that were no higher than in a number of other states. Moreover, low human development indicators betrayed the fact that the populations of the tribal belt and ghettoized Muslims had been excluded from "Vibrant Gujarat."[27] The slickness of the Modi campaign, however, overcame these criticisms. Alongside his popularity, the stalling of India's rapid economic growth, the corruption scandals surrounding the Congress government, and Rahul Gandhi's lack of appeal to ordinary voters all ensured a decisive BJP victory.

Economic Liberalization

Modi's Gujarat economy was growing at around 10 percent beginning in 2005. It was thus keeping pace with the leading states and just topped the national rate, whose performance led not only to the domestic India Shining copy but to international portrayal of the country's economy as an "emerging giant."[28] India, after a generation of an annual "Hindu rate of growth" of around 3 percent, was growing more rapidly than all other Asian economies except China's.[29] Rapid economic growth was accompanied by increasing exports of goods and services, a dramatic rise in foreign investment, and a revolution in the telecommunications sector of the economy. Merchandise exports, for example, rose fivefold from 1990–91 to reach $102.7 billion in 2005–6; services exports stood at $60.6 billion in 2005–6. Foreign investment rose from $6 billion in 2002–3 to $20.2 billion in 2005–6.[30] Telephone connections increased from 23 million in 1999 to about 672 million in 2010, a more rapid growth than anywhere else in the world.[31] The slowing of India's rapid economic progress in the two years before the 2014 polls was a major factor in the disillusionment with the Congress rule of outgoing Prime Minister Manmohan Singh.

The roots of India's economic transformation can be traced back to Rajiv Gandhi's period in office, October 1984–December 1989, although the crucial changes occurred only beginning in 1991. The earlier period has been termed one of "liberalization by stealth" with respect to industrial deregulation. The asset limit under which businesses were controlled by the 1969 Monopolies and Restrictive Trade Practices Act (MRTP) was raised by Rajiv from two hundred million rupees ($4.3 million) to one billion rupees ($21.5 million). The cement industry, among others, was decontrolled. The conditions were laid for later development in the telecommunications industry by creating a Department of Telecommunications (1985) and ending the government monopoly on the manufacture of telecommunications equipment. The opening of the first technology park in Bangalore and the liberalization of imports of electronic equipment further boosted technological development.[32] The conditions were thus being created for the 1990s boom.[33] Nonetheless, Rajiv failed to achieve a major liberalization of the economy because "he was not able to change the mindset of his colleagues or overcome the opposition of powerful groups that had benefited the most from planned economic development."[34]

Drastic economic reform was delayed until the severe balance of payments and fiscal deficit crisis in July 1991. It culminated years of increasing government borrowing, lack of economic competitiveness, and a closed economy. The rise in the cost of oil imports following Iraq's invasion of Kuwait in August 1990 was the tipping point. India was left virtually bankrupt, with foreign exchange reserves roughly equal to two weeks' imports; a current account deficit close to 35 percent of GDP; and a fiscal deficit of around 8.5 percent GDP. The urgent need for IMF and World Bank conditional lending assistance led to a major liberalization of trade and the domestic economy. This was successfully sustained by growing awareness within domestic policy-making circles of the need to change tack. Rajiv's earlier reforms had seen growth quicken. The collapse of the Soviet Union and the growing outward economic orientation of China were also important factors in New Delhi's transformed economic approach.

P. V. Narasimha Rao's appointment of Dr. Manmohan Singh as finance minister in June 1991 boosted those Indian technocrats like the commerce secretary, Montek Singh Ahluwalia, who favored liberalization.[35] Singh reduced tariff rates, ended import licensing on capital goods, and devalued the rupee. These moves created the conditions for the export boom we have already seen, especially in IT and services. Deregulation enabled India's competitive advantages in this sector, arising from low-cost, English-speaking engineers, to be fully exploited. Tariff liberalization increased Indian industry's competitiveness. The successful Tata group exploited the new globalization opportunities to expand overseas with eventual acquisition of the Jaguar and Land Rover automobile industries. The Indian middle class, increasingly wealthy as a result of rapid economic growth, provided a market for its Indica brand. Finally, Tata introduced the world's cheapest car, the Nano, designed for the home Asian market.

Rao, aside from backing Manmohan Singh's approach, took a hands-on role in the economic reforms. He became industry minister and used this role to both drastically reduce licensing and encourage greater foreign investment. The latter process was assisted by the establishment of a National Stock Exchange in 1993. It was not until 2001, however, following a major scandal, that trading rules were made transparent. The Air Corporations Act (1994) was another important liberalization measure, which allowed private airlines to operate. There was a resulting surge in air traffic and the emergence of such companies as Jet, Kingfisher, and Spice, which became familiar to visitors and domestic passengers.

The Vajpayee BJP–led government matched the pace of economic reform and of growth of the Rao period. There were further stock market reforms and encouragement for private sector involvement in telecommunications and for international investment. As we have seen, however, the India Shining trademark on these successes did not avert election defeat. The government's defeat raised the wider issue of whether the reforms had increased social inequalities and regional disparities.[36] States such as Maharashtra, Tamil Nadu, and Gujarat grew much faster in the early postreform period than the less-advantaged Bihar and UP. The latter lacked the infrastructure and human capital to reap the growth opportunities.[37]

Even in the most-developed states, infrastructural problems threatened long-term growth. While the power sector was in better shape than in neighboring Pakistan, it was still beset by rampant theft, the charging of higher prices to industrial customers than to others, and outages resulting from the inability to meet supply peaks.[38] The agricultural sector remained a drag on India's economy. It remained a large employer—the 2001 census showed 58 percent of the population employed in farming—but was subsidy reliant and growing at a much slower rate, less than 3 percent, than the rest of the economy. The human costs of agricultural distress were starkly revealed in the wave of farmer suicides in such states as Andhra Pradesh, Maharashtra, Madhya Pradesh, and Karnataka.[39] Such policies as the Mahatma Gandhi National Rural Employment Guarantee Act (2005) were adopted by the Manmohan Singh–led coalition government to address the issue of poverty alleviation in the countryside.[40] The Sikh prime minister's final term in office was accompanied by a slowdown in growth, accompanied by infrastructural problems, labor market inflexibilities, and the marginalization of large sections of the population. Popular attention focused more on corruption, however, than on India's social inequalities, as seen in public support for the campaigns of Anna Hazare in 2011 and the stunning electoral debut of his protégé Arvind Kerijiwal at the head of the Aam Aadmi Party in the Delhi state elections a year later.

During the three-plus decades since Indira Gandhi's assassination, India has undergone significant political and economic transformation. The country is wealthier, with a large consumerist middle class. The communications revolution has improved the lives of huge numbers of people living in both the towns and countryside. India is becoming increasingly urbanized. Malnutrition and agrarian distress, however, remain problems not just in "poor" UP and Bihar but in states that have experienced rapid growth, such as Maharashtra and Gujarat. India is also not shining for the increasingly ghettoized urban Muslim populations. Where communal peace reigns, as it has in Gujarat since the 2002 pogrom, it is because there is no political necessity for violence, as the BJP has become the preeminent electoral force.

The past decades have been an era mainly of coalition politics, in which regional parties align themselves with the Congress or the BJP. Both national parties have needed to broaden election strategies to address the rise of the OBCs. This development has meant that caste remains a hugely significant source of political identity. Lower-caste empowerment has been linked with the "criminalization" of politics in such states as Bihar. Conversely, it could be regarded as a deepening of democracy: a more rough-and-tumble type of patron-client politics than the upper-caste patronage networks that traditionally dominated state institutions, with the result that the poor were marginalized and the constitutional rights abridged. Laloo promised his lower-caste supporters "dignity" and a "voice." The 2014 Modi wave swept aside Laloo's influence.

Rent-seeking politics has undoubtedly increased at state level. This has hindered international companies that wish to do business in India, even though there has been considerable national political consensus on the issue of economic liberalization. The power of vested interests has slowed reforms since the heady days of the Rao period.[41] The continuing institutional barriers to foreign and domestic investment, however, threaten continued high rates of growth less than do infrastructural weaknesses and the problems of achieving socially and regionally inclusive patterns of growth. Alongside these issues are the environmental challenges we have seen earlier. The state's ability to address the political, economic, and environmental challenges facing its billion-plus inhabitants in the years ahead will determine whether India fulfills the rhetoric of its emerging global power.

SIXTEEN

The Contemporary International Relations of South Asia

The Jaswant Garh War Memorial at Nuranang, Arunachal Pradesh, stands beside the rugged road to the nearby Buddhist monastery town of Tawang. Tourists are requested to stop by to "Have a Cup of Tea, Be Part of History." Exhausted by the hairpin bends of the hazardous terrain of the Sela Pass, they are happy to take advantage of the snack store run by the Garhwal Rifles and to look around the templelike memorial. It commemorates the heroism of a rifleman, Jaswant Singh Rawat, who singlehandedly repulsed Chinese invaders for seventy-two hours at this outpost during the 1962 Sino-Indian War. Rawat's uniform, cap, and watch are displayed at the memorial beside his garlanded bronze bust.

Despite the tourist presence, this area is heavily militarized, for as we have seen, Arunachal Pradesh ("Land of the rising sun") is claimed by China as South Tibet. Since 2008, China has vigorously asserted its old territorial claims and engaged in aggressive patrolling of the border areas. In March 2009 Beijing attempted to block a $2.9 billion loan to India from the Asian Development Bank (ADB) because it included flood relief projects in what it termed the "disputed territory" of Arunachal Pradesh. When Manmohan Singh visited the state in October 2009, Beijing termed it "unhelpful." The more belligerent tone was accompanied by renewed territorial claims and military incursions in western Bhutan's Dolam Plateau, where Bhutan, Tibet, and India meet. These moves threaten the Siliguri corridor, which connects the northeastern states with the remainder of India. Paradoxically, these moves occurred when trade between India and China was booming. From 2000 to 2010 trade increased twentyfold, to $61.7 billion, with China becoming India's leading trading partner.[1] Some analysts have wondered whether, despite Beijing's official rhetoric of cooperation and economic engagement, events in Arunachal Pradesh and the neighboring Tibetan plateau will in the coming decades define future international relations and strategic planning in South Asia as much as the Kashmir dispute has done to date.[2]

Sino-Indian engagement and increasing strategic competition represent one of three profound transformations in South Asia's post–Cold War international relations. The second major change involves an increasingly close Indo-US relationship. Finally, India and Pakistan have emerged during this period as nuclear weapons powers, and Afghanistan has become a significant theater for Indo-Pakistani rivalry.[3] These transformations coexist with long-standing constants in South Asia's international relations. These include Pakistan's Indocentric foreign policy, with the Kashmir dispute playing a critical role, and Pakistan's support of proxy Islamist forces against India. The latter strategy has had a blowback destabilizing effect and led to the 1999 Kargil War. "Terrorism" real and perceived continues to bedevil Indo-Pakistani relations. The rocky relationship between New Delhi and Islamabad has continued to stymie attempts to encourage regional economic and political cooperation through the institution of the South Asian Association for Regional Cooperation (SAARC).

The Impact of China's Rise on South Asia
Sino-Indian Relations

China's claim on Arunachal Pradesh rests in part on the region's cultural affinity with neighboring Tibet. Fortified *gompas*, prayer wheels, and red-robed monks milling around the precincts of the large seventeenth-century Buddhist monastery founded in Tawang by the Tibetan Buddhist Mera Lama Ladre Gyasto all attest to this. Moreover, it was through the Tawang Valley that the Dalai Lama and his followers entered India as they fled the Chinese repression of the abortive 1959 Tibetan rebellion. Roadside billboards proudly draw attention to this history. China's renewed assertiveness followed shortly after monk-led spring 2008 unrest in Tibet. The discontent was a response to increased economic exploitation and an influx of Han Chinese following the opening of the China-Tibet railway. Chinese development in Tibet has had profound ecological consequences, which have in turn appalled native inhabitants who witnessed the pollution of sacred rivers and lakes, such as Lake Yamdrok Tso southwest of Lhasa.

The title of a book by a former army officer, *Tibet's Waters Will Save China*, sums up official Chinese attitudes. Control of China's western frontier in Tibet is vital to the ambitious hydrological plans to feed, with water diverted from the Brahmaputra River, the parched plains of North China, home to nearly half of the country's population.[4] This would involve constructing the world's largest dam at Motuo just before the river enters India. The dam would feed the water supply diverted through canals and tunnels into the Yellow River, forming the "great western route" component of China's South-North Water Transfer Project. It would also make a significant hydroelectric power contribution (thirty-eight gigawatts) to China's voracious energy demands. To contextualize this, Motuo would be nine times bigger than America's Hoover Dam in terms of hydro-generating capacity and the equivalent of Australia's 2010 electricity capacity from all energy sources.[5]

The harnessing of the Brahmaputra not only would decrease Indian rice cultivation in Assam but, as we have seen, could have a major effect downstream in Bangladesh. Smaller dam projects in Tibet that are part of the Three Rivers Development Project have already had adverse environmental impacts downstream. Indeed, India's application to the ADB for funding was specifically to address the flooding problems in Arunachal Pradesh caused by breaches in dams, release of excess water, and resultant deforestation in Tibet. According to Brahma Chellaney, "Water is becoming a key security issue in India-China relations as a result of China's water megaprojects on the Tibetan Plateau. . . . Water indeed adds an ominous new dimension to an India-China situation characterized by territorial disputes, deep-seated mistrust, border tensions, and geo-political rivalry."[6] He further maintains that "Between nuclear-armed, continental-sized China and India, the water bomb is no less potent than the nuclear bomb."[7]

China's claims on Arunachal Pradesh have to be set in the context of the wider strategic rivalry to which Chellaney alludes. The claims followed shortly after the improvement of US-Indian ties was signaled by a nuclear deal between the two countries. They could, viewed in this light, be seen as a deterrent to further strategic partnership between Washington and New Delhi. Another factor explaining China's new assertiveness is the military modernization that has accompanied the country's spectacular economic development. This has encouraged a more muscular diplomacy not just in the sensitive Tawang area but in the Indian Ocean and especially the waters of the South China Sea.

China's "string of pearls" policy of acquisition of port facilities in the Indian Ocean has added a naval dimension to the Chinese-Indian geopolitical competition. This strategy includes military agreements with such countries as Cambodia and Myanmar, as well as a commercial presence in the Indian Ocean secured through the funding of the development of Gwadar in Pakistan and the building of container ports at Chittagong and Hambantota (Sri Lanka).[8] Indian financial support for the reconstruction of Chabahar port in Iran was a direct response to Gwadar. China's increasing strategic expansion in the Indian Ocean prompted New Delhi's decision to establish its Far Eastern Command in the Andaman and Nicobar islands. The Indian navy increasingly participates in exercises involving the United States, Japan, and Australia. Ties with Japan have also been strengthened by the joint development of natural gas in the Andaman Sea.[9] India has also helped Vietnam's naval development.

India sees China's string of pearls as part of a containment policy. This perception was reinforced by Beijing's agreement with Myanmar for the construction of a highway linking Kunming in southeastern China through the country to Chittagong. This would provide Beijing with direct access to the Bay of Bengal.[10] India still has the upper hand with respect to naval power, unlike in the nuclear, border transport development, and hydrological fields.[11] But Beijing's interest in extending its maritime influence in the Indian Ocean is a clear component of a growing bilateral divergence. This has led some analysts to see the unprecedented simultaneous rise of China (the world's "back factory") and of India (the world's "back office") as generating a rivalry that will become a defining feature of the twenty-first century. This rivalry has already spread from economic to military competition and includes not just Asia but Africa, where China has stolen a significant march in obtaining minerals and energy assets, and the Gulf States, where both countries are involved in deepening engagement.[12] The Gulf not only is vitally important for Indian oil supplies but, as we have seen, is the destination for much migrant labor. The Indian diaspora has been most important in encouraging commercial and strategic ties, however, in Singapore. Indian migrants form part of a "look east" policy in line with Indian response to strategic rivalry with China.

The "look east" policy, initiated by the United Front government, is intended to extend New Delhi's reach into Southeast Asia. India has attempted to cash in on long-term cultural and trade links in the region and to exploit growing concerns about both China's expansionism in the South China Sea and the impact of its hydroengineering projects. Chinese projects on the Mekong River affect fishing and rice cultivation in downstream states such as Laos, Thailand, Cambodia, and Vietnam. Beginning in the early 1990s, China has built a number of dams on the Mekong's upper reaches, as it cascades from Tibet through Yunnan Province. Some of the schemes are massive. The Xiaowan Dam, which is higher than the Eiffel Tower, threatens the downstream flow of water and silt on which the lives of millions in the Indochina Peninsula depend.

India has developed close strategic and commercial ties with such countries as Vietnam and Singapore. In 1995 it obtained full dialogue partner status with the Association of Southeast Asian Nations (ASEAN).[13] The possibility of improving communication between India's Northeast and Southeast Asia through Myanmar is being explored through such projects as the Kaladan Multi Modal Plan, connecting Kolkata and Sittwe by sea and then Sittwe to Mizoram, as well as the two thousand–mile Trilateral Highway Project. The highway, which could be completed in 2016, will link Manipur to Thailand via Myanmar.

India's "soft power," as seen in the popularity of Bollywood films throughout Southeast Asia, has also contributed to its increased standing in the region.[14] Such cities as Singapore (for films like *Krrish* and *Pyaar Impossible!*),

Bangkok, and Kuala Lumpur both provide film locations and host awards ceremonies. By 2009 more than a hundred Indian films were being shot annually in Thailand. They contributed to Bangkok's Hindi film dance exercise craze. "Rukhsters"—fans of the Bollywood superstar Shahrukh Khan— have organized dance events in Indonesia. Spurred by the influence of Bollywood, traditional Indian dance, art, and music have all become more prominent, as seen in Singapore's annual Indian Festival of Arts held at the Esplanade theater complex each November.

China's Presence in South Asia

Beijing's strategy appears to be to hem in India. It has used its border disputes and South Asian countries' hostility to India's dominance as factors in this policy, along with a growing naval presence. Neighbors' apprehensions regarding Indian hegemony were not entirely unfounded in the light of New Delhi's annexation of Sikkim in 1975, intervention in Sri Lanka in 1987–90, and blocking of goods into Nepal in 1989.

In an attempt to dispel the view of a "big brother" India United Front government Prime Minister Inder Kumar Gujral set out his famous five principles of foreign relations in 1996.[15] The Gujral Doctrine, with its emphasis on nonintervention and respect for territorial integrity and sovereignty, lightened the regional mood for a time. It especially led to a warming in the relationship between New Delhi and Colombo. This thaw was also encouraged by the decline in Indian pro-Tamil sentiment following Rajiv Gandhi's assassination, and by the election of Chandrika Kumaratunga as president of Sri Lanka in 1994. He worked with a series of prime ministers to free up trade with India and to resolve such long-standing political issues as citizenship rights for Tamils of Indian origin.

But China has become an important arms supplier to Sri Lanka, along with such South Asian countries as Nepal and Myanmar. Indeed, Colombo's ultimately successful war against the Liberation Tigers of Tamil Eelam would have been impossible without Chinese weapons. Pakistan, however, is the main recipient of Chinese armaments and has also for more than four decades jointly produced military equipment with the Chinese. This has been of vital importance for Islamabad's attempts to keep pace with India, especially during periods of US military embargo. By 2010 Chinese economic aid to Pakistan was exceeding America's. Trade had also burgeoned and was annually running at around $7 billion. China has financed the important Karakoram Highway linking the countries, and the deep-sea Gwadar Port at the entrance of the Arabian Sea.

China has also increased its trade and security relationships with Nepal and Bangladesh, providing both countries with opportunities to balance India's dominant regional power. Nepalese concerns about excessive Indian interference can be traced back to the "unequal" Treaty of Peace and Friendship concluded between India and Nepal on 31 July 1950 which recognized Nepal's independence but regulated arms imports.[16] Nehru's visit at the end of the decade was condemned in Kathmandu as being marked by a "big brother" attitude. It was a factor in King Mahendra's dismissal in 1960 of the Congress government of B. P. Koirala, who was seen as an Indian puppet. The king visited China shortly afterward. Unlike the smaller Himalayan Kingdom of Bhutan, Nepal is anxious to avoid a semiprotectorate status. The Indian annexation of Sikkim, in which ethnic Nepalis played a role, and the presence of a considerable number of Indian settlers from Eastern UP and Bihar in Nepal's Terai region caused further concern in Kathmandu. The 1983 Gurung Committee Report into Indian migration in the Terai led to press reports about India's "demographic invasion." In 1989, Indo-Nepalese relations reached their nadir when New Delhi suspended its trade and transit arrangements to demonstrate its disapproval of Kathmandu's decision to import arms from China through its border with Tibet. Another low point occurred at the Dhaka Summit in 2005, when King Gyanendra raised the prospect of China's admission to SAARC.[17] New Delhi remained aloof the following year when the constitutional parties, along with the Maoists, moved against the monarchical absolutism Gyanendra had introduced in February 2005.

Unsurprisingly, Nepal has been less ready than Bhutan to develop hydroelectric projects with India. The Indo-Bhutanese projects at Chukha, Kurichhu, and Tala (which at 1,020 megawatts is the biggest) have become the country's largest source of revenue.[18] The hydro power sector accounts for as much as 45 percent of government revenues and 12 percent of GDP. While Bhutan has prospered in providing energy to its neighboring giant, Nepal not only remains sunk in poverty but needs to import electricity from India, despite the hydro power potential of the Kosi and Gandak Rivers. Fewer than one Nepalese resident in five has access to electricity. China thus provides the possibility of economic development and strategic balance. India retains the upper hand, but China is emerging as a significant donor and commercial partner, with trade between China and Nepal rising twentyfold in 2005–9 to reach $414 million. Cultural and academic ties have also increased with the establishment of a Confucius Centre at Kathmandu University.

Western sanctions following government repression of the pro-democracy movement in Myanmar in 1988 and 1990 served as a prelude to growing Chinese influence. In addition to providing military assistance, China has assisted in building up the infrastructure of its Burmese southern neighbor. It has also established listening posts to monitor Indian naval activity. The China National Petroleum Company is also engaged in oil exploration in the waters off the communally disturbed western Rakhine state, home of the embattled Muslim Rohingya community. India has responded to the Chinese presence by its own road-building projects and by increasing trade. The agreement of June 2010 was an important liberalization measure. India has also engaged the Myanmar military government in an attempt to secure cooperation against insurgents in the Northeast who had based themselves in the country.[19]

Relations between India and Bangladesh, after the honeymoon post–liberation war era, have been marked by mistrust, tension, and resentfulness.[20] We have seen that issues of water management, illegal migration, and claims that the Chittagong Hill Tracts provided sanctuaries for Indian insurgents have all undermined bilateral relations. The India-"locked" Bangladesh territory that has been the legacy of the Radcliffe Award has created issues over transit. During interludes of military rule and BNP governments, Bangladeshi attitudes have become increasingly pro-Pakistan and open to Chinese influence.

Changing Domestic Foreign Policy Contexts

Geopolitical strategic moves by the two Asian giants are complicated by domestic political developments not only within Bangladesh but in other countries of Southeast and South Asia. The coming to power of the Liberal Democratic Party in Japan in 2009, for example, temporarily threatened an emerging Japan-India relationship to counter China as it raised the thorny issue of nuclear proliferation. This trajectory was resumed, however, after a diplomatic spat between Tokyo and Beijing over the Senkaku Islands.

India's influence in Nepal was threatened by the loss of power of its traditional monarchical ally, and by the Maoists coming down from the hills into government following the April 2008 Constituent Assembly elections.[21] The Maoist leader Pushpa Kamal Dahal ("Prachandra") became prime minister. This added a new and uncertain dimension to Indian and Chinese jockeying for influence. Prachandra broke with the tradition of previous Nepali prime ministers, who visited India before China, when he attended the closing ceremony of the Beijing Olympics shortly after assuming office. China had in fact placed realpolitik before ideological support for the Maoists. During the decadelong Maoist insurgency, which claimed more than thirteen thousand lives, Beijing supplied arms to the Royal Nepal Army.

China's growing role as an arms supplier to Bangladesh and in infrastructural development (symbolized by the construction of "friendship bridges") coincided with the periods of military rule and the civilian governments of the BNP. The signing of deals on the peaceful use of nuclear power (2005) and for the sale of F-7 fighters to Dhaka occurred during the last BNP-led government. The former agreement opened the way for Chinese financing of the Rooppur nuclear power project. When the Awami League returned after the December 2008 polls, relations with India became markedly warmer. The September 2009 visit of the Bangladeshi foreign minister to New Delhi was marked by increased transit trade and communication agreements.[22] This paved the way for Sheikh Hasina's visit at the beginning of 2010, which resulted in further agreements. Nonetheless, Sheikh Hasina has always sought to simultaneously maintain ties with China. She visited

Beijing in March 2010. In June the then–Chinese vice president Xi Jenping traveled to Dhaka. China promised assistance for building an $8.7 billion deep-sea port at Chittagong.[23]

The transition from an absolute to a constitutional monarchy in Bhutan (2006–8) created a new context for the traditional special relationship between Thimphu and New Delhi. This had deepened in the wake of the 1962 Sino-Indian War and has been marked by generous Indian economic aid and the presence of Indian troops in the land of the thunder dragon. Bhutan's new constitutional monarch Jigme Khesar Namgyel Wangchuck received a warm welcome on his official visit to New Delhi in August 2008. The previous year Indo-Bhutanese relations had been refreshed with the signing of a new treaty of friendship.

Indo-US Relations

The post–Cold War era has been a time of much closer ties between India and the United States. This movement reflects both a convergent strategic interest stemming from the rise of China and India's enhanced global economic presence following the post-1991 liberalization. The end of the Cold War also eliminated the thorny issue of Indo-Soviet security relations, which had alienated Washington since the time of Indira Gandhi.[24]

There are numerous accounts of the back story of the strained relations between America and the "world's largest democracy."[25] New Delhi certainly had its US advocates in Ambassadors John Kenneth Galbraith and Chester Bowles and such White House insiders as Robert Komer in the late 1950s and early 1960s. Both Eisenhower and Kennedy risked alienating their long-term Pakistani ally by providing considerable economic aid to New Delhi. Nevertheless US-Indian relations were never easy because of New Delhi's nonalignment policy. Indian criticism of the US role in Vietnam, its "flawed" economic policy in US eyes, and the emergence of the Soviet Union as India's largest trading partner further strained bilateral ties. The "short tether" food policies of 1966 and the tilt to Pakistan five years later were the lowest points in the US-Indian relationship. There followed years of "benign neglect" while the relationship between Washington and Islamabad exuded warmth in the aftermath of the Soviet invasion of Afghanistan.

We will examine the emergence of India and Pakistan as nuclear powers in the next section. Suffice it to say here that after the initial sanctions, Washington moved to adopt a more balanced approach to its diplomacy. In the period after 9/11, while Pakistan resumed its long-accustomed role as military ally, Washington progressively improved its relations with New Delhi. The process began during the second Clinton administration, following the president's visit to India in 2000, but fully flowered during the George W. Bush administration. The long-standing policy of denying nuclear technology to New Delhi was overturned by the adoption of a new strategic partnership in 2005. The United States amended its Atomic Energy Act to enable civil nuclear cooperation with India. The new strategic architecture was finally approved after rancorous debates in both countries in 2008. The important Indian diaspora lobby in Washington assisted in securing Senate approval. Islamabad regarded the new relationship as a major snub, after the United States turned down a Pakistani request for a similar deal. The shift undoubtedly raised India's global as well as regional status. India remains committed to "strategic autonomy" from Washington, but both countries are increasingly conscious of their common Asia-wide interests.

Indo-Pakistani Relations: The Nuclear Rubicon and the Afghanistan Theater

Nuclear weapons acquisition and jockeying for influence in Afghanistan were historically rooted in the postcolonial Indo-Pakistani rivalry. India began its tenure as a "nuclear pariah" following its peaceful explosion of a nuclear bomb in 1974. Bhutto's decision to produce a nuclear weapon predated this test by two years. It was motivated by the need to deter India's military superiority after the Bangladesh war and to restore Pakistan's place in the world after its defeat. It was during the rule of Bhutto's nemesis Zia that Pakistan eventually acquired its "Islamic" bomb. Pakistan used the US need for its support in Afghanistan in the 1980s as a window of opportunity to build a "bomb in the basement," circumventing nonproliferation through clandestine dealings. The United States responded in 1990 by cutting off aid and halting arms sales until Pakistan agreed to a verifiable capping of its nuclear program.

The BJP's ascent to power was a key factor in New Delhi's decision to detonate five nuclear devices at Pokhran in Rajasthan in mid-May 1998. Economic sanctions were considered a cost worth paying to signal India's national rise. The tests were also designed to send a message to Pakistan, which had the previous month test-fired a long-range missile capable of hitting any target in India. It was named Ghauri, after the Turkish invader of India in 1192. On 29 May, Pakistan under Nawaz Sharif's leadership conducted its own five nuclear explosions at the Chaghai test site in Balochistan. Henceforth Pakistan and India were to face each other across the Wagah border armed with "Islamic" and "Hindu" bombs. The scene was set for the Subcontinent to gain the unenviable sobriquet of the most dangerous place on earth.

The tests led to greater US engagement with South Asia. The significance of the mission by Robert M. Gates, deputy US national security adviser, in avoiding war in 1990, in the early stages of Pakistani support for the Kashmiri insurgency, is still vigorously debated.[26] The Kashmiri "intifada" had its roots in domestic politics, but presented Pakistan with a strategic opportunity that it eagerly seized.[27] The United States could not prevent the launching of the Pakistani invasion into Kargil in April 1999, but ensured that Islamabad's infringement against the line of control led to its diplomatic isolation.[28]

The Kargil military conflict revealed that even under the protective nuclear umbrella, Pakistan could not fight a conventional war to "free" Kashmir. Nonetheless, to keep up pressure on New Delhi, Pakistan continued to support Kashmiri jihadist organizations. Pakistan's military ruler Pervez Musharraf sought to distinguish between Kashmir-focused groups and other "terrorists" in the wake of 9/11, when Pakistan abandoned the Taliban regime in Afghanistan that it had helped create and which had hosted Osama bin Laden.[29] Pakistan supported the US-led Operation Enduring Freedom by granting overflight and landing rights and sharing intelligence. Islamabad gained leverage and acceptance from the international community, where its standing was low after the October 1999 coup and because of nuclear proliferation. However, its abandonment of the Taliban was a serious strategic setback. The new Afghan regime, headed by Hamid Karzai, brought non-Pakhtuns to the corridors of power. Tajiks and Uzbeks gained influence: two ethic groups traditionally associated with the Northern Alliance, which had looked to India for support. In the wake of 9/11, increasing Indian influence in Afghanistan, seen in substantial financial aid for reconstruction and capacity-building activities and the opening of five Indian consulates, raised fears of encirclement in some Pakistan security analysts' minds. This was not a totally irrational response, as Pakistani intelligence claimed Indian involvement in the growing insurgency in Balochistan.[30]

India's growing economic aid to Afghanistan was accompanied by a "partnership council" to enhance cooperation on security and law-enforcement issues. Manmohan Singh's visit to Kabul in May 2011, during which he addressed a joint session of the Afghan Parliament, provided a further sign of the growing Indian presence. Some commentators have claimed that New Delhi's post-2001 influence in Afghanistan could become as important a source of tension with Pakistan as the long-running Kashmiri flashpoint.[31]

Pakistan's continued logistical and financial support for militant groups engaging India, such as Lashkar-e-Toiba (LeT) and Jaish-e-Muhammad (JeM), brought India and Pakistan to a dangerous military standoff in the wake of the 13 December 2001 terrorist attack on the Indian Parliament. Seven years later another spectacular terrorist attack in Mumbai (26 November 2008), in which LeT was implicated, halted the attempted peace process that had restarted in 2004.[32]

Musharraf was an unlikely partner for dialogue, as he was seen in New Delhi as the architect of the Kargil War, which had claimed more than one thousand lives. Nonetheless, he had revealed greater flexibility than previous civilian leaders in declaring that the UN Security Council Resolutions calling for a free and fair plebiscite under UN auspices to enable the people of Jammu and Kashmir to determine whether they wish to join India or Pakistan, which had been the center point of Pakistani diplomacy over six decades, could be set aside. He also raised a series of proposals for soft borders, demilitarization, self-governance, and joint mechanisms of supervision for the Kashmir region. In reality, however, the Pakistani military still regarded India as the country's main strategic threat, despite the improvement in diplomatic relations from the nadir of 2001–2.

SAARC and Regionalism

The post–Cold War era was marked by the global establishment of new instruments of regional cooperation, such as the Asia-Pacific Economic Cooperation and the North American Free Trade Agreement, as well as the deepening of existing agreements, including the European Union and the Association of Southeast Asian Nations. But despite the formation of the South Asian Association for Regional Cooperation, in December 1985, South Asia, in the words of Bjorn Hette, continued with a very low level of "regionness."[33] This resulted from India and Pakistan's "conflict unending" and from the smaller countries' apprehensions regarding Indian hegemony. SAARC did not, as a result, become stronger in the new multipolar world. It has consequently remained a pale shadow of ASEAN.

The World Trade Organization imperative for trade liberalization did result in the SAARC members signing up to the South Asian Free Trade Agreement (SAFTA) in 2004. This built on the initial attempt to promote trade through regional agreement (South Asian Preferential Trade Agreement, December 1995). Despite the completion of three rounds of negotiations, SAPTA had little effect in encouraging intraregional trade, which at less than 5 percent of the total volume of trade with the rest of the world contrasted adversely with all other regional groupings.

SAFTA set the goal of a phased removal of all import tariffs to group members, except for items reserved under a negative "sensitive" list. Not only did the agreement allow for the list to be extensive and to "protect" a high percentage by value of a nation's imports, but unlike the ASEAN Free Trade Agreement, SAFTA established no time frame for the pruning of the negative lists. Moreover, SAFTA did not make a commitment to deal with nontariff barriers. These limitations have reduced the impact of SAFTA on regional trade. India, which would be the main driver of greater intraregional trade and economic integration, is increasingly trading with East Asia and has deepened links with ASEAN+3 (ASEAN countries plus China, Japan, and the Republic of Korea, initiated in 1997). Trade liberalization in South Asia is occurring on a bilateral rather than multilateral basis, as epitomized by the 1998 Indo–Sri Lankan Free trade Agreement.

SAFTA's stagnation reflects the political barriers to increased regional economic cooperation. It also reduces the possibility of any spillover political effects arising from its successful process. SAARC, in theory, provides a multilateral forum for dialogue when members' bilateral relations have broken down. Not only has it failed to play this role, but its own functioning has been disrupted by tense relations in the region. Differences of opinion over the presence of the Indian peacekeeping force in Sri Lanka led to the postponement of the fourth SAARC summit, scheduled for Colombo. The eleventh summit was also postponed in 1999 because of Indo-Pakistani tensions.

The large Bhutan SAARC building facing the prominent Thimphu landmark of the pink-roofed Tashichhoe Dzong (Fortress of the glorious religion) hosted SAARC's silver jubilee summit in late April 2010. Manmohan Singh noted in a speech that SAARC was not yet "empowered" sufficiently to be "more proactive."[34] The same point applied to SAFTA. South Asia's growing Asian and global presence owes little to an emergent regional organization. It has rather been rooted first in India's post-1991 economic dynamism and second in Pakistan's continuing geopolitical importance.

Sovereignty trade-offs, which lie at the heart of regional integration, have been impossible in South Asia, where domestic politics are shaped by mistrust and fear of neighbors. In the absence of trust, relations remain unstable. The emergence of a Chinese colossus has exacerbated the political issues that since decolonization have stood in the way of both a cooperative security architecture and an economic and infrastructural framework.

Thus issues relating to trade, water, and energy, which could be effectively addressed on a regional basis, have in South Asia become matters of interstate conflict, or at best bilateral agreements. Despite the creation of a SAARC Energy Centre in 2006, there is no prospect of a subcontinental power pool equivalent to that established by the South African development community.[35] Paradoxically, however, while individual nations jealously guard their resources and trade within South Asia, the region as a whole is connecting with areas to its southeast much more vigorously than at any other time in the postcolonial era.

Rise and Fall of the East India Company

1600	Grant of a royal charter to the East India Company
1612	East India Company builds a factory at Surat
1639	East India Company trading post at Madras, followed by Bombay (1668) and Calcutta (1690)
1756	Beginning of Seven Years' War, in which the French military threat in India is defeated
1757	Clive defeats the forces of Siraj ud Daulah at the Battle of Plassey
1793	Permanent settlement of Bengal
1799	Defeat and death of Tipu Sultan in Fourth Anglo-Mysore War
1813	East India Company Act deprives the Company of its trade monopoly, except for trade in tea and trade with China
1818	Publication of James Mill's history of India
1824	First Anglo-Burma War
1829	Abolition of sati by Governor General Bentinck
1833	East India Company's remaining trade monopolies are abrogated
1835	"Minute on Education" by Macaulay
1845	First Anglo-Sikh War. Punjab annexed in its entirety after Second War (1848–49)
1852–53	Second Anglo-Burma War
1856	Annexation of Awadh under the Doctrine of Lapse
1857	Civilian and military uprising against East India Company rule
1858	East India Company abolished and British Crown assumes direct control

The British Raj and Indian Responses

1860	British annex the Chittagong Hill Tracts; spread of railways through India
1875	Foundation of the Arya Samaj; establishment of the Muhammadan Anglo-Oriental College at Aligarh
1876	Victoria becomes empress of India
1880s	Civic development of hill stations
1882	*Ananda Math*, containing the famous hymn "Bande Mataram," is published by Bengali author Bankim Chandra Chatterjee
1885	Foundation of the Indian National Congress at Bombay
1885–86	After Third Anglo-Burma War, Burma becomes a province of British India
1903	Delhi Darbar celebrates coronation of Edward VII as emperor of India
1905	Partition of Bengal leads to the launching of the swadeshi movement
1906	Foundation of the All-India Muslim League at Dacca
1908	Construction of Jamshedpur officially begins
1909	Morley-Minto constitutional reforms create separate electorates for Muslims
1910	Gandhi's *Hind Swaraj* is published in English
1914	Ghadr movement
1916	Lucknow Pact between the All-India Muslim League and the Congress allows cooperation between the two organizations in the Khilafat movement
1919	Montagu-Chelmsford reforms; Jallianwala Bagh massacre; Gandhi leads noncooperation movement, his first all-India Satyagraha
1923	V. D. Savarkar publishes the Hindu nationalist text *Hindutva: Who Is a Hindu?*
1925	Foundation of Rashtriya Swayam Sevak Sangh (RSS)
1930	Gandhi's salt march
1932	Communal award provides separate representation for Sikhs and Untouchables; Gandhi's fast leads to Poona Pact with B. R. Ambedkar

Toward Independence and Partition

1933	Rahmat Ali coins the term "Pakistan"
1935	Government of India Act introduces provincial autonomy
1937	Muslim League polls poorly in Muslim-majority provinces; Congress forms governments in seven of the eleven Indian provinces
1939	Muslim League celebrates Day of Deliverance following the resignation of Congress provincial governments

1940   Muslim League adopts Lahore Resolution; Linlithgow sets out his "August offer"

1942   Fall of Singapore; Cripps mission; Quit India movement

1943   Wavell replaces Linlithgow as viceroy; Bengal famine

1944   Gandhi-Jinnah talks fail, but Jinnah's prestige is further enhanced

1945   Failure of Simla Conference

1946   Cabinet mission (March–June); Muslim League Direct Action Day leads to the "great Calcutta killing," 16–18 August; communal violence in Noakhali and Bihar

1947   Attlee announces on 20 February that Britain will leave India by June 1948 and that Mountbatten will succeed Wavell; Mountbatten arrives in India on 22 March; 3 June, Partition plan; Mountbatten announces independence will be brought forward to 15 August; celebration of independence to backdrop of large-scale massacres and migrations in Punjab

Postindependence India

1947–50   Integration of Princely States; Naga secessionist movement begins

1948   Kashmir War; Gandhi assassinated

1950   Indian Constitution comes into effect; India is the first republic within the British Commonwealth

1951   Dr. S. P. Mookherjee, former president of the Hindu Mahasabha, forms the Jana Sangh

1952   Congress election victories establish the pattern of one-party dominance

1953   Beginning of the formation of linguistic states in India with the creation of Andhra Pradesh; Akali Dal launches demand for Punjabi subha

1956   Militant phase of the Naga insurgency begins

1957   Second five-year plan emphasizes Indian import substitution industrialization; development of license-permit raj

1959   Dalai Lama flees Tibet for Indian exile

1962   Sino-Indian War

1963   State of Nagaland created

1964   Death of Nehru; Shastri succeeds him as prime minister

1965   Indo-Pakistani War

1966   Death of Shastri at Tashkent; Syndicate chooses Indira Gandhi as prime minister

1967   Elections mark the end of the Congress system of dominance

1969   Indira Gandhi splits Congress

1971   Gandhi triumphs in elections

1974	India conducts its first nuclear detonation at Pokhran on 18 May, describing it as a "peaceful" nuclear explosion; JP movement, taking its name from the leadership and inspiration provided by the veteran Gandhian Jayaprakash Narayan, is initiated by students to protest Congress misrule and corruption in Bihar
1975	Proclamation of Indian emergency
1976–77	Sterilization program; "beautification" of Delhi
1977	Janata Front wins March parliamentary elections; Moraji Desai becomes prime minister
1980	Indira Gandhi returns to power following the disintegration of the Janata Party; Jana Sangh renamed the Bharatiya Janata Party (BJP)
1981	Death of Sanjay Gandhi; Mandal Commission Report
1984	Operation Bluestar; assassination of Indira Gandhi; Delhi riots; Rajiv Gandhi secures Congress election triumph
1986	Shah Bano case; Babri Masjid Committee formed
1987	Bofors scandal; V. P. Singh forms the Janata Dal; state of Mizoram created
1989	National Front wins election, marking the BJP's rise to prominence; implementation of Mandal Report by V. P. Singh; insurgency begins in Kashmir
1990	L. K. Advani's *rath yatra*; secessionist violence in Assam
1991	Assassination of Rajiv Gandhi; Narasimha Rao Congress government begins economic liberalization in the wake of economic crisis
1992	Destruction of the Babri Masjid on 6 December
1996	Thirteen-day minority BJP government; United Front coalition government led first by Deve Gowde and then by I. K. Gujral
1998	BJP-led coalition headed by Atal Bihari Vajpayee takes office; nuclear tests
1999	Vajpayee loses vote of confidence but has resounding victory in fresh parliamentary elections
2001	Terrorist attack on Parliament Building in New Delhi leads India and Pakistan to the brink of war
2002	Pogrom against Muslim communities in Gujarat ruled by BJP Chief Minister Narendra Modi; rapid Indian economic growth
2004	The Congress-led United Progressive Alliance unexpectedly wins the parliamentary elections; Manmohan Singh becomes prime minister
2005	National Rural Employment Guarantee Act; introduction of value added tax; initiation of negotiations on Indo-US civilian nuclear agreement
2007	GDP growth rate 9 percent, second-highest in world; aid increased to Afghanistan

2008	Indo-US civilian nuclear agreement ratified; Mumbai bombings
2009	United Progressive Alliance wins elections
2010	Allahabad High Court rules that the disputed holy site of Ayodhya should be divided between Muslims and Hindus
2011	Anna Hazare stages twelve-day hunger strike in Delhi to protest state corruption; mobile phone license corruption trial begins
2012	Gang rape and murder of a student in Delhi leads to nationwide protests
2013	Supreme Court reverses a 2009 Delhi High Court order that had decriminalized homosexual acts
2014	Landslide victory for the BJP and its prime ministerial candidate Narendra Modi in sixteenth parliamentary elections

Postindependence Pakistan

1948	Death of Mohammad Ali Jinnah
1951	Assassination of Liaquat Ali Khan
1952	Killing of "language martyrs" in Dhaka
1954	Ghulam Muhammad dismisses Constituent Assembly; Muslim League defeated in East Bengal provincial elections; dismissal of United Front government
1955	Introduction of One Unit scheme; Pakistan becomes a member of CENTO and SEATO
1956	Pakistan Constitution introduces presidential system
1958	Pakistan's first military coup led by Ayub Khan
1959	Introduction of Public Offices Disqualification Order and Elective Bodies Disqualification Order; introduction of Basic Democracy scheme
1962	New Constitution for Pakistan
1965	India-Pakistani War
1966	Awami League launches six-point program
1967	Foundation of the Pakistan People's Party (PPP)
1968	Popular uprising against Ayub Khan
1969	Yahya Khan replaces Ayub
1970	Cyclone kills up to half a million people in Bengal delta; Pakistan's first national elections; Awami League sweeps board in East Pakistan
1971	Operation Searchlight; Civil War in East Pakistan; Indian military intervention leads to emergence of Bangladesh; Zulfiqar Ali Bhutto replaces Yahya Khan as president
1972	Introduction of land reforms, labor reforms, and nationalization
1973	Pakistan's third Constitution; Bhutto becomes prime minister; Balochistan insurgency begins

1974	Holding of Islamic Summit in Lahore
1977	PPP wins elections but is accused of rigging; introduction of martial law by Zia-ul-Haq
1979	Soviet occupation of Afghanistan; Bhutto executed; Harkat-ul-Jihad al-Islami founded
1980	Federal Shariat Court established
1983	Movement for the restoration of democracy
1984	Law of evidence
1985	"Partyless" elections; Eighth Amendment to Pakistan Constitution gives president power to dismiss prime minister and dissolve National Assembly
1986	Benazir Bhutto returns to Pakistan
1988	Death of Zia; restoration of democracy; Benazir Bhutto leads PPP government; Nawaz Sharif establishes rival Punjab powerbase
1990	President Ghulaqm Ishaq Khan dismisses Benazir Bhutto; Ghulam Mustafa Jatoi caretaker prime minister; cessation of US aid under terms of the Pressler Amendment; PPP claims Nawaz Sharif's crushing electoral victory was rigged
1991	Privatization of eighty-nine state enterprises; collapse of Cooperative Societies in Punjab; Shariat Act
1992	Yellow Taxi scheme; Benazir Bhutto's long march to Islamabad
1993	Political crisis following Nawaz Sharif's dismissal; president steps down; Moeen Qureshi caretaker government; Benazir Bhutto returns to power after elections
1994	Insurgency in Karachi
1995	Waiving of Pressler Amendment
1996	Killing of Mir Murtaza Bhutto widens breach between Benazir and President Farooq Leghari and leads to her dismissal; caretaker administration of Meraj Khalid
1997	Nawaz Sharif secures crushing election victory; removal of president's power to dismiss prime minister
1999	Kargil conflict; coup of Pervez Musharraf
2000	Beginning of Baloch insurgency
2001	Pakistani support for Operation Enduring Freedom in Afghanistan
2002	Elections held without Benazir Bhutto and Nawaz Sharif; PML-Q takes office
2004	Beginning of military intervention in Tribal Areas
2005	Composite dialogue and confidence-building measures with India
2007	Formation of Tehrik-e-Taliban Pakistan; terrorist incidences surge in the wake of military operation against the Red Mosque in Islamabad; introduction of emergency, suspension of Chief Justice Iftikhar Muhammad Chaudhry; assassination of Benazir Bhutto on 27 December

2008	PPP wins elections; Asif Ali Zardari elected president after Musharraf's resignation on 18 August
2009	Military operation wrests control of Swat from militants
2010	Parliamentary approval of constitutional reforms reducing the power of the president
2011	Osama bin Laden is killed by US special forces in Abbottabad
2012	Supreme Court disqualifies Prime Minister Gilani from holding office; Taliban attack campaigner for girls' education Malala Yousafzai
2013	Nawaz Sharif returns to power for third time after May elections
2014	Former president Pervez Musharraf goes on trial on treason charges; government and Taliban begin peace talks

Bangladesh Since Independence

1972	Sheikh Mujibur Rahman heads Awami League government
1973	Bangladesh's first general elections
1975	Constitutional coup and autocratic rule by Sheikh Mujibur Rahman; August army coup, Sheikh Mujibur Rahman and family killed in Dhaka; two more army coups before Ziaur Rahman assumes power; beginning of war in Chittagong Hill Tracts
1978	Leaders of Jamaat-i-Islami (JI) return from exile in Pakistan; Zia creates Bangladesh Nationalist Party (BNP)
1981	Ziaur Rahman assassinated in Chittagong
1982	General Ershad assumes power
1986	Ershad founds Jatiya Party
1990	Popular rising forces Ershad from office
1991	Elections won by BNP, led by Zia's widow, Khaleda Zia
1993	Fatwa against Taslima Nasrin; groundwater arsenic poisoning discovered
1996	Awami League wins general elections, Sheikh Hasina becomes prime minister; agreement with India over the division of Ganges waters.
1997	Peace agreement in Chittagong Hill Tracts conflict
2001	BNP wins general elections and Khaleda Zia returns as prime minister in alliance with JI
2006	Nobel Prize for Muhammad Yunus, founder of Grameen Bank
2007	General elections postponed; military-backed interim government led by Fakhruddin Ahmed
2008	Awami League–led Grand Alliance sweeps to power in general elections
2010	Five former army officers executed for the 1975 murder of Sheikh Mujibur Rahman
2011	Constitutional change scraps the provision for a neutral caretaker government to oversee elections

2012	Key figures of Jamaat-e-Islami are charged with war crimes by a government tribunal
2013	Major clashes following the conviction of Ghulam Azam, leader of JI; Supreme Court upholds death sentence of Abdul Kader Mullah; BNP boycotts elections, which return Sheikh Hasina for third term in office
2014	Khaleda Zia sent for trial on corruption charges

Introduction

1. Alexander Evans, *The United States and South Asia After Afghanistan* (New York: Asia Society, 2012), 27.
2. See, for example, the World Bank "South Asia Countries," last modified 28 December 2012, http://www.worldbank.org/WBSITE/EXTERNAL/COUNTRIES SOUTHASIAEXT/0,,pagePK:158889~piPK:146815~theSitePK:223547,00.html.
3. Asia-Pacific POPIN Consultative Workshop Report, Asia-Pacific POPIN Bulletin 7, no. 12 (1995), 7–11.
4. See Commonwealth Consultative Committee on South and South East Asia: The Colombo Plan, IOR/V/27/270/27 (1950), British Library.
5. Guy Wint, *What Is the Colombo Plan?* (London: Batchworth, 1952).
6. India's population was estimated in July 2012 at 1.2 billion, Pakistan's at 190 million, and Bangladesh's at 161 million. See Central Intelligence Agency, "The World Factbook," last modified 14 December 2012, https://www.cia.gov/library/publications/the-world-factbook/wfbExt/region_sas.html.
7. See Daniel Bass, *Everyday Ethnicity in Sri Lanka: Up-Country Tamil Identity Politics* (Abingdon: Routledge, 2013), 168 ff.
8. Nalini Ranjan Chakravarti, *The Indian Minority in Burma: The Rise and Decline of an Immigrant Community* (London: Institute of Race Relations, 1971).
9. Michael Twaddle, ed., *Expulsion of a Minority: Essays on Ugandan Asians* (London: Athlone, 1975); J. D. Kelly and M. Kaplan, *Represented Communities: Fiji and World Decolonization* (Chicago: University of Chicago Press, 2001).
10. The best works in this crowded field are Barbara D. Metcalf and Thomas R. Metcalf, *A Concise History of Modern India*, 3rd ed. (Cambridge: Cambridge University Press, 2012); and Judith M. Brown, *Modern India: The Origins of an Asian*

Democracy, 2nd ed. (Oxford: Oxford University Press, 1994). For contemporary India see Stuart Corbridge, John Harriss, and Craig Jeffrey, *India Today: Economics, Politics, and Society* (Cambridge; Polity, 2013).

11. The notable exceptions are, of course, Sugata Bose and Ayesha Jalal, *Modern South Asian History: Culture and Political Economy* (London: Routledge, 1998); and David Ludden, *India and South Asia: A Short History* (Oxford: Oneworld, 2007).

12. See, for example, Stanley Wolpert, *India and Pakistan: Continued Conflict or Co-Operation?* (Berkeley: University of California Press, 2011); and Strobe Talbott, *Engaging India: Diplomacy, Democracy, and the Bomb* (New Delhi: Penguin, 2007).

13. William B. Milam, *Bangladesh and Pakistan: Flirting with Failure in South Asia* (London: Hurst, 2009).

14. On the Maoists see Nirmalangshu Mukherji, *The Maoists in India: Tribals Under Siege* (London: Pluto, 2012).

15. For an interesting collection of essays on the historical roots of the Sinhala-Tamil conflict see Jonathan Spencer, ed., *Sri Lanka: History and Roots of Conflict* (London: Routledge, 2000).

16. Lok Raj Baral, *Nepal: Nation-State in the Wilderness; Managing State, Democracy, and Geo-Politics* (New Delhi: Sage, 2012).

17. Evans, *The United States and South Asia*, 20.

18. Subir Bhaumik, *Troubled Periphery: Crisis of India's North East* (New Delhi: Sage, 2009), 156.

19. See Nicholas Dirks, *Castes of Mind: Colonialism and the Making of Modern India* (Princeton: Princeton University Press, 2001).

20. Eugene F. Irschick, *Dialogue and History: Constructing South India, 1795–1895* (Berkeley: University of California Press, 1994).

21. Markus Daechsel has recently creatively used the papers preserved in Athens by the Greek architect and planning consultant Constantinos A. Doxiadis to reflect on the politics of development in early postindependence Pakistan. *On the Road to Islamabad: The Politics of Development in Postcolonial Pakistan* (Cambridge: Cambridge University Press, 2013).

22. For examples of their use see Yunas Samad, *A Nation in Turmoil: Nationalism and Ethnicity in Pakistan, 1937–1958* (New Delhi: Sage, 1995); Ian Talbot, *Pakistan: A Modern History*, 3rd ed. (London: Hurst 2009); Ayesha Jalal, *The State of Martial Rule: The Origins of Pakistan's Political Economy of Defence* (Cambridge: Cambridge University Press, 1990); Antara Datta, *Refugees and Borders in South Asia: The Great Exodus of 1971* (London: Routledge, 2013).

23. See Ayesha Jalal, *The Pity of Partition: Manto's Life, Times, and Work Across the India-Pakistan Divide* (Princeton: Princeton University Press, 2013).

24. Brij V. Lal, ed., *Bittersweet: The Indo-Fijian Experience* (Canberra: Pandanus, 2004).

25. Mark Tully, *No Full Stops in India* (London: Penguin, 1992).

26. William van Schendel, *The Bengal Borderland: Beyond State and Nation in South Asia* (London: Anthem, 2005).

1. Borders and Boundaries

1. *The Hindu* (Kolkata), 4 February 2002.

2. Jagat Mani Acharya, Manjita Gurung, and Ranabir Samaddar, *Chronicles of a No-Where People on the Indo-Bangladesh Border* (Kathmandu: South Asia Forum for Human Rights, 2003), 1.

3. Veena Das and Deborah Poole, "The State and Its Margins," in *Anthropology in the Margins of the State*, ed. Veena Das and Deborah Poole (Santa Fe, NM: School of American Research Press, 2004), 22.

4. Sujata Ramachandran, *Indifference, Impotence, and Intolerance: Transnational Bangladeshis in India*, Global Migration Prospects 42 (Geneva: Global Commission on International Migration, 2005), 7.

5. See South Asia Forum for Human Rights, "What People Don't Want: Violence and Violations in the Bengal Borderland," accessed 3 January 2013, http://www.safhr.org/index.php?view=article&catid=187:indo-bangladesh&id=316%3Awhat-people-dont-want.

6. See Michael Hutt, *Unbecoming Citizens: Culture, Nationhood, and the Flight of Refugees from Bhutan* (New Delhi: Oxford University Press, 2005).

7. For details of the display at Hussainiwalla in the Ferozepore district and at Sadqi in the Fazilka district see: http://www.punjabnewsline.com/content/retreat-ceremony-hussainiwalla-wherebhagat-rajguru-and-sukhdev-were-cremated/38671, accessed 4 January 2013; S. P. Sharma, "Border Sentinels," *Tribune* (Chandigarh), 14 August 2011.

8. See Ian Talbot, *Divided Cities: Partition and Its Aftermath in Lahore and Amritsar, 1947–1957* (Karachi: Oxford University Press 2006).

9. See, for example, the famous BBC video of the traveler and former member of the Monty Python comedy troupe Michael Palin at the border ceremony, www.youtube.com/watch?v=n9y2qtaopbE.

10. Navtej Purewal and Virinder Kalra, "The Strut of the Peacocks: Partition, Travel, and the Indo-Pak Border," in *Travel Worlds: Journeys in Contemporary Cultural Politics*, ed. Raminder Kaur and John Hutnyk (London: Zed, 1999), 54–68.

11. Ibid., 56.

12. Stephen Alter, *Amritsar to Lahore: A Journey Across the India-Pakistan Border* (Philadelphia: University of Pennsylvania Press, 2001).

13. Tridivesh Singh Maini, "Not Just Another Border," *Himal Southasia* (Kathmandu), 15 August 2012.

14. Sarota Kumari Sodha, "Home and Heart," *Himal Southasia* (Kathmandu), 15 August 2012.

15. See Bani Gill, "The Border Dialogues in Sindh and Rajasthan," www.wiscomp .org/pp-v4-n2/borderdialogues.pdf, accessed 27 March 2015.

16. For details see Brian Cloughley, *A History of the Pakistan Army: Wars and Insurrections* (Karachi: Oxford University Press, 1999), 61–62; Farooq Bajwa, *From Kutch to Tashkent: The Indo-Pakistan War of 1965* (London: Hurst, 2013), 77–80.

17. For further details see CRO Circular no. 118, "The Dispute Between India and Pakistan over the Rann of Kutch," 28 April 1965, PREM 13/391, NA.

18. BBC, "India and Pakistan in Border Talks," http://news.bbc.co.uk/go/pr/fr/-/1/hi/ world/south_asia/6202399.stm modified 22 December 2006.

19. See chapter 3 of Charu Gupta anf Mukul Sharma, *Contested Coastlines: Fisherfolk, Nations, and Borders in South Asia* (Abingdon: Routledge, 2008).

20. For details see Neville Maxwell, *India's China War* (New York: Pantheon, 1971).

21. "Chinese Intentions Against India," Joint Intelligence Committee Report, 22 November 1962, CAB 158/47 NA.

22. Ananth Krishnan, "China Will Not Accept LAC as Solution to Border Dispute, Says Commentary," *The Hindu*, 25 October 2012, http://www.thehindu.com/news/ national/china-will-not-accept-lac-as-solution-to-border-dispute-says-commentary/ article4031786.ece, accessed 6 January 2013.

23. Both the Afghan and Pakistani Taliban comprise a number of tribal and sectarian militias that draw on Deobandi and Salafi interpretations of Islam to inspire their jihadist activities. For further reading on their cross-border activities see Ian Talbot, *Pakistan: A New History* (London: Hurst, 2012).

24. Anatol Lieven, *Pakistan: A Hard Country* (London: Allen Lane, 2011), 187.

25. Pervez Musharraf, *In the Line of Fire* (London: Simon and Schuster, 2006), 68–69.

26. Irfan Ghauri, "Tales from LoC-3: Neelum Valley People Thirst for Peace," *Express Tribune*, 4 July 2011, http://www.tribune.com.pk/story/202001/tales-from-loc-3 -neelum-valley-people-thirst-for-peace, accessed 6 January 2013.

27. The shorter route reopened after the cease-fire took five hours; www.thehindu .com/todays-paper/tp-national/ceasefire-opens-up-old-routes-in-pak/article3176019 .ece, accessed 6 January 2013.

28. Raj Chengappa, "On the Line of Caution: The Other Kashmir Looks for a Change in the Narrative Between India and Pakistan," *Tribune* (Chandigarh), 2 May 2011.

29. See Praveen Swami, *India, Pakistan, and the Secret Jihad: The Covert War in Kashmir, 1947–2001* (Milton Park, Abingdon: Routledge, 2007).

30. Ibid., 60–63.

31. Basharat Peer, *Curfewed Night: A Frontline Memoir of Life, Love, and War in Kashmir* (London: Harper, 2010), 35.

32. Ibid.
33. The construction cost about 4.4 million rupees per mile. Vinay Kumar, "LOC Fencing in Jammu Nearly Complete," *The Hindu*, 1 February 2004, http://www .hindu.com/2004/02/01/stories/2004020109130800.htm, accessed 6 January 2013.
34. Willem van Schendel, *The Bengal Borderland: Beyond State and Nation in South Asia* (London: Anthem, 2005), 56.
35. The chars account for about 1.5 percent of Bangladesh's land area.
36. Schendel, *The Bengal Borderland*, 62.
37. Ibid., 63.
38. Ibid., 73n38.
39. On the massacres in the Chittagong Hill Tracts see Wolfgang May, ed., *They Are Now Burning Village After Village: Genocide in the Chittagong Hill Tracts* (Copenhagen: International Work Group for Indigenous Affairs, 1984). The best account of India's "war" in the northeast is contained in Marcus Franke, *War and Nationalism in South Asia: The Indian State and the Nagas* (London: Routledge, 2009).
40. Subir Bhaumik, *Troubled Periphery: Crisis of India's North East* (New Delhi: Sage, 2009), 154–55.
41. Schendel, *The Bengal Border*, 49.
42. For details see Bhaumik, *Troubled Periphery*.
43. See Ashok Kapur and A. Jeyaratnam Wilson, *Foreign Policies of India and Her Neighbours* (Basingstoke: Macmillan, 1996), 118 ff.; K. M. De Silva and W. H. Wriggins, *J. R. Jayewardene of Sri Lanka: A Political Biography* (Honolulu: University of Hawaii Press, 1988).
44. David Waines, *The Odyssey of Ibn Battuta: Uncommon Tales of a Medieval Adventurer* (London: I. B. Tauris, 2012).
45. On the 1988 military coup and India's Operation Cactus response see I. H. Zaki and Regina Mulay Parakh, *Small States Security Dilemma: A Maldivian Perception* (New Delhi: Lancers', 2008), 101.

2. Land, Society, Environment

1. "Pleas from Pakistan: Flood Victims Tell Their Stories," http://www.thestar.com/ news/world/pakistan/article/850957, modified 22 August 2010.
2. "Flooding During Monsoon Period of 2010 in Pakistan," http://www.pakmet.com .pk/FFD/cp/floodpage.asp, accessed 9 January 2013.
3. This figure was quoted by the World Bank President Robert Zoellick; *Dawn* (Karachi), 14 August 2010.
4. See Ian Talbot, "Pakistan After the Floods: Prospects for Stability and Democratic Consolidation," Institute of South Asian Studies working paper 122 (National University of Singapore: ISAS, 2011), 3.

5. Willem van Schendel, *A History of Bangladesh* (Cambridge: Cambridge University Press, 2009), 3.

6. See Rita P. Wright, *The Ancient Indus: Urbanism, Economy, and Society* (Cambridge: Cambridge University Press, 2010).

7. See Christopher V. Hill, *South Asia: An Environmental History* (Santa Barbara, CA: ABC-CLIO, 2008).

8. Bernard S. Cohn, "Regions Subjective and Objective: Their Relations to the Study of Modern Indian History and Society," in *An Anthropologist Among the Historians and Other Essays*, ed. Bernard S. Cohn (Delhi: Oxford University Press, 1987), 100–136.

9. The idea of the god-king celebrated at Angkor Wat did not develop in India, where royal authority was expressed in devotion to dominant deities in lavish temple construction. This reveals that the cultural interaction with Southeast Asia was more complex than is acknowledged in some Indian nationalist celebrations of "Greater India."

10. "Amarnath Yatra: Record 6.34 Lakh Visit Shrine" http://www.zeenews.india.com/news/nation/amarnath-yatra-record-634-lakh-visit-shrine_25854.html, accessed 10 January 2013.

11. *Amrit Nectar of Immortality* website, http://www.amritfilm.net, accessed 10 January 2013.

12. For the history of Varanasi as a pilgrimage site, see Diana L. Eck, *Banaras: City of Light* (New York: Columbia University Press, 1982).

13. Richard M. Eaton, *The Rise of Islam and the Bengal Frontier* (Berkeley: University of California Press, 1993); Nile Green, "Migrant Sufis and Sacred Space in South Asia," *Contemporary South Asia* 12, no. 4 (December 2003), 493–509.

14. Marcia Hermansen, "Imagining Space and Society: Collective Memory in South Asian Biographical Literature (Tazkirahs)," *Studies in Contemporary Islam* 4, no. 2 (2002), 1–21.

15. Richard M. Eaton, "The Political and Religious Authority of the Shrine of Baba Farid in Pakpattan Punjab," paper presented at History Research Seminar, University of California, Berkeley, 7 June 1979.

16. Burton Stein, *A History of India* (Oxford: Blackwell, 1998), 13.

17. For a survey of the development of Hinduism see Gavin Flood, *An Introduction to Hinduism* (Cambridge: Cambridge University Press, 1996).

18. K. W. Jones, *Arya Dharm: Hindu Consciousness in 19th-Century Punjab* (Berkeley: University of California Press, 1976).

19. On Hinduism's philosophic traditions see Pratima Bowes, *The Hindu Religious Tradition: A Philosophical Approach* (London: Routledge, 1977).

20. There are numerous studies on caste. Useful works include Susan Bayly, *Caste, Society, and Politics in India from the Eighteenth Century to the Modern Age*

(Cambridge: Cambridge University Press, 2001); Christophe Jaffrelot, *India's Silent Revolution: The Rise of the Lower Castes* (London: Hurst, 2003); Louis Dumont, *Homo Hierarchicus: The Caste System and Its Implications*, 2nd ed. (Chicago: University of Chicago Press, 1981).

21. On the *bhakti* (devotional tradition) in Hinduism see Krishna Sharma, *Bhakti and the Bhakti Movement: A New Perspective* (Delhi: Munshiram Manoharlal, 1987).

22. For a classic exposition of the "great" and "little" traditions in Hinduism see Ruth S. Freed and Stanley A. Freed, "Two Mother Goddess Ceremonies of Delhi State in the Great and Little Tradition," *Southwestern Journal of Anthropology* 18, no. 3 (Autumn 1962), 246–77.

23. On the Jain tradition see Paul Dundas, *The Jains* (London: Taylor and Francis, 2002); and John E. Cost, *Jains in the World: Religious Values and Ideology* (Oxford: Oxford University Press, 2011). There is an extremely rich literature on Buddhism; see, for example, Peter Harvey, *An Introduction to Buddhism: Teachings, History, and Practices* (Cambridge: Cambridge University Press, 1990); and Richard F. Gombrich, *Theravada Buddhism: A History from Ancient Benares to Modern Colombo*, 6th ed. (London: Routledge, 2002).

24. The "Guru's place" is not only a place of worship where people sit and listen to scriptural recitation from the Guru Granth Sahib (the Sikh scripture), which is installed in a position of honor, but serves also as a center for social activity.

25. Mark Juergensmeyer, *Radhoasami Reality: The Logic of a Modern Faith* (Princeton: Princeton University Press, 1991).

26. There are many works on the Singh Sabha reform movement; see, for example, Harjot Oberoi, *The Construction of Religious Boundaries: Culture, Identity, and Diversity in the Sikh Tradition* (Chicago: University of Chicago Press, 1994).

27. The Deoband movement, which has become immensely influential in contemporary Pakistan, was organized around the Islamic school founded in 1867. It emphasized a conservative Islamic faith that had no place for modern science or the study of English. The Ahl-e-Hadith was an even more puritanical movement. For the emergence of the Deoband movement see Barbara D. Metcalf, *Islamic Revival in British India: Deoband, 1860–1900* (Princeton: Princeton University Press, 1982).

28. Stein, *A History of India*, 55.

29. Eaton, *The Rise of Islam*.

30. David Gilmartin, "Environmental History, *Biraderi*, and the Making of Pakistani Punjab," in *Punjab Reconsidered: History, Culture, and Practice*, ed. Anshu Malhotra and Farina Mir (New Delhi: Oxford University Press, 2012), 289.

31. See Graham P. Chapman, *The Geo-Politics of South Asia: From Early Empires to the Nuclear Age*, 2nd ed. (Aldershot: Ashgate, 2003), 112–14.

32. Ira Klein, "Malaria and Mortality in Bengal, 1840–1921," *Indian Economic and Social History Review* 9, no. 2 (1972), 132–60.

33. See chapter 7 of Iftekhar Iqbal, *The Bengal Delta: Ecology, State, and Social Change, 1840–1943* (New York: Palgrave Macmillan, 2010).

34. For a history of the Chipko movement see Thomas Weber, *Hugging the Trees: The Story of the Chipko Movement* (Harmondsworth: Penguin, 1999); and Ramachandra Guha, *The Unquiet Woods: Ecological Change and Peasant Resistance in the Himalaya* (Berkeley: University of California Press, 1990).

35. Ahsan Uddin Ahmed, *Bangladesh: Climate Change Impact and Vulnerability. A Synthesis* (Dhaka: Climate Change Cell, Department of Environment, 2006), 38–39.

36. Winston H. Yu et al., *Climate Change Risks and Food Security in Bangladesh* (London: Earthscan, 2010), 5.

37. Ahmed, *Bangladesh*, 44.

38. The findings of the UN Human Development report for 2007–8 are cited in Bangladesh Institute of International and Strategic Studies and Saferworld, *Climate Change and Security in Bangladesh: A Case Study* (Dhaka, 2009), 8.

39. Randeep Ramesh, "Paradise Almost Lost: Maldives Seek to Buy a New Homeland," *Guardian* (London), 10 November 2008.

40. R. Vidayasagar and K. Suman Chandra, *Farmers' Suicides in Andhra Pradesh and Karnata* (Hyderabad: National Institute of Rural Development, 2004).

41. P. Sainath, "17,368 Farm Suicides in 2009," *The Hindu* (Mumbai), 27 December 2010), http://www.thehindu.com/opinion/columns/sainath/17368-farm-suicides-in-2009/article995824ece. According to the same article, there had been 44,276 farm suicides since 1999 in Maharashtra, the worst affected state.

42. Ahmed, *Bangladesh*, 1.

3. The South Asian Diasporas

1. M. C. Lall, *India's Missed Opportunity: India's Relationship with Non-Resident Indians* (Ashgate: Aldershot, 2001).

2. Ruth Maxey, *South Asian Atlantic Literature* (Edinburgh: Edinburgh University Press, 2012).

3. See, for example, Ashin Dasgupta, "Indian Merchants and Trade in the Indian Ocean 1500–1700," in *The World of the Indian Ocean Merchant, 1500–1800: Collected Essays of Ashin Dasgupta*, compiled by Umar Dasgupta (New York: Oxford University Press, 2001), 59–87.

4. See Kernial Singh Sandhu, *Indians in Malaya: Some Aspects of Their Immigration and Settlement, 1786–1957* (Cambridge: Cambridge University Press, 1969); Lomarsh Roopnarine, *Indo-Caribbean Indenture: Resistance and Accommodation, 1838–1920* (Kingston: University of the West Indies Press, 2007); Oscar H. K. Spate, *From the Punjab to Fiji* (Canberra: Australian National University, 1991); Brij V.

Lal, ed., *Bittersweet: An Indo-Fijian Experience* (Canberra: Australian National University, Pandanus, 2004); Manjit Singh Sidhu, *The Sikhs in Kenya* (Chandigarh: Punjab University, n.d.); and S. Bhana, ed., *Essays on Indentured Indians in Natal* (Leeds: Peepal Tree, 1991).

5. Hugh Tinker, *A New System of Slavery: The Export of Indian Labour Overseas, 1830–1920* (London: Oxford University Press, 1974).

6. Judith M Brown, *Global South Asians: Introducing the Modern Diaspora* (Cambridge: Cambridge University Press, 2006), 30.

7. This was known as the *kangany* system.

8. See Brown, *Global South Asians*.

9. On the Indian presence in Hong Kong see B. S. White, *Turbans and Traders: Hong Kong's Indian Communities* (Oxford: Oxford University Press, 1994).

10. Sumita Mukherjee, *Nationalism, Education, and Migrant Identities: The England-Returned* (Abingdon: Routledge, 2010).

11. Rozina Visram, *Ayahs, Lascars, and Princes: Indians in Britain, 1700–1947* (London: Pluto, 1986); Michael Herbert Fisher, Shompa Lahiri, and Shinder S. Thandi, *A South Asian History of Britain: Four Centuries of Peoples from the Indian Subcontinent* (Westport, CT: Greenwood, 2007); Sushila Nasta, *India in Britain: South Asian Networks and Connections, 1858–1950* (Basingstoke: Palgrave Macmillan, 2012); M. Fisher, *Counterflows to Colonialism: Indian Travellers and Settlers in Britain, 1600–1857* (Delhi: Permanent Black, 2003).

12. See Bruce La Brack, *The Sikhs of Northern California, 1904–1975* (New York: AMS, 1988); and Joan M. Jensen, *Passage from India: Asian Indian Immigrants in North America* (New Haven: Yale University Press, 1988).

13. Sunil S. Amrith, *Migration and Diaspora in Modern Asia* (New York: Cambridge University Press, 2011), 30, table 1.1.

14. Edward St. J. Jackson, *Report of a Commission on Immigration into Ceylon* (Colombo: Ceylon Government Press, 1938), 26; L/I/1/603 Indians Overseas, India Office Records (IOR), British Library.

15. Brown, *Global South Asians*, 35.

16. Amrith, *Migration and Diaspora*, 30.

17. Ibid., 31.

18. Jackson, *Report*, appendix IV, table C.

19. Ibid., 10–11, 16, 20–22.

20. Government of India, Settlers Abroad: Position Reviewed, Simla, 21 September 1938; L/I/1/603 Indians Overseas (IOR), British Library.

21. Amrith, *Migration and Diaspora*, 93.

22. Sugata Bose, *A Hundred Horizons: The Indian Ocean in the Age of Global Empire* (Cambridge: Harvard University Press, 2006).

23. M/3/514 B 3932/38 (ii) Burma Riots (IOR), British Library.

24. Jackson, *Report*, 25.

25. Caroline Adams, *Across Seven Seas and Thirteen Rivers: Life Stories of Pioneer Sylheti Settlers in Britain* (London: Tower Hamlets Arts Project, 1987).

26. See Christopher McDowell, *A Tamil Asylum Diaspora: Sri Lankan Migration, Settlement, and Politics in Switzerland* (Oxford: Berghahn, 1996).

27. Dubai is the driving force in the economic growth of the UAE. Sharjah is most famous for its sporting development, hosting India-Pakistan cricket matches when political conditions have not permitted those contests on the Subcontinent's soil. The smaller emirates Abu Dhabi, Ajman, Al Fujayrah, Ra's al khaymah, and Umm al Qaywayn have not experienced such hectic development.

28. In 2005 there were 2.7 million migrant workers on the UAE, making up 95 percent of the private sector workforce.

29. Human Rights Watch, *Bad Dreams: Exploitation and Abuse of Migrant Workers in Saudi Arabia*, 14 July 2004, http://www.hrw.org/reports/2004/07/13/bad-dreams, accessed 17 January 2013, 4–5.

30. Ibid.

31. In 2005, there were more than 300,000 construction workers in the UAE alone. The vast majority of these were from South Asia. Human Rights Watch, *Building Towers, Cheating Workers: Exploitation of Migrant Construction Workers in the United Arab Emirates*, 12 November 2006, http://www.hrw.org/reports/2006/11/11/building-towers-cheating-workers-0, accessed 17 January 2013, 4–5.

32. Ibid., 6.

33. Human Rights Watch, *Bad Dreams*, 6.

34. Ibid., 8.

35. Saritha Rai, "Some Silicon Valley Style Pioneers Head East," *Epoch Times*, 13 October 2012, http://www.theepochtimes.com/n2/opinion/some-silicon-valley-style-pioneers-head-east-302990.html, accessed 17 January 2013.

36. Ian Talbot, *India and Pakistan* (London: Arnold, 2000), 245.

37. "How Indians Defied Gravity and Achieved Success in Silicon Valley," *Forbes*, 15 October 2012, http://www.forbes.com/sites/singularity/2012/10/15/how-indians-defied-gravity-and-achieved-success-in-silicon-valley/, accessed 17 January 2012.

38. Sean Randolph, "Silicon Valley Expats Spur Innovation in India," *YaleGlobal*, 2 September 2010, http://yaleglobal.yale.edu/content/silicon-valley-spur-innovation, accessed 17 January 2013.

39. Brown, *Global South Asians*, 54.

40. See Anupama Jain, *How to Be South Asian in America: Narratives of Ambivalence and Belonging* (Philadelphia: Temple University Press, 2011); Lavina Dhingra Shankar and Rajini Srikanth, eds., *A Part, Yet Apart: South Asian Americans on Asian America* (Philadelphia: Temple University Press, 1998).

41. A notable exception is provided by Latha Varadarajan, *The Domestic Abroad: Diasporas in International Relations* (New York: Oxford University Press, 2010).

42. Aarti is the offering of light from wicks soaked in ghee or camphor to deities as part of worship. See http://www.youtube.com/watch?v=ygoZQOolMsVI, accessed 18 January 2013.

43. See, for example, Devesh Kapur and John McHale, "Migration's New Payoff," *Foreign Policy*, 1 November 2003, 49–57.

44. See I. Talbot, *Pakistan: A New History* (London: Hurst, 2012), 28.

45. M. Ghazanfar Ali Khan, "More Workers to Be Hired from Bangladesh," *Arab News* (Jeddah), 23 October 2003.

46. Human Rights Watch, *Bad Dreams*, 4–5.

47. See http://www.bapscharities.org.uk/our_services.php, accessed 18 January 2013.

48. On the Swaminarayan sect see Raymond Williams, *Introduction to Swaminarayan Hinduism* (Cambridge: Cambridge University Press, 2001).

49. Marie C. Lal, *India's Missed Opportunity: India's Relationship with the Non-Resident Indians* (Aldershot: Ashgate, 2001).

50. Shinder Thandi, "*Vilayati Paisa*: Some Reflections on the Potential of Disapora Finance in the Socio-Economic Development of Indian Punjab," in *People on the Move: Punjabi Colonial and Post-Colonial Migration*, ed. Ian Talbot and Shinder Thandi (Karachi: Oxford University Press, 2004), 210–25.

51. Kabbadi was the focus of a Kannada-language film that flopped at the box office in 2009. Three years later a more successful Punjabi film was released, *Kabbadi Once Again*.

52. Brown, *Global South Asians*, 86.

53. Darshan Singh Tatla, *The Sikh Diaspora: The Search for Statehood* (London: University College Press, 1999).

54. For details see International Crisis Group, *The Sri Lankan Tamil Diaspora After the LTTE*, Asia report no. 186, 23 February 2010, 5–16.

55. Patricia Ellis and Zafar Khan, "Diasporic Mobilization and the Kashmir Issue in British Politics," *Journal of Ethnic and Migration Studies* 24, no. 3 (1998), 471–88; Vernon Hewitt and Mark Wickham-Jones, "New Labour and the Politics of Kashmir," in *New Labour's Foreign Policy: A New Moral Crusade?*, ed. Richard Little and Mark Wickham-Jones (Manchester: Manchester University Press, 2000), 201–18.

56. Katy Gardner, "Desh-Bidesh: Sylheti Images of Home and Away," *Man*, n.s. 28, no. 1 (March 1993), 13.

57. Ibid., 12.

58. For a history, see John Eade, *The Politics of Community: The Bangladeshi Community in East London* (Aldershot: Avebury, 1989).

59. Katy Gardner, *Global Migrants, Local Lives: Travel and Transformation in Rural Bangladesh* (Oxford: Clarendon, 1995); Katy Gardner, *Songs at the River's Edge: Stories from a Bangladeshi Village* (London: Pluto, 1997); Katy Gardner, "Desh-Bidesh: Sylheti Images of Home and Away," *Man*, n.s. 28, no. 1 (March 1993), 1–15.

60. Gardner, "Desh-Bidesh," 10.
61. Gardner, *Global Migrants*, 92.
62. Gardner, "Desh-Bidesh," 4.

4. British Rule

1. For a recent more "traditional" understanding, however, see C. Brad Faught, *Clive: Founder of British India* (Washington, DC: Potomac, 2013).
2. For further details see Michael W Charney, *A History of Modern Burma* (Cambridge: Cambridge University Press, 2008).
3. For a historiographical overview of the issues of continuity and change in this period see Ian J. Barrow and Douglas E Haynes, "The Colonial Transition: South Asia, 1780–1840," *Modern Asian Studies* 38, no. 3 (2004), 469–78. This should be read alongside more detailed case studies, for example, Ratnalekha Ray, *Change in Bengal Agrarian Society, 1760–1850* (Delhi: Manohar, 1979).
4. On elements of continuity and change see David Washbrook, "Progress and Problems: South Asian Economic and Social History c. 1720–1860," *Modern Asian Studies* 22, no. 1 (1988), 57–96.
5. See, for example, Mountstuart Elphinstone, *History of India*, 2 vols. (London: John Murray, 1841, 1843); Jadunath Sarkar, *Fall of Mughal India*, 4th ed. (New Delhi: Longman, 1988).
6. See Charles Raikes, *The Englishman in India* (London: Longmans, Green, 1867); and George Bruce Malleson, *The Founders of the Indian Empire: Lord Clive* (London: Allen, 1882).
7. See C. A. Bayly, *Imperial Meridian: The British Empire and the World, 1780–1830* (London: Longman, 1989); P. J. Marshall, *"A Free Though Conquering People": Eighteenth-Century Britain and Its Empire* (Aldershot: Ashgate Variorum, 2003); and Nicholas B. Dirks, *The Scandal of Empire: India and the Creation of Imperial Britain* (Cambridge: Harvard University Press, 2008).
8. See C. A. Bayly, *Rulers, Townsmen, and Bazaars: North Indian Society in the Age of British Expansion, 1770–1870* (Cambridge: Cambridge University Press, 1983); C. A. Bayly, *Indian Society and the Making of the British Empire* (Cambridge: Cambridge University Press, 1988); Richard B. Barnett, *North India Between the Empires: Awadh, Mughals, and the British* (Berkeley: University of California Press, 1980).
9. See David Washbrook, "Law, State, and Agrarian Society in Colonial India," *Modern Asian Studies* 15, no. 3 (1981), 649–721; Burton Stein, "State Formation and Economy Reconsidered," *Modern Asian Studies* 19, no. 3 (1985), 415–80.
10. This view also finds support in Prasannan Parthasarathi, "Merchants and the Rise of Colonialism," in *Institutions and Economic Change in South Asia*, ed. Burton Stein and Sanjay Subrahmanyan (Delhi: Oxford University Press, 1996), 85–104.

11. Burton Stein, *A History of India* (Oxford: Blackwell, 1998), 210.

12. Washbrook, "Progress and Problems," 76.

13. The links with Awadh made its sepoys resentful of the Company's recent annexation of the state, while their high-caste status made them sensitive to the "pollution" of the new Enfield rifle cartridges, which were greased with beef and pork fat and had to be bitten before being loaded.

14. C. A. Bayly, *Origins of Nationality in South Asia: Patriotism and Ethical Government in the Making of Modern India* (New Delhi: Oxford University Press, 2001), 251.

15. Cited in J. M. Brown, *Modern India: The Origins of an Asian Democracy*, 2nd ed. (Oxford: Oxford University Press, 1994).

16. For details see Stein, *A History*, 216 ff.

17. See Bruce Carlisle Robertson, *Raja Rammohan Roy: The Father of Modern India* (New Delhi: Oxford University Press, 1995).

18. See Lata Mani, *Contentious Traditions: The Debate on Sati in Colonial India* (Berkeley: University of California Press, 1998).

19. For a discussion of the "contextual" as opposed to the "essentialized" understanding of thugee see chapter 2 of Parama Roy, *Indian Traffic: Identities in Question in Colonial and Post-Colonial India* (Berkeley: University of California Press, 1998).

20. A useful examination of this process at work is contained in Anand Yang, *The Limited Raj: Agrarian Relations in Colonial India: Saran District, 1793–1920* (Berkeley: University of California Press, 1989).

21. For the intellectual milieu of what has been termed the Bengal Renaissance, of which the Brahmo Samaj was a part, see David Kopf, *British Orientalism and the Bengal Renaissance: The Dynamics of Indian Modernization, 1773–1835* (Berkeley: University of California Press, 1969).

22. Barrow and Haynes, *The Colonial Transition*, 474.

23. David Washbrook, "South India, 1770–1840: The Colonial Transition," *Modern Asian Studies* 38, no. 3 (2004), 479–516.

24. On the appreciation for Indian culture in the 1780s see S. N. Mukherjee, *Sir William Jones: A Study in Eighteenth-Century British Attitudes to India* (Cambridge: Cambridge University Press, 1968).

25. Ayesha Jalal, *Partisans of Allah: Jihad in South Asia* (Cambridge: Harvard University Press, 2008) 137–38.

26. Brown, *Modern India*, 90.

27. S. B. Chaudhuri, *Civil Rebellion in the Indian Mutinies* (Calcutta: World Press, 1957), 21.

28. Eric Stokes, *The Peasant and the Raj: Studies in Agrarian Society and Peasant Rebellion in Colonial India* (Cambridge: Cambridge University Press, 1978).

29. Rudrangshu Mukherjee, *Awadh in Revolt: A Study of Popular Resistance* (Delhi: Oxford University Press, 1984).

30. Thomas R. Metcalf, *The Aftermath of Revolt: India, 1857–1880* (Princeton: Princeton University Press, 1965), 68.

31. Mukherjee, *Awadh*, 62–64.

32. Tapti Roy, "Visions of the Rebels: A Study of 1857 in Bundelkhand," *Modern Asian Studies* 27, no. 1 (1993), 210.

33. Vinayak Damodar Savarkar, *The Indian War of Independence, 1857* (New Delhi: R. Granthagar, 1970).

34. Bayly, *Origins*, 86.

35. On the wider impact of 1857 on the British imagination see Gautam Chakravarty, *The Indian Mutiny and the British Imagination* (New Delhi: Cambridge University Press, 2006).

36. For evidence of the brutal British reprisals see Andrew Wood, *Our Bones Are Scattered: The Cawnpore Massacres and the Indian Mutiny of 1857* (London: John Murray, 1996).

37. See Carol Hills and Daniel C. Silverman, "Nationalism and Feminism in Late Colonial India: The Rani of Jhansi Regiment, 1943–1945," *Modern Asian Studies* 27, no. 4 (1993), 741–60.

38. For a synopsis and trailer of *The Rising: Ballad of Mangal Pandey* see www.sbs.com.au/movies/movie/rising-ballad-mangal-pandey, accessed 24 January 2013.

39. Hugh Purcell, *After the Raj: The Last Stayers-On and the Legacy of British India* (Brimscombe Port, Stroud: History Press, 2011), 272–75.

5. The "High Noon" of Empire

1. Ian J. Kerr, "Bombay and Lahore: Colonial Railways and Colonial Cities: Some Urban Consequences of the Development and Operation of Railways in India, c. 1850–c. 1947," 5 http:// www.docutren.com/HistoriaFerroviaria/Aranjuez2001/pdf/07.pdf, accessed 28 January 2013, 5.

2. The accolade comes from Jan Morris, *Stones of Empire: The Buildings of the Raj* (Oxford: Oxford University Press, 1983), 133.

3. On both the building of New Delhi and architecture's representation of British power in India see the essays in Thomas R. Metcalf, *Forging the Raj: Essays on British India in the Heyday of Empire* (New Delhi: Oxford University Press, 2005).

4. Beginning in the late 1860s, India was ravaged by famines in such regions as Orissa, Mysore, Hyderabad, and Rajasthan, which affected millions of people and claimed hundreds of thousands of lives.

5. Stanley Wolpert, *A New History of India*, 4th ed. (New York: Oxford University Press, 1993), 231.

6. On the representation of the British woman in India see Indrani Sen, *Woman and Empire: Representations in the Writings of British India, 1858–1900* (London: Sangam, 2002).

7. Eric Hobsbawm and Terence Ranger, eds., *The Invention of Tradition* (Cambridge: Cambridge University Press, 1984).

8. See *Hindoo Patriot* (Calcutta), 30 December 1902; *Amrita Bazaar Patrika* (Calcutta), 25 December 1902.

9. Government of India, *Census of India Report, 1881* (Calcutta: Government Printing Press, 1881), 1: 19 (emphasis added).

10. Government of India, *Census of India Report, 1911* (Calcutta: Government Printing Press, 1911), 1: 118.

11. Thomas Blom Hansen, *The Saffron Wave: Democracy and Nationalism in Modern India* (Princeton: Princeton University Press, 1999), 66.

12. E. M. Collingham, *Imperial Bodies: The Physical Experience of the Raj, c. 1800–1947* (Cambridge: Polity, 2001), 86.

13. See Pamela Kanwar, *Imperial Simla: The Political Culture of the Raj* (Delhi: Oxford University Press, 1990).

14. See A. D. King, *The Colonial Bungalow-Compound Complex: A Study in the Cultural Use of Space* (London: R.I.B.A. 1974).

15. Mary A. Procida, *Married to the Empire: Gender, Politics, and Imperialism in India, 1883–1947* (Manchester: Manchester University Press, 2002), 58.

16. Collingham, *Imperial Bodies*, 104–5.

17. On the memsahib see Margaret MacMillan, *Women of the Raj* (New York: Thames and Hudson, 1988).

18. Procida, *Married to Empire*, 6.

19. Cited in Pran Nevile, *Sahib's India: Vignettes from the Raj* (New Delhi: Penguin, 2010), 143.

20. See Maria Misra, *Business, Race, and Politics in British India* (Clarendon: Oxford, 1999).

21. Nevile, *Sahib's India*, 128.

22. See Dhara Anjaria, "Curzon and the Limits of Viceregal Power: India, 1899–1905," Ph.D. diss., University of London, 2009.

23. For further details of this episode see Chris Furedy, "Lord Curzon and the Reform of the Calcutta Corporation, 1899: A Case of Imperial Decision Making," *South Asia: Journal of South Asian Studies* 1, no. 1 (1978), 75–89.

24. Curzon to Hamilton, 11 October 1899, Curzon Papers F111/158 (IOR), British Library.

25. Ian Talbot, *India and Pakistan* (London: Arnold, 2000), 80.

26. Quoted in Sumit Sarkar, *The Swadeshi Movement in Bengal, 1903–1908* (New Delhi: People's Publishing, 1973), 262.

27. Bharati Ray, "Women in Calcutta: The Years of Change," in *Calcutta: The Living City* Vol. 2 (New Delhi: Oxford University Press, 1999), edited by Sukanta Chaudhri, 37.

6. Indians and the Raj

1. Frederick Charles Temple, *Report on Town Planning: Jamshedpur, November 1919* (Bombay: Commercial, 1919), 4.
2. Frank R. Harris, *Jamsetjee Nusserwanjee Tata: A Chronicle of His Life* (London: Blackie, 1958), 204.
3. Ibid., 275.
4. The Maharaja of Mysore had donated four hundred acres of land for the institute.
5. T. M. Luhrmann, *The Good Parsi: The Fate of a Colonial Elite in a Postcolonial Society* (Cambridge: Harvard University Press, 1996), 90.
6. Parsis played a leading role in the founding of all Bombay's major banks, as well as the stock exchange, which was established in 1860. Their wealth, as epitomized by the career of the famous merchant Sir Jamsetjee Jeejeebhoy (1783–1859), rested initially on trade (opium) with China. Parsis were the earliest Indian community to take up the game of cricket, in the early 1840s. Twice in the 1880s, Parsi teams toured England. See Ramachandra Guha, *A Corner of a Foreign Field: An Indian History of a British Sport* (London: Picador, 2001).
7. *Tourist's Handbook to Bombay and India*, cited in Luhrmann, *The Good Parsi*, 89–90.
8. See A. Guha, *More About the Parsi Seths: Their Roots, Entrepreneurship, and Comprador Role, 1650–1918.* Centre for Studies in the Social Sciences, Calcutta, occasional paper no. 50, 1982.
9. Dadabhai Naoroji is known as the "Grand Old Man of India." He was one of the first writers to popularize the notion that Britain was "draining" India of wealth.
10. See *Tata Steel Diamond Jubilee, 1907–1967* (Bombay: Tata, 1967), 78.
11. Dileep M. Wagle, "Imperial Preference and the Indian Steel Industry, 1924–1939," *Economic History Review* 34, no. 1 (February 1981), 120–31.
12. Luhrmann, *The Good Parsi*, 87.
13. R. A. Wadia, *The Bombay Dockyard and the Wadia Master Builders* (Mumbai: Bombay Parsi Panchayat, 2004), 207–13.
14. R. P. Masani, *N. M. Wadia and His Foundation* (Mumbai: Parsi Panchayat, 2004), 20–21.
15. Medha Kudaisya, "Marwari and Chettiar Merchants, c. 1850s-1950s: Comparative Trajectories," in *Chinese and Indian Business: Historical Antecedents*, ed. Medha Kudaisya and Ng Chin-Keong (Leiden: Koninklijke Brill, 2009), 107.
16. Medha Kudaisya, *The Life and Times of G. D. Birla* (New Delhi: Oxford University Press, 2006), 8.
17. See Thomas A Timberg, "Three Types of the Marwari Firm," in *Entrepreneurship and Industry in India, 1800–1947*, ed. Rajat Kanta Ray (Delhi: Oxford University Press, 1992), 127–57.

18. Ibid., 146–49.
19. B. R. Tomlinson, *The Political Economy of the Raj, 1914–1947: The Economics of Decolonization in India* (London: Macmillan, 1979)
20. Kudaisya, "Marwari and Chettiar Merchants," 103–5.
21. For details see Kudaisya, *Life and Times of G. D. Birla*, 35–37.
22. See D. A. Low, "The Forgotten Bania: Merchant Communities and the Indian National Congress," in *Eclipse of Empire* (Cambridge: Cambridge University Press, 1991), 101–19.
23. Kudaisya, *Life and Times of G. D. Birla*, 126.
24. Ibid., 164.
25. Ibid., 165.
26. "Gandhi House: Gandhi Smriti or 'Birla House,' New Delhi, India," YouTube, http://www.youtube.com/watch?v=bcJi9Xnn4tc, accessed 3 February 2013.
27. Cited in S. H. Rudolph, "The New Courage: An Essay on Gandhi's Psychology," in *Modern India: An Interpretative Anthology*, ed. T. R. Metcalf (London: Macmillan, 1971), 248.
28. See Kenneth W. Jones, *Arya Dharm: Hindu Consciousness in 19th Century Punjab* (Berkeley: University of California Press, 1976); Kenneth W. Jones, "Ham Hindu Nahin: Arya-Sikh Relations, 1877–1905," *Journal of Asian Studies* 32, no. 3 (May 1973), 457–75; J. E. Llewellyn, *The Arya Samaj as a Fundamentalist Movement: A Study in Comparative Fundamentalism* (Delhi: Manohar, 1993).
29. Madhu Kishwar, "Arya Samaj and Women's Education: Kanya Mahavidyalaya Jalandhar," *Economic and Political Weekly* 29, no. 17 (26 April 1986), ws-9–ws-24.
30. Ian Talbot, *India and Pakistan* (London: Arnold, 2000), 101.
31. On Vivekananda's legacy of social service see Gwilym Beckerlegge, *Swami Vivekananda's Legacy of Service: A Study of the Ramakrishna Math and Mission* (New Delhi: Oxford University Press, 2006).
32. See Jeffrey J. Kripal, *Kali's Child: The Mystical and the Erotic in the Life and Teachings of Ramakrishna* (Chicago: University of Chicago Press, 1995).
33. On Vivekananda see Pandya Dushyanta, *Swami Vivekananda: The Monarch of Monks* (New Delhi: Readworthy, 2009).

7. The Nation and Beyond

1. For an overview see Arun Coomer Bose, *Indian Revolutionaries Abroad, 1905–1922, in the Background of International Developments* (Patna: Bharati Bhawan, 1971).
2. See "German Schemes for Raising Revolt in India," 17/8/1915 L/P&S/11/103/1916, British Library.
3. Latha Varadarajan, *The Domestic Abroad: Diasporas in International Relations* (New York: Oxford University Press, 2010), 61.

4. See Karen A. Roy, "Roots of Ambivalence: Indenture, Identity, and the 'Indian Freedom Struggle,'" in *Ethnicity, Identity, Migration: The South Asian Context*, ed. Milton Israel and N. K. Wagle (Toronto: University of Toronto Press, 1993), 269–90.

5. There are numerous studies on the Ghadr movement. For a useful recent one see Maia Ramnath, *Haj to Utopia: How the Ghadr Movement Charted Global Radicalism and Attempted to Overthrow the British Empire* (Berkeley: University of California Press, 2011).

6. On Har Dayal see Emily C. Brown, *Har Dayal: Hindu Revolutionary and Rationalist* (Delhi: Manohar, 1976); and Benjamin Zachariah, "A Long Strange Trip: The Lives in Exile of Har Dayal," *South Asian History and Culture* 4, no. 4 (2013), 574–92.

7. The photographs of such Ghadrite prisoners as Pandit Jagat Ram, Baba Gurdit Singh, and Baba Madan Singh can be seen in the freedom fighter gallery in the prison.

8. Cited in Tatla, *The Sikh Diaspora*, 89.

9. The many works on Bhagat Singh are frequently hagiographical in approach. See P. Kumar, *Bhagat Singh: A Great Son of India* (New Delhi: Mahaveer, 2008). For a useful account of Bhagat Singh's role in popular Indian culture see Kamla Maclean, "The History of a Legend: Accounting for Popular Histories of Revolutionary Nationalism in India," *Modern Asian Studies* 46, no. 6 (2012), 1540–71.

10. Dharm Vir, "Dar Hardyal," in *Punjab's Eminent Hindus*, ed. N. B. Sen (Lahore: New Book Society, 1943), 67.

11. See Ayesha Jalal, *Partisans of Allah: Jihad in South Asia* (Cambridge: Harvard University Press, 2008), 179 ff.

12. Ibid., 192.

13. *Zamindar* was not alone in its pro-Turkish sentiments; Lahore's reading public could also encounter these in Maulana Abul Kalam Azad's *Al-Hilal*, which was published in Calcutta, and Mohammad Ali's *Hamdard* (Delhi).

14. By 1900, *Paisa Akhbar* was selling thirteen thousand copies a week. See "Report on 'Native Newspapers in the Punjab,' Week Ending 11 November 1900," NAI.

15. "Turkish Intrigues Among Indian Muhammadans," 19 March 1914 L/P&S/ 11 P4651 (IOR), British Library.

16. See M. S. Leigh, *Punjab and War* (Lahore: Government Printing, 1922); I. Talbot, *Punjab and the Raj, 1849–1947* (New Delhi: Manohar, 1988).

17. Maulana Obaidallah Sindhi was a convert from Sikhism who was admitted to the Darul Uloom Deoband in 1888. He was the home member in Mahendra Pratap's provisional government of India. He had to leave Afghanistan for Moscow in 1922, but unlike some of the mujahideen, he did not abandon pan-Islamic ideals for socialism. For the imperial view of Obaidullah's activities see "The Silk Letter

Conspirators," L/P&S/12/1760 Col 3/163 (IOR), British Library. This should be read alongside Muhammad Hajjan Shaikh, *Maulana Ubaid Ullah Sindhi: A Revolutionary Scholar* (Islamabad: National Institute of Historical and Cultural Research, 1986).

18. See Gail Minault, *The Khilafat Movement: Religious Symbolism and Political Mobilization in India* (New York: Columbia University Press, 1982).

19. On the Sikh Gurdwara reform movement see Mohinder Singh, *The Akali Movement* (Delhi: Macmillan, 1978); and J. S. Grewal, *The Sikhs of the Punjab* (Cambridge: Cambridge University Press, 1991).

20. On the Moplah uprising see K. N. Panikkar, *Against Lord and State: Religion and Peasant Uprisings in Malabar, 1836–1921* (Delhi: Oxford University Press, 2001).

21. Cited in Sekhar Bandyopadhyay, *From Plassey to Partition: A History of Modern India* (Hyderabad: Orient Longman, 2004), 338.

22. Sugata Bose, *A Hundred Horizons: The Indian Ocean in the Age of Global Empire* (Cambridge: Harvard University Press, 2006), 152–70.

23. See Eric Itzkin, *Gandhi's Johannesburg: Birthplace of Satyagraha* (Johannesburg: Witwatersrand University Press, Global, 2001).

24. Madhu Kishwar, "Gandhi on Women," *Economic and Political Weekly*, 5 October 1985, 1691–1720.

25. A. Basu, "Gujarati Women's Response to Gandhi, 1920–1942," *Samya Shakti* 1, no. 2 (1984), 6–16.

26. See Lanka Sundaram, *Indians Overseas: A Study in Economic Sociology* (Madras: G. A. Natesan, 1933); and Nagendranath Gangulee, *Indians in the Empire Overseas: A Survey* (London: New India, 1947).

27. Varadarajan, *The Domestic Abroad*, 62.

28. On the history of the Indian National Army see Gerard H. Corr, *The War of the Springing Tigers* (London: Osprey, 1975); and Peter Ward Fay, *Forgotten Army: India's Armed Struggle for Independence, 1942–45* (Ann Arbor: University of Michigan Press, 1995).

29. See Sugata Bose, *His Majesty's Opponent: Subhas Chandra Bose and India's Struggle Against Empire* (Cambridge: Belknap Press of Harvard University Press, 2011); *The Essential Writings of Netaji Subhas Chandra Bose*, ed. Sisir K. Bose and Sugata Bose (Delhi: Oxford University Press, 1997); *Netaji: Collected Works*, ed. Sisir K. Bose (Calcutta: Netaji Research Bureau, 1980–2007).

30. Bose, *A Hundred Horizons*, 179.

31. This paragraph draws on the insights from Bose, *A Hundred Horizons*, 180–81.

32. The persistent rumors that Bose did not die in the plane crash at Taipei on 18 August 1945 have been the subject of three government of India–sponsored commissions and numerous private investigations. For Bose's period in Nazi Germany and a discussion of his views regarding Nazism, see Romain Hayes, *Subhas*

Chandra Bose in Nazi Germany: Politics, Intelligence, and Propaganda, 1941–1943 (London: Hurst, 2011). Bose denounced Nazi racism but was prepared to ally with Hitler in the context of the Second World War in the endeavor to achieve India's freedom.

33. Bose, *His Majesty's Opponent*, 324.

8. Independence with Partition

1. Penderel Moon, ed., *Wavell: The Viceroy's Journal* (London: Oxford University Press, 1973), 402.
2. Mohandas Gandhi, "Statement to the Press," *Harijan*, 3 March 1946, cited in *Towards Freedom: Documents on the Movement for Indepdendence in India 1946*, ed. Sumit Sarkar (New Delhi: Oxford University Press, 2007), 59.
3. Extract from Sardar Patel's correspondence, cited in Sarkar, *Towards Freedom*, 3.
4. T. B. Sapru to M. R. Jayakar 3 March 1946 (extracts from Sapru papers), cited in Sarkar, *Towards Freedom*, 64.
5. See Latif Ahmed Sherwani, *The Partition of India and Mountbatten* (Karachi: Council for Pakistan Studies, 1986).
6. Mountbatten's detractors include Andrew Roberts, *Eminent Churchillians* (London: Weidenfeld and Nicholson, 1994), 55–137; and Stanley Wolpert, *Shameful Flight: The Last Years of the British Empire in India* (New York: Oxford University Press, 2006). His supporters include Philip Ziegler, *Mountbatten: The Official Biography* (London: Collins, 1985); H. V. Hodson, *The Great Divide: Britain-India-Pakistan* (London: Hutchinson, 1969); and A. Campbell-Johnson, *Mission with Mountbatten* (London: Hamilton, 1985).
7. For details see David Page, *Prelude to Partition: The Indian Muslims and the Imperial System of Control* (Cambridge: Cambridge University Press, 1985).
8. Bipan Chandra, *India's Struggle for Independence* (Harmondsworth: Penguin, 1989), 324.
9. Hodson, *The Great Divide*, 84–85.
10. Cited in Nicholas Owen, "The Cripps Mission of 1942: A Reinterpretation," *Journal of Imperial and Commonwealth History* 30, no. 1 (2002), 61–98.
11. Ibid., 80.
12. Cited in B. R. Nanda, "The Triumph and Tragedy of Mahatma Gandhi," in *The Partition in Retrospect*, ed. Amrik Singh (New Delhi: Anamika, 2000), 48–60.
13. For details see chapter 3 of I. Talbot and G. Singh, *The Partition of India* (Cambridge: Cambridge University Press, 2009).
14. Ian Talbot, *Pakistan: A Modern History* (London: Hurst, 2008); Ian Talbot, *Punjab and the Raj, 1949–1947* (Delhi: Manohar, 1988); Ian Talbot, "The 1946 Punjab Elections," *Modern Asian Studies* 14, no. 1 (1980), 65–91.

15. Lucy Chester, *On the Edge: Borders, Territory, and Conflict in South Asia* (Manchester: Manchester University Press, 2008).

16. On the operation of the Punjab Boundary Force, see Robin Jeffrey, "The Punjab Boundary Force and the Problem of Order, August 1947," *Modern Asian Studies* 8, no. 4 (1974), 491–520.

17. Joya Chatterji, *The Spoils of Partition: Bengal and India, 1947–1967* (Cambridge: Cambridge University Press, 2007), 314.

18. Ibid., 19.

19. Talbot, *Pakistan: A Modern History*, 152.

20. See Anindita Dasgupta, "Denial and Resistance: Sylheti Partition 'Refugees' in Assam," *Contemporary South Asia* 10, no. 3 (2001), 345.

9. Nehru and the "New" India

1. See Jane Drew, "Le Corbusier as I Knew Him," in *The Open Hand: Essays on Le Corbusier* (Cambridge: MIT Press, 1977), 364–74.

2. Vikramaditya Prakash, *Chandigarh's Le Corbusier: The Struggle for Modernity in Post-Colonial India* (Seattle: University of Washington Press, 2002), 146–47.

3. Cited in Madhu Sarin, *Urban Planning in the Third World: The Chandigarh Experience* (London: Mansell, 1982), 26.

4. Prakash, *Chandigarh's Le Corbusier*, 10.

5. *Time*, 21 April 1958.

6. Ravi Kalia, *Gandhinagar: Building National Identity in Post-Colonial India* (Columbia: University of South Carolina Press, 2004), 2.

7. Sunil Khilnani, *The Idea of India* (New Delhi: Penguin, 1999), 128.

8. Quoted ibid., 135.

9. Ravi Kalia, *Bhubaneswar: From a Temple City to a Capital City* (Carbondale: Southern Illinois University Press, 1994).

10. For details see chapter 3 of Kalia, *Gandhinagar*.

11. Ibid., 107.

12. Khilnani, *The Idea of India*, 135.

13. As early as November 1908, a plan was mooted for a storage reservoir on the Sutlej River. In the late colonial period, various specification plans were made, and a draft agreement was signed in 1945 between the raja of Bilaspur and the Punjab government.

14. Developmental History of Bhakra—Nangal Dam Project, http://www.bbmb.gov.in/english/history_nangal_dam.asp, accessed 4 March 2013.

15. Judith M. Brown, *Nehru: A Political Life* (New Haven: Yale University Press, 2003), 190.

16. For an assessment of the contingencies that influenced Nehru, see Khilnani, *The Idea of India*, 166–70.

17. The clash between the prime minister and his deputy was reported to the US embassy by Matthai, the minister of transport. See I. Talbot, *India and Pakistan* (London: Arnold, 2000), 164.

18. Brown, *Nehru*, 198. Nehru provided a detailed statistical breakdown to his old friend Mountbatten, who loved such things. Nehru to Mountbatten, 26 March 1952, MB1/G28, folder 1, Mountbatten Papers, University of Southampton.

19. Robert L. Hardgrave, *India: Government and Politics in a Developing Nation*, 3rd ed. (New York: Harcourt, Brace, Jovanovich, 1980), 192.

20. For the important role of the physicist and statistician Prasaanta Chandra Mahalanobis on the Planning Committee see Khilnani, *The Idea of India*, 82–87.

21. See Brown, *Nehru*, 300–301, for a discussion of socioeconomic change and the problem of population pressures.

22. Neville Maxwell, *India, Nagas, and the North-East* (London: Minority Rights Group, 1980), 4.

23. S. Gupta, *India Redefines Its Role* (Oxford: Oxford University Press and IISS, 1995), 25.

24. Paul M. McGarr, *The Cold War in South Asia: Britain, the United States, and the Indian Subcontinent, 1945–1965* (Cambridge: Cambridge University Press, 2013), 174–75.

25. Sandys to Gore-Booth, 20 December 1961, MS Gorebooth 85, Paul Gore-Booth Papers, Bodleian Library, University of Oxford.

26. For details see Robert L. Hardgrave, *Essays in the Political Sociology of South India* (New Delhi: Usha, 1979), 225.

27. This comment was made in 1953 by Paul Appleby, an American academic and consultant in public administration; quoted in Brown, *Nehru*, 205.

28. Vijayalakshmi Pandit to Earl Mountbatten, 14 February 1962, MB1/J325, folder 1 Mountbatten Papers, University of Southampton.

29. McGarr, *The Cold War in South Asia*, 251.

30. Nehru to Mountbatten, 25 March 1951, MB1/H167, Mountbatten Papers, University of Southampton.

31. Nehru to Mountbatten, 8 March 1960, MB1/J303, Mountbatten Papers, University of Southampton.

32. Nehru to Mountbatten, 24 May 1964, MB1/J302, Mountbatten Papers, University of Southampton.

33. As early as 1952, Edwina and her husband had been urging Nehru to look for and groom suitable successors. Mountbatten to Nehru, 18 February 1952, MB1/G28, folder 1 Mountbatten Papers, University of Southampton.

34. McGarr, *The Cold War in South Asia*, 246–47.

35. Mountbatten to Nehru, 30 January 1964, MB1/J302, Mountbatten Papers, University of Southampton.

36. Brown, *Nehru*, 335.
37. McGarr, *The Cold War in South Asia*, 260.

10. Pakistan's Failure in Democratic Consolidation

1. See Jinnah Mausoleum, http://www.youtube.com/watch?v=u1LGPfdCs6Y, uploaded by sightsandsoundsofpak, 21 February 2007.
2. R. LaPorte, *Power and Privilege: Influence and Decision-Making in Pakistan* (Berkeley: University of California Press, 1975), 36.
3. See K. L. Kamal, *Pakistan: The Garrison State* (New Delhi: Intellectual Publishing House, 1982); and Ayesha Jalal, *The State of Martial Rule: The Origin of Pakistan's Political Economy of Defence* (Cambridge: Cambridge University Press, 1990).
4. Claude Markovits, *Indian Business and Nationalist Politics, 1931–1939: The Indigenous Capitalist Class and the Rise of the Congress Party* (Cambridge: Cambridge University Press, 1985), appendix 1.
5. Ian Talbot, *Pakistan: A Modern History* (London: Hurst, 2005), 54–65.
6. M. Waseem, *The 1993 Elections in Pakistan* (Lahore: Vanguard, 1994), 30–31.
7. C. Dewey, "The Rural Roots of Pakistani Militarism," in *The Political Inheritance of Pakistan*, ed. D. A. Low (Basingstoke: Macmillan, 1991), 255–84.
8. Allen McGrath, *The Destruction of Pakistan's Democracy* (Karachi: Oxford University Press, 1996).
9. For a detailed analysis see Yaqoob Khan Bangash, "The Integration of the Princely States of Pakistan, 1947–55," D. Phil. diss., University of Oxford, 2011.
10. See *Nawa-e-Waqt* (Lahore), 19 April 1945; *Eastern Times* (Lahore), 27 May 1945.
11. Translation of a pamphlet issued by the election board of the Punjab Muslim Students' Federation Freedom Movement Archives.
12. Pirs issued fatwas to their disciples commanding them to vote for Muslim League candidates, while landlords directed their tenants to vote for the League. Wherever strong biraderis existed, the Muslim League endeavored to choose their leaders as candidates. See *Eastern Times* (Lahore), 27 October 1945; *Nawa-e-Waqt* (Lahore), 3 and 19 January 1946.
13. See I. Talbot, *Provincial Politics and the Pakistan Movement: The Growth of the Muslim League in North-West and North-East India, 1937–47* (Karachi: Oxford University Press, 1988).
14. Deputy High Commissioner's Report for East Bengal, 12–18 January 1948, L/P&J/5/322 (IOR), British Library.
15. *Eastern Times* (Lahore), 29 January 1947.
16. *Nawa-e-Waqt* (Lahore), 9 January 1946.
17. See *Statesman* (Calcutta), 28 October 1950.

18. Yunas Samad, *A Nation in Turmoil: Nationalism and Ethnicity in Pakistan, 1937–1958* (New Delhi: Sage, 1995), 127.
19. Sarah Ansari, *Life After Partition: Migration, Community, and Strife in Sindh, 1947–1962* (Karachi: Oxford University Press, 2005), 130.
20. Cited in Chaudhuri Muhammad Ali, *The Emergence of Pakistan* (New York: Columbia University Press, 1967), 376.
21. Samad, *A Nation in Turmoil*, 128.
22. Jalal, *The State of Martial Rule*, 299–300.
23. M. Ayub Khan, *Friends Not Masters: A Political Biography* (London: Oxford University Press, 1967), 55.
24. Cited in Jalal, *The State of Martial Rule*, 227.
25. Ibid., 273.
26. See Fazal Muqeem Khan, *Story of the Pakistan Army* (Karachi: Oxford University Press, 1963), 202. Mirza in his memoir dismissed this as an "absurd" fabrication to justify Ayub's action.
27. See Mazhar Aziz, *Military Control: The Parallel State* (London: Routledge, 2008).

11. Challenges to Nehruvian India

1. For biographies of this "forgotten" political figure see L. P. Singh, *Portrait of Lal Bahadur Shastri* (Delhi: Ravi Dayal, 1996); and C. P. Srivastava, *Lal Bahadur Shastri: A Life of Truth in Politics* (New Delhi: Oxford University Press, 1995).
2. "Mr Lal Bahadur Shastri," June 1964, PREM 11/4864, NA.
3. See Bruce Muirhead, "Differing Perspectives: The World Bank and the 1963 Aid India Negotiations," *India Review* 4, no. 1 (January 2005), 1–22.
4. On the Green Revolution see Francine R. Frankel, *India's Green Revolution: Economic Gains and Political Costs* (Princeton: Princeton University Press, 1971).
5. John R. Westley, *Agriculture and Equitable Growth: The Case of Punjab-Haryana* (Boulder, CO: Westview, 1986); G. S. Bhalla, *Green Revolution and the Small Peasant: A Study of Income Distribution Among Punjab Cultivators* (New Delhi: Concept, 1983).
6. On the cultural dimensions of Sikh "fundamentalism" see, for example, Cynthia Keppley Mahmood, "Sikh Rebellion and the Hindu Concept of Order," *Asian Survey* 29, no. 3 (1989), 326–40; and Angela Dietrich, "The Khalsa Resurrected: Sikh Fundamentalism in the Punjab," in *Studies in Religious Fundamentalism*, ed. Lionel Caplan (Albany: State University of New York, 1987), 122–37.
7. Indira Gandhi moved Jha to the Reserve Bank of India in September 1967 and replaced him with the more "loyal" P. N. Haksar.
8. See Asok Kapur, *India's Nuclear Option: Atomic Diplomacy and Decision Making* (New York: Praeger, 1976).

9. Farooq Bajwa, *From Kutch to Tashkent: The Indo-Pakistan War of 1965* (London: Hurst, 2013), 371.

10. A number of conspiracy theories still surround Shastri's death.

11. For a variety of views see Krishnan Bhatia, *Indira: Biography of Prime Minister Gandhi* (New York: Praeger, 1974); Dilip Hiro, *Inside India Today* (New York: Monthly Review Press, 1979); Zareer Masani, *Indira Gandhi: A Biography* (New York: Crowell, 1976); David Selbourne, *An Eye to India: The Unmasking of a Tyranny* (New York: Penguin, 1977); and Uma Vasudev, *Two Faces of Indira Gandhi* (New Delhi: Vikas, 1978).

12. P. N. Dhar, *Indira Gandhi, the "Emergency," and Indian Democracy* (New Delhi: Oxford University Press, 2000), 289, 282–83.

13. See Biplap Dasgupta, *The Naxalite Movement* (Bombay: Allied, 1974); Asish Kumar Roy, *The Spring Thunder and After* (Calcutta: Minerva, 1975); and Marcus F. Franda, *Radical Politics in West Bengal* (Cambridge: M.I.T. Press, 1971). For fictional references see Mahasweta Devi, *Hajar Churashir Maa* (Calcutta: Karuna Prakashani, 1974); and Michael Palin, *The Truth* (London: Weidenfield and Nicholson, 2012).

14. See W. H. Morris-Jones, "India Elects for Change—and Stability," *Asian Survey* 11 (August 1971), 727.

15. Dhar, *Indira Gandhi*, 135.

16. Ibid., 123.

17. Ibid., 351.

18. Ibid., 223.

19. Among the numerous accounts see Michael Henderson, *Experiment with Untruth: India Under the Emergency* (Columbia, MO: South Asia Books, 1977); and Kuldip Nayer, *The Judgement* (New Delhi: Vikas, 1977). The major source is the three-volume Shah Commission of Inquiry Report, dealing with the prelude and excesses of the emergency period. Gandhi was to use its proceedings, however, to present herself as a persecuted victim. When she returned to power in January 1980, she attempted to recall all copies of the Commission's findings. Shah Commission of Inquiry, *Interim Report 1: March 11, 1978* (New Delhi: Government of India Press, 1978); *Interim Report 2: April 26, 1978* (New Delhi: Government of India Press, 1978); *Third and Final Report: August 6, 1978* (New Delhi: Government of India Press, 1978).

20. A national emergency had been declared under Article 352 of the Constitution during the 1962 war with China and the 1971 Bangladeshi war, but these were responses to external aggression.

21. See Ghanshayam Shah, *Protest Movements in Two Indian States: A Study of the Gujarat and Bihar Movements* (Delhi: Ajanta, 1977).

22. Dawn E. Jones and Rodney W. Jones, "Urban Upheaval in India: The 1974 Nav Nirman Riots in Gujarat," *Asian Survey* 16 (November 1976), 1012–23.

23. Natish R. De, "Gherao as a Technique for Social Intervention," *Economic and Political Weekly* 5, annual number (January 1970), 201–8.

24. Ghanshyam Shah, "The 1975 Gujarat Assembly Elections in India," *Asian Survey* 16 (March 1976), 270–82.

25. Dhar, *Indira Gandhi*, 260–61.

26. Ibid., 324.

27. Ibid., 341–51.

28. Rohinton Mistry, *A Fine Balance* (Toronto: McCelland and Stewart, 1995).

29. Salman Rushdie, *Midnight's Children* (London: Jonathan Cape, 1981).

30. Nayantara Saghal, *Rich Like Us* (London: Heinemann, 1985).

31. Rahi Masoom Raza, *Katra Bi Arzoo* (New Delhi: Rajkamal Prakashan, 2002).

32. The BLD was itself the product of a merger in 1974; its main components were the Bharatiya Kranti Dal, led by Charan Singh; the free-enterprise Swatantra Party; and Raj Narain's Socialist grouping. The BLD was a vehicle for the prosperous agriculturalist castes of North India.

33. The AIDKM was founded in 1972 by the charismatic actor "MGR" (M. G. Ramachandran), who used his fan clubs to mobilize support. He attracted a range of support, including upper castes, backward castes, and Dalits. See Narendra Sub-ramanian, "Identity Politics and Social Pluralism: Political Sociology and Political Change in Tamil Nadu," in *Decentering the Indian Nation*, ed. Andrew Wyatt and John Zavos (London: Frank Cass, 2003), 125–39.

34. Dhar, *Indira Gandhi*, 355.

35. For a brief and incisive assessment of Charan Singh see Paul Brass, "Chaudhuri Charan Singh: An Indian Political Life," *Economic and Political Weekly* 28 (September 25, 1993), 2087–90.

36. James Manor, "Where Congress Survived: Five States in the Indian General Election of 1977," *Asian Survey* 17 (December 1977), 1207–20.

37. Francine Frankel, "The Middle Classes and Castes in India's Politics" in *India's Democracy: An Analysis of Changing State-Society Relations*, ed. Atul Kohli (Princeton: Princeton University Press, 1990), 256–59.

38. The Telegu Desam Party had its main support base among the backward castes, who felt that Congress had bypassed them in favor of the Dalits. See K. C. Suri, "Telegu Desam Party," in *India's Political Parties*, ed. Peter Ronald deSouza and E. Sridharan (New Delhi: Sage, 2006), 283–87.

39. Among the vast literature on this topic see Paul R. Brass, *The Production of Hindu-Muslim Violence in Contemporary India* (Seattle: University of Washington Press, 2003); Asghar Ali Engineer, *Communal Riots in Post-Independence India* (Hyderabad: Sangam, 1984); and Steven I. Wilkinson, *Votes and Violence: Electoral Competition and Ethnic Riots in India* (Cambridge: Cambridge University Press, 2004).

40. For background to the Punjab crisis see Gurharpal Singh, *Ethnic Conflict in India: A Case Study of Punjab* (Basingstoke: Macmillan, 2000).
41. Mark Tully and S. Jacob, *Amritsar: Mrs Gandhi's Last Battle* (London: Cape, 1985).
42. Uma Chakravarti and Nandita Haksar, *The Delhi Riots: Three Days in the Life of a Nation* (New Delhi: Lancer International 1987); *Who Are the Guilty? Report of a Joint Report into the Causes and Impact of the Riots in Delhi from 31 October to 10 November* (Delhi: People's Union for Civil Liberties, 1984).

12. Pakistan's National Crisis and the Birth of Bangladesh

1. As with the events of 1857, different interpretations are wrapped up in the terms used, which vary from "liberation war," or "muktijuddho," to the Indo-Pakistani War of 1971. See Antara Datta, *Refugees and Borders in South Asia: The Great Exodus of 1971* (London: Routledge, 2013), 2.
2. The Pakistani government's denial of genocide is based on the notion that accounts of atrocities by such reporters as Anthony Mascarenhas were "Indian propaganda." The Hamoodur Rahman account of casualties during the civil war puts these at just twenty-six thousand, while the most conservative credible numbers are usually regarded as between 300,000 and 500,000 (Mark Dummett, "Bangladesh War: The Article that Changed History," www.bbc.co.uk/news/world-asia-16207201), with some writers claiming up to 3 million deaths. Bose was regarded by Bangladeshis as a "genocide denier." She played down the role of the Pakistan Army in atrocities, which she portrayed as resulting more from ethnic clashes between Biharis and Bengalis. Sarmila Bose, *Dead Reckoning: Memories of the 1971 Bangladesh War* (New York: Columbia University Press, 2011).
3. Harun-or-Rashid, *The Foreshadowing of Bangladesh: Bengal Muslim League and Muslim League Politics, 1936–1947* (Dhaka: Asiatic Society of Bangladesh, 1987), 177–79.
4. Quoted ibid., 45.
5. Quoted ibid., 181.
6. Deputy High Commissioner's Reports for East Bengal, Period Ending 11 July 1948, L/P&J/5/322 (IOR), British Library.
7. Ian Talbot, *Pakistan: A New History* (London: Hurst, 2012), 71.
8. Ibid., 72.
9. Ayesha Jalal, *The State of Martial Rule*, 189.
10. For further details on the Basic Democracies scheme see I. Talbot, *Pakistan: A Modern History*, 2nd ed. (London: Hurst, 2009), 154–56.
11. A. T. Rafiqur Rahman, *Basic Democracies at the Grass Roots* (Comilla: Pakistan Academy for Village Development, 1962), 253.

12. Hasan-Askari Rizvi, *Military, State, and Society in Pakistan* (Basingstoke: Macmillan, 2000), 89.

13. M. Waseem, *Politics and the State in Pakistan* (Lahore: Progressive, 1989), 155.

14. Consul-General Dacca to Department of State, 8 February 1962, 790.D.00/2-162, National Archives at College Park.

15. Z. Niazi, "Towards a Free Press," in *Old Roads, New Highways: Fifty Years of Pakistan*, ed. Victoria Schofield (Karachi: Oxford University Press, 1997), 182.

16. American Consul-General Lahore to Department of State, 22 January 1963, 790.D.00/1-1663, National Archives at College Park.

17. For details see Talbot, *Pakistan: A New History*, 88–91.

18. For a detailed account see Farooq Bajwa, *From Kutch to Tashkent: The Indo-Pakistan War of 1965* (London: Hurst, 2013).

19. Philip E. Jones, *The Pakistan People's Party: Rise to Power* (Karachi: Oxford University Press, 2003).

20. Ibid., 361.

21. Morrice James, *Pakistan Chronicle* (London: Hurst, 1992), 157.

22. Pakistan had been engaged in diplomatic realignment since the October 1962 Sino-Indian War. Bhutto encouraged a tilt to China in its wake. British and US emergency military aid to India was unpopular in Islamabad. Anti-Americanism intensified with the US arms embargo during the 1965 war. On the war's impact on the rise of "Bhuttoism" see Jones, *The Pakistan People's Party*. The best account of the Pakistan Army's long-term links with jihadist groups to advance its strategic aims in Kashmir can be found in Praveen Swami, *India, Pakistan, and the Secret Jihad: The Covert War in Kashmir, 1947–2001* (Milton Park, Abingdon: Routledge, 2007).

23. Tariq Rahman, "Language and Politics in a Pakistan Province: The Sindhi Language Movement," *Asian Survey* 35, no. 11 (November 1995), 1010–11.

24. Tariq Rahman, *Language and Politics in Pakistan* (Karachi: Oxford University Press, 1996), 99.

25. Rounaq Jahan, *Pakistan: Failure in National Integration* (New York: Columbia University Press, 1972), 74–75.

26. Ayesha Siddiqa, *Military Inc.: Inside Pakistan's Military Economy* (London: Pluto Press, 2007), 131.

27. Fazal Muqeem Khan, *Pakistan's Crisis in Leadership* (Islamabad: National Book Foundation, 1973), 16.

28. H. Zaheer, *The Separation of East Pakistan: The Rise and Realization of Bengali Muslim Nationalism* (Karachi: Oxford University Press, 1995), 124–25.

29. Sharif al Mujahid, "Pakistan: First General Elections," *Asian Survey* 11 (January 1971), 166.

30. Iftikhar Ahmad, *Pakistan General Elections, 1970* (Lahore: South Asia Institute, Punjab University, 1976); Javed Kamran Bashir, *NWFP Elections, 1970* (Lahore: Progressive Publishers, 1973).

31. Golam Waheed Choudhury, *The Last Days of United Pakistan* (London: Hurst, 1974), 161.
32. Richard Sisson and Leo E. Rose, *War and Secession: Pakistan, India, and the Creation of Bangladesh* (Berkeley: University of California Press, 1990), 57.
33. Ibid., 272.
34. Ibid., 67.
35. Willem Van Schendel, *A History of Bangladesh* (Cambridge: Cambridge University Press, 2009), 190.

13. Bangladesh Since Independence

1. Numerous works have been written on the issues of aid, dependency, and development. See, for example, M. Akhlaqur Rahman, *Foreign Aid and Self-Reliant Growth: The Case of Bangladesh* (Dhaka: Dhaka University, 1984). On the arsenic poisoning see Allan H. Smith et al., "Contamination of Drinking-Water by Arsenic in Bangladesh: A Public Health Emergency," *Bulletin of the World Health Organization* 78, no. 9 (2006), 567–74. The renowned Bangladeshi social anthropologist Katy Gardner has recently produced a study of the impact on rural Bangladeshi lives of gas mining operations. See Katy Gardner, *The Discordant Development: Global Capitalism and the Struggle for Connection in Bangladesh* (London: Pluto, 2012).
2. On the weaknesses of media coverage as a result of lack of contextualization and on the Indian claims that ISI was seeking to destabilize India by its activities in Bangladesh, see the Introduction of Ali Riaz, *God Willing: The Politics of Islamism in Bangladesh* (Lanham, MD: Rowman and Littlefield, 2004).
3. These parties are not solely based in rural areas. Hizbut Tahrir, for example, has recently emerged with an urban-educated class base of support.
4. Md. Shamsul Islam, "Political Violence in Bangladesh," in *Political Islam and Governance in Bangladesh*, ed. Ali Riaz and C. Christine Fair (London: Routledge, 2011), 27–46.
5. Manmay Zafar, "Under the Gaze of the State: Policing Literature and the Case of Taslima Nasrin," *Inter-Asia Cultural Studies* 6, no. 3 (2005), 410–21.
6. The establishment of a tribunal had formed part of the Awami League platform in the December 2008 general election. The war crimes tribunal issued its first indictments in 2010. These involved leading figures within the Bangladesh JI who had been involved in the Al-Badr and Al-Shams volunteer movements, which had carried out atrocities during the liberation war.
7. *Daily Star* (Dhaka), 6 February 2013.
8. For her immensely influential autobiographical account of the atrocities by pro-Pakistan groups in the liberation war see Jahanara Imam, *Of Blood and Fire: The Untold Story of Bangladesh's War of Independence*, trans. Mustafizur Rahman (New Delhi: Sterling, 1989).

9. Nick Cohen, "The Agonies of Bangladesh Come to London," *Observer* (London), 17 February 2013.

10. Dina Mahnaz Siddiqi, "Political Culture in Contemporary Bangladesh: Histories, Ruptures, and Contradictions," in Riaz and Fair, *Political Islam and Governance in Bangladesh*, 10.

11. William B. Milam, *Bangladesh and Pakistan: Flirting with Failure in South Asia* (London: Hurst, 2009), 37.

12. Talukder Maniruzzaman, "Bangladesh in 1975: The Fall of the Mujib Regime and Its Aftermath," *Asian Survey* 16, no. 2 (1976), 119–29.

13. See Habib Zafarullah, ed., *The Zia Episode in Bangladesh Politics* (New Delhi: South Asian Publishers, 1996).

14. Golam Hossain, *General Ziaur Rahman and the BNP: Political Transformation of a Military Regime* (Dhaka: Bangladesh University Press, 1988).

15. Milam, *Bangladesh and Pakistan*, 60.

16. Ibid., 32.

17. S. Abdul Hakim, *Begum Khaleda Zia of Bangladesh: A Political Biography* (New Delhi: Vikas, 1992).

18. Sirajuddin Ahmed, *Sheikh Hasina: Prime Minister of Bangladesh* (New Delhi: UBS, 1998).

19. Milam, *Bangladesh and Pakistan*, 127–28.

20. Ibid., 194.

21. Ibid., 133.

22. Election Commission, Bangladesh, Election Results 2008, http://www.ecs.gov.bd, accessed 9 April 2013.

23. Aminul Faraizi, Taskinur Rahman, and Jim McAllister, *Micro-Credit and Women's Empowerment: A Case Study of Bangladesh* (London: Routledge, 2011).

24. Ibid., 20, 42, 111–12.

25. See Muhammad Yunus with Alan Jolis, *Banker to the Poor: The Autobiography of Muhammad Yunus, Founder of Grameen Bank* (London: Arum, 1998).

26. A. Aziz Khan and M. Solaiman, *The Academy at Comilla: A Brief Review of Its Establishment, Programmes, and Contributions to Rural Development in Bangladesh* (Comilla: Bangladesh Academy for Rural Development, 1978).

27. Faraizi, Rahman, and McAllister, *Micro-Credit*, 45.

28. Ibid., 14.

29. Nabiha Syed, *Replicating Dreams: A Comparative Study of Grameen Bank and Its Replication, Kashf Foundation Pakistan* (Karachi: Oxford University Press, 2009).

30. Faraizi, Rahman, and McAllister, *Micro-Credit*, 50–51.

31. Ibid., 45.

32. Aminur Rahman, *Women and Micro-Credit in Rural Bangladesh: An Anthropological Study of Grameen Bank Lending* (Boulder, CO: Westview, 2002), 73.

33. For a classic account of domestic violence see Betsey Hartmann and James K. Boyce, *A Quiet Violence: A View from a Bangladesh Village* (London: Zed, 1983). On microcredit and domestic violence see Rahman, *Women and Micro-Credit*, 125–26.

34. Rahman, *Women and Micro-Credit*, 133.

35. Faraizi, Rahman, and McAllister, *Micro-Credit*, 107.

36. Elora Shehabuddin, *Reshaping the Holy: Democracy, Development, and Muslim Women in Bangladesh* (New York: Columbia University Press, 2008).

37. Riaz, *God Willing*, 8.

38. Ibid., 39–40.

39. For further details on this incident and on the growing campaign against the Ahmadis see "Bangladesh Breach of Faith: Persecution of the Ahmadiyya Community in Bangladesh," *Human Rights Watch* 17, 6 (i) (June 2005).

14. Pakistan Since 1971

1. See Ian Talbot, *Pakistan: A Modern History*, 2nd ed. (London: Hurst, 2009).

2. Ibid., 98.

3. For further details see chapter 3 of Farzana Shaikh, *Making Sense of Pakistan* (London: Hurst, 2009).

4. Ibid., 64–68.

5. Hasan-Askari Rizvi, *Military, State, and Society in Pakistan* (Basingstoke: Macmillan, 2000), 142–43.

6. S. J. Burki, *Pakistan Under Bhutto, 1971–1977* (London: Macmillan, 1980), 105, table 2.

7. Z. A. Bhutto, *If I Am Assassinated* (New Delhi: Vikas, 1979), 19.

8. For a perceptive comparison of the PPP and Muslim League experience see Philip E. Jones, *The Pakistan People's Party Rise to Power* (Karachi: Oxford University Press, 2003), 459.

9. For a military insider account see General Khalid Mahmud Arif, *Working with Zia: Pakistan's Power Politics, 1977–1988* (Karachi: Oxford University Press, 1995).

10. Z. A. Bhutto, "Address to the Nation Announcing Nationalization of Ten Categories of Industries," 12 January 1972, *Speeches and Statements, 20 December 1971–31 March 1972* (Karachi, 1972), 33.

11. Cited in Iftikhar H. Malik, *State and Civil Society in Pakistan: Politics of Authority, Ideology, and Ethnicity* (Basingstoke: Macmillan, 1997), 92.

12. For further details see Robert Wirsing, *Pakistan's Security Under Zia, 1977–88: The Policy Imperatives of a Peripheral Asian State* (Basingstoke: Macmillan, 1991).

13. Iqbal Akhund, *Memoirs of a Bystander: A Life of Diplomacy* (Karachi: Oxford University Press, 1988), 353.

14. They included Maulana Masood Azhar, who was a leading figure in Harkat-ul-Ansar and founder of Jaish-e-Muhammad (JeM), organizations that conducted terrorist activities in India and were closely associated with Osama bin Laden on his return to Afghanistan from Sudan at the beginning of 1996.
15. In 1992 alone, ten blasphemy cases were instituted against Ahmadis. In 1994 there were twenty-five blasphemy cases against Christians. For details see Amnesty International, *Pakistan: Violations of Human Rights of Ahmadis* (ASA 33/15/91); and Amnesty International, *Pakistan: Use and Abuse of the Blasphemy Laws* (ASA 33/08/94).
16. See M. Sahibuddin Ghausi, "The Great Bank Robbery," *Herald* (Karachi), September 1993.
17. On the rigging of the 1990 polls see People's Democratic Alliance, *How an Election Was Stolen: The PDA White Paper on the Pakistan Elections, 1990* (Islamabad: Midasia 1991); and W. L. Richter, "The 1990 General Elections in Pakistan," in *Pakistan in 1992*, ed. C. H. Kennedy (Boulder, CO: Westview, 1993), 19–43.
18. Ayesha Siddiqa, *Military Inc: Inside Pakistan's Military Economy* (London: Pluto Press, 2007).
19. S. P. Cohen, *The Idea of Pakistan* (New Delhi: Oxford University Press, 2005), 154.
20. On the 1997 polls see Zahid Hussain, "Clean Sweep," *Newsline* (Karachi), February 1997.
21. On Musharraf's local government reform see National Reconstruction Bureau, *Local Government, Final Plan, 2000* (Islamabad: G. A. Publishers, 2000).
22. See chapter 7 of Ian Talbot, *Pakistan: A New History* (London: Hurst, 2012).
23. On the Zardari era, which ended with the return of Nawaz Sharif to power following the May 2013 elections, see chapter 8 of Talbot, *Pakistan: A New History*.
24. For a more nuanced approach see Ayesha Jalal, *Democracy and Authoritarianism in South Asia: A Comparative and Historical Perspective* (Cambridge: Cambridge University Press, 1995).

15. India Shining

1. See Park Square Mall website, http://www.parksquaremall.com, accessed 21 March 2013.
2. On Mayawati see Ajoy Bose, *Behenji: A Political Biography of Mayawati* (New Delhi: Penguin, 2008). For a perceptive account of the development of the BSP under Kanshi Ram see chapter 11 of Christophe Jaffrelot, *India's Silent Revolution: The Rise of the Lower Castes in North India* (London: Hurst, 2003).
3. For an overview see Kanchan Chandra, *Why Ethnic Politics Succeed: Patronage and Ethnic Head Counts in India* (Cambridge: Cambridge University Press, 2004).
4. For an analysis of the Mandalization of politics see Jaffrelot, *India's Silent Revolution*.

5. Singh had uncovered details of the kickback scandal involving the Swedish arms manufacturer Bofors and had quit Congress after his dismissal as finance minister. Allegations surrounding Rajiv shattered his image as "Mr. Clean," although he was posthumously cleared of direct involvement. Singh formed a government that relied on the support of the BJP. When this was withdrawn, Chandra Shekhar of Janata Dal became prime minister, now dependent on the Congress.

6. OBCs number double the combined population of Scheduled Castes and Scheduled Tribes and around three and a half times the Muslim population.

7. *Laloo in the Dock: CBI's Charge Sheet in the Fodder Scam Case* (Calcutta: Statesman, 1997).

8. See Manoj Chaurasia, *Rabri Devi: Lalu's Masterstroke* (New Delhi: Vitasta, 2008).

9. Laloo's career has evoked contrasting hagiographical and condemnatory works. See Wahab Ashrafi, *Laloo Prasad: An Apostle of Social Justice* (Delhi: Education Publishing House, 1994); K. C. Yadav, *The Laloo Phenomenon: Paradoxes of Changing India* (Gurgaon: Hope India2001); and Sankarshan Thakur, *The Making of Laloo Yadav: The Unmaking of Bihar* (New Delhi: HarperCollins India, 2000).

10. Jaffrelot, *India's Silent Revolution*, 484–86.

11. For a discussion of the evolution of the controversy surrounding the site see S. Gopal, ed., *Anatomy of a Confrontation: The Babri Masjid-Ram Janmabhumi Controversy* (New Delhi: Penguin, 1991).

12. On the post-1989 insurgency in Kashmir see Sumit Ganguly, *The Crisis in Kashmir: Portents of War, Hopes of Peace* (New York: Cambridge University Press, 1997). For Pakistan's involvement see Arif Jamal, *Shadow War: The Untold Story of Jihad in Kashmir* (Brooklyn, NY: Melville, 2009).

13. Sumit Ganguly and Rahul Mukherji, *India Since 1980* (Cambridge: Cambridge University Press, 2011), 129.

14. For the full Sachar Committee Report see http://www.minorityaffairs.gov.in/sites/upload_files/moma/files/pdfs/sachar_comm.pdf. For further reflection on the Muslim experience of increasing marginalization in contemporary India see C. Jaffrelot and L. Gayer, eds., *Muslims in Indian Cities: Trajectories of Marginalisation* (London: Hurst, 2012); and Christophe Jaffrelot, "Muslims in Indian Politics," paper presented at the annual meeting of the British Association of South Asian Studies, London, 30 November 2012.

15. The VHP (World Hindu Congress) had been founded in 1964 as an offshoot of the RSS with the goal of creating an umbrella Hindu organization that would counteract sectarian and caste-based divisions.

16. V. L. Farmer, "Mass Media: Images, Mobilization, Communalism," in *Contesting the Nation: Religion, Community, and the Politics of Democracy in India*, ed. David Ludden (Philadelphia: University of Pennsylvania Press, 1996), 102.

17. For details see S. D. Muni, *The Pangs of Proximity: India and Sri Lanka's Ethnic Crisis* (New Delhi: Sage, 1993).

18. See Adish C. Aggarwala, *P. V. Narasimha Rao: Scholar Prime Minister* (New Delhi: Amish, 1995); and Janak Raj Jai, *Narasimha Rao: The Best Prime Minister?* (New Delhi: Regency, 1996).

19. Dipankar Gupta, *Nativism in a Metropolis: The Shiv Sena in Bombay* (New Delhi: Manohar, 1982).

20. For details see Jim Masselos, "The Bombay Riots of January 1993: The Politics of Urban Conflagration," in *Politics of Violence: From Ayodhya to Behrampada*, ed. J. McGuire, P. Reeves, and H. Brasted (New Delhi: Sage 1996), 111–27.

21. Flavia Agnes, "Behrampada: The Busti That Did Not Yield," ibid., 49–71.

22. Thomas Blom Hansen, "The Ethics of Hindutva and the Spirit of Capitalism," in *The BJP and the Compulsions of Politics in India*, ed. Thomas Bloom Hansen and Christophe Jaffrelot (New Delhi: Oxford University Press, 1998), 306.

23. See Siddharth Varadarajan, ed., *Gujarat: The Making of a Tragedy* (New Delhi: Penguin, 2002).

24. Asghar Ali Engineer, "The Gujarat Carnage," in *The Deadly Embrace: Religion, Politics, and Violence in India and Pakistan, 1947–2002*, ed. Ian Talbot (Karachi: Oxford University Press, 2007), 139.

25. Ibid., 141.

26. For this campaign in action see http://www.narendramodi.in/tag/vibrant-gujarat, accessed 26 March 2012. A more detailed study is contained in Christophe Jaffrelot, *Saffron "Modernity" in India: Narendra Modi and His Experiment with Gujarat* (London: Hurst, 2014).

27. Neera Chandhoke, "Modi's Gujarat and Its Little Illusions," *Economic and Political Weekly* 47, no. 49 (8 December 2012), commentary.

28. Barry Eichengreen, Poonam Gupta, and Rajiv Kumar, eds., *Emerging Giants: China and India in the World Economy* (Oxford: Oxford University Press, 2010).

29. See, for example, Arvind Panagariya, *India: The Emerging Giant* (New York: Oxford University Press, 2008).

30. Ibid., xvi.

31. Ganguly and Mukherji, *India Since 1980*, 93.

32. Panagariya, *India*, 93.

33. For further details see Vibha Pingle, *Rethinking the Developmental State* (New Delhi: Oxford University Press, 1999), 126–41.

34. P. N. Dhar, *Indira Gandhi, the "Emergency," and Indian Democracy* (New Delhi: Oxford University Press, 2000), 379.

35. See R. J. Venkateswaran, *Reforming the Indian Economy: The Narasimha and Manmohan Singh Era* (New Delhi: Vikas, 1996). A definitive account of Manmohan Singh's subsequent period as India's fourteenth prime minister has yet to be written.

36. On the issue of the inclusivity of the postreforms' growth see S. Mahendra Dev, *Inclusive Growth in India* (New Delhi: Oxford University Press, 2008).

37. Montek S. Ahluwalia, "State-Level Performance Under Economic Reforms," in *Economic Policy Reforms and the Indian Economy*, ed. Anne O. Krueger (New Delhi: Oxford University Press, 2002), 91–122.

38. Ganguly and Mukherji, *India Since 1980*, 96.

39. D. Narasimha Reddy and Srijit Misra, "Agriculture and the Reforms Regime," in *Agrarian Crisis in India*, ed. D. Narasimha Reddy and Srijit Misra (New Delhi: Oxford University Press, 2009), 3–43.

40. Ministry of Rural Development, *Mahatma Gandhi National Rural Employment Guarantee Act 2005: Report to the People 2nd Feb. 2006–2nd Feb. 2010* (New Delhi: Government of India, 2010).

41. Nuashad Forbes, "Doing Business in India," in Krueger, *Economic Policy Reforms*, 129–68.

16. The Contemporary International Relations of South Asia

1. M. Taylor Fravel, "China Views India's Rise: Deepening Cooperation, Managing Differences," in *Asia Responds to Its Rising Powers: China and India*, ed. Ashley J. Tellis, Travis Tanner, and Jessica Keogh (Seattle: National Bureau of Asia Research, 2011), 65–101.

2. On the shift of Indian military planners' future strategic focus from Pakistan to China, see Harsh V. Pant, "India Comes to Terms with a Rising China," in Tellis, Tanner, and Keogh, *Asia Responds*, 101–31.

3. Other elements of post–Cold War foreign policy rebalancing, such as the transformation in relations with Israel since 1992, are beyond the scope of this book.

4. More than a hundred Chinese cities are said to be experiencing important water scarcities, including Beijing and Tianjin. Jian Xie et al., *Addressing China's Water Scarcity: A Synthesis of Recommendations for Selected Water Resource Management Issues* (Washington, DC: World Bank, 2009), 8.

5. Brahma Chellaney, *Water: Asia's New Battleground* (Washington, DC: Georgetown University Press, 2011), 132.

6. Ibid., 157, 144.

7. Ibid., 175.

8. Gurpreet Khurana, "China's 'String of Pearls' in the Indian Ocean and Its Security Implications," *Strategic Analysis* 32, no. 1 (January 2008), 1–22.

9. Harsh V. Pant, "India in the Indian Ocean: Growing Mismatch Between Ambitions and Capabilities," *Pacific Affairs* 82, no. 2 (Summer 2009), 279–97.

10. Ajay Banerjee, "Dragon Closing In on India?" *Tribune* (Chandigarh), 2 October, 2010.

11. For further details on the nuclear issue and China's development of roads and railways in the Yunnan, Tibet, and Xinjiang provinces bordering India, see Pant, "India Comes to Terms," 113–18.

12. On India's belated response to China's investments in resource-rich areas of Africa see Rhys Blakeley, "India Takes on China over Africa's Riches," *Times* (London), 9 April 2008. For India's deepening engagement with the Gulf States see Pant, "India Comes to Terms," 125.

13. F. B. Yahya, *Economic Cooperation Between Singapore and India: An Alliance in the Making?* (New York: Routledge, 2008); F. Grare and A. Mattoo, eds., *India and ASEAN: The Politics of India's Look East Policy* (New Delhi: Manohar, 2001); K. Reddy Raja, ed., *India and ASEAN: Foreign Policy Dimensions for the Twenty-First Century* (New Delhi: New Century, 2005).

14. Much has been written on India's "soft power" capabilities as a result of the reach of its cultural affinities. Attention has been devoted to, among other things, culture, food, handicrafts, and cricket. See Shashi Tharoor, "Indian Strategic Power: Soft," *Global Brief* 13 (May 2009), http://globalbrief.ca/blog/2009/05/13/soft-is-the-word. For a brief discussion of Indian soft power in the Southeast Asian context see David M. Malone, *Does the Elephant Dance? Contemporary Indian Foreign Policy* (Oxford: Oxford University Press, 2011), 218–19.

15. I. K. Gujral, *A Foreign Policy for India* (New Delhi: Ministry of External Affairs, 1998), 69–81.

16. Raj Kumar Jha, *The Himalayan Kingdoms in Indian Foreign Policy* (Ranchi: Maitryee, 1986), 347–50.

17. Gyanendra had become king following the murder of his brother Birendra in the palace massacre of June 2001.

18. Chellaney, *Water*, 286.

19. See the two following articles for material on India's strategic interests and aims in Myanmar: Renaud Egreteau, "India's Ambitions in Burma," *Asian Survey* 48, no. 6 (November–December 2008), 936–57; and Dominic J. Nardi, "Cross-Border Chaos: A Critique of India's Attempts to Secure Its Northeast Tribal Areas Through Cooperation with Myanmar," *SAIS Review* 28, no. 1 (Winter–Spring 2008), 161–71.

20. For an overview see J. N. Dixit, *Liberation and Beyond: Indo-Bangladesh Relations* (Delhi: Kornak, 1999); Zaglul Haider, *The Changing Pattern of Bangladesh Foreign Policy: A Comparative Study of the Mujib and Zia Regimes* (Dhaka: University Press, 2006); and Kirti Singh Chauhan, *Foreign Policy of Bangladesh* (New Delhi: Kaveri, 2012).

21. On the background to the Maoist insurgency and relations between Nepal and India see V. R. Raghavan, ed., *Internal Conflict in Nepal: Transnational Conse-quences* (Chennai: Vij, 2011); and Indu Bala, *Compulsions of a Land-Locked State: A Study of Nepal-India Relations* (New Delhi: Batra, 2001).

22. India gave Bangladesh transit access to Nepal and Bhutan. This move was designed to encourage Dhaka to address the sensitive issue of opening road cor-ridors in Bangladesh for India to access its northeastern states at a lower cost than at present. On the transit issue, see Mohammad Humayn Kabir, "Obstacles to

Bangladesh-India Cooperation: An International Relations Theory Perspective," in *International Relations Theory and South Asia*, vol. 1, ed. E. Sridharan (New Delhi: Oxford University Press, 2011), 329–69.

23. Iftekhar Ahmed Chowdhury, "Bangladesh: Opportunities and Challenges," in *A Resurgent China: South Asian Perspectives* (Abingdon: Routledge, 2012), 62–63.

24. For discussion of the background to the 1971 Indo-Soviet treaty and its implications see Surinder Nihal Singh, *The Yogi and the Bear* (Riverdale, MD: Riverdale, 1988); and Robert Horn, *Soviet-Indian Relations: Issues and Influence* (New York: Praeger, 1982).

25. See P. K. Chaudhury and M. Vanduzer-Snow, eds., *The United States and India: A History Through the Archives; The Formative Years* (New Delhi: Sage, 2008); Dennis Kux, *India and the United States: Estranged Democracies, 1941–91* (Washington, DC: National Defense University Press, 1992); Rudra Chaudhuri, *Forged in Crisis: India and the United States Since 1947* (London: Hurst, 2013); and Paul M. McGarr, *The Cold War in South Asia: Britain, the United States, and the Indian Subcontinent, 1945–1965* (Cambridge: Cambridge University Press, 2013).

26. Devin Hagerty, *The Consequences of Nuclear Proliferation* (Cambridge: MIT Press, 1998).

27. On the domestic background to the insurgency see Sumit Ganguly, *The Crisis in Kashmir: Portents of War, Hopes of Peace* (Cambridge: Cambridge University Press, 1997); and Victoria Schofield, *Kashmir in the Crossfire* (New York: I. B. Tauris, 1996).

28. On the Kargil conflict, see Praveen Swami, *The Kargil War* (New Delhi: Leftword, 2000).

29. Musharraf's autobiography provides a colorful account of this volte face. P. Musharraf, *In the Line of Fire: A Memoir* (London: Simon and Schuster, 2006).

30. Ian Talbot, *Pakistan: A New History* (London: Hurst, 2012), 185, 197–99.

31. Hilary Synnott, *Transforming Pakistan: Ways Out of Instability* (Abingdon: Routledge, 2009), 137–39.

32. On Lashkar-e-Taiba's involvement in the Mumbai attacks see Stephen Tankel, *Storming the World Stage: The Story of Lashkar-e-Taiba* (London: Hurst, 2011).

33. Aparajita Biswas, "SAARC: The Search for a Regional Security Model," in *International Relations Theory and South Asia*, ed. E. Sridharan (New Delhi: Oxford University Press, 2012), 121.

34. See Sandeep Dikshit, "SAARC Meet Begins in Thimpu on Introspectve Note," *The Hindu*, 29 April 2010, www.thehindu.com/news/national/saarc-meet-beins-in-thimpu-on-introspective-note/article413768.ece, accessed 28 March 2015.

35. Aparna Shivpuri Singh, "Regional Integration in South Asia and Energy Cooperation: Opportunities and Challenges," in *The Geopolitics of Energy in South Asia*, ed. Marie Lall (Singapore: Institute of Southeast Asian Studies, 2009), 77–80.

GLOSSARY

Adi Granth	sacred scripture of the Sikhs
ahimsa	nonviolence
anjuman	association
"Bande Mataram"	"Hail to Thee, Mother"
bhadralok	gentlefolk
bhakti	devotional worship
chakra	wheel
char	silt bank, island
dalit	oppressed; self-designation of Untouchables
darbar	court of a ruler
dhoti	loincloth
Durga	the goddess as consort of Shiva
fatwa	ruling by an expert in Muslim religious law
fiqh	jurisprudence
ganj	rural market
ghadr	revolution
goonda	hired thug
grameen	rural
hajj	pilgrimage to Mecca
hartal	strike
hawala	banking system
hijrat	Muslim religious flight
intifada	uprising
jagirdar	landholder
jai	victory
jati	occupational caste group

jihad	holy war
karma	actions, behavior
kar sevaks	temple volunteers
Khalsa	Sikh brotherhood instituted by Guru Gobind Singh
kisan	peasant
kshatriya	member of warrior and ruler caste
lathi	wooden club
lingam	phallus, symbol of Shiva
madrassah	Muslim college
Mahatma	great souled one; title given to M. K. Gandhi
mofussil	countryside
mullah	preacher
murid	disciple of a *pir*
pandit	scholar
pir	Muslim saint, spiritual guide
pradesh	province, state
raiyat	tenant
roti	flatbread
sabha	council of elders
sadhu	holy man, ascetic
sant	peripatetic Sikh teacher or preacher
sati	"true one"; widow sacrificed on husband's funeral pyre
satyagreha	truth force or soul force; nonviolent struggle
sharia	Muslim law
shuddhi	purification rite, which became a vehicle for conversion to Hinduism
sufi	Muslim mystic
swadeshi	"own country"; indigenous
swaraj	independence
thana	police station
ulama	Muslims learned in Islamic religious sciences
urs	death anniversary of a *sufi* saint
varna	caste
zamindar	landlord, tax collector
zindabad	long live

Private Papers

Caroe Papers, India Office Records, Mss. Eur F203
Paul Gore-Booth Papers, Bodleian Library, University of Oxford
Mountbatten Papers, University of Southampton MB1
Mudie Papers, India Office Records, Mss. Eur F164
Quaid-e-Azam Papers, National Archives of Pakistan, Islamabad

Government Records

India Office Records

Records of the Military Department, 1940–42
Records of the Political and Secret Department, 1928–47
Records of the Public and Judicial Department, 1929–47

National Archives, UK

Records of the Cabinet Office
Records of the Commonwealth Relations Office
Records of the Prime Minister

National Archives, India

Records of the Home Political Department, 1927–45

National Archives, US, College Park, MD

State Department Central Files, 1960–63, 1964–66

National Security Archives, George Washington University

India-Pakistan (4 boxes)
LBJ Presidential Files Country Files (Pakistan)

National Archives of Pakistan, Islamabad, National Freedom Movement Archives

All-India Muslim League Records
Committee of Action, 1944–47
Provincial Muslim League Records
Working Committee, 1932–37

Select Printed Works

Ali, Chaudhri Muhammad. *The Emergence of Pakistan*. New York: Columbia University Press, 1967.

Ali, Imran. *The Punjab Under Imperialism, 1885–1947*. Princeton: Princeton University Press, 1988.

Ali, S. Mahmud. *The Fearful State: Power, People, and Internal Wars in South Asia*. London: Zed, 1993.

——. *Understanding Bangladesh*. London: Hurst, 2010.

Ali, Tariq. *Pakistan: Military Rule or People's Power*. New York: William Morrow, 1970.

Alter, Stephen. *Amritsar to Lahore: A Journey Across the Indo-Pakistan Border*. Philadelphia: University of Pennsylvania Press, 2001.

Amrith, Sunil S. *Migration and Diaspora in Modern South Asia*. Cambridge: Cambridge University Press, 2011.

Ansari, Sarah. *Sufi Saints and State Power: The Pirs of Sind, 1843–1947*. Cambridge: Cambridge University Press, 1992.

——. *Life After Partition: Migration, Community, and Strife in Sindh, 1947–1962*. Karachi: Oxford University Press, 2005.

Ayres, Alyssa. *Speaking Like a State: Language and Nationalism in Pakistan*. Cambridge: Cambridge University Press, 2009.

Aziz, Mazhar. *Military Control: The Parallel State*. London: Routledge, 2008.

Bala, Indu. *Compulsions of a Land-Locked State: A Study of Nepal-India Relations*. New Delhi: Barea, 2001.

Baral, Lok Raj. *Nepal: Nation-State in the Wilderness; Managing State, Democracy, and Geo-Politics*. New Delhi: Sage, 2012.

Bayly, C. A. *Rulers, Townsmen, and Bazaars: North Indian Society in the Age of British Expansion, 1770–1870*. Cambridge: Cambridge University Press, 1983.

——. *Indian Society and the Making of the British Empire*. Cambridge: Cambridge University Press, 1988.

————. *Imperial Meridian: The British Empire and the World, 1780–1830*. London: Longman, 1989.

————. *Origins of Nationality in South Asia: Patriotism and Ethical Government in the Making of Modern India*. New Delhi: Oxford University Press, 2001.

Bhatmik, Subir. *Troubled Periphery: Crisis of India's North East*. New Delhi: Sage, 2009.

Bhutto, Benazir. *Daughter of the East: An Autobiography*. Rev. ed. London: Simon and Schuster, 2007.

Bose, Sarmila. *Dead Reckoning: Memories of the 1971 Bangladesh War*. London: Hurst, 2012.

Bose, Sugata. *A Hundred Horizons: The Indian Ocean in the Age of Global Empire*. Cambridge: Harvard University Press, 2006.

————. *His Majesty's Opponent: Subhas Chandra Bose and India's Struggle Against Empire*. Cambridge: Belknap Press of Harvard University Press, 2011.

Bose, Sugata, and Ayesha Jalal. *Modern South Asia: History, Culture, and Political Economy*. New York: Routledge, 1998.

Brass, Paul R. *The Production of Hindu-Muslim Violence in Contemporary India*. Seattle: University of Washington Press, 2003.

Brown, J. M. *Gandhi's Rise to Power: Indian Politics, 1915–1922*. Cambridge: Cambridge University Press, 1972.

————. *Modern India: The Origins of an Asian Democracy*. New York: Oxford University Press, 1994.

————. *Nehru: A Political Life*. New Haven: Yale University Press, 2003.

————. *Global South Asians*. Cambridge: Cambridge University Press, 2006.

Burki, Shahid Javeed. *Pakistan Under Bhutto, 1971–77*. Basingstoke: Macmillan, 1980.

Butalia, Urvashi. *The Other Side of Silence: Voices from the Partition of India*. New Delhi: Penguin, 1998.

Butt, Usama, and N. Ilahi, eds. *Pakistan's Quagmire: Security, Strategy, and the Future of the Islamic-Nuclear Nation*. New York: Continuum, 2010.

Campbell-Johnson, A. *Mission with Mountbatten*. London: Hamilton, 1985.

Chakravarti, Uma, and Nandita Haksar. *The Delhi Riots: Three Days in the Life of a Nation*. New Delhi: Lancer International, 1987.

Chakravarty, Gautam. *The Indian Mutiny and the British Imagination*. New Delhi: Cambridge University Press, 2006.

Chandavarkar, Rajnayarayan. *Imperial Power and Popular Politics: Class, Resistance, and the State in India, 1850–1950*. Cambridge: Cambridge University Press, 1998.

Chandra, Kanchan. *Why Ethnic Politics Succeed: Patronage and Ethnic Head Counts in India*. Cambridge: Cambridge University Press, 2004.

Chapman, Graham P. *The Geo-Politics of South Asia: From Early Empires to the Nuclear Age*. 2nd ed. Aldershot: Ashgate, 2003.

Chatterji, Joya. *Bengal Divided: Hindu Communalism and Partition, 1932–1947*. Cambridge: Cambridge University Press, 1994.

——. *The Spoils of Partition: Bengal and India, 1947–1967*. Cambridge: Cambridge University Press, 2007.

Chaudhuri, Rudra. *Forged in Crisis: India and the United States Since 1947*. London: Hurst, 2013.

Chellaney, Brahma. *Water: Asia's New Battleground*. Washington, DC: Georgetown University Press, 2011.

Chester, Lucy. *On the Edge: Borders, Territory, and Conflict in South Asia*. Manchester: Manchester University Press, 2008.

Cloughley, Brian. *A History of the Pakistan Army: Wars and Insurrections*. Karachi: Oxford University Press, 1999.

Cohen, Bernard S., ed. *An Anthropologist Amongst the Historians and Other Essays*. Delhi: Oxford University Press, 1987.

Cohen, S. P. *The Pakistan Army*. Karachi: Oxford University Press, 1998.

——. *The Idea of Pakistan*. Washington, DC: Brookings Institution, 2004.

Datta, Antara. *Refugees and Borders in South Asia: The Great Exodus of 1971*. London: Routledge, 2013.

Dev, S. Mahendra. *Inclusive Growth in India*. New Delhi: Oxford University Press, 2008.

Devji, Faisal. *Landscapes of the Jihad: Militancy, Morality, Modernity*. Ithaca, NY: Cornell University Press, 2005.

Dewey, Clive. "The Rural Roots of Pakistani Militarism." In *The Political Inheritance of Pakistan*, ed. D. A. Low, 255–84. Basingstoke: Macmillan, 1991.

Dhar, P. N. *Indira Gandhi, the "Emergency," and Indian Democracy*. New Delhi: Oxford University Press, 2000.

Dirks, Nicholas B. *The Scandal of Empire: India and the Creation of Imperial Britain*. Cambridge: Harvard University Press, 2008.

Dixit, J. N. *Liberation and Beyond: Indo-Bangladesh Relations*. Delhi: Kornak, 1999.

Dundas, Paul. *The Jains*. London: Taylor and Francis, 2002.

Eade, John. *The Politics of Community: The Bangladeshi Community in East London*. Aldershot: Avebury, 1989.

Eaton, Richard M. *The Rise of Islam and the Bengal Frontier*. Berkeley: University of California Press, 1993.

Eichengreen, Barry, Poonam Gupta, and Rajiv Kumar, eds. *Emerging Giants: China and India in the World Economy*. Oxford: Oxford University Press, 2010.

Engineer, Asghar Ali. *Communal Riots in Post-Independence India*. Hyderabad: Sangam, 1984.

Faraizi, Aminul, Taskinur Rahman, and Jim McAllister. *Micro-Credit and Women's Empowerment: A Case Study of Bangladesh*. London: Routledge, 2012.

Forbes, Geraldine. *Women and Modern India*. Cambridge: Cambridge University Press, 1996.

Franda, Marcus F. *Radical Politics in West Bengal*. Cambridge: MIT Press, 1971.

Frankel, Francine R. *India's Green Revolution: Economic Gains and Political Costs*. Princeton: Princeton University Press, 1971.

Ganguly, Sumit. *The Crisis in Kashmir: Portents of War, Hopes of Peace*. Cambridge: Cambridge University Press, 1997.

———. *Conflict Unending: India-Pakistan Tensions Since 1947*. New York: Columbia University Press, 2001.

Ganguly, Sumit, and Rahul Mukherji. *India Since 1980*. New York: Cambridge University Press, 2011.

Gardner, Katy. *Songs at the River's Edge: Stories from a Bangladesh Village*. London: Pluto, 1997.

———. *Global Migrants, Local Lives: Travel and Transformation in Rural Bangladesh*. Oxford: Oxford University Press, 2001.

———. *The Discordant Development: Global Capitalism and the Struggle for Connection in Bangladesh*. London: Pluto, 2012.

Gayer, Laurent, and Christophe Jaffrelot, eds. *Muslims in Indian Cities: Trajectories of Marginalisation*. London: Hurst, 2012.

Gilmartin, David. *Empire and Islam: Punjab and the Making of Pakistan*. Berkeley: University of California Press, 1998.

Gombrich, Richard F. *Theravada Buddhism: A History of Ancient Benares to Modern Colombo*. 6th ed. London: Routledge, 2002.

Gupta, Charu, and Mukul Sharma. *Contested Coastlines: Fisherfolk, Nations, and Borders in South Asia*. Abingdon: Routledge, 2008.

Gupta, Dipankar. *Nativism in a Metropolis: The Shiv Sena in Bombay*. New Delhi: Manohar, 1982.

Hansen, Thomas Blom. *The Saffron Wave: Democracy and Nationalism in Modern India*. Princeton: Princeton University Press, 1999.

Hansen, Thomas Blom, and Christophe Jaffrelot, eds. *The BJP and the Compulsions of Politics in India*. New Delhi: Oxford University Press, 1998.

Haqqani, Husain. *Pakistan: Between Mosque and Military*. Washington, DC: Carnegie Endowment for International Peace, 2005.

Hartmann, Betsey, and James K Boyce. *A Quiet Violence: A View from a Bangladeshi Village*. London: Zed, 1983.

Hassan, Abbas. *Pakistan's Drift into Extremism: Allah, the Army, and America's War on Terror*. Armonk, NY: M. E. Sharpe, 2005.

Hills, Christopher V. *South Asia: An Environmental History*. Santa Barbara: ABC-Clio, 2008.

Hobsbawm, Eric, and Terence Ranger, eds. *The Invention of Tradition*. Cambridge: Cambridge University Press, 1984.

Hodson, H. V. *The Great Divide: Britain-India-Pakistan*. London: Hutchinson, 1969.

Hopkins, Benjamin D., and Magnus Marsden. *Fragments of the Afghan Frontier*. New York: Columbia University Press, 2011.

Hutt, Michael. *Unbecoming Citizens: Culture, Nationhood, and the Flight of Refugees from Bhutan*. New Delhi: Oxford University Press, 2005.

Iqbal, Iftekhar. *The Bengal Delta: Ecology, State and Social Change, 1840–1943*. Basingstoke: Palgrave Macmillan, 2010.

Irschick, Eugene F. *Politics and Social Conflict in South India: The Non-Brahmin Movement and Tamil Separatism, 1916–1929*. Berkeley: University of California Press, 1969.

Jaffrelot, Christophe. *India's Silent Revolution: The Rise of the Lower Castes in North India*. London: Hurst, 1999.

——. *Dr Ambedkar and Untouchability: Analysing and Fighting Caste*. London: Hurst, 2005.

Jahan, Rounaq. *Pakistan: Failure in National Integration*. New York: Columbia University Press, 1972.

Jain, Anupuma. *How to be South Asian in America: Narratives of Ambivalence and Belonging*. Philadelphia: Temple University Press, 2011.

Jalal, Ayesha. *The Sole Spokesman: Jinnah, the Muslim League and the Demand for Pakistan*. Cambridge: Cambridge University Press, 1985.

——. *The State of Martial Rule: The Origin of Pakistan's Political Economy of Defence*. Cambridge: Cambridge University Press, 1990.

——. *Democracy and Authoritarianism in South Asia: A Comparative and Historical Perspective*. Cambridge: Cambridge University Press, 1995.

——. *Self and Sovereignty: Individual and Community in South Asian Islam Since 1850*. London: Routledge, 2000.

——. *Partisans of Allah: Jihad in South Asia*. Cambridge: Harvard University Press, 2008.

Jamal, Arif. *Shadow War: The Untold Story of Jihad in Kashmir*. Brooklyn, NY: Melville, 2009.

Jensen, Joan M. *Passage from India: Asian Indian Immigrants in North America*. New Haven: Yale University Press, 1988.

Jha, Raj Kumar. *The Himalayan Kingdoms in Indian Foreign Policy*. Ranchi: Maitryee, 1986.

Johnson, Rob. *A Region in Turmoil: South Asian Conflicts Since 1947*. London: Reaktion, 2008.

Jones, K. W. *Arya Dharm: Hindu Consciousness in 19th Century Punjab*. Berkeley: University of California Press, 1976.

Jones, Philip E. *The Pakistan People's Party: Rise to Power*. Karachi: Oxford University Press, 2003.

Juergensmeyer, M. *Radhaosmi Reality: The Logic of a Modern Faith*. Princeton: Princeton University Press, 1991.

Kanwar, Pamela. *Imperial Simla: The Political Culture of the Raj*. Delhi: Oxford University Press, 1990.

Kapur, Asok, with A. Jeyaratnam Wilson. *The Foreign Policy of India and Her Neighbours*. Basingstoke: Macmillan, 1996.

Kessinger, T. G. *Vilyatpur, 1848–1968: Social and Economic Change in a North Indian Village*. Berkeley: University of California Press, 1974.

Khan, Yasmin. *The Great Partition: The Making of India and Pakistan*. New Haven: Yale University Press, 2007.

Khilnani, Sunil. *The Idea of India*. New Delhi: Penguin, 1999.

Kudaisya, Medha M. *The Life and Times of G. D. Birla*. New Delhi: Oxford University Press, 2006.

Kux, Dennis. *The United States and Pakistan, 1947–2000: Disenchanted Allies*. Washington, DC: Woodrow Wilson International Center for Scholars; Baltimore: Johns Hopkins University Press, 2001.

Lall, Marie, ed. *The Geopolitics of Energy in South Asia*. Singapore: Institute of South-East Asian Studies, 2009.

Lelyveld, David. *Aligarh's First Generation: Muslim Solidarity in British India*. Princeton: Princeton University Press, 1978.

Lewis, David. *Bangladesh: Politics, Economy, and Civil Society*. Cambridge: Cambridge University Press, 2011.

Lieven, Anatol. *Pakistan: A Hard Country*. London: Allen Lane, 2011.

Low, D. A., ed. *The Political Inheritance of Pakistan*. Basingstoke: Macmillan, 1991.

Ludden, David. *India and South Asia: A Short History*. Oxford: Oneworld, 2007.

——, ed. *Contesting the Nation: Religion, Community, and the Politics of Democracy in India*. Philadelphia: University of Pennsylvania Press, 1996.

Luhrmann, T. M. *The Good Parsi: The Fate of a Colonial Elite in a Postcolonial Society*. Cambridge: Harvard University Press, 1996.

Malhotra, Anshu, and Farina Mir, eds. *Punjab Reconsidered: History, Culture, and Practice*. New Delhi: Oxford University Press, 2012.

Malik, Iftikhar Haider. *State and Civil Society in Pakistan: Politics of Authority, Ideology, and Ethnicity*. Basingstoke: Macmillan, 1997.

Malone, David M. *Does the Elephant Dance? Contemporary Indian Foreign Policy*. Oxford: Oxford University Press, 2011.

Mani, Latta. *Contentious Traditions: The Debate on Sati in Colonial India*. Berkeley: University of California Press, 1998.

Mascarenhas, Anthony. *The Rape of Bangladesh*. Delhi: Vikas, 1971.

Maxwell, Neville. *India's China War*. New York: Pantheon, 1971.

McGarr, Paul M. *The Cold War in South Asia: Britain, the United States, and the Indian Subcontinent, 1945–1965*. Cambridge: Cambridge University Press, 2013.

McGrath, Allen. *The Destruction of Pakistan's Democracy*. Karachi: Oxford University Press, 1996.

Metcalf, Barbara D. *Islamic Revival in British India: Deoband, 1860–1900*. Princeton: Princeton University Press, 1982.

Metcalf, Barbara D., and Thomas R. Metcalf. *A Concise History of Modern India*. 3rd ed. Cambridge: Cambridge University Press, 2012.

Metcalf, Thomas R. *Forging the Raj: Essays on British India in the Heyday of Empire*. New Delhi: Oxford University Press, 2005.

Milam, William B. *Bangladesh and Pakistan: Flirting with Failure in South Asia*. London: Hurst, 2009.

Minault, Gail. *The Khilafat Movement: Religious Symbolism and Political Mobilization in India*. New York: Columbia University Press, 1982.

Mukherjee, Sumita. *Nationalism, Education, and Migrant Identities: The England-Returned*. Abingdon: Routledge, 2010.

Mumtaz, Khawar, and Farida Shaheed, eds. *Women of Pakistan: Two Steps Forward, One Step Back?* London: Zed, 1987.

Muni, S. D., and Tan Tai Yong, eds. *A Resurgent China: South Asian Perspectives*. Abingdon: Routledge, 2012.

Murshid, T. M. *The Sacred and the Secular: Bengal Muslim Discourses, 1871, 1977*. Calcutta: Oxford University Press, 1995.

Musharraf, Pervez. *In the Line of Fire: A Memoir*. London: Simon and Schuster, 2006.

Nasta, Sushila. *India in Britain: South Asian Networks and Connections, 1858–1950*. Basingstoke: Palgrave Macmillan, 2012.

Nayer, Kuldeep. *The Judgement*. New Delhi: Vikas, 1977.

Oberoi, Harjot. *The Construction of Religious Boundaries: Culture, Identity, and Diversity in the Sikh Tradition*. Chicago: University of Chicago Press, 1994.

O'Hanlon, Rosalind. *Class, Conflict, and Ideology: Mahatma Jotirao Phule and Lower Caste Protest in Nineteenth Century Western India*. Cambridge: Cambridge University Press, 1985.

Page, David. *Prelude to Partition: The Indian Muslims and the Imperial System of Control*. Cambridge: Cambridge University Press, 1985.

Panagaroya, Arvind. *India: The Emerging Giant*. New York: Oxford University Press, 2008.

Pandey, Gyanendra, and Yunas Samad. *Remembering Partition: Violence, Nationalism, and History*. Cambridge: Cambridge University Press, 2002.

——— . *Fault Lines of Nationhood*. Delhi: Roli, 2007.

Paul, T. V. *The India-Pakistan Conflict: An Enduring Rivalry*. Cambridge: Cambridge University Press, 2005.

Peer, Basharat. *Curfewed Night: A Frontline Memoir of Life, Love, and War in Kashmir*. London: HarperPress, 2010.

Purcell, Hugh. *After the Raj: The Last Stayers-On and the Legacy of British India*. Stroud: History Press, 2011.

Rahman, Aminur. *Women and Micro-Credit in Rural Bangladesh: An Anthropological Study of Grameen Bank Lending*. Boulder, CO: Westview, 2002.

Rahman, Tariq. *Language and Politics in Pakistan*. Karachi: Oxford University Press, 1996.

Ramnath, Maia. *Haj to Utopia: How the Ghadr Movement Charted Global Radicalism and Attempted to Overthrow the British Empire*. Berkeley: University of California Press, 2011.

Rashid, Harun-or. *The Foreshadowing of Bangladesh: Bengal Muslim League and Muslim League Politics, 1936–1947*. Dhaka: Asiatic Society of Bangladesh, 1987.

Riaz, Ali. *God Willing: The Politics of Islamism in Bangladesh*. Lanham, MD: Rowman and Littlefield, 2004.

Riaz, Ali, and C. Christine Fair, eds. *Political Islam and Governance in Bangladesh*. London: Routledge, 2011.

Rizvi, Hasan Askari. *Military, State, and Society in Pakistan*. London: Palgrave Macmillan, 2003.

Robinson, Francis. *Separatism Among Indian Muslims: The Politics of the United Provinces' Muslims, 1860–1923*. Cambridge: Cambridge University Press, 1974.

Roopnarine, Lomarsh. *Indo-Caribbean Indenture: Resistance and Accommodation, 1838–1920*. Kingston: University of West Indies Press, 2007.

Samad, Yunas. *A Nation in Turmoil: Nationalism and Ethnicity in Pakistan, 1937–1958*. New Delhi: Sage, 1995.

Sarkar, Sumit. *Modern India, 1885–1947*. New York: St. Martin's, 1989.

Schendel, Willem van. *The Bengal Borderland: Beyond State and Nation in South Asia*. London: Anthem, 2005.

———. *A History of Bangladesh*. Cambridge: Cambridge University Press, 2009.

Schofield, Victoria. *Kashmir in the Crossfire*. London: I. B. Tauris, 1996.

Shaikh, Farzana. *Making Sense of Pakistan*. London: Hurst, 2009.

Shehabuddin, Elora. *Reshaping the Holy: Democracy, Development, and Muslim Women in Bangladesh*. New York: Columbia University Press, 2008.

Sherman, Taylor C. *State Violence and Punishment in India*. London: Routledge, 2010.

Siddiqa, Ayesha. *Military Inc.: Inside Pakistan's Military Economy*. London: Pluto, 2007.

Singh, Gurharpal. *Ethnic Conflict in India: A Case Study of Punjab*. Basingstoke: Macmillan, 2000.

Singh, Surinder Nihal. *The Yogi and the Bear: Story of Indo-Soviet Relations*. Riverdale, MD: Riverdale, 1998.

Sisson, Richard, and Leo E. Rose. *War and Secession: Pakistan, India, and the Creation of Bangladesh*. Berkeley: University of California Press, 1990.

Sridharan, E., ed. *International Relations Theory and South Asia: Security, Political Economy, Domestic Politics, Identities, and Images*, vol. 1. New Delhi: Oxford University Press, 2011.

Stein, Burton. *A History of India*. Oxford: Blackwell, 1998.

St. John, Ian. *The Making of the Raj: India Under the East India Company*. Santa Barbara: Praeger, 2012.

Swami, Praveen. *India, Pakistan, and the Secret Jihad: The Covert War in Kashmir, 1947–2001*. Abingdon: Routledge, 2007.

Talbot, Ian. *Punjab and the Raj, 1949–1947*. Delhi: Manohar, 1988.

——. *India and Pakistan*. London: Arnold, 2000.

——. *Khizr Tiwana, the Punjab Unionist Party, and the Partition of India*. Karachi: Oxford University Press, 2002.

——. *Divided Cities: Partition and Its Aftermath in Lahore and Amritsar, 1947–1957*. Karachi: Oxford University Press, 2006.

——, ed. *The Deadly Embrace: Religion, Politics, and Violence in India and Pakistan, 1947–2002*. Karachi: Oxford University Press, 2007.

——. *Pakistan: A Modern History*. 2nd ed. London: Hurst, 2009.

——. *Pakistan: A New History*. London: Hurst, 2012.

Talbot, Ian, and Gurharpal Singh, eds. *The Partition of India*. Cambridge: Cambridge University Press, 2009.

Tankel, Stephen. *Storming the World Stage: The Story of Lashkar-e-Taiba*. London: Hurst, 2011.

Tatla, Darshan Singh. *The Sikh Diaspora: The Search for Statehood*. London: University College Press, 1999.

Tellis, Ashley J., Travis Tanner, and Jessica Keough, eds. *Asia Responds to Its Rising Powers: China and India*. Washington, DC: National Bureau of Asian Research, 2011.

Tinker, Hugh. *A New System of Slavery: The Export of Indian Labour Overseas, 1830–1920*. London: Oxford University Press, 1974.

Tomlinson, B. R. *The Political Economy of the Raj, 1914–1947: The Economics of Decolonization in India*. London: Macmillan, 1979.

Tully, Mark. *No Full Stops in India*. London: Penguin, 1992.

Tully, Mark, and Satish Jacob. *Amritsar: Mrs. Gandhi's Last Battle*. London: Cape, 1985.

Varadarajan, Siddharth, ed. *Gujarat: The Making of a Tragedy*. New Delhi: Penguin, 2002.

Venkateswaran, R. J. *Reforming the Indian Economy: The Narasimha and Manmohan Singh Era*. New Delhi: Vikas, 1996.

Wagner, Kim A. *Thuggee: Banditry and the British in Early Nineteenth Century India*. Basingstoke: Palgrave Macmillan, 2007.

Waseem, Mohammad. *Politics and the State in Pakistan*. Islamabad: National Institute of Cultural and Historical Research, 1994.

White, B. S. *Turbans and Traders: Hong Kong's Indian Communities*. Oxford: Oxford University Press, 1994.

Wint, Guy. *What Is the Colombo Plan?* London: Batchworth, 1952.

Wirsing, Robert. *Pakistan's Security Under Zia, 1977–88: The Policy Imperatives of a Peripheral Asian State.* Basingstoke: Macmillan, 1991.

Wolpert, Stanley. *Jinnah of Pakistan.* New York: Oxford University Press, 1984.

——. *Shameful Flight: The Last Years of the British Empire in India.* New York: Oxford University Press, 2006.

——. *India and Pakistan: Continued Conflict or Co-operation.* Berkeley: University of California Press, 2011.

Yahya, F. B. *Economic Cooperation between Singapore and India: An Alliance in the Making?* New York: Routledge, 2008.

Yang, Anand. *The Limited Raj: Agrarian Relations in Colonial India: Saran District, 1793–1920.* Berkeley: University of California Press, 1989.

Zaki, I. H., and Regina Mulay Parakh. *Small States' Security Dilemma: A Maldivian Perception.* New Delhi: Lancer's, 2008.

Zaman, Muhammad Qasim. *The Ulama in Contemporary Islam: Custodians of Change.* Princeton: Princeton University Press, 2002.

Zamindar, Vazira-Fazila Yacoobali. *The Long Partition and the Making of Modern South Asia: Refugees, Boundaries, Histories.* New York: Columbia University Press, 2007.

Maps 1–3 courtesy of University of Southampton
Figure 1 copyright © The India Today Group/Getty Images
Figure 2 copyright © Majority World/UIG/Getty Images
Figures 3, 4, 11, 13–18 copyright © Special Collections, Hartley Library, University of Southampton
Figures 5, 6, 20, photos by author
Figures 7–10, 12, 19, National Army Museum